The Mini **Rough Guide** to

# Paris

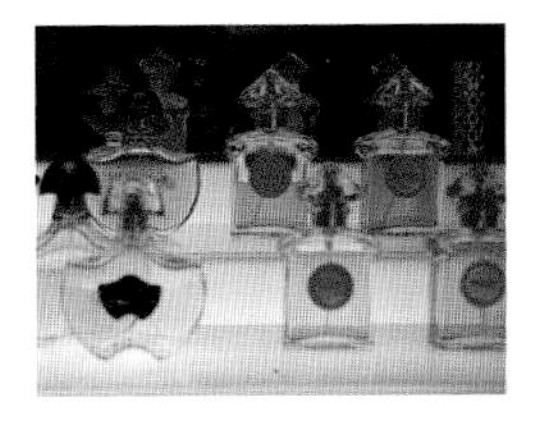

written and researched by


**Ruth**

**Jam**

www.roughguides.com

Domaine
le Garrigon
VISAN

# Contents





◂◂ Perfumes at Guerlain ◂ Wine barrels at Le Baron Rouge

# Introduction to

# Paris

**Paris does grandeur like no other city. Few sights match the splendour of the vista leading up the Champs-Elysées to the Arc de Triomphe, the nobility of Notre-Dame towering above the Seine, or the still-shocking impact of the Eiffel Tower seen up close. Paris excels in these great architectural set pieces, which are the legacy of its powerful rulers. Almost every king, emperor or president has left the stamp of their authority on the city, from the elegant royal squares of place de la Concorde and place des Vosges to the bold Grands Projets of the modern-day presidents – most famously the insanely inside-out Pompidou Centre and the futuristic glass pyramid in the Louvre.**

With all its great monuments, Paris can seem inhumanly magnificent at times, yet it's also made up of *quartiers* operating on a delightfully human scale, where life revolves around the local boulangerie and café. In fact this is where much of the appeal of Paris lies. It can feel like a collection of little villages, full of atmospheric streets, charming architectural details, cafés with loyal, local customers and fiercely independent shops.

Much of the allure and romance of the city stems from the days when it was the artistic and intellectual capital of the world. At the beginning of the twentieth century, artists such as Picasso and Modigliani flocked here, and writers Ernest Hemingway and F. Scott Fitzgerald made it their home for a while. Jazz musicians, such as Sidney Bechet, fleeing racism in America, found a haven in the city, as did political exiles – White Russians escaping Communism and Jews seeking refuge from Hitler.

Partly as a legacy of its years of artistic pre-eminence and partly as a result of Napoleon's acquisitive tendencies, Paris has an **art collection** that's second to none. The greatest works are spread among the Louvre, Musée d'Orsay and the Pompidou Centre, but some of the most satisfying places to visit are the numerous smaller museums, many of which are dedicated to individual artists.

The city is equally well endowed with **restaurants and cafés**, ranging from ultra-modern fashion temples to traditional, mirrored palaces, and from tiny *bistrots* where the emphasis is all on the cooking to bustling Vietnamese diners. You could blow out on the meal of a lifetime in one of the city's famed gastronomic restaurants or sample any number of cheeses and *saucissons* from one of the many open-air markets.

▲ Place du Tertre, Montmartre

After dark, Paris's theatres and concert halls host inventive and world-leading productions of **theatre** and **dance**, while many classical concerts take place in fine settings, such as churches and museums. **Jazz and world music** have a strong following, with many Malian and Algerian stars choosing to base themselves in the capital, reflecting France's strong links with these countries. Above all, Paris is a real **cinema** capital, with well over three hundred *salles*.

# What to see

The city is divided into twenty arrondissements, or districts, which spiral out from the centre in a clockwise direction. The central arrondissements (1er–8e) contain the main sights and are the most alluring – you can easily explore this area on foot. Through the middle of the city flows the **Seine**, spanned by 37 bridges. The river encircles two islands at the heart of the capital: the **Ile de la Cité**, the kernel from which Paris grew, is the site of the Gothic cathedral of **Notre-Dame** and the **Sainte-Chapelle**, renowned for its magnificent stained-glass windows, while the smaller **Ile Saint-Louis** is packed with handsome townhouses and fringed with leafy *quais*.

▼ Jardin des Tuileries

North of the river, the Right Bank (*rive droite*) is characterized by broad avenues, lined with Neoclassical buildings, radiating out from grand squares. The chief attraction here is the splendid **Louvre** palace and museum. Extending from the Louvre west is the city's longest and grandest vista – the Voie Triomphale – incorporating some of the capital's most famous landmarks: the **Tuileries** gardens, the **Champs-Elysées**, the **Arc de Triomphe** and the **Grande Arche de la Défense**. The area around the Champs-Elysées is currently one of the city's hottest spots, a hub of new and fashionable bars, cafés and shops.

▲ Passage du Grand-Cerf

North of the Louvre lies the commercial and financial quarter, bounded by the busy **Grands Boulevards**. Here you'll find the large department stores Galeries Lafayette and Printemps, as well as smaller and more unusual boutiques hidden in the *passages*, nineteenth-century shopping arcades. More mainstream stores congregate in the 1970s **Les Halles** underground shopping complex, weathering badly compared to its neighbour the **Pompidou Centre**, which still wows visitors with its "inside-out" architecture and houses a superb collection of modern art. East of the Louvre, the **Marais** was the prestige address in the seventeenth century; along with the nearby **Bastille** and **Canal St-Martin**, it's one of the most exciting areas of the city, alive with trendy shops, cafés and nightlife.

The south bank of the river, or Left Bank (*rive gauche*), is quite different in character from the Right Bank, quieter and more village-like. The **Quartier Latin** is the traditional domain of the intelligentsia, along with **St-Germain**, which becomes progressively snootier as you travel west towards the ministries, embassies and museums that surround the **Eiffel Tower**. Once you move towards glitzy **Montparnasse** and the southern swathe of the Left Bank, high-rise flats alternate with charming bourgeois neighbourhoods.

Back on the Right Bank, many of the outer or higher-number arrondissements were once outlying villages, and were gradually absorbed by the expanding city in the nineteenth century – some, such as **Montmartre** in the north, **Belleville** on the eastern edges, and **Passy** in the west, have succeeded in maintaining something of their village identity. The areas to the east were traditionally poor and working class, while those to the west were affluent – divisions that to some extent hold true today.

# When to go

**Spring** is deservedly the classic time to visit Paris, when the weather is mild, with bright days balanced by rain showers. **Autumn**, similarly mild, and **winter** can be very rewarding, but on overcast days – all too common – the city can feel very melancholy; winter sun on the other hand is the city's most flattering light, and hotels and restaurants are relatively uncrowded in this season. By contrast, high **summer** is not the best time to go: large numbers of Parisians desert the capital between July 15 and the end of August for the beach or mountains, and many restaurants and shops close down for much of this period.

Paris's climate

| | Jan | Feb | Mar | Apr | May | Jun | Jul | Aug | Sep | Oct | Nov | Dec |
|---|---|---|---|---|---|---|---|---|---|---|---|---|
| **Average daily temperature** | | | | | | | | | | | | |
| Max/Min (°F) | 43/34 | 45/34 | 54/39 | 60/43 | 68/49 | 73/55 | 76/58 | 75/58 | 70/53 | 60/46 | 50/40 | 44/36 |
| Max/Min (°C) | 6/1 | 7/1 | 12/4 | 16/6 | 20/10 | 23/13 | 25/15 | 24/14 | 21/12 | 16/8 | 10/5 | 7/2 |
| **Average monthly rainfall** | | | | | | | | | | | | |
| Rainfall (In/mm) | 2.2/56 | 1.8/46 | 1.4/35 | 1.7/42 | 2.2/56 | 2.1/54 | 2.3/59 | 2.5/64 | 2.2/56 | 2.0/50 | 2.0/50 | 2.0/50 |

# 13 things not to miss

*It's not possible to see everything that Paris has to offer in one trip – and we don't suggest you try. What follows is a selective taste of the city's highlights: its best landmarks, most engaging museums and liveliest neighbourhoods. They're arranged, in no particular order, in five colour-coded categories, which you can browse through to find the very best things to see and experience. All highlights have a page reference to take you straight into the guide, where you can find out more.*

**01 Pompidou Centre** Page **69** • The inside-out, multi-coloured architecture of the Pompidou Centre is a superb advert for the museum of modern art inside.

**02 Jardin du Luxembourg** Page **109** • A favourite with students, families and visitors alike, the Jardin du Luxembourg is the largest and loveliest of central Paris's parks.

**03 Eiffel Tower** Page **116** • An exhilarating landmark, worth seeing by day and by night.

**05 Musée d'Orsay** Page **113** • A brilliantly converted railway station makes a magnificent setting for the works of the French Impressionists and their contemporaries.

**04 Place des Vosges** Page **76** • A serene architectural gem from the seventeenth century: pink, arcaded townhouses surround a lovely garden square.

**06 Markets** Page **268** • Paris's street markets are living testimony to the city's love of food, and great places for people-watching.

**07 The Louvre** Page 37 • More than the *Mona Lisa* and the glass pyramid: the Louvre is simply the greatest art gallery in the world, and a fine museum of antiquities to boot.

**08 Eastern Paris nightlife** Page 240 • For the city's hippest bars and cutting-edge sounds, you need to venture out to the gritty eastern districts.

**09 Montmartre** Page 129 • The cobbled slopes of Paris's highest hill, Montmartre, have a unique, deliciously villagey feel – albeit a village packed with bars, restaurants and some of the city's coolest fashion boutiques.

**10 Brasseries** Page **199** • The combination of antique decor, the hum of conversation and mouthwatering, classic dishes makes a meal at one of Paris's traditional brasseries a must.

**11 Notre-Dame** Page **33** • The massive, solemn cathedral of Our Lady is the ancient heart of Paris – climb the towers for a fine view.

**12 Père-Lachaise** Page **144** • The last resting place of Paris's famous – and infamous – dead is a wonderful place for a wander.

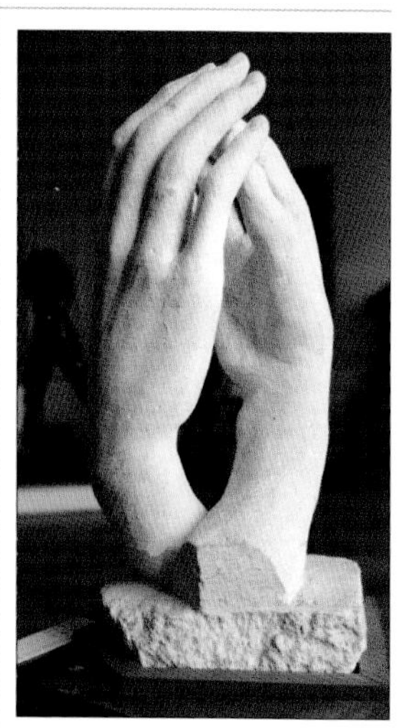

**13 Musée Rodin** Page **120** • Rodin's most intimate and thought-provoking sculptures are housed in an exquisite eighteenth-century mansion.

# Basics

# Basics

# Arrival



**Many British travellers to Paris arrive by Eurostar at the central Gare du Nord train station, while more far-flung visitors are likely to land at one of Paris's two main airports: Charles de Gaulle and Orly.**

## By air

The two main Paris **airports** dealing with international flights are Roissy-Charles de Gaulle and Orly. Information on them can be found on Ⓦwww.aeroportsdeparis.fr. A third airport, Beauvais, is used by low-cost airline Ryanair.

### Roissy-Charles de Gaulle Airport

Roissy-Charles de Gaulle Airport (24hr information in English Ⓣ01.70.36.39.50), usually referred to as **Charles de Gaulle** and abbreviated to CDG or Paris CDG, is 23km northeast of the city. The airport has three terminals: CDG 1, CDG 2 and CDG T3.

The cheapest and quickest way to the centre of Paris is the **Roissyrail** train link, which runs on RER line B (every 15min from 5am until midnight; 30min; €8.40 one-way). You can pick it up direct from CDG T3 and most parts of CDG 2 but from CDG 1 and CDG 2A and 2B you have to get a shuttle bus (*navette*) to the RER station. Ordinary commuter trains also run on this line; they only take about five minutes more than the Roissyrail to get to the centre, though have fewer facilities for luggage storage.

Various **bus** companies provide services from the airport direct to a number of city-centre locations, but they're slightly more expensive than Roissyrail and may take longer. The **Roissybus,** for instance, connects CDG 1 and CDG 2 with the Opéra Garnier (corner of rues Auber and Scribe; ⓂOpéra/RER Auber); it runs every fifteen minutes from 5.45am to 11pm, costs €9.10 one-way and takes around 45 minutes to an hour. There are also two **Air France buses**: the green line 2 stops outside Charles-de-Gaulle-Etoile RER/métro while the yellow line 4 stops at the Gare de Lyon before terminating near the Gare Montparnasse. The timings are similar to the Roissybus, but tickets are more expensive at €24 return; for detailed information on routes and prices see ⓦwww.cars-airfrance.com.

**Taxis** (metered) into central Paris from CDG cost around €40–50, including a small luggage supplement (€1 per piece of luggage), and should take a little under an hour. Slightly less expensive is the minibus door-to-door service, **Paris Blue**, which costs from €30 for two people, with no extra charge for luggage. It operates round-the-clock but bookings must be made at least 24 hours in advance on ⓣ01.30.11.13.00 or via their website ⓦwww.paris-blue-airport-shuttle.fr. Note that if your flight gets in after midnight your only means of transport is a taxi or the minibus.

## Orly Airport

**Orly Airport** (information in English daily 6am–11.30pm, ⓣ01.70.36.39.50), 14km south of Paris, has two terminals, Orly Sud (south, for international flights) and Orly Ouest (west, for domestic flights), linked by shuttle bus but easily walkable. Probably the easiest way into the centre is the fast **Orlyval train shuttle** link to RER line B station Antony, followed by métro connection stops at Denfert-Rochereau, St-Michel and Châtelet-Les Halles; it runs every four to seven minutes daily from 6am to 11pm (€9.30 one-way; 35min to Châtelet). Alternatively, you can take a **"Paris par le train" shuttle bus** (*navette*) to RER line C station Pont de Rungis, from where trains leave every twenty minutes from 5am to 11.30pm for the Gare d'Austerlitz and other métro connection stops on the Left Bank (train 25min, total journey around 45min; €6.10 one-way). Leaving Paris, the trains run from Gare d'Austerlitz from 5.40am to 10.40pm.

Two bus services are also worth considering: the **Orlybus**, which runs to Denfert-Rochereau RER/métro station in the 14e (every 15–20min, 6am–11.30pm; €6.10 one-way; around 30min); and **bus 285**, which runs to métro Villejuif-Louis-Aragon (line 7) every ten to twenty minutes (every 30min on Sun) between 5.05am and 1am (€1.70; 15min).

**Taxis** take about 35 minutes to reach the centre of Paris and cost at least €30.

---

**Disneyland Paris is linked by bus from both Charles de Gaulle and Orly airports; for details of these services, plus train links from the centre to the purpose-built Marne-La-Vallée TGV, see p.171.**

---

## Beauvais airport

**Beauvais airport** (Ⓣ08.92.68.20.66, Ⓦwww.aeroportbeauvais.com), 65km northwest of Paris, is served by Ryanair from Dublin, Shannon, Glasgow and East Midlands. It's sometimes called Paris Beauvais-Tillé airport. **Coaches** (€13 each way) shuttle between the airport and Porte Maillot in the 17e arrondissement, where you can pick up métro line 1 to the centre. The journey takes about an hour in total. The coach leaves between fifteen and thirty minutes after the flight has arrived and three hours and fifteen minutes before the flight departs on the way back. Tickets can be bought online via the airport's website, at Arrivals or from the Beauvais shop at 1 boulevard Pershing, near the Porte Maillot terminal.

## By rail

**Eurostar** (Ⓣ08.92.35.35.39, Ⓦwww.eurostar.com) terminates at the busy **Gare du Nord**, rue Dunkerque, in the northeast of the city. Coming off the train, turn left for the métro and the RER, and the tourist office. Turn right for taxis (roughly €10 to the centre) and the secure left luggage (daily 6.15am–11.15pm; around €7 for 24 hours, depending on the locker size), both down the escalators opposite the Avis car rental desk. You can get a shower (€7 for 20min) in the public toilets (daily 6am–midnight; small charge payable) at the bottom of the métro escalators, and change money at two bureaux de change at the station (daily 7.30am–11.40pm). The Eurostar offices and check-in point for departures are both located on the mezzanine level, above the main station entrance. The Gare du Nord is also the arrival point for trains from Calais and other north European countries. Watch out for scammers offering to "help" with tickets or taxis.

Nearby, the **Gare de l'Est** (place du 11-Novembre-1918, 10e) serves eastern France and central and eastern Europe; the **Gare St-Lazare** (place du Havre, 8e) serves the Normandy coast and Dieppe; **Gare de Lyon** (place Louis-Armand, 12e) serves trains from Italy and Switzerland and TGV lines from southeast France. South of the river, on the Left Bank, the **Gare Montparnasse** on boulevard de Vaugirard, 15e, is the terminus for Chartres, Brittany, the Atlantic coast and TGV lines from southwest France. **Gare d'Austerlitz**, on boulevard de l'Hôpital, 13e, serves the Loire Valley and the Dordogne. The **motorail** station, Gare de Paris-Bercy, is down the tracks from the Gare de Lyon on boulevard de Bercy, 12e; it's also used by sleeper trains to Italy.

All the stations are equipped with cafés, restaurants, *tabacs*, ATMs and bureaux de change (long waits in season), and all are connected with the métro system; most also offer free wi-fi access. The **tourist offices** at Gare du Nord, Gare de l'Est and Gare de Lyon can book same-day accommodation (see p.24). Left-luggage facilities are available at all train stations under heavy security, but are limited in number.

## By road

Almost all the buses coming into Paris arrive at the main **gare routière** at 28 avenue du Général-de-Gaulle, Bagnolet, at the eastern edge of the city; métro Gallieni (line 3) links it to the centre. If you're driving into Paris yourself, don't try to go straight across the city to your destination unless you know what you're doing. Use the ring road – the *boulevard périphérique* – to get around to the nearest "*porte*"; except at rush hour, it's very quick – sometimes frighteningly so – and relatively easy to navigate.

# City transport

Finding your way around Paris is remarkably easy, as the city proper, stripped of its suburbs, is compact and relatively small, with an integrated public transport system – the RATP (Régie Autonome des Transports Parisiens). The system is cheap, fast and meticulously signposted, comprising buses, underground métro and suburban express trains, known as RER (Réseau Express Régional) trains. Even the Batobus along the river comes under the same network. For information on all RATP services visit ⓦwww.ratp.fr. Cycling is an increasingly popular way to get around since the introduction of Vélib', the city's popular bike rental scheme. Building on this success, the city council is launching an electric car-sharing scheme called Autolib', in 2011. Some 2000 cars will be available to pick up and drop off at various locations around the city.

## Tickets and passes

The standard **RATP ticket** at €1.60 (or €1.70 if bought on buses) is valid for any one-way métro, bus or RER express rail ride anywhere within the city limits and immediate suburbs (zones 1 and 2). Only one ticket is ever needed on the métro system, but you can't switch between buses or between bus and métro/RER on the same ticket. For a short stay in the city consider buying a reduced-price **carnet** of ten tickets (€11.40). Tickets are available at stations and *tabacs* (newsagents/tobacconists). Children under 4 travel free, and kids aged 4 to 11 pay half price.

**At its widest point, Paris is only about 12km across, which, at a brisk pace, is not much more than a two-hour walk.**

If you're travelling beyond the city limits (zones 3 to 5), to La Défense, for example, you'll need to buy a separate RER ticket. If you're doing a number of journeys in one day, it might be worth getting a **mobilis day pass** (from €6.10 for the city to €17.30 to include the outer suburbs, though not the airports), which offers unlimited access to the métro, buses and, depending on which zones you choose, the RER. If you've arrived early in the week and are staying more than three days, it's more economical to buy a **Navigo** weekly pass (*le passe Navigo découverte*). It costs €18.35 for zones 1 and 2 and is valid for an unlimited number of journeys from Monday morning to Sunday evening. You can only buy a ticket for the current week until Wednesday; from Thursday you can buy a ticket to begin the following Monday. A monthly pass costs €60.40 for zones 1 and 2. The Navigo swipe card itself costs €5, and you'll also need a passport photo.

Other possibilities, though not as good value as the mobilis and Navigo cards, are the **Paris Visite** passes (ⓦwww.ratp.info/touristes), one-, two-, three- and five-day visitors' passes at €9, €14.70, €20 and €28.90 for Paris and close suburbs, or €18.90, €28.90, €40.50 and €49.40 to include the airports, Versailles and Disneyland Paris (make sure you buy this one when you arrive at Roissy-Charles de Gaulle or Orly to get maximum value). A half-price child's version is also available. You can buy them from métro and RER stations, tourist offices and online from ⓦwww.helloparis.co.uk or ⓦwww.parismetro.com. Paris Visite passes become valid on the first day you use them and entitle you to unlimited travel (in the zones you have chosen) on bus, métro, trams, RER, SNCF, the Montmartrobus around Montmartre and the Montmartre funicular between the hours of 5.30am and 1.30am; they also allow you discounts at certain monuments, museums and tours, including day tickets to Disneyland Paris.

## The métro and RER

The **métro** (Ⓜ), combined with the **RER** suburban express lines, is the simplest way of moving around the city. Both run from around 5.30am to roughly 12.30am (1.30am on Saturdays). Lines are colour-coded and designated by numbers for the métro and letters for the RER. Platforms are signposted using the name of the terminus station; travelling north from Montparnasse to Châtelet, for example, you need to follow the signs for "Direction Porte-de-Clignancourt", at the northernmost end of the line. For RER journeys beyond the city, make sure that the station you want is illuminated on the platform display board. **Stations** are evenly spaced and usually very close together, though interchanges can involve a lot of legwork.

Free maps of varying sizes and detail are available at most stations: the largest and most useful is the *Grand Plan de Paris numéro 2*, which overlays the métro, RER and bus routes on a map of the city so you can see exactly how transport lines and streets match up. If you just want a handy pocket-sized métro/bus map ask for the *Petit Plan de Paris* or the smaller *Paris Plan de Poche*.

**A map of the Paris métro can be found at the back of this guide.**

## Buses and trams

**Buses** are often rather neglected in favour of the métro, but can be very useful. Naturally you see much more, plus journeys have become quicker with the introduction of bus lanes. Free **route maps** are available at métro stations, bus terminals and the tourist office; the best, showing the métro and RER as well, is the *Grand Plan de Paris*. Every bus stop displays the numbers of the buses that stop there, a map showing all the stops on the route, and the times of the first and last buses. Generally speaking, buses run from 7am to 8.30pm with some services continuing to 12.30am. However, many lines don't operate on Sundays and holidays – log onto Ⓦwww.ratp.fr for a map of the most useful tourist routes.

Some bus routes are particularly good for **sightseeing**, notably bus #29, which has an open platform at the back, and traverses the Right Bank from Opéra to Bastille; bus #24, along the Left Bank; and bus #73, down the Champs-Elysées. Most bus lines are now easily **accessible** for **wheelchairs** and prams; these are indicated on the *Grand Plan de Paris* and on Ⓦwww.ratp.fr.

On Sunday afternoons and holidays from mid-April to mid-September, a special **Balabus service** (not to be confused with Batobus, see p.22) passes all the major tourist sights between the Grande Arche de la Défense and Gare de Lyon (every 15–20min noon–9pm).

Bus stops are marked "Balabus", and you'll need one to three bus tickets, depending on the length of your journey. Paris Visite and Mobilis passes are also valid. **Night buses** (Noctilien; ⓦwww.noctilien.fr) run on 45 routes at least every hour (with extra services on weekends) from 1am to 5.30am between place du Châtelet, west of the Hôtel de Ville, and the suburbs. Details of routes are available online.

There are currently four **tram lines** in and around Paris, with more planned; currently the most useful is line T3, which runs along the southern edge of the city from the Pont du Garigliano on the Seine in the 15e arrondissement to Pont d'Ivry métro. Trams run every five or ten minutes or so between 4.50am and 11.40pm; stops are marked by a large T.

## Taxis

The best place to get a **taxi** is at a taxi rank (*arrêt taxi* – there are around 470 of them) – usually more effective than hailing from the street. Currently, the large white light signals the taxi is free and the orange light means it's in use, though by the end of 2011 this is set to change: a green light will mean that the taxi is free, a red light that the taxi is occupied. Finding a taxi at lunchtime and any time after 7pm can be almost impossible and your best bet might be to call one. The main firms are all on one number: ⓣ01.45.30.30.30.

Taxis are metered and charges are fairly reasonable: between €6 and €12 for a central daytime journey, though considerably more if you call one out. There's a minimum charge of €6.10, a pick-up charge of €2.10, an extra charge of €0.70 if you're picked up from a mainline train station, and a €1 charge for each piece of luggage carried. Taxi drivers do not have to take more than three passengers (they don't like people sitting in the front); if a fourth passenger is accepted, an extra charge of €2.95 will be added. A tip of 10 percent, while optional, is generally expected.

## Batobus

The **river-boat** service, Batobus (ⓦwww.batobus.com), operates all year round (apart from January), stopping at eight points along the Seine between the Eiffel Tower and the Jardin des Plantes. Boats run every fifteen to thirty minutes (Feb to mid-March,

Nov & Dec 10.30am–4.30pm; mid-March to June, Sept & Oct 10am–7pm; June–Aug 10am–9.30pm). The total journey time from one end to the other is around thirty minutes and you can hop on and off as many times as you like – a day pass costs €13, two consecutive days €17 and five consecutive days €20 (kids half price). Information on day-tripper "Bateaux-Mouches" and other trips is given in "Activities" on p.288.

## Cycling

The easiest way to rent a bike is to pick up one of the town hall's 24,000 **Vélib'** machines from one of the 1750 stations found every 300m or so across the city and neighbouring suburbs. First buy a subscription card from one of the bigger bike stations, or any shop that displays the Vélib' logo, or online at Ⓦwww.velib.paris.fr. The *carte Vélib'* can be valid for one day (€1), seven days (€5) or one year (€29). Put your card into the vending machine at every bike station, type in how much time you want and pay the amount displayed. The first half-hour is free; after that you have to pay a €1 supplement for the second half-hour, €2 for the third, and €4 per half-hour thereafter. Once your card is paid up, you simply press it against the automatic readers to release a bike. Since its inception in 2007, the scheme has proved very popular, though the incidence of theft and vandalism is high and there is talk of higher charges in order to offset this.

Several outlets run **cycle tours** and **rent bikes** by the hour, day, weekend or week. Prices are about €15–20 a day, or upwards of €50 for a week.

**Fat Tire Bike Tours** 24 rue Edgar Faure, 15e Ⓣ01.56.58.10.54, Ⓦfattirebiketours.com/paris. ⓂDupleix.
**Paris à Vélo C'est Sympa** 22 rue Alphonse Baudin, 11e Ⓣ01.48.87.60.01, Ⓦwww.parisvelosympa.com. ⓂRichard Lenoir.
**Paris Bike Tour** 38 rue de Saintonge, 3e Ⓣ01.42 74 22 14, Ⓦwww.parisbiketour.net. ⓂFilles du Calvaire/République.

# Information

**The main Paris tourist office is at 25 rue des Pyramides, 1er (June–Oct daily 9am–7pm; Nov–May Mon–Sat 10am–7pm, Sun 11am–7pm; Ⓦwww.parisinfo.com; ⓂPyramides/RER Auber). The other main branch offices are at the Gare du Nord (daily 8am–6pm); at the Gare de Lyon (Mon–Sat 8am–6pm) by the Grandes Lignes arrivals; on the corner of the Champs-Elysées and avenue de Marigny (June–Oct daily 10am–7pm; ⓂChamps-Elysées-Clémenceau); and opposite 72 boulevard Rochechouart (daily 10am–6pm; ⓂAnvers). The tourist offices give out information on Paris and the suburbs, and all can book hotel accommodation and also sell the Carte Musées et Monuments (see p.25) and Paris Visite travel passes (see p.20). It's also worth picking up a free map of Paris.**

Alternative sources of information are the **Hôtel de Ville information office** – Bureau d'Accueil – at 29 rue de Rivoli (Mon–Sat 9.30am–6pm; Ⓣ01.42.76.43.43, Ⓦwww.paris.fr; ⓂHôtel-de-Ville), and the **Espace du Tourisme d'Ile de France**, within the Carrousel du Louvre, underground below the triumphal arch at the east end of the Tuileries (daily 10am–6pm; Ⓣ08.92.68.30.00), which has information on the region around Paris.

For detailed what's-on information you'll need to buy one of Paris's **listings magazines**, *Pariscope* (€0.40) or *L'Officiel des Spectacles* (€0.35), available from all newsagents and kiosks. On Wednesdays, *Le Monde* and *Le Figaro* also bring out free listings supplements, while for more detail, the Webzines *Paris Voice* (Ⓦwww.parisvoice.com) and *GoGo Paris* (Ⓦwww.gogoparis.com) cover the latest events. The free monthly magazine *Paris Voice* (Ⓦwww.parisvoice.com), available online and from English-language bookshops, has good listings and reviews as well as ads for flats and courses. In addition, a number of pocket independent nightlife guides (*Lylo* is a good one) can be picked up in stores and cafés all over the city for free.

The **maps** in this guide and the free *Paris Map* should be adequate for a short sight-seeing stay, but for a more detailed map your best bet is one of the pocket-sized *L'indispensable* series booklets, sold everywhere in Paris.

## Museums and monuments

Entrance tickets to **museums and monuments** can really add up, though the permanent collections at municipal museums are **free** all year round, while all national museums (including the Louvre, Musée d'Orsay and Pompidou Centre) are free on the first Sunday of the month – see Ⓦwww.rmn.fr for a full list.

Each institution has its own policy for **children** and **teenagers**. In many museums under 18s go free, while all monuments are free for under 12s. Under 4s almost always get free admission. Half-price or reduced admission is normally available for 5- to 18-year-olds and students, though some commercial attractions charge adult rates from 12. The ISIC card (Ⓦwww.isiccard.com) is often the only card accepted for reduced-price **student** admission – often around a third off. For those **over 60 or 65**, reductions are sometimes available; you'll need to carry your passport around with you as proof of age.

If you are going to take in a lot of museums, consider buying the **Carte Musées et Monuments** (€32 two-day, €48 three-day, €64 five-day; Ⓦwww.parismuseumpass.com). Available online, from the tourist office and participating museums, it's valid for 35 or so of the most important museums and monuments including the Pompidou Centre, the Louvre and the Château de Versailles, and allows you to bypass ticket queues (though not the security checkpoints); it often doesn't cover the cost of special exhibitions. The Paris Visite multi-day transport pass (see p.20) also offers discounts on a number of museum admissions.

## Opening hours and holidays

Most **shops** and **businesses** are open from 9 or 10am through to 7 or 8pm. Bigger stores open Monday to Saturday, but smaller shops may close on Monday and often at lunchtime, roughly between 12.30 and 2pm. **Sunday opening** is currently restricted to just a few areas of

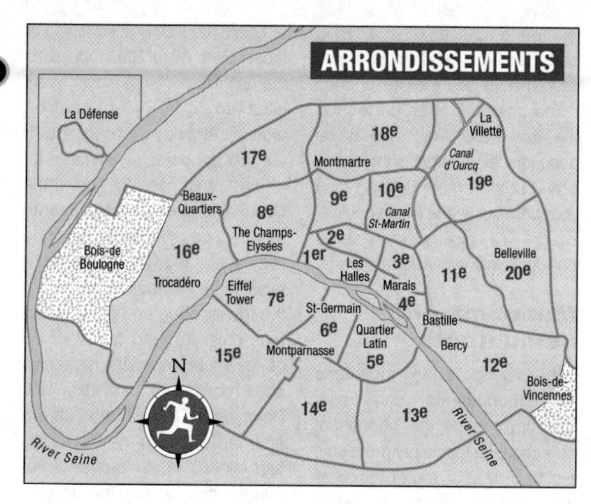


the city, including the Marais, Champs-Elysées, Bercy Village and the Carrousel du Louvre.

**Restaurants**, bars and cafés often close on Sunday or Monday, and quite a few restaurants also close at noon on Saturday and sometimes in the evening, too. It's common for bars and cafés to stay open to 2am, and even extend hours on a Friday and Saturday night, closing earlier on Sunday. Restaurants won't usually serve after 10pm, though some brasseries cater for night owls and serve meals till the early hours. Many restaurants and shops take a holiday between the middle of July and the end of August, and over Easter and Christmas.

Don't be caught out by museum closing days – usually Monday or Tuesday, and sometimes both. France celebrates eleven **national holidays**: January 1; Easter Monday; May 1; May 8; Ascension Day; Whitsun; Whit Monday; July 14; August 15; November 11; December 25. Note that the opening hours we give for Sundays also apply to these public holidays, and that with three and sometimes four holidays, May is a particularly festive month.

# Guide

# Guide

# 1

# The Islands

There's no better place to start a tour of Paris than its two river islands. On the **Ile de la Cité**, the city's ancient core, lie the capital's most treasured monuments – the Gothic cathedral of Notre-Dame and the stunning Sainte-Chapelle – while to the east is the charming, village-like **Ile St-Louis**.

## Ile de la Cité

**Map 2, G8.** Ⓜ Cité.

The **Ile de la Cité** is where Paris began. It was settled in around 300 BC by a Celtic tribe, the Parisii, and in 52 BC was overrun by Julius Caesar's troops. A natural defensive site commanding a major east–west river trade route, the island was an obvious candidate for a bright future – the Romans garrisoned it and laid out one of their standard military town plans. Lutetia Parisiorum, as the settlement was named by the Romans, developed into an important administrative centre and was endowed with a palace-fortress that served as the stronghold of the Merovingian kings, then of the counts of Paris, who in 987 became kings of France. The Frankish kings set about transforming the old Gallo-Roman fortress into a splendid palace, of which the Gothic **Sainte-Chapelle** and **Conciergerie** prison survive today. At the other end of the island, they erected the great cathedral of **Notre-Dame**. By the early thirteenth century the tiny Ile de la Cité teemed with life, somehow managing to accommodate twelve parishes, not to mention numerous chapels and monasteries.

Today, it takes quite a stretch of the imagination to picture what this medieval city must have looked like, for most of it was erased in the nineteenth century by the over-zealous Baron Haussmann, Napoleon III's Préfet de la Seine (a post equivalent to mayor of Paris – for more on Haussmann see Contexts, p.323). He demolished the homes of around 25,000 people, as well as churches, shops and ninety lanes – though it has to be said that these narrow, dark streets were notoriously squalid and dangerous at night. In their place Haussmann raised several vast Neoclassical edifices, including the Préfecture de Police, an extension to the Palais de Justice law courts and the Hôtel-Dieu hospital. He also cleared the space in front of the cathedral of **Notre-Dame**, creating a large square with shades of a military parade ground about it, but it does at least allow uncluttered views of the cathedral's facade. The few corners of the island that escaped Haussmann's attentions include the leafy **square du Vert-Galant** and the charming **place Dauphine**.

The island's chief attractions, the cathedral, Conciergerie and Sainte-Chapelle, inevitably attract large crowds and it's not unusual to have to queue for entry. Things are generally a bit quieter if you visit in the early morning or late afternoon.

## Pont Neuf and square du Vert-Galant

**Map 2, F6 & E6.** Ⓜ Pont-Neuf.

A popular approach to the Ile de la Cité is via the graceful, twelve-arched **Pont Neuf**, linking the island's western tip with both the Left and Right banks. Built in 1607 by Henri IV, it was the first in Paris not to have the usual medieval complement of houses built on it, hence the name "new bridge". This daring construction was, in its day, as potent a symbol of Paris as the

Eiffel Tower is today. Henri is commemorated with a bronze equestrian statue halfway across the structure, and he also lends his nickname to the **square du Vert-Galant**, enclosed within the triangular "stern" of the island and reached via steps leading down behind the statue. "Vert-Galant", meaning a "green" or "lusty gentleman", is a reference to Henri's legendary amorous exploits, and he would no doubt have approved of this tranquil, tree-lined garden, a popular haunt of lovers. The prime spot to make for is the knoll dotted with trees at the extreme point of the island, where you can watch the sun set over the Seine. At the other end of the garden is the dock for the river boats, the Bateaux-Vedettes du Pont-Neuf.

For more information on river boats, see p.22.

## Place Dauphine

**Map 2, F7.** Ⓜ Cité.

On the eastern side of the bridge, across the street from the statue of Henri IV, seventeenth-century houses flank the entrance to **place Dauphine**, one of the city's most secluded and attractive squares. Here, the noise of traffic recedes and is replaced by nothing more intrusive than the gentle tap of boules being played in the shade of the giant chestnuts. At the far end of the square looms the hulking mass of the **Palais de Justice**, the site of the old palace occupied by the Frankish kings until Etienne Marcel's bloody revolt in 1358 frightened them off to the greater security of the Louvre.

## Sainte-Chapelle

**Map 2, F7.** 4 bd du Palais. Daily: March–Oct 9.30am–6pm; Nov–Feb 9am–5pm; €8, combined admission to the Conciergerie €11; Ⓜ Cité.

Within the Palais de Justice complex and accessed from the boulevard du Palais, the only part of the old palace that remains in its entirety is Louis IX's chapel, the **Sainte-Chapelle**, its delicate spire soaring above the Palais buildings. It was built in 1242–48 to house a collection of holy relics, including the supposed Crown of Thorns and fragments of the True Cross, that Louis had bought for extortionate rates – far more than it cost to build the Sainte-Chapelle – from the bankrupt empire of Byzantium. Though damaged in the Revolution, the chapel was sensitively restored in the mid-nineteenth century and remains one of the finest achievements of French High Gothic. There are actually two chapels: the simple **lower chapel**, which would have been used by servants, gives no clue as to the splendour that lies ahead in the upper chapel, a truly dazzling sight, its walls made almost entirely of magnificent stained glass. The seemingly pencil-thin supports, made possible by the minimal use of structural masonry, coupled with the sheer vastness of the windows, combine to create what appears to be a huge uninterrupted expanse of glowing jewel-like blues, reds and emerald-greens. The windows tell the story of the Book of Genesis (on the left), followed by various other books of the Old Testament, continuing with the Passion of Christ (east end), the history of the relics (on the right) and ending with the Book of Revelation in the rose window. Each window panel is read from the bottom up and from left to right.

---

**The Sainte-Chapelle is the splendid setting for regular evening classical music concerts. Tickets cost €21–27.50 and can be booked in advance from branches of FNAC (see p.263) or Virgin Megastore (main branch at 52 av des Champs-Elysées; Ⓜ Franklin-D. Roosevelt; map 7, H3), though you stand a good chance of getting in on the door if you turn up half an hour or so beforehand.**

---

## The Conciergerie

**Map 2, G7.** 2 bd du Palais. Daily: March–Oct 9.30am–6pm; Nov–Feb 9am–5pm; €7, combined ticket with Sainte-Chapelle €11; Ⓜ Cité.

Also in the Palais de Justice complex is the medieval **Conciergerie**, the oldest prison in Paris. One of its towers, on the corner of the quai de l'Horloge, bears Paris's first public clock, built in 1370. The Conciergerie was where Marie-Antoinette and, in their turn, the leading figures of the Revolution were incarcerated before execution; you can see the queen's cell as well as various other reconstructed rooms, such as the innocent-sounding "salle de toilette", where the condemned had their hair cropped and shirt collars ripped in preparation for the guillotine. The other main point of interest is the enormous vaulted late-Gothic **Salle des Gens d'Armes**, canteen and recreation room of the royal household staff.

## The Cathédrale de Notre-Dame

**Map 2, H8.** Cathedral daily 8am–6.45pm; free. Towers April–June & Sept daily 10am–6.30pm; July & Aug Mon–Fri 10am–6.30pm, Sat & Sun 10am–11pm; Oct–March daily 10am–5.30pm; last entry 45min before closing time; €8; Ⓦwww.cathedraledeparis.com; ⓂCité.

The **Cathédrale de Notre-Dame** is one of the masterpieces of the Gothic age. The Romanesque influence is still visible, not least in its solid H-shaped west front, but the overriding impression is one of lightness and grace, created in part by the filigree work of the rose windows and galleries and the exuberant flying buttresses. Built on the site of the Merovingian cathedral of Saint-Etienne, Notre-Dame was begun in 1160 under the auspices of Bishop de Sully and completed around 1345. The cathedral's seminaries became an ecclesiastical powerhouse, churning out six popes in the course of the thirteenth and fourteenth centuries, though it subsequently lost some of its pre-eminence to other sees, such as Reims and St-Denis. The building fell into decline over the centuries, suffering its worst depredations during the Revolution when the frieze of Old Testament kings on the facade was damaged by enthusiasts who mistook them for the kings of France.

It was only in the 1820s that the cathedral was at last given a much-needed **restoration**, a task entrusted to the great architect-restorer Viollet-le-Duc. He carried out a thorough – arguably too thorough – renovation, remaking much of the statuary on the facade (the originals can be seen in the Musée National du Moyen Age, see p.98) and adding the steeple and baleful-looking gargoyles, which you can see close up if you climb the **towers**.

The facade was meticulously cleaned in the run-up to the millennium, removing years of accumulated grime and allowing the magnificent **carvings** over the portals to make their full impact. Over the central portal is the *Day of Judgement*: the lower frieze is a whirl of movement as the dead rise up from their graves, while above Christ presides, sending those on his right to heaven and those on his left to grisly torments in hell. The left portal shows Mary being crowned by Christ, with scenes of her life in the lower friezes, while the right portal depicts the Virgin enthroned and, below, episodes from the life of St Anne (Mary's mother) and the life of Christ.

**Inside**, you're immediately struck by the dramatic contrast between the darkness of the nave and the light falling on the first great clustered pillars of the choir. The end walls of the transepts admit all this light, as they are nearly two-thirds glass, including two magnificent rose windows coloured in imperial purple. These windows, the vaulting and the soaring shafts reaching to the springs of the vaults, are all definite Gothic elements, though there remains a strong sense of Romanesque in the stout round pillars of the nave.

Free guided **tours** (1hr–1hr 30min) take place in English (Wed & Thurs 2pm, Sat 2.30pm) and in French (Mon–Fri, though not 1st Fri of the month, 2pm & 3pm, Sat & Sun 2.30pm); gather at the welcome desk near the entrance.

## Kilomètre Zéro and the Crypte Archéologique

**Map 2, G8.**

Notre-Dame isn't only the heart of Paris, it's also the symbolic centre of France – outside on the pavement by the west door is a spot, marked by a bronze star, known as **Kilomètre Zéro**, from which all main-road distances in France are calculated. At the other end of the square, steps lead down to the atmospherically lit **Crypte Archéologique** (Tues–Sun 10am–6pm; €4), a large excavated area revealing remains of the original cathedral, as well as vestiges of the streets and houses that once clustered around Notre-Dame: most are medieval, but some date as far back as Gallo-Roman times.



### Le Mémorial de la Déportation

**Map 2, H9.** Daily 10am–noon & 2–5pm; free; ⓂCité.

At the eastern tip of the island is the **Mémorial de la Déportation**, the symbolic tomb of the 200,000 French who died in Nazi concentration camps during World War II – Resistance fighters, Jews and forced labourers. Their poignant memorial, barely visible above ground, is a kind of bunker-crypt studded with thousands of quartz pebbles representing the dead. Above the exit are the words "Pardonne. N'oublie pas" (Forgive. Do not forget).

## Ile St-Louis

**Map 2, I9.** ⓂPont-Marie/Sully-Morland.

Edged with attractive tree-lined *quais*, the compact **Ile St-Louis** feels somewhat removed from the rest of Paris and has a village-like air about it. Unlike its larger neighbour, it has no monuments or sights as such, save for a small **museum** at 6 quai d'Orléans, devoted to the Romantic Polish poet **Adam Mickiewicz** (Thurs 2–6pm, or by appointment on ⓣ01.43.54.35.61; free). Instead you'll find austerely beautiful houses on single-lane streets, assorted restaurants and cafés, and interesting little shops.

For centuries, the Ile-St-Louis was nothing but swampy pastureland, owned by Notre-Dame, until Christopher Marie, the seventeenth-century version of a property developer, had the bright idea of filling it with elegant mansions. By 1660, the island was transformed into the landscape we see today. In the

1840s, the island became a popular Bohemian hangout. The Club des Hachichins, whose members included Baudelaire, Dumas, Delacroix and Daumier, met every month and got high on hashish at the **Hôtel Lauzun**, 17 quai d'Anjou. Baudelaire, in fact, lived for a while in the attic where he wrote *Les Fleurs du Mal*. The *hôtel*, built in 1657, has an intact interior, complete with splendid trompe l'oeil decorations; it's often used for government receptions, and is occasionally open to the public for guided tours – details are given in the "Visites conferences" section in *Pariscope* (see p.24).

# 2

# The Louvre



The palace of the **Louvre** cuts a magnificent Classical swathe right through the centre of the city – a fitting setting for one of the world's grandest and most gracious art galleries. Originally little more than a feudal fortress, begun by Philippe-Auguste in the 1190s, the castle was enlarged by Charles V in the 1360s. However, it wasn't until 1546 that the first stones of the Louvre we see today were laid. Over the next century and a half, France's rulers continued to enlarge and aggrandize their palace without significantly altering its style, and the result is an architecturally harmonious whole that perfectly reflects the palace's central role in French history, and its central place in the French capital.

The origins of the **Musée du Louvre** lie in the personal art collection of François I. While the royal academy mounted exhibitions, known as *salons*, in the palace as early as 1725, the Louvre was only opened as an art gallery in 1793, the year of Louis XVI's execution. Within a decade, Napoleon's wagonloads of war booty transformed the Louvre's art collection into the world's largest – and not all the loot has been returned.

Napoleon's pink marble Arc du Carrousel has always looked a bit out of place at the end of the main courtyard, but the emperor's nephew, Napoleon III, returned to form in the late nineteenth century, with the conservative courtyard facades of the Richelieu and Denon wings. It was only in 1989, when I.M. Pei's controversial Pyramide erupted from the centre of the Cour Napoléon like a visitor from another architectural planet, that the Louvre received its first radical makeover. Since then, the museum has palpably basked in its status as a truly first-class art gallery.

## 2 Tickets and practicalities



Map 2, E5.

The **main entrance** is via the Pyramide, but if it's raining or the queues look too long make for the **alternative entrances**: via the Porte des Lions, just east of the Pont Royal, or directly under the Arc du Carrousel; the latter can also be accessed from 99 rue de Rivoli and from the line #1 platform of the Palais Royal-Musée du Louvre métro stop. If you've already got a ticket or a museum pass (see p.25) you can also enter from the passage Richelieu. **Disabled access** is via the futuristic rising and sinking column in the middle of the Pyramide.

**Opening hours** for the permanent collection are 9am to 6pm every day except Tuesday, when the museum is closed. On Wednesday and Friday the museum stays open till 9.45pm. Note that almost a quarter of the museum's rooms are closed one day a week on a rotating basis, though the most popular rooms are always open. See Ⓦwww.louvre.fr for details on current exhibitions.

The **entry fee** is €9.50, or €6 for the twice-weekly evening openings. Under-18s get in free, as do under-26s from or studying in EU countries who have proof of residency; on the first Sunday of each month admission is free for everyone. **Tickets** can be bought in advance by phone or online at Ⓦwww.louvre.fr, but you'll have to pay for them to be posted. For a smaller commission, you can buy tickets at branches of FNAC (see p.263) and Virgin Mega-store – and conveniently, there's a Virgin store right outside the entrance under the Arc du Carrousel. The ticket allows you to step outside for a break, though the museum itself has three good **cafés** – the quiet and elegant *Café Richelieu* (first floor, Richelieu), with its summer terrace, the cosy *Café Denon* (lower ground floor, Denon) and the busier *Café Mollien* (first floor, Denon), whose summer terrace looks down onto the main courtyard. The various cafés and restaurants directly under the Pyramide are less attractive.

## Orientation and highlights

From the Hall Napoléon under the **Pyramide**, stairs lead into each of the three wings: Denon (south), Richelieu (north) and Sully (east, around the giant quadrangle of the Cour Carré). Few visitors will be able to resist the allure of the *Mona Lisa* (see p.42), which haunts the **Denon** wing, together with the Italian paintings and sculptures and the large-scale French nineteenth-century canvases. A relatively peaceful alternative would be to focus on the grand chronologies of French painting and sculpture in the **Richelieu** wing. For a complete change of scene, descend to the **Medieval Louvre** section on

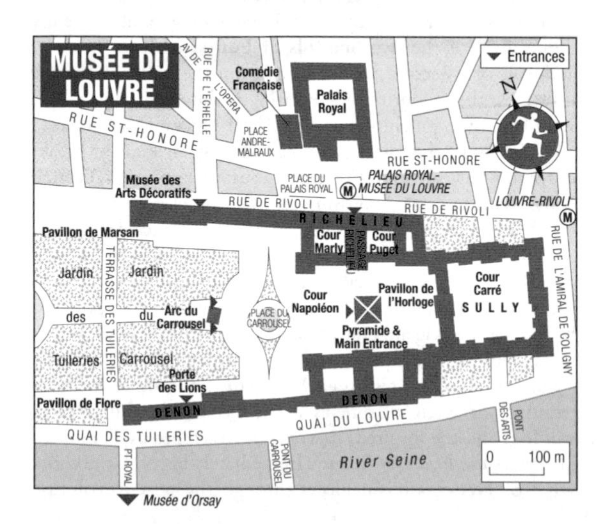

the lower ground floor of Sully where you'll find the dramatic stump of Philippe-Auguste's keep and vestiges of Charles V's medieval palace walls.

A **floor plan**, available free from the information booth in the Hall Napoléon, will help you find your way around. It's wise not to attempt to see too much – even if you spent the entire day here you'd only see a fraction of the collection. The museum's size does at least make it easy to get away from the crowds – beyond the Denon wing you can explore the Louvre in relative tranquillity. For a really **quiet visit**, come for the evening opening on Wednesdays and Fridays.



## Painting

The development of **French painting** is traced in one grand chronological circuit, beginning on the second floor of the Richelieu wing. The preliminary Richelieu section is chiefly of interest for the portraits of French kings and the edgy atmosphere of the two **Schools of Fontainebleau** (rooms 9 and 10). In a Second School piece from the 1590s, Gabrielle d'Estrées, the favourite of Henri IV, is shown sharing a bath with her sister, pinching her nipple as if plucking a cherry.

It's not until the seventeenth century, when Poussin breaks onto the scene (room 13), that the style known as **French Classicism** emerges. Poussin's *Arcadian Shepherds* shows four shepherds interpreting the inscription "et in arcadia ego" (I, too, in Arcadia) – meaning that death exists even in pastoral paradise. You'll need a healthy appetite for Classical bombast in the next suite of rooms, but there are some arresting portraits by Hyacinthe Rigaud and Philippe de Champaigne as well as some idiosyncratically mystical works by Georges de la Tour.

Moving into the **eighteenth century**, the more intimate paintings of Watteau come as a relief, as do Chardin's intense still lifes and the inspired, hasty rococo sketches by Fragonard known as the *Figures of Fantasy*. Immediately beyond, the chilly wind of **Neoclassicism** blows through the post-Revolution paintings of Gros, Gérard, Prud'hon, David and Ingres. This in turn contrasts with the more sentimental style launched by Greuze, which flows into the **Romanticism** of Géricault and Delacroix. The final set of rooms covers Millet, Corot and the **Barbizon school** of painting, the precursor of Impressionism. For anything later than 1848 you'll have to head over to the Musée d'Orsay (see p.113).

## Northern European painting

The western end of Richelieu's second floor is given over to **German**, **Flemish** and **Dutch** paintings. Here you'll find no fewer than twelve paintings by Rembrandt – look out for *Bathsheba* and *The Supper at Emmaus* in room 31 – and two serene canvases from Vermeer, *The Astronomer* and *The Lacemaker*, in room 37. An awesome set of two dozen works by Rubens can be found in the **Galerie Médicis** (room 18), the entire cycle dedicated to the glory of Queen Marie de Médicis.

## The Grande Galerie

Over in the Denon wing, the first floor is dominated by the staggering **Italian collection**. The high-ceilinged **Salon Carré** (room 3) has been used to exhibit paintings since the first exhibition or "salon" of the Académie Royale in 1725 and now displays thirteenth- to fifteenth-century works from Italian painters such as Giotto, Cimabue and Fra Angelico, as well as one of Uccello's panels depicting the *Battle of San Romano*.

To the west of the Salon, the famous **Grande Galerie**, originally built to link the palaces of the Louvre and the now-destroyed Tuileries, stretches into the distance. It begins with Mantegna's opulent *Madonna of Victory*, and continues through Giovanni Bellini, Filippo Lippi, Raphael, Correggio and Titian. Leonardo da Vinci's *Virgin of the Rocks*, *St John the Baptist* and *Virgin and Child with St Anne* are on display just after the first set of pillars, while the Mannerists make their entrance roughly halfway along.

The relatively small **Spanish Collection** is relegated to the far end of Denon but has a few gems, notably Murillo's tender *Beggar Boy* and the *Marquise de Santa Cruz* amongst the Goya portraits.



## Large-format French painting and the Mona Lisa

Running parallel to the Grande Galerie are two giant rooms labelled "large-format French paintings" on the plan. The Salle Mollien (room 75), dedicated to post-Revolution **French Nationalism**, boasts David's epic *Coronation of Napoleon I*. In the Salle Daru (room 77), early to mid-nineteenth-century

### The Mona Lisa

The **Mona Lisa** receives some six million visitors a year, many of whom wonder how such a diminutive, murky portrait acquired such amazing celebrity. The answer lies in the painting's story. It was probably brought to France by Leonardo himself, when he came to work for François I in 1516, but it remained largely neglected until the nineteenth-century poet and novelist Théophile Gautier turned his hand to a guidebook for the Louvre. Her "sinuous, serpentine mouth", he wrote, "turned up at the corners in a violet penumbra, mocks the viewer with such sweetness, grace and superiority that we feel timid, like schoolboys in the presence of a duchess".

In the Anglophone world the painting was made famous by the critic Walter Pater in 1869. According to Pater, her presence "is expressive of what in the ways of a thousand years men had come to desire". But the *Mona Lisa* only really hit the international big time when she was stolen by an Italian security guard in August 1911. By the time she was recovered, in December 1913, her face had graced the pages of endless books and newspapers. Then, in 1919, the Dadaist Marcel Duchamp bought a cheap postcard reproduction, coloured in a goatee beard and

**Romanticism** is heralded by Géricault's dramatic *Raft of the Medusa*, showing shipwrecked survivors despairing as sails disappear over the horizon. The model for the dead figure lying face down with his arm extended was Delacroix, whose iconic *Liberty Leading the People* also hangs in this room.

The **Salle des Etats** (room 6) is the proud setting for Leonardo da Vinci's **Mona Lisa** (see box below). If you want to meet *La Joconde* without the usual camera-toting swarm for company, be the first to arrive, the last to leave, or schedule your visit for one of the evening opening sessions. Elsewhere in the room, you can't miss Paolo Veronese's resplendent *Marriage at Cana*.

scrawled underneath "L.H.O.O.Q.", which when pronounced in French translates as "she's got a hot ass". Since Duchamp, the *Mona Lisa*'s celebrity has fed on itself, and critics have complained about the painting in vain. Bernard Berenson, for example, decided Lisa was "watchful, sly, secure, with a smile of anticipated satisfaction and a pervading air of hostile superiority", while Roberto Longhi claimed to prefer Renoir's women to this "wan fusspot".

In recent years, the *Mona Lisa*'s fame has only swelled as a result of her bit-part appearance in Dan Brown's conspiracy thriller, *The Da Vinci Code*, which suggests (among other wilder theories) that the *Mona Lisa* is a Leonardo self-portrait in drag. (It is at least true that the artist was known for painting androgynous-looking figures.) Visitors today often find the painting surprisingly small – and very dark. Basically, it's filthy, and while the new, air-conditioned glass frame adds a corrective tint, no art restorer has yet dared to propose actually working on the picture. Eventually, time may force the museum's hand, as the thin poplar panel on which the image is painted is slowly warping.

## Sculpture

**French sculpture** is arranged on the lowest two levels of the Richelieu wing, with the more monumental pieces housed in two grand, glass-roofed courtyards. Many sculptures removed from the park at Marly grace the **Cour Marly**, notably the four triumphal equestrian statues known as the *Marly Horses*. The **Cour Puget** has Pierre Puget's dynamic *Milon de Crotone* as its centrepiece. The surrounding rooms trace the development of sculpture in France from painful Romanesque Crucifixions to smooth Neoclassicism. Among the startlingly realistic Gothic pieces, you can't miss the Burgundian *Tomb of Philippe Pot*. Towards the end of the course, however, you may find yourself crying out for an end to all the gracefully perfect nudes and grandiose busts of noblemen. The only real antidote is Rodin, and you'll have to head west to the Musée d'Orsay (see p.113) or Musée Rodin (see p.120) to see any of his works.

Alternatively, make for the smaller, more intense **Italian sculpture** section in the long Galerie Mollien (room 4), on the ground and basement floors of Denon. Here you'll find two of Michelangelo's writhing *Slaves*, the anonymous *Veiled Woman* and Canova's irresistible *Cupid and Psyche*. In the old stables on the lower ground floor (room 1), you can admire early Italian sculpture, notably Duccio's virtuoso *Virgin and Child Surrounded by Angels*. For a more intimate approach, visit the **Tactile Gallery**, where you can run your hands over copies of some of the most important sculptures from the collection. In the small adjacent rooms A–C you can seek out some severe but impressive **Gothic Virgins** from Flanders and Germany.

### Pavillon des Sessions

The **Pavillon des Sessions**, at the far western end of the Denon wing, is an outpost of the new Musée du Quai Branly (see p.117), whose collections encompass all non-Western art. The sculptures displayed here are the artistic cherry-pickings, including anything from exquisitely abstracted sculpted heads and totem-like figures from West Africa to bird-like masks from northern Canada and wooden breast ornaments from Easter Island. After the endless pale ranks of serene Classical statuary elsewhere in the Louvre, the Pavillon can provide a jolt of much-needed visceral energy.



## Objets d'art

The vast **Objets d'art** section, on the first floor of the Richelieu wing, presents the finest tapestries, ceramics, jewellery and furniture commissioned by France's wealthiest and most influential patrons. Walking through the entire 81-room chronology affords a powerful sense of the evolution of aesthetic taste at its most refined and opulent. The exception is the **Middle Ages** section, which is of a decidedly pious nature, while the apotheosis of the whole experience comes towards the end, as the circuit passes through the breathtakingly plush **apartments** of Napoleon III's Minister of State.

## Antiquities

The enormous **Antiquities** collection practically forms a parallel museum of its own, taking up most of the Sully wing, aside from the top floor. **Oriental Antiquities** (Richelieu wing, ground floor) covers the sculptures, stone-carved writings, pottery and other relics of the Mesopotamian, Sumerian, Babylonian, Assyrian and Phoenician civilizations, plus the art of ancient Persia. Watch out for the black, 2m-high *Code of Hammurabi*, a hugely important find from the Mesopotamian civilization, dating from around 1800 BC. The utterly refined **Arts of Islam** collection lies below, on the lower ground floor.

### Egyptian antiquities

The Louvre's collection of **Egyptian Antiquities** is the most important in the world after that of the Egyptian Museum in Cairo. Starting on the ground floor of the Sully wing, the thematic circuit takes the visitor through the everyday life of pharaonic Egypt by way of cooking utensils, jewellery, musical instruments, sarcophagi and a host of mummified cats. Among the major exhibits of the first floor's chronological tour are: the *Great Sphinx*, carved from a single block of pink granite; the polychrome *Seated Scribe* statue; the striking, life-size wooden statue of Chancellor Nakhti; and a bust of Amenophis IV.

### Greek and Roman antiquities

The lower ground ("*entresol*") floor of Denon contains the fascinating **Pre-Classical Greece** section, while on the ground-floor level the handsomely vaulted room to the south of the main pyramid hall (room A) houses Italian Renaissance copies and restorations of antique sculptures. Immediately west of here, the Galerie Mollien begins the Italian sculpture section, while mirroring it to the east is the long **Galerie Daru** (room B). This kicks off the main Antiquities section with the poised energy of Lysippos's *Borghese Gladiator*. At the eastern end of the gallery, Lefuel's imperial **Escalier Daru**, or Daru staircase, rises triumphantly under the billowing famous feathers of the *Winged Victory of Samothrace*.

Skirt this staircase to continue through the **Etruscan and Roman** collections and on into the Sully wing, where you enter Lescot's original sixteenth-century palace. In the **Salle des Caryatides** (room 17), which houses Roman copies of Greek works, the musicians' balcony is supported by four giant caryatids, sculpted in 1550 by Jean Goujon. The celebrated *Venus de Milo* is found in room 12, surrounded by hordes of less familiar Aphrodites.

## Les Arts Décoratifs

**Map 2, D4.** 107 rue de Rivoli. Tues–Fri 11am–6pm, Sat & Sun 10am–6pm; €8; Ⓦwww.lesartsdecoratifs.fr; ⓂPalais Royal–Musée du Louvre/Tuileries.

The westernmost wing of the Palais du Louvre, on the north side, houses a second, newly revamped and entirely separate museum entitled **Les Arts Décoratifs**, which could be translated as "the art of design" or, more prosaically, as "applied arts".

## Musée des Arts Décoratifs

The biggest of the three museums, the **Musée des Arts Décoratifs**, takes you on a long – sometimes over-long – journey through French design, and French furniture in particular.

Medieval benches and tapestries slowly give way to an endless parade of gilt consoles and commodes before you arrive at graceful Art Deco armchairs and the contemporary designs of Philippe Starck and his rivals. The best rooms are the complete reconstructions: the medieval section holds a fifteenth-century bedchamber, for instance, complete with original wall panelling, canopied bed, fireplace and windows, while the eighteenth-century section features a room of gorgeous *singerie* panelling from the 1720s – decorated with then-fashionable frescoes of monkeys cavorting in human clothing. In the fabulous Art Deco and Art Nouveau section, there's a complete 1903 bedroom by métro designer Hector Guimard, and an entire apartment created in the early 1920s for the *couturière* Jeanne Lanvin. Towards the end there's even a part-reconstruction of a 1980s TGV carriage.

The second floor of the museum is occupied by themed galleries. One houses a progression of **toys** from wooden soldiers and china dolls to Star Wars figures and (interactive) computer games. Another gallery is devoted to over a thousand pieces of **jewellery**; there are a number of older pieces but the focus is on twentieth-century designs, and you'll find most of the great names represented here, notably the Art Nouveau jeweller René Lalique.

## Musée de la Mode et du Textile and Musée de la Publicité

The **Musée de la Mode et du Textile** holds high-quality temporary exhibitions drawn from the large permanent collection, aimed at demonstrating the most brilliant and cutting-edge of Paris fashions from all eras. Recent exhibitions have included Sonia Rykiel's couture designs and a personal "history of fashion" curated by Christian Lacroix. On the third floor, directly above the fashion museum, the **Musée de la Publicité** shows off its collection of advertising posters and video through cleverly themed, temporary exhibitions. The space is appropriately trendy – half exposed brickwork and steel panelling, and half crumbling Louvre finery.

3

# The Champs-Elysées and around

Synonymous with Parisian glitz and glamour, the **Champs-Elysées** cuts through one of the city's most exclusive districts, studded with luxury hotels and top fashion boutiques. The avenue forms part of a grand, 9km axis that extends from the Louvre at the heart of the city to the Grande Arche de la Défense in the west. Often referred to as the Voie Triomphale, or Triumphal Way, it offers impressive vistas along its length and is punctuated with some of the city's most recognizable landmarks – including the **place de la Concorde**, **Tuileries gardens** and the **Arc de Triomphe** – erected over the centuries by kings and emperors, presidents and corporations, each a monumental gesture aimed at promoting French power and prestige.

## The Champs-Elysées

Map 7, E2–L5.

Tree-lined and broad, the celebrated **avenue des Champs-Elysées** sweeps down from the Arc de Triomphe towards the place de la Concorde. Seen from a distance it's an impressive sight, though as you get up close it can seem a little disappointing, with its constant stream of traffic, its fast-food places and chain stores.

Over the last decade or so, however, the Champs has regained something of its former cachet as a chic address, enjoying a renaissance that started with a mid-1990s facelift, when the rows of trees that the Nazis removed during World War II were replanted and pavements were widened and repaved. A number of exclusive designers, such as Louis Vuitton, have subsequently moved in, luxury hotels have appeared, formerly dowdy shops such as the Publicis drugstore and the Renault car showroom have undergone stylish makeovers and acquired cool bar-restaurants, while new, fashionable cafés and restaurants in the streets around are constantly injecting fresh buzz and glamour.

The Champs-Elysées began life as a leafy promenade, an extension of the Tuileries gardens. It was transformed into a fashionable thoroughfare during the Second Empire, when members of the *haute bourgeoisie* built themselves splendid mansions along its length and high society frequented its cafés and theatres. Most of the mansions finally gave way to office blocks and the *beau monde* moved elsewhere, but remnants of this glitzy heyday live on at the *Lido* cabaret, *Fouquet's* café-restaurant (see p.202), the perfumier Guerlain's shop, occupying an exquisite 1913 building, and the former *Claridges* hotel, now a swanky shopping arcade.

The area bounded by the Champs-Elysées and, to the south, **avenue Montaigne** and **rue Francois 1^er^**, is nicknamed the **Triangle d'Or** (Golden Triangle) on account of its exclusive character: this is the domain of flagship designer stores, including Dior, Prada, Chanel and Givenchy, as well as luxury hotels, such as the *Plaza Athénée* and *George V*.

The less commercial stretch of the Champs-Elysées, between place de la Concorde and the Rond-Point roundabout, is bordered by chestnut trees and attractive flowerbeds. On the north side stand the guarded walls of the presidential **Elysée Palace**. The gigantic building with grandiose Neoclassical exteriors, glass roofs and exuberant flying statuary rising above the greenery to the south, is the Grand Palais, created with its neighbour, the Petit Palais, for the 1900 Exposition Universelle. Today, both the Grand Palais and Petit Palais contain permanent museums and host major exhibitions.

## The Petit Palais

**Map 7, K5.** Av Winston Churchill. Tues–Sun 10am–6pm; free; ⓦwww.petitpalais.paris.fr; ⓂChamps-Elysées-Clemenceau.

The **Petit Palais**, facing the Grand Palais, holds the **Musée des Beaux Arts de la Ville de Paris**. It's hardly "petit", but is certainly palatial, with its highly decorated Neoclassical exterior, interior garden with Tuscan colonnade, beautiful spiral wrought-iron staircases and a grand gallery similar to Versailles' Hall of Mirrors. The museum's extensive holdings of paintings, sculpture and decorative artworks are displayed on two floors and range from the ancient Greek and Roman period up to the early twentieth century. At first sight it looks like it has mopped up the leftovers after the city's other galleries have taken their pick, but there are some real gems here, such as Monet's *Soleil couchant sur la Seine à Lavacourt*, Courbet's provocative *Demoiselles du bord de la Seine* and Pissarro's delicate *Le Pont Royal et le Pavillon de Flore*, painted a few months before he died. Decorative arts feature strongly, especially eighteenth-century furniture and porcelain. There's also fantasy Art Nouveau jewellery, an elegant dining room in pear wood by Hector Guimard (who designed the original Paris métro stations) and a fine collection of seventeenth-century Dutch landscape painting. Changing exhibitions allow the museum to display works from its vast reserves. If your own reserves are running low you could head for the smart café, which opens out onto the restored interior garden.

**Popular lunchtime concerts are held most Thursdays at the Petit Palais by Radio France (turn up about an hour in advance to collect a ticket).**

## The Grand Palais

**Map 7, J5.** Av Winston Churchill Ⓦwww.grandpalais.fr; ⓂChamps-Elysées-Clemenceau/Franklin D. Roosevelt.

The 44m-high glass cupola of the huge, Neoclassical **Grand Palais** can be seen from most of the city's viewpoints and forms the centrepiece of the *nef* (nave), a huge, impressive exhibition space, whose glass and steel ceiling allows light to flood the interior. After extensive restoration work, now more or less complete, the *palais* has resumed its role as the city's premier special events venue, hosting music festivals and art exhibitions, as well as trade fairs and fashion shows.

In the west wing of the building the **Galeries Nationales** (Mon & Wed–Sun 10am–8pm, till 10pm on Wed; €11; Ⓦwww.grandpalais.fr) is one of the city's major exhibition spaces and well known for its blockbuster shows, such as the major Turner exhibition in 2010. The Grand Palais' east wing houses the **Palais de la Découverte** (Tues–Sat 9.30am–6pm, Sun & hols 10am–7pm; €7, combined ticket with planetarium €10.30; Ⓦwww.palais-decouverte.fr), Paris's original science museum, opened in the late 1930s. It has plenty of interactive exhibits, some engaging temporary exhibitions on subjects such as climate change, dinosaurs and the history of clay, as well as an excellent **planetarium**.

# The Arc de Triomphe

**Map 7, D2.** Daily: April–Sept 10am–11pm; Oct–March 10am–10.30pm; €9; ⓂCharles-de-Gaulle-Etoile.

The best views of the Champs-Elysées are to be had from the terrace at the top of the **Arc de Triomphe**. Modelled on the ancient Roman triumphal arches and impressive in scale, it was begun by Napoleon in 1806 in homage to his Grande Armée, but wasn't actually finished until 1836 by Louis-Philippe, who dedicated it to the French army in general. Later, in 1871 and 1942, victorious German armies would make a point of marching through the arch to compound the humiliation of the French. After the Prussians' triumphal parade in 1871, the Parisians lit bonfires beneath the arch and down the Champs-Elysées to eradicate the "stain" of German boots. Still a potent symbol of the country's military might, the arch is the starting point for the annual Bastille Day procession, a bombastic march-past of tanks, guns and flags. A more poignant ceremony is conducted every evening at 6.30pm, when the continually burning flame on the tomb of an unknown soldier, killed in the Great War, is stoked up by war veterans. In the little museum, just below the viewing terrace, is a small collection of prints and photos depicting illustrious scenes from the history of the arch, as well as preliminary drawings for the glorious friezes and sculptures that adorn the pillars. The Champs-Elysées side in particular boasts a fine high-relief sculpture, *La Marseillaise* by François Rude.

Access to the Arc de Triomphe is gained from stairs on the north corner of the Champs-Elysées. Views from the top are at their best towards dusk on a sunny day when the marble of the Grande Arche de la Défense sparkles in the setting sun and the Louvre is bathed in warm light. Your attention is also likely to be caught by the mesmerizing traffic movements below in place Charles-de-Gaulle or the Etoile, the world's first roundabout, otherwise popularly known as place de la Traffic.

## Etoile and around

**Map 7, D2.** Ⓜ Charles-de-Gaulle-Etoile.

Twelve avenues make up the star of the **Etoile**, with the Arc de Triomphe at its centre. The avenues striking off into the northern 16^e^ and eastern 17^e^ arrondissements are for the most part cold and soulless, and the huge fortified apartments here are empty much of the time, as their owners – royal, exiled royal, ex-royal or just extremely rich – move between their other residences dotted about the globe. The 8^e^ arrondissement, north of the Champs-Elysées, however, has more to offer commercially and culturally, with some of the *hôtels particuliers* (mansions) housing fine museums, best of which is the splendid Musée Jacquemart-André.

## Musée Jacquemart-André

**Map 7, off I1.** 158 bd Haussmann. Daily 10am–6pm; €10; Ⓦwww.musee-jacquemart-andre.com; ⓂMiromesnil/St-Philippe-du-Roule.

The Haussmannian Hôtel André houses the magnificent art collection of the **Musée Jacquemart-André**, accumulated by the art lover Edouard André and his wife, former society portraitist Nélie Jacquemart, while on their travels. They loved Italian art above all; a stunning series of fifteenth- and sixteenth-century Italian works, including some by Tiepolo, Botticelli, Donatello, Mantegna and Uccello, forms the core of their collection. Almost as compelling as the splendid interior and artworks is the insight into an extraordinary marriage and grand nineteenth-century lifestyle.

The Musée Jacquemart-André has a fabulously elegant *salon de thé*. See p.202.

## Musée Nissim de Camondo

**Map 7, off I1.** 63 rue de Monceau. Wed–Sun 10am–5.30pm; €6; ⓂMonceau/Villiers.

A grand mansion in the style of the Petit Trianon at Versailles is the fitting setting for an impressive collection of eighteenth-century decorative art and painting. The **Musée Nissim de Camondo** was built up by Count Moïse de Camondo, son of a wealthy Sephardic Jewish banker who emigrated from Istanbul to Paris in the late nineteenth century. The ground-floor rooms, decorated in original eighteenth-century panelling, overflow with Gobelin tapestries, paintings of pastoral scenes by Huet and Vigée-Lebrun, gilded furniture and delicate Sèvres porcelain; an excellent free audioguide, available in English, helps you get the most out of the exhibits.

The upper-floor rooms, where the family spent most of their time, are cosier and less museum-like, affording glimpses into the home life of an early twentieth-century aristocratic family. These rooms take on a progressively melancholy air, however, as you learn more about the tragic fate of the Camondo family: after a few years of marriage Moïse's wife left him for the head groom; his beloved son, Nissim, after whom the museum is named, died on a flying mission in World War I, while his remaining child, Béatrice, perished together with her children in the camps in World War II.

### Musée Cernuschi

**Map 7, I1.** 7 av Vélasquez. Tues–Sun 10am–5.40pm; free; ⓂMonceau/Villiers.

Further north, ancient Chinese art reigns at the **Musée Cernuschi**. The art was bequeathed to the state by the banker Cernuschi, who narrowly escaped execution for giving money to the insurrectionary Commune of 1871. The ground floor hosts temporary exhibitions, while the first floor displays the permanent collection, among which are some exquisite pieces, including intricately worked bronze vases from the Shang era (1550–1050 BC) and some unique ceramics detailing everyday life in ancient China.

## Place de la Concorde

**Map 2, A3.** ⓂConcorde.

Marking the beginning of the Champs-Elysées' graceful gradients is the grand **place de la Concorde**, marred only by the constant stream of traffic around its perimeter. At the centre of the *place* is an obelisk from the temple of Ramses at Luxor, offered to Louis-Philippe in a favour-currying gesture by the viceroy of Egypt in 1829. Despite the harmony implied in its name, the square's history is anything but peaceful: the equestrian statue of Louis XV that formerly stood at the centre of the square was toppled by revolutionaries in

1792 and, between 1793 and 1795, some 1300 people died here beneath the guillotine, among them Louis XVI, Marie-Antoinette, Danton and Robespierre. From the centre of the square there are magnificent views of the Champs-Elysées and Tuileries, and you can admire the alignment and symmetry of the Assemblée Nationale, on the far side of the Seine, with the church of the Madeleine at the end of rue Royale, to the north. The Neoclassical *Hôtel de Crillon* – the ultimate luxury address for visitors to Paris – and its twin, the Hôtel de la Marine, housing the Ministry of the Navy, flank the entrance to rue Royale.

## Jardin des Tuileries

**Map 2, B4.** Ⓜ Tuileries/Concorde.

With its splendid vistas, grand avenues, fountains and manicured lawns, the **Jardin des Tuileries**, extending from the place de la Concorde to the Louvre, is the formal French garden *par excellence*. It's especially popular on Sunday mornings when half the city seems to be in the park jogging; families come to promenade and children push toy boats around the central pond and get treated to pony rides. Named after the medieval warren of tilemakers (*tuileries*) that once occupied the site, the Tuileries gardens are all that survive of the palace and grounds commissioned by Catherine de Médicis in the mid-sixteenth century (the palace was burned down during the Paris Commune in 1871). A hundred years after that, Le Nôtre, who landscaped the grounds at Versailles, created the current schema of the gardens, laying out a grand central alley, *terrasses* and pools both round and octagonal in shape. Later, sculptures were brought here from Versailles and Marly, including Coysevox's rearing horses *Fama* and *Mercury*. The originals are now housed in the Richelieu wing of the Louvre and have been replaced here by copies.

During the eighteenth century, fashionable Parisians came to the gardens to preen, parade and relax, and in 1783 the

Montgolfier brothers, Joseph and Etienne, launched the first successful hot-air balloon here. The first serious replanting was carried out after the Revolution and, in the nineteenth century, rare species such as honey locusts and pagoda trees were added to the garden, at this time dominated by chestnut trees. Sadly, some of the oldest specimens were lost in the December 1999 storms: the centennial chestnuts around the two central oval ponds are now the most senior.

At the eastern end of the gardens in front of the Louvre is the **Jardin du Carrousel**, a raised terrace where the Palais des Tuileries was sited. It's now planted with trim yew hedges, between which stand oddly static bronzes of buxom female nudes by Maillol.

---

**One of the best of the pleasant shady cafés in the Jardin des Tuileries is *Café Véry* (see p.202).**

---

## Musée de l'Orangerie

**Map 2, A4.** Jardin des Tuileries. Wed–Sat & Sun 12.30–7pm, Fri till 9pm; groups only 9am–12.30pm; €6.50; Ⓦwww.musee-orangerie.fr; ⓂConcorde.

The **Musée de l'Orangerie** is an elegant Neoclassical-style building, originally designed to protect the Tuileries' orange trees, and now housing a private art collection, including eight of Monet's giant water lily paintings. It re-opened in 2006 after six years of renovations designed to bring Monet's masterpieces "back into the light". In the 1960s a concrete ceiling was added to accommodate a new storey; this has been removed, and once again the natural light illumines the water lilies – exactly how Monet wished them to be seen. These vast, mesmerizing canvases were executed in the last years of the artist's life, a period when he almost obsessively painted the pond in his garden at Giverny, attempting to capture the fleeting light and changing colours.

On the lower floor of the museum is an excellent collection of paintings by Monet's contemporaries. Highlights include a number of Cézanne still lifes and portraits, some sensuous nudes by Renoir, vibrant landscapes by Derain and a collection of more expressionistic canvases by Soutine.

## 3 Jeu de Paume

**Map 2, A3.** 1 place de la Concorde. Tues noon–9pm, Wed–Fri noon–7pm, Sat & Sun 10am–7pm; €6; Ⓦwww.jeudepaume.org; ⓂConcorde.

Opposite the Orangerie stands the Neoclassical **Jeu de Paume**, once a royal tennis court and now a major exhibition space dedicated to photography and video art; it's not as well lit as you might expect from the soaring, light-filled foyer, but this is one of the top venues for catching major retrospectives of well-known photographers, such as Martin Parr. It has a sister site at the Hôtel de Sully (see p.77).

4

# The Grands Boulevards and around

Built in the eighteenth century on the site of the city's fourteenth-century ramparts, the **Grands Boulevards** extend in a long arc from the Eglise de la Madeleine in the west to the Bastille in the east. The streets off the Grands Boulevards are home to grandiose financial, cultural and state institutions and are associated with established commerce such as the clothing trade, plus well-heeled shopping. Crisscrossing the boulevards, attractive nineteenth-century shopping arcades or **passages** conceal chic boutiques, while the classy department stores Galeries Lafayette and Printemps (see p.252) stand nearby in the 9$^{e}$ arrondissement, just north of the **Palais Garnier** opera house. Catering to the seriously rich, the boutiques at the western end of the 1$^{er}$, around the church of the **Madeleine** and **place Vendôme**, display the wares of top couturiers, jewellers and art dealers. The peaceful gardens of the **Palais Royal**, to the south, make for an ideal rest stop and are a handy shortcut to the venerable **Bibliothèque Nationale**.

# The Grands Boulevards

The **Grands Boulevards** is the collective name given to the eight streets that form one continuous, broad thoroughfare running from the Madeleine to République, then down to the Bastille. Lined with solid Haussmann-era mansion blocks, imposing banks, cinemas, theatres, brasseries and neon-lit fast-food outlets, these broad boulevards are busy and vibrant, if not the most alluring or glamorous parts of Paris. This was not always so: the western section, from the Madeleine to Porte St-Denis, was especially fashionable in the nineteenth century. Parisians came in droves to stroll and sit out drinking lemonade or beer in the numerous cafés, and the chic café clientele of the **boulevard des Italiens** set the trends for all of Paris in terms of manners, dress and conversation. The eastern section, meanwhile, developed a more colourful reputation, derived from its association with street theatre, mime, juggling, puppets, waxworks and cafés of ill repute. It earned itself the nickname the *boulevard du Crime* and was immortalized in the film *Les Enfants du Paradis*. Much of this area was swept away in the latter half of the nineteenth century by Baron Haussmann when he created the huge place de la République.

On boulevard St-Denis, you get a powerful sense of the old city limits; two triumphal arches stand at either end of the street, now looking oddly out of place in the midst of motor traffic and shop hoardings. The **Porte St-Denis** (map 3, K9; ⓂStrasbourg-St-Denis) was erected in 1672 to celebrate Louis XIV's victories on the Rhine. With France's northern frontier secured, Louis ordered Charles V's city walls to be demolished and replaced by leafy promenades; these became known as the *boulevards* after the Germanic word for an earth rampart, a *bulwark*. Two hundred metres east, the more graceful **Porte St-Martin** (map 3, L9) was built two years after its sibling, in celebration of further victories.

As recently as the 1950s, a visitor to Paris would, as a matter of course, have gone for a stroll along the Grands Boulevards to see *Paris vivant*. Something of this tradition still survives in the theatres and cinemas (including the Max Linder and Grand Rex – the latter an extraordinary building inside and out, see p.273) and numerous brasseries and cafés.

### Musée Grévin

**Map 3, H8.** 10 bd Montmartre. Mon–Fri 10am–6.30pm, Sat & Sun 10am–7pm; last admission 1hr beforehand; €20, children up to 14 years €12; Ⓦwww.grevin.com; ⓂGrands Boulevards.

The waxworks in the **Musée Grévin** are a remnant from the fun-loving times of the Grands Boulevards. The collection comprises mainly French literary, media and political personalities as well as the usual bunch of Hollywood actors. Perhaps the best things about the museum are the original rooms: the magical Palais des Mirages (Hall of Mirrors), built for the World Fair in 1900; the theatre, with its sculptures by Bourdelle; and the 1882 Baroque-style Hall of Columns where, among other unlikely juxtapositions, Lara Croft prepares for action a few steps away from a dignified Charles de Gaulle, while Voltaire smiles across at the billowing skirts of Marilyn Monroe.

## The Opéra (Palais Garnier)

**Map 3, D8.** Interior daily 10am–4.30pm; €9; Ⓦwww.operadeparis.fr; ⓂOpéra.

Set back from the boulevard des Capucines is the dazzling nineteenth-century Opéra de Paris – now commonly referred to as the **Palais Garnier** to distinguish it from the new opera house at the Bastille. The architect, Charles Garnier, drew on a number of existing styles and succeeded in creating a magnificently ornate building the like of which Paris had never seen before. Its **exterior** is a fairy-tale concoction of white, pink and green marble, colonnades, rearing horses, winged angels and gleaming gold busts of composers. Four allegorical sculptures punctuate the facade, one of which, Carpeaux's *La Danse*, caused a scandal on its unveiling on account of its sensuous, naked figures, and even had ink thrown over it; the original is now in the Musée d'Orsay and has been replaced by a copy. The opera house took fourteen years to complete and was opened in 1875. Part of the reason construction took so long was the discovery of a water table that had to be drained and replaced by a huge concrete well, giving rise to the legend of an underground lake, popularized by Gaston Leroux's *Phantom of the Opera*. By day, you can visit the sumptuous gilt-marble **interior**, including the auditorium, as long as there are no rehearsals – your best chance is between 1 and 2pm. The colourful ceiling, depicting opera and ballet scenes, is easily recognized as the work of **Chagall**.

For information on booking opera tickets see p.282.

## Paris-Story

**Map 3, D8.** 11bis rue Scribe. Daily with shows on the hour 10am–6pm; €10; ⓂOpéra/Chaussée-d'Antin-La-Fayette & RER Auber.

West of the Opéra and next door to the main tourist office, the **Paris-Story** multimedia show is an enjoyable, if partial and highly romanticized, history of Paris "narrated" by Victor Hugo, with simultaneous translation in English. The 45-minute film uses a kaleidoscope of computer-generated images and archive footage, set against a luscious classical-music soundtrack.

## Madeleine

**Map 3, B9.** ⓂMadeleine.

South of boulevard Haussmann, occupying nearly the whole of the place de la Madeleine, is the huge, imperious-looking **Eglise de la Madeleine**, the parish church of Parisian high society. Modelled on the Parthenon, the church is surrounded by 52 Corinthian columns and fronted by a huge pediment depicting *The Last Judgement*. Originally intended as a monument to Napoleon's army, the building narrowly escaped being turned into a railway station before finally being consecrated to Mary Magdalene in 1845. Inside, the wide, single nave is decorated with Ionic columns and surmounted by three huge domes – the only source of natural light. A theatrical stone sculpture of the Magdalene being swept up to heaven by two angels draws your eye to the high altar. The half-dome above is decorated with a fresco by Jules-Claude Ziegler (1804–56), a student of Ingres; entitled *The History of Christianity*, it commemorates the concordat signed between the church and state after the end of the Revolution, and shows all the key figures in Christendom, with Napoleon centre-stage, naturally.

If the Madeleine caters to spiritual needs, the rest of the square is given over to nourishment of an earthier kind, for this is where Paris's top **gourmet food stores**, Fauchon and Hédiard (see p.265), are located. Their remarkable displays are a feast for the eyes, and both have restaurants where you can sample some of their epicurean treats. On the east side of the church is one of the city's oldest **flower markets**, dating back to 1832 and open every day except Monday. Also nearby are some rather fine Art Nouveau public toilets, built in 1905 and definitely worth inspecting.

## Place Vendôme and around

**Map 2, C2.** Ⓜ Madeleine/Tuileries.

Built by Hardouin-Mansart, **Place Vendôme** is one of the city's most impressive set pieces. It's a pleasingly symmetrical, eight-sided *place*, enclosed by a harmonious ensemble of elegant mansions, graced with Corinthian pilasters, *mascarons* (decorative masks) and steeply pitched roofs. Once the grand residences of tax collectors and financiers, they now house such luxury establishments as the *Ritz*, one of the three original *Ritz* hotels, along with those in London and Madrid, established by César Ritz at the start of the last century. Elsewhere in the square top-flight jewellers Cartier, Bulgari and others reinforce the air of exclusivity. Somewhat out of proportion with the rest of the *place*, the centrepiece is a towering triumphal **column**, surmounted by a statue of Napoleon dressed as Caesar. It was raised in 1806 to celebrate the Battle of Austerlitz – bronze reliefs of scenes from the battle, cast from 1200 recycled Austro-Russian cannons, spiral their way up the column.

An air of luxury also pervades the surrounding streets, especially ancient **rue St-Honoré**, a preserve of top fashion designers and art galleries; you can marvel at John Galliano's extravagant creations at no. 392 or join the style-conscious young Parisians perusing the latest designs at the Colette concept store at no. 213.

## The *passages*

The 2e and 9e arrondissements are scattered with around twenty **passages**, or shopping arcades, that have survived from the early nineteenth century. Built at a time when pavements were unknown in Paris, they were places where people could shop, dine and drink, protected from mud and horse-drawn vehicles. Their popularity declined with the advent of department stores in the latter half of the nineteenth century and most were demolished by Haussmann to make way for his building projects. The remaining *passages* were left to crumble and decay, and it's only over the last decade or so that many have now been renovated and restored to something approaching their former glory; their tiled floors and glass roofs have been repaired and chic boutiques have moved in alongside the old-fashioned traders and secondhand dealers. Their entrances are easy to miss, and where you emerge at the other end can be quite a surprise. Most are closed at night and on Sundays.

### Galerie Véro-Dodat

**Map 2, E4.** Ⓜ Louvre-Rivoli.

Between rue Croix-des-Petits-Champs and rue Jean-Jacques Rousseau, **Galerie Véro-Dodat**, named after the two pork butchers who set it up in 1824, is the most homogeneous and aristocratic of the *passages*, with painted ceilings and mahogany-panelled shop fronts divided by faux-marble columns. Some of the older businesses are still quietly plying their trade here, such as *luthier* R and F Charle, selling and repairing stringed instruments, while others have given way to luxury boutiques, such as Christian Louboutin.

## Galerie Vivienne

**Map 2, E2.** Ⓜ Bourse.

The flamboyant decor of Grecian and marine motifs in **Galerie Vivienne**, linking rue Vivienne with rue des Petits-Champs, establishes the perfect ambience in which to buy Jean-Paul Gaultier gear, browse in the antiquarian bookshop, Librairie Jousseaume, which dates back to the *passage*'s earliest days, and take a tea break in *A Priori Thé* (see p.205).

## Passage Choiseul

**Map 2, D2.** Ⓜ Pyramides.

Alluringly dark and dingy-looking, the **passage Choiseul** shelters takeaway food shops, discount clothes and book stores, bars, galleries and Lavrut, at no. 52, a well-known supplier of artists' materials. Also here is an entrance to the Théâtre des Bouffes Parisiens, where Offenbach conducted the first performance of *Orpheus in the Underworld*.

## Passage des Panoramas

**Map 3, G8.** Ⓜ Grands Boulevards.

Slightly scruffier is the **passage des Panoramas**, the grid of arcades north of the Bibliothèque Nationale, beyond rue St-Marc. Most of the eateries here make no pretence at style, but one old brasserie, now a tearoom, *L'Arbre à Cannelle* (see p.205), has fantastic carved wood panelling, and there are still bric-a-brac shops, stamp dealers and an old print shop with its original 1867 fittings. It was around the Panoramas, in 1817, that the first Parisian gas lamps were installed.

## Passage Jouffroy and passage Verdeau

**Map 3, H8/7.** ⓂGrands Boulevards.

**Passage Jouffroy**, across boulevard Montmartre, is full of the kind of stores that make shopping an adventure rather than a chore. One of them, M & G Segas, sells walking canes and theatrical antiques opposite a shop displaying every conceivable fitting and furnishing for a doll's house. Near the romantic *Hôtel Chopin*, Paul Vulin sets out his second-hand books along the passageway, and Ciné-Doc appeals to cinephiles with its collection of old film posters. Crossing rue de la Grange-Batelière, you enter the equally enchanting **passage Verdeau**, sheltering antiquarian books, old prints and postcards.

## Passage du Grand-Cerf

**Map 2, H3.** ⓂEtienne-Marcel.

Back in the 2e arrondissement the three-storey **passage du Grand-Cerf**, between rue St-Denis and rue Dessoubs, is stylistically the most impressive of all the *passages*. The wrought-iron work, glass roof and plain-wood shop fronts have all been cleaned, attracting chic arts, crafts and design shops. There's always something quirky and original on display in the window of Le Labo (no. 4), specializing in lamps and other lighting fixtures made from recycled objects, while As'Art, opposite, is a treasure trove of home furnishings and objects from Africa.

# The Palais Royal

**Map 2, E3–E4.** ⓂPalais Royal-Musée du Louvre.

At the heart of the 1er arrondissement stands the **Palais Royal**, a handsome, colonnaded palace built for Cardinal Richelieu in 1629, though little remains of the original edifice. It now houses various government and constitutional bodies, as well as the **Comédie Française**, longstanding venue for the classics of French theatre.

North of the palace lie sedate **gardens** surrounded by stately eighteenth-century buildings built over arcades, housing quirky antique and design shops. The gardens are an attractive and peaceful oasis, with avenues of clipped limes, fountains and flowerbeds. You'd hardly guess that for many years this was a site of gambling dens, brothels (it was here that Napoleon lost his virginity to a prostitute in 1787) and funfair attractions – there was even a *café mécanique*, where you sat at a table, sent your order down one of its legs, and were served via the other. The prohibition on public gambling in 1838, however, put an end to the fun. Folly, some might say, has returned though, in the form of Daniel Buren's black-and-white striped pillars, rather like sticks of Brighton rock, dotted about the main courtyard in front of the palace. Installed in 1986, they're a rather disconcerting sight, but seem popular with children and rollerbladers, who treat them as an adventure playground and obstacle course respectively.

## The Bibliothèque Nationale Richelieu

**Map 2, E2.** 58 rue de Richelieu. Library reading rooms: Mon–Fri 9/10am–6pm, Sat 10am–5pm; exhibitions Tues–Sun 10am–7pm; €7; Ⓦwww.bnf.fr; ⓂBourse. Cabinet des Monnaies, Médailles et Antiques: Mon–Fri 9am–6pm, Sat 9am–5pm; free.

Cutting through the Palais Royal gardens brings you to the forbidding wall of the **Bibliothèque Nationale Richelieu**, much of whose enormous collection has been transferred to the new François Mitterrand site in the 13$^{e}$. The library's origins go back to the 1660s, when Louis XIV's finance minister Colbert deposited a collection of royal manuscripts here, and it was first opened to the public in 1692. There's no restriction on entering the library, nor on peering into the atmospheric reading rooms; the central room, with its slender iron columns supporting nine domes, is a fine example of the early use of iron-frame construction. Visiting the library's temporary exhibitions will give you access to the beautiful **Galerie Mazarine**, with its panelled ceilings painted by Romanelli (1617–62). It's also worth calling into the **Cabinet des Monnaies, Médailles et Antiques**, a permanent display of coins, Etruscan bronzes, ancient Greek jewellery and some exquisite medieval cameos. One of the highlights is Charlemagne's ivory chess set, its pieces made up of malevolent-looking characters astride elephants.

5

# Beaubourg and Les Halles

Straddling the 3e and 4e arrondissements, the **quartier Beaubourg** hums with lively cafés, shops and art galleries. At its heart stands the **Pompidou Centre**, one of the city's most popular attractions. The ground-breaking "inside-out" architecture of this huge arts centre provoked a storm of controversy on its opening in 1977, but since then it has won over critics and public alike. Now it is one of the city's most recognizable landmarks, drawing large numbers to its excellent modern art museum and high-profile exhibitions. By contrast, nearby **Forum des Halles**, a massive underground shopping complex built around the same time as the Pompidou Centre to replace the centuries-old **Les Halles** food market, has never really endeared itself to the city's inhabitants. It's probably the least inspired of all the urban developments undertaken in Paris in the last thirty years; the good news is that it's currently undergoing a major revamp.

## The Pompidou Centre

**Map 2, H5.** Ⓦwww.cnac-gp.fr; ⓂRambuteau/Hôtel-de-Ville.

The **Pompidou Centre**, also known locally as Beaubourg, is one of the twentieth century's most radical buildings. In an effort to move away from the traditional idea of galleries as closed treasure chests, the architects Renzo Piano and Richard Rogers stripped the "skin" off the building and made all the "bones" visible. The infrastructure was put on the outside: escalator tubes and utility pipes, brightly colour-coded according to their function, climb around the exterior in snakes-and-ladders fashion.

The centre's main draw is the excellent modern art museum, the **Musée National d'Art Moderne**. Major retrospectives of modern and contemporary artists are frequently held on the top floor, and there's also a huge public library, two cinemas and performance spaces. One of the treats of visiting the museum is that you get to ascend the transparent **escalator** on the outside of the building, affording superb views over the city.

## Musée National d'Art Moderne

Daily except Tues 11am–10pm; €10, under 18s plus EU residents aged 18–25 free, free to all first Sun of the month; tickets bookable online.

The **Musée National d'Art Moderne** is spread over floors four and five of the Pompidou Centre, with the latter covering the period 1905 to 1960, and the former 1960 to the present day. Thanks to an astute acquisitions policy and some generous gifts, the collection is a near-complete visual essay on the history of twentieth-century art and is so large that only a fraction of the fifty thousand works are on display at any one time (they're frequently rotated).

The collection on **floor five** starts in a blaze of colour with the **Fauvists** – **Braque**, **Derain**, **Vlaminck** and **Matisse**. A fine example of the movement's desire to create form rather than imitate nature is Braque's *L'Estaque* (1906); colour becomes a way of composing and structuring a picture, with trees and sky reduced to blocks of vibrant reds and greens.

Shape is broken down even further in Picasso and Braque's early **Cubist** paintings. One of the highlights here is **Picasso**'s portrait of his lover Fernande (*Femme assise dans un fauteuil;* 1910), in which different angles of the figure are shown all at once, giving rise to complex patterns and creating the effect of movement.

One room is devoted to the nihilistic Dada movement; art students cluster round leading Dadaist **Marcel Duchamp**'s notorious *Fontaine* (1917), a urinal elevated to the rank of "art" simply by being taken out of its ordinary context and put on display.

The museum possesses a particularly fine collection of works by **Kandinsky**; you can follow the artist's experiments with abstract art through his series "Impressions, Improvisations and Compositions". Fellow abstract-art pioneers, **Robert and Sonia Delaunay**, set the walls ablaze with a number of their characteristically colourful paintings.

**Surrealist painters** Magritte, Dalí and Ernst figure in later rooms. **Ernst**'s *Ubu Imperator* (1923), typical of the movement's exploration of the darker recesses of the mind, depicts a figure that is part man, part Tower of Pisa and part spinning top, apparently symbolizing the perversion of male authority.

American **abstract expressionists** Jackson Pollock and Mark Rothko are also represented. In Pollock's splattery *Number 26A, Black and white* (1948), the two colours seem to struggle for domination; the dark bands of colour in Rothko's large canvas *No. 14 (Browns over Dark)*, in contrast, draw the viewer in. **Matisse**'s later experiments with form and colour are usually on show. His cut-out gouache technique is perfected in his masterpiece *La Tristesse du Roi* (1952), a meditation on old age and memory.

The collection continues on the **fourth floor** with **contemporary art**, as well as displays of architectural models and contemporary design. Of the more established artists, **Yves Klein** stands out for his series of "body prints", in which he turned female models into human paintbrushes, covering them in paint to create his artworks. Other established French artists you're likely to come across include Annette Messager, Sophie

Calle, Christian Boltanski and Daniel Buren. **Boltanski** is known for his large *mise-en-scène* installations, often containing veiled allusions to the Holocaust. **Buren**'s works are easy to spot: they all bear his trademark stripes, exactly 8.7cm in width.

Some space is dedicated to **video art**, with changing installations by artists such as Jean-Luc Vilmout, Dominique Gonzalez-Foerster, the up-and-coming Melik Ohanian and current star of the scene Pierre Huyghe.

### Atelier Brancusi

Daily except Tues 2–6pm; free.

Down some steps off the Pompidou Centre's piazza, in a small, separate building, is the **Atelier Brancusi**, the reconstructed studio of the sculptor **Constantin Brancusi**, who bequeathed the contents of his *atelier* to the state on a condition that the rooms be arranged exactly as he left them. Studios one and two are crowded with fluid sculptures of highly polished brass and marble and his trademark abstract bird and column shapes. In studios three and four, Brancusi's private quarters, you get a vivid sense of how the artist lived and worked.

## Quartier Beaubourg

**Map 2, H5.** ⓂHôtel-de-Ville.

The lively **quartier Beaubourg** around the Pompidou Centre also offers much in the way of visual art. The colourful moving sculptures and fountains in the pool in front of Eglise St-Merri on **place Igor Stravinsky**, on the south side of the Pompidou Centre, were created by Jean Tinguely and Niki de Saint Phalle; this squirting set of waterworks pays homage to Stravinsky – each fountain corresponds to one of his compositions (*The Firebird*, *The Rite of Spring*, etc) – though shows scant respect for passers-by. Stravinsky's music in many ways steered the course for the pioneering work of **IRCAM** (Institut de la Recherche et de la Coordination Acoustique/Musique), whose entrance is on the west side of the square. Founded by the composer Pierre Boulez, it's a research centre for contemporary music and a concert venue, much of it underground, with an overground extension by Renzo Piano.

North of the Pompidou Centre, numerous commercial galleries take up the contemporary art theme on **rue Quincampoix**, the most attractive street in the area: narrow, pedestrianized and lined with handsome *hôtels particuliers*.

## Hôtel de Ville

**Map 2, H7.** Ⓜ Rambuteau/Hôtel-de-Ville.

South of the Pompidou Centre stands the **Hôtel de Ville**, the seat of the city's mayor. It's a mansion of gargantuan proportions in florid neo-Renaissance style, modelled almost entirely on the previous building which was burned down during the Commune in 1871. A succession of conservative governments decided that Paris was too unruly to be allowed its own administration and it was only in 1977 that the office of mayor was restored – with Jacques Chirac winning the post. The huge square in front of the Hôtel de Ville, a notorious guillotine site during the Revolution, becomes the location of a popular **ice-skating rink** from December to March; it's free and you can hire skates for €5.

## Les Halles and around

**Map 2, F4–G5.** Ⓜ Les-Halles/RER Châtelet-Les-Halles.

**Les Halles** was the site of the city's main food market for over eight hundred years until it was moved out to the suburbs in 1969, despite widespread opposition. It was replaced by landscaped gardens and a large underground shopping and leisure complex, known as the Forum des Halles. Unsightly, rundown, even unsavoury in parts, the complex is now widely acknowledged as an architectural disaster – so much so that steps are underway to give Les Halles a major facelift. The

French architect, David Mangin, who won the competition to redevelop the site, plans to suspend a vast glass roof over the forum, allowing light to flood in, while also redesigning the gardens and creating a wide promenade modelled on Barcelona's Las Ramblas. Work is expected to be complete by 2014.

For now, the Forum comprises a busy métro/RER station, some 180 shops spread over four levels, a swimming pool and a number of cinemas, including the recently revamped **Forum des Images**, which has five screens and an archive of some 5500 films, all connected with Paris and any of which you can watch in your own private booth (€5 for four hours, free weekdays after 7.30pm). The shops, housed in aquarium-like arcades and arranged around a sunken patio, are mostly devoted to high-street fashion, though there's a decent FNAC bookshop and the Forum des Créateurs, an outlet for young fashion designers.

You can still catch a flavour of the old market atmosphere on pedestrianized **rue Montorgueil** to the north, where traditional grocers, horse butchers and fishmongers still ply their trade, jostling for space with the trendy cafés that have sprung up over the last few years. Hard to pass by without stopping to gaze at its exquisite cakes and beautiful old decor is Stohrer's pâtisserie (see p.266), in business since 1730.

## St-Eustache

Map 2, G4. ⓂLes-Halles/RER Châtelet-Les-Halles.

For an antidote to the steel and glass troglodytism of Les Halles head for the soaring vaults of the beautiful church of **St-Eustache**, on the north side of the gardens. Built between 1532 and 1637, it's Gothic in structure, with lofty naves and graceful flying buttresses, and Renaissance in decoration, with Corinthian columns, pilasters and arcades. Molière, Richelieu and Madame de Pompadour were baptized here, while Rameau and Marivaux were buried here. The church has a long musical tradition and is an atmospheric venue for concerts and organ recitals.

## Fontaine des Innocents

**Map 2, G5.** ⓂLes-Halles/RER Châtelet-Les-Halles.

Another remnant of the Renaissance can be seen on the other side of Les Halles in the shape of the perfectly proportioned **Fontaine des Innocents** (1549). Adorned with reliefs of water nymphs, it looks slightly marooned amid the fast-food joints, tattoo parlours and shoe shops of the place Jean du Bellay. On warm days shoppers sit around its edge, drawn to the cool of its cascading waters. The fountain takes its name from the cemetery that used to occupy this site, the Cimetière des Innocents. Full to overflowing, the cemetery was closed down in 1786 and its contents transferred to the catacombs in Denfert-Rochereau.

6

# The Marais

Comprising most of the 3e and 4e arrondissements, the **Marais** is one of the most seductive districts of Paris. Having largely escaped the heavy-handed attentions of Baron Haussmann, and unspoiled by modern development, the *quartier* is full of handsome Renaissance *hôtels particuliers* (mansions), narrow lanes and inviting cafés and restaurants. There's a significant Jewish community here, established in the twelfth century and centred on **rue des Rosiers**, and with its long-lasting reputation for tolerance of minorities, the area has become popular with gay Parisians.

Prime streets for wandering are **rue des Francs-Bourgeois**, lined with fashion and interior design boutiques, **rue Vieille-du-Temple** and **rue des Archives**, their trendy cafés and bars abuzz at all times of day and night, and **rue Charlot and rue de Poitou** with their art galleries and chic fashion outlets. The Marais' animated streets and atmospheric old buildings would be reason enough to visit, but the *quartier* also boasts a high concentration of excellent museums, not least among them the **Musée Picasso**, the **Carnavalet** history museum and the **Musée d'Art et d'Histoire du Judaïsme**, all set in fine *hôtels particuliers*.

## Place des Vosges and around

**Map 4, D11.** ⓂChemin-Vert/St-Paul/Bastille.

Arguably the city's most beautiful square, the **place des Vosges** is a masterpiece of aristocratic elegance. Bordered by arcaded pink-brick and stone mansions, with a formal garden at its centre, the *place* is the first example of planned development in the history of Paris. It was commissioned in 1605 by Henri IV and was inaugurated in 1612 for the wedding of Louis XIII and Anne of Austria; it is Louis' statue – or, rather, a replica of it – that stands hidden by chestnut trees in the middle of the grass and gravel gardens. The gardens' shady benches are ideal for a break from sightseeing, or you can dine alfresco at one of the restaurants under the arcades while buskers fill the air with jazz or classical music. Children can play in the sandpits and make the most of the fact that this is one of the few parks in Paris where the grass isn't out of bounds.

Through all the vicissitudes of history, the *place* has never lost its cachet as a smart address. Among the many celebrities who made their homes here was Victor Hugo; his house, at no. 6, where he wrote much of his novel *Les Misérables*, is now a museum, the **Maison de Victor Hugo** (Tues–Sun 10am–6pm; closed public hols; free). Hugo's life, including his nineteen years of exile in Jersey and Guernsey, is evoked through a somewhat sparse collection of memorabilia, portraits, photographs and first editions of his works. What you do get, though, is an idea of his prodigious creativity: as well as being a prolific writer, he drew – a number of his ink drawings are exhibited – and designed his own furniture; he even put together a Chinese-style dining room, recreated in its entirety here.

From the southwest corner of the *place*, a door leads through to the formal château garden, *orangerie* and exquisite Renaissance facade of the **Hôtel de Sully**. The garden, with its benches, makes for a peaceful rest stop; it's also a handy shortcut through to rue St-Antoine. Temporary photographic exhibitions, usually with social, historical or anthropological themes, are mounted in the *hôtel* by the **Jeu de Paume** (Tues–Fri noon–7pm, Sat & Sun 10am–7pm; €7; Ⓦwww.jeudepaume.org). The attached bookshop has an extensive collection of books on Paris, some in English.

The Marais is one of the few areas of the city where most shops, cafés and restaurants remain open on a Sunday (shops usually 2–6pm) – many Parisians come here for brunch (see p.199) and spend the afternoon browsing the shops and strolling around place des Vosges.



## Musée Carnavalet

**Map 4, C10.** 23 rue de Sévigné. Daily except Mon 10am–6pm; free; ⓂSt-Paul.

Just off rue des Francs-Bourgeois is the fascinating **Musée Carnavalet**, charting the history of Paris from its origins up to the *belle époque* through an extraordinary collection of paintings, sculptures, decorative arts and archeological finds. The museum's setting alone, in two beautiful adjacent Renaissance mansions, Hôtel Carnavalet and Hôtel Le Peletier, surrounded by attractive gardens, is reason enough to visit.

The **ground floor** displays nineteenth- and early twentieth-century shop and inn signs and engrossing models of Paris through the ages, accompanied by maps and plans, illustrating how much Haussmann's boulevards changed the face of the city. The renovated **orangerie** houses a significant collection of Neolithic finds, including a number of wooden dug-out canoes unearthed during the redevelopment of the Bercy riverside area in the 1990s.

On the **first floor**, decorative arts feature strongly, with numerous recreated salons and boudoirs full of richly sculpted wood panelling and tapestries from the time of Louis XII to Louis XVI, rescued from buildings that had to be destroyed to make way for Haussmann's boulevards. Room 21 is devoted to the famous letter writer **Madame de Sévigné**, who lived in the Carnavalet mansion and corresponded almost on a daily basis with her daughter, vividly portraying high-society life during the reign of Louis XIV. You can see her Chinese lacquered writing desk, as well as portraits of her and various contemporaries, such as Molière and Corneille. Rooms 128 to 148 are largely devoted to the **belle époque**, evoked through numerous paintings from the period and some wonderful **Art Nouveau** interiors, among which is the sumptuous peacock-green interior designed by Alphonse Mucha for Fouquet's jewellery shop in rue Royale. Also well preserved is José-Maria Sert's **Art Deco** ballroom, with its extravagant gold-leaf decor and grand-scale paintings, including one of the Queen of Sheba with a train of elephants. Nearby is a section on literary life at the beginning of the twentieth century. You can see a reconstruction of **Proust's bedroom** (room 147) with its cork-lined walls, designed to muffle external noise and allow the writer to work in peace – he spent most of his last three years closeted away here, penning his great novel, *A la recherche du temps perdu*.

The **second floor** rooms are full of mementoes of the **French Revolution**: models of the Bastille, original declarations of the Rights of Man and the Citizen, sculpted allegories of Reason, crockery with revolutionary slogans, glorious models of the guillotine and execution orders to make you shed a tear for the royalists.

## Musée Cognacq-Jay

**Map 4, C10.** 8 rue Elzévir. Daily except Mon 10am–5.40pm; free; ⓂSt-Paul/Chemin-Vert.

The **Musée Cognacq-Jay**, occupying the fine Hôtel Donon, houses artworks collected by the family who built up the Samaritaine department store, which closed down in 2005. As well as being noted philanthropists, the Cognacq-Jays were lovers of European art. Their small collection of eighteenth-century pieces includes a handful of works by Canaletto, Fragonard, Greuze, Tiepolo and Fantin de la Tour, as well as an early Rembrandt and an exquisite still life by Chardin, displayed in beautifully carved wood-panelled rooms.

## Rue des Rosiers and the Jewish Quarter

**Map 4, B10–C11.** ⓂSt-Paul.

Narrow, pedestrianized **rue des Rosiers**, one block south of the rue des Francs-Bourgeois, has been the heart of the city's **Jewish quarter** ever since the twelfth century. Despite incursions by trendy fashion boutiques in recent times, it just about manages to retain a Jewish flavour, with the odd delicatessen, kosher food shop and Hebrew bookstore, as well as a number of falafel takeaways – testimony to the influence of the **North African Sephardim**, who, since the end of World War II, have sought refuge here from the uncertainties of life in the French ex-colonies. They have replenished Paris's Jewish population, depleted when its Ashkenazim, having escaped the pogroms of Eastern Europe, were rounded up by the Nazis and the French police and transported back east to concentration camps in 1942–44.

## Musée de l'Histoire de France and around

**Map 4, B9.** 60 rue des Francs-Bourgeois. Mon–Fri 10am–12.30pm & 2–5.30pm, Sat & Sun 2–5.30pm; €3; ⓂRambuteau/St-Paul.

The entire block from rue des Quatre Fils and rue des Archives, and from rue Vieille-du-Temple to rue des Francs-Bourgeois, was once filled by a magnificent early eighteenth-century palace complex. Only half remains standing today, but what's left is utterly splendid, especially the grand colonnaded courtyard of the **Hôtel Soubise**, with its vestigial fourteenth-century towers on rue des Quatre Fils. The *hôtel* holds the city archives and the **Musée de l'Histoire de France**, which mounts changing exhibitions drawn from the archives.

The adjacent **Hôtel de Rohan**, recently renovated, is also part of the archives complex and is sometimes used when there are large exhibitions. It has more fine interiors, including the Chinese-inspired Cabinet des Singes, whose walls are painted with monkeys acting out various aristocratic scenes.



**Chamber music recitals (€10) are held most Saturdays at 6.30pm in the Chambre du Prince, on the ground floor of the Hôtel Soubise.**

## Musée d'Art et d'Histoire du Judaïsme

**Map 4, B9.** 71 rue du Temple. Mon–Fri 11am–6pm, Sun 10am–6pm; €6.80; Ⓦwww.mahj.org; ⓂRambuteau.

Housed in the attractively restored Hôtel de Saint-Aignan, the **Musée d'Art et d'Histoire du Judaïsme** traces the culture and history of the Jews in France, though there are also many artefacts from the rest of Europe and North Africa. The result is a comprehensive collection, as educational as it is beautiful. The free audio-guides in English are well worth picking up if you want to get the most out of the museum.

Highlights include a Gothic-style Hanukkah lamp, one of the very few French Jewish artefacts to survive from the period before the expulsion of the Jews from France in 1394; an Italian gilded circumcision chair from the seventeenth century; and a completely intact late nineteenth-century Austrian *Sukkah*, a temporary dwelling for the celebration of the Harvest, decorated with paintings of Jerusalem and the Mount of Olives. Among other artefacts are Moroccan wedding garments, highly decorated marriage contracts from eighteenth-century Modena and gorgeous, almost whimsical, spice containers.

The museum also holds the Dreyfus archives, and appropriately enough, one room is devoted to the notorious **Dreyfus affair** of the 1890s, in which Alfred Dreyfus, a captain in the

French army and a Jew, was wrongly convicted of spying for the Germans, and only released after a high-profile campaign by prominent left-wing intellectuals and republicans. The affair is documented with photographs, press clippings and letters – including some from Dreyfus to his wife speaking of his terrible loneliness and suffering in the penal colony of Devil's Island in French Guiana.

The last few rooms contain a significant collection of paintings and sculpture by **Jewish artists** – Marc Chagall, Samuel Hirszenberg, Chaïm Soutine and Jacques Lipchitz – who came to live in Paris at the beginning of the twentieth century.

The Holocaust is only briefly touched on, since it's dealt with in depth by the Musée de la Shoah (see p.86). There's an installation by contemporary artist Christian Boltanski: one of the exterior walls of a small courtyard is covered with black-bordered death announcements printed with the names of the Jewish artisans who once lived in the building, a number of whom were deported.

## Musée Picasso

**Map 4, C9.** 5 rue de Thorigny. Daily except Tues: April–Sept 9.30am–6pm; Oct–March 9.30am–5.30pm; €5.50, free on the first Sun of the month; Ⓦwww.musee-picasso.fr; ⓂChemin Vert/St-Paul.

Closed until 2012 for a major renovation and the addition of an extension, the **Musée Picasso** is set in a magnificent classical seventeenth-century mansion, the Hôtel Salé. The museum houses the world's largest collection of the artist's works, representing most periods of his life from 1905 onwards, though there are some gaps, notably the early Blue and Rose periods. Many of the paintings were owned by Picasso and on his death in 1973 were offered by the family to the state in lieu of taxes owed. The result is an unedited body of work, which, though not containing the most recognizable masterpieces, nevertheless provides a sense of the artist's development and an insight into the person behind the myth.

The collection includes paintings from the late Blue period, studies for the *Demoiselles d'Avignon*, and experiments with Cubism and Surrealism, as well as larger-scale works on themes of war and peace (such as *Massacre in Korea*, 1951). The artist's later preoccupations with love and death are reflected in the Minotaur and bullfighting paintings. Perhaps some of the most engaging works are Picasso's more personal ones – those of his children, wives and lovers – such as *Olga pensive* (1923), in which his first wife is shown lost in thought, the deep blue of her dress reflecting her mood. Portraits of his later lovers, Dora Maar and Marie-Thérèse (both painted in 1937), show how the two women inspired Picasso in very different ways: Dora Maar is painted with strong lines and vibrant colours, suggesting a passionate, vivacious personality, while Marie-Thérèse's muted colours and soft contours convey serenity and peace.

The museum also holds a substantial number of Picasso's **engravings**, **ceramics** and **sculpture**, reflecting the remarkable ease with which the artist moved from one medium to another. Some of the most arresting sculptures are those he created from recycled household objects, such as the endearing *La Chèvre* (The Goat), whose stomach is made from a basket, and the *Tête de Taureau* (Bull's head), an ingenious pairing of a bicycle seat and handlebars. Interspersed throughout the collection are paintings that Picasso bought or were given by his contemporaries, as well as his collection of African masks and sculptures, his Communist party membership cards and sketches of Stalin, and photographs of him in his studio taken by Brassaï.

## The Haut Marais

Formerly a quiet backwater, the northern part of the Marais, often referred to as the "**haut Marais**" (the "upper Marais"), is currently the favoured strolling ground of *bobo* (bourgeois bohemian) Parisians, drawn by the burgeoning number of design shops, chichi fashion boutiques and commercial art galleries that have sprung up, especially along **rue Charlot**, rue de Poitou and rue Saintonge.



### Rue Charlot

**Map 4 C8.** ⓂFilles-du-Calvaire.

Rue Charlot, with its attractive seventeenth-century shuttered townhouses, has fast become one of the city's design and fashion hotspots. Nordic design from the 1950s to 1970s features primarily at Galerie Dansk, at 31 rue Charlot; slinky mohair and cashmere knits in vibrant colours make for a colourful display at Samy Chalon at no. 24, while the boutique of cutting-edge fashion designer Gaspard Yurkievich, at no. 43, is full of energetic, verging on the outlandish, clothes. At no. 9 you could check out what's happening at **Passage de Retz** (daily except Mon 10am–7pm; €8), an art gallery that stages changing exhibitions of fine art and design from young artists and is attractively set in an old mansion; there's also a bookshop and café.

### Marché des Enfants-Rouges

**Map 4, C8.** Tues–Sat 8.30am–1pm & 4–7.30pm, Sun 8.30am–2pm; ⓂFilles-du-Calvaire.

Further north, just short of the vibrant rue de Bretagne, is the easily missed entrance to the **Marché des Enfants-Rouges**, one of the smallest and oldest food markets in Paris, dating back to 1616, and purveying mostly traditional produce. In recent years several cheap eateries with outdoor tables have opened up, and it is now possible to sample Moroccan, Italian, Afro-Cajun and Lebanese food here. **Rue de Bretagne** itself has an agreeable provincial air and is full of traditional food shops such as cheesemongers, bakeries and coffee merchants.

## The Musée des Arts et Métiers

**Map 4, A6.** 60 rue de Réaumur. Daily except Mon 10am–6pm, Thurs till 9.30pm; €6.50; ⓦwww.arts-et-metiers.net; ⓂArts-et-Métiers.

Part of the Conservatoire des Arts et Métiers, the **Musée des Arts et Métiers** is a fascinating museum of technological innovation, and incorporates the former Benedictine priory of St-Martin-des-Champs, its original chapel dating from the fourth century. Extensively revamped a number of years ago, the museum happily combines creaky old floors and spacious rooms with high-tech, twenty-first-century touches. Its most important exhibit is **Foucault's pendulum**, which the scientist used to demonstrate the rotation of the earth in 1851, a sensational event held at the Panthéon and attended by a huge crowd eager to "see the earth go round". The orb itself, a hollow brass sphere, is under glass in the chapel and there's a working model set up nearby.

Other exhibits include the laboratory of Lavoisier, the French chemist who first showed that water is a combination of oxygen and hydrogen, and, hanging as if in mid-flight, above the grand staircase is the elegant "Avion 3", a flying machine complete with feathered propellers, which was donated to the Conservatoire after several ill-fated attempts to fly it.

## The Quartier St-Paul-St-Gervais

The **Quartier St-Paul-St-Gervais**, below rues de Rivoli and St-Antoine, is less buzzy than the rest of the district, its quiet, atmospheric streets lined with attractive old houses. The chief sights are the moving **Mémorial de la Shoah**, with its museum documenting the fate of French Jews in World War II, and the **Maison Européenne de la Photographie**, which hosts exhibitions by contemporary photographers.

The first landmark you come to, starting at the western end of the district near the Hôtel de Ville, is the late-Gothic **church of St-Gervais-St-Protais** (map 4, A11). On the outside, the church is somewhat battered owing to a direct hit from a shell fired from Big Bertha in 1918.

However, it's more pleasing inside, with some lovely stained glass, carved misericords and a seventeenth-century organ, Paris's oldest.



## Mémorial de la Shoah

**Map 4, B12.** 17 rue Geoffroy l'Asnier. Mon–Fri & Sun 10am–6pm; free; Ⓦwww.memorialdelashoah.org; ⓂSt-Paul/Pont-Marie.

The grim fate of French Jews in World War II is commemorated at the **Mémorial de la Shoah**. Since 1956 this has been the site of the Mémorial du Martyr Juif Inconnu (Memorial to an Unknown Jewish Martyr), a sombre crypt containing a large black marble star of David, with a candle at its centre. In 2005, President Chirac opened a new museum here and unveiled a **Wall of Names**, four giant slabs of marble engraved with the names of the 76,000 French Jews – around a quarter of the wartime population – sent to death camps from 1942 to 1944. Ten researchers spent two and a half years trawling Gestapo documents and interviewing French families to compile the list.

The highly absorbing **museum** focuses mainly on events in France leading up to and during World War II, but also gives useful background on the history of Jews in France and in Europe as a whole. Individual stories are illustrated with photos, ID cards, letters and other documents, and there are some drawings and letters from Drancy, the holding station outside Paris from which French Jews were sent on to camps in Germany. The museum ends with the Mémorial des Enfants, an overwhelming collection of photos of 2500 French children, each marked with the date of their birth and the date of their deportation.

## Maison Européenne de la Photographie

**Map 4, B11.** 4 rue de Fourcy. Wed–Sun 11am–8pm; €6.50, free Wed after 5pm; Ⓦwww.mep-fr.org; ⓂSt-Paul/Pont-Marie.

Between rues de Fourcy and François-Miron, a gorgeous Marais mansion, the early eighteenth-century Hôtel Hénault de Cantobre, has been turned into the **Maison Européenne de la Photographie**, dedicated to the art of contemporary photography. Temporary shows combine with a revolving exhibition of the Maison's permanent collection; young photographers and photojournalists get a look in, as well as artists using photography in multimedia creations or installation art. A library and *vidéothèque* can be freely consulted, and there's a stylish café.

# Bastille and around

Indissolubly linked with events that triggered the French Revolution of 1789, the **Bastille quarter** traditionally belongs in spirit and in style to the working-class districts of eastern Paris. With the construction of the new opera house in the 1990s, however, the area has become more diverse, with artists, fashion folk and younger residents moving in, bringing with them trendy shops and an energetic nightlife. These days, as the cutting edge moves further east, the bars cater more for out-of-towners and tourists. Much of the action takes place on **rue de Lappe**, continuing a tradition that goes back to the nineteenth century when migrant workers from the Auvergne colonized this street and opened dancehalls and music clubs. Cocktail haunts and theme bars now dominate, edging out the old tool shops, cobblers and ironmongers. Some of the working-class flavour lingers on, though, especially in the furniture workshops off **rue Faubourg St-Antoine**, east of Bastille, testimony to a long history of cabinet-making and woodworking in the district.

South of Bastille, the relatively unsung **12$^{e}$** arrondissement offers an authentic slice of Paris, traditionally working-class and full of neighbourhood shops and bars. Much has changed here too, though, and a fashionable crowd has moved in, attracted by new developments, such as the landscaping of a large park in the **Bercy** riverside area and the conversion of the old Bercy wine warehouses into attractive cafés and shops. One of the most imaginative projects has been the creation of the **Promenade Plantée**, an ex-railway line converted into an elevated garden walkway, running from Bastille right across the 12$^{e}$ arrondissement to the green expanse of the **Bois de Vincennes** in the east.

## Place de la Bastille

**Map 4, E12.** Ⓜ Bastille.

The huge **place de la Bastille** is where Parisians congregate to celebrate Bastille Day, France's most important national holiday. It marks the storming of the Bastille prison on July 14, 1789, which kicked off the French Revolution. Hardly anything survives now of the prison – the few remains have been transferred to square Henri-Galli at the end of boulevard Henri IV. A Société Générale bank is situated on the former site of the prison and the square is where the fortress's ramparts originally stood. A gleaming, gold, winged figure of Liberty stands atop a bronze column at the centre of the square, erected to commemorate not, as you might expect, the surrender of the prison, but the July Revolution of 1830, which replaced the autocratic Charles X with the "Citizen King" Louis-Philippe. When Louis-Philippe fled in the more significant 1848 Revolution, his throne was burnt beside the column. The victims – some seven hundred – of both conflicts are buried in vaults underneath the monument and their names inscribed around the shaft of the column. The square is still an important rallying point for political protest, and it's an obligatory halt on the route of any left-wing march.

The Bicentennial of the Revolution in 1989 was marked by the inauguration of the **Opéra Bastille**, which fills almost the entire block between rues de Lyon, Charenton and Moreau. This rather amorphous glass and steel structure, likened by one critic to a "hippopotamus in a bathtub", is not the loveliest of buildings, but with time, use and familiarity, Parisians seem to have become reconciled to the new opera house, and happily sit on its steps, wander into its shops and libraries, and camp out all night for the free performance on July 14.

For information on tickets and performances given at the Opéra Bastille, see p.282.

## The Port de l'Arsenal and Maison Rouge

Port de l'Arsenal: **Map 4, E13.** Maison Rouge: **Map 4, E14.** 10 bd de la Bastille. Wed–Sun 11am–7pm, Thurs till 9pm; €7; Ⓦwww.lamaisonrouge.org; ⓂBastille/Quai de la Rapée.

Just south of the place de la Bastille is the **Port de l'Arsenal** marina, occupying part of what was once the moat around the Bastille. The Canal St-Martin starts here, flowing underneath the square and emerging much further north, just past place de la République, a route plied by canal pleasure boats run by Canauxrama (see p.290). Some two hundred boats are moored up in the marina, and the landscaped banks, with children's playgrounds, make it a pleasant spot for a wander.

One of the former industrial spaces bordering the Arsenal has been converted into a light and spacious contemporary art gallery, **La Maison Rouge – Fondation Antoine de Galbert**. Founded in 2004 by collector Antoine de Galbert, the Maison Rouge, which takes its name from the bright red pavilion at the centre of the building, holds changing exhibitions, either devoted to an individual artist, or a private collection, such as the recent exhibition of Argentine artist Mika Rottenberg's video installations on the female body.

# Rue de Lappe and around

**Map 4, F12.** ⓂBastille.

Northeast of place de la Bastille, off rue de la Roquette, narrow, cobbled **rue de Lappe** is a lively nightspot, crammed with bars drawing a largely teenage and touristy crowd. At no. 32, *Balajo* is one remnant of a very Parisian tradition: the *bals musettes*, or music halls of 1930s *gai Paris* established by the area's large Auvergnat population and frequented between the wars by Edith Piaf, Jean Gabin and Rita Hayworth. It was founded by one Jo de France, who introduced glitter and spectacle into what were then seedy gangster dives, enticing Parisians from the other side of the city to drink absinthe and savour the rue de Lappe low-life. Parisians are still drawn to the area and frequent the hip bars and restaurants of the nearby section of **rue de la Roquette** and **rue de Charonne**, the latter also home to trendy fashion boutiques and wacky interior designers; and **rue Keller**, clustered with alternative, hippy outfits, indie record stores and young fashion designers.

# The Promenade Plantée

**Map 4, F14.** ⓂBastille/Ledru-Rollin.

The **Promenade Plantée**, also known as the Coulée Verte, is an excellent way to see a little-visited part of the city – and from an unusual angle. This stretch of disused railway line, much of it along a viaduct, has been ingeniously converted into an elevated garden walk and planted with a profusion of trees and flowers – cherry trees, maples, limes, roses and lavender. The walkway starts near the beginning of **avenue Daumesnil**, just south of the Bastille opera house, and is reached via a flight of stone steps – or lifts – with a number of similar access points all the way along. From there it extends to the Parc de Reuilly, then descends to ground level and continues nearly as far as the *périphérique*, from where you can follow signs to the Bois de Vincennes. The whole walk is around 4.5km long, but if you don't feel like doing the entire thing you could just walk the first part – along the viaduct – which also happens to be the most attractive stretch, running past venerable old mansion blocks and giving you a bird's-eye view of the street below.

The arches of the viaduct itself, collectively known as the **Viaduc des Arts**, have been transformed into attractive spaces for artisans' studios and craft shops. The workshops house a wealth of creativity: furniture and tapestry restorers, interior designers, cabinet-makers, violin- and flute-makers, embroiderers and fashion and jewellery designers.

# Bercy

**Map 1 & map 5, N5.** Ⓜ Bercy/Cour St-Emilion.

Over the last decade or so, the former warehouse district of **Bercy**, where for centuries the capital's wine supplies were unloaded from river barges, has been altered by a series of ambitious, ultramodern developments designed to complement the grand-scale Seine Rive Gauche project on the opposite bank. The heart of this development is **Bercy village**, a complex of old wine warehouses stylishly converted into shops, restaurants and, appropriately enough, wine bars – popular places to come before or after a film at the giant Bercy multiplex cinema at the eastern end of Cour Saint-Emilion.

West of here extends the **Parc de Bercy**, which incorporates elements of the old warehouse site such as disused railway tracks and cobbled lanes. The western section of the park is a fairly unexciting expanse of grass with a huge stepped fountain (popular with children) set into one of the grassy banks. But the area east has arbours, rose gardens, lily ponds, an *orangerie* and the **Maison du Jardinage** (March–Oct Tues–Fri 1–5.30pm, Sat & Sun 1–6.30pm; Nov–Feb Tues–Sat 1–5.30pm), a garden exhibition centre where you can consult gardening books and magazines and visit the adjoining greenhouse and vegetable garden.

## The Cinémathèque

**Map 1.** 51 rue de Bercy ⓦwww.cinematheque.fr; ⓂBercy.

Of the new buildings surrounding the park, the most striking is the **Cinémathèque**, on the north side. Designed by Guggenheim Bilbao architect Frank Gehry, it's made from zinc, glass and limestone and resembles a falling pack of cards: according to Gehry, the inspiration was Matisse's collages, done "with a simple pair of scissors". There's a huge archive of films dating back to the earliest days of cinema, and regular retrospectives of French and foreign films are screened in its four cinemas. It also has an engaging **museum** (Mon & Wed–Sat noon–7pm, Sun 10am–8pm; €5) tracing the history of cinema, with lots of early cinematic equipment, magic lanterns, silent-film clips and costumes, such as the dress worn by Vivien Leigh in *Gone with the Wind* and outfits from Eisenstein's *Ivan the Terrible*.

# Bois de Vincennes

**Map 1.** ⓂChâteau de Vincennes.

East of Bercy, beyond the *périphérique* (ringroad), lies the **Bois de Vincennes**, one of the largest parks that the city has to offer. Unfortunately, it's so crisscrossed with roads that countryside sensations don't stand much of a chance, but it has some pleasant corners, including the attractive **Parc Floral** (daily: summer 9.30am–8pm; winter 9.30am–dusk; €1; ⓦwww.parcfloraldeparis.com; ⓂChâteau de Vincennes, then bus #112 or a fifteen-minute walk). Flowers are always in bloom in the Jardin des Quatre Saisons, and you can picnic beneath pines, then wander through concentrations of camellias, rhododendrons, cacti, ferns, irises and bonsai trees. Between April and September there are art and horticultural exhibitions in several pavilions, free jazz and classical music concerts, and numerous activities for children, including a mini-golf course of Parisian monuments.

If you feel like a lazy day out in the park, you can go boating on the **Lac Daumesnil** (ⓂPorte-Dorée), near the

Porte Dorée entrance. North of the Lac Daumesnil, at 53 avenue de St-Maurice, is the city's largest **zoo**, which closed for a much-needed renovation in late 2008 and is unlikely to reopen before 2012.

## Château de Vincennes

**Map 1.** Daily: May–Aug 10am–6pm; Sept–April 10am–5pm; *donjon* €8, Chapelle Royale €8, combined ticket €12; ⓦwww.chateau-vincennes.fr; ⓂChâteau-de-Vincennes.

On the northern edge of the *bois* rears up the **Château de Vincennes**, erstwhile royal medieval residence, then state prison, porcelain factory, weapons dump and military training school. Enclosed by a high defensive wall and surrounded by a (now empty) moat, it presents a rather austere aspect on first sight, but it has two visitable attractions worth stopping for:

the Flamboyant Gothic **Chapelle Royale**, completed in the mid-sixteenth century and decorated with superb Renaissance stained-glass windows, and the lofty fourteenth-century **donjon** (keep), built by Charles V. You can see some fine vaulted ceilings, graffiti left by prisoners and Charles V's bedchamber, where the English king Henry V died in 1422, shortly before he was to join forces with his Burgundian allies.



## Cité Nationale de l'Histoire de l'Immigration

**Map 1.** 293 av Daumesnil. Tues–Fri 10am–5.30pm, Sat & Sun 10am–7pm; €5; Ⓦwww.histoire-immigration.fr; ⓂPorte Dorée.

Just outside the Bois de Vincennes, across the way from the Porte Dorée entrance, a huge Art Deco building, the Palais de la Porte Dorée, houses the **Cité Nationale de l'Histoire de l'Immigration**. It deals with the history of immigration to France over the last two centuries (15 million French citizens have foreign roots) through a collection of photographs, artefacts and illustrations. Artworks themed around immigrants' struggles to integrate into French society and images of vehicles loaded with possessions arriving at the border are among the thought-provoking exhibits. Perhaps the most poignant items on display, though, are the suitcases brought over by immigrants, containing photos of loved ones, religious texts and teddy bears. There are also regular temporary exhibitions, such as one on Paris's *banlieues* (suburbs), which house a large proportion of the city's immigrants.

On the lower ground floor you can visit the popular **aquarium** (same times; €6.50, children €5), with its crocodile pit and large collection of tropical fish, left over from the *palais*' previous incarnation as the Musée des Arts Africains et Océaniens (whose exhibits have been transferred to the Musée du Quai Branly, see p.117).

8

# The Quartier Latin and the southeast



The traditional heartland of the **Quartier Latin** lies between the river and the Montagne-Ste-Geneviève, a modest hill once crowded with medieval colleges and now proudly crowned by the giant dome of the **Panthéon**. In medieval times, the *quartier*'s name was a simple description of its Latin-speaking, learned inhabitants. Today, the name has stuck, often used – as here – to refer to the modern 5e arrondissement, an area defined by the boulevard St-Michel to the west, and the river to the north. It's an increasingly trendy quarter, these days, but still deeply scholarly: the northern half of the arrondissement alone boasts the famous **Sorbonne** and Jussieu campuses, plus a cluster of stellar academic institutes. While few students can afford the rents these days, they still maintain the *quartier*'s traditions in the cheaper bars, cafés and *bistrots*, decamping to the Luxembourg gardens (see p.109) on sunny days.

The area's medieval heritage is superbly displayed in the **Musée National du Moyen Age**, which is worth visiting for the stunning tapestry series, the *Lady with the Unicorn*, alone. Out towards the eastern end of the 5e, the flavour is more Arabic than Latin in the brilliantly designed **Institut du Monde Arabe** and **Paris Mosque**. Nearby, you'll find the flowerbeds, zoo and natural history museum of the leafy **Jardin des Plantes**.

The southern half of the 5e is less interesting, with the exception of the ancient, romantic thoroughfare of the **rue Mouffetard**, which still snakes its way south to the boundary of the 13e arrondissement and the **Gobelins tapestry works**. Deep in the otherwise undistinguished southern swathe of Paris, **Chinatown** and the **Butte-aux-Cailles** are worth seeking out for their restaurants and bars, while the dramatic library towers of the **Bibliothèque Nationale de France** form the centrepiece of a new riverfront quarter.

## Place St-Michel and around

**Map 2, F8.** Ⓜ St-Michel/RER St-Michel-Notre-Dame.

The pivotal point of the Quartier Latin is **place St-Michel**, where the tree-lined boulevard St-Michel begins. The name is redolent of student chic, though these days dull commercial outlets have largely taken over the famous "boul' Mich". Nevertheless, the cafés and shops around the square are constantly jammed with young people: either students or, in summer, foreign backpackers. A favourite meeting point is the fountain at the back end of the *place*, which spills down from a statue of the archangel Michael stomping on the devil.

The touristy scrum is at its ugliest on and around **rue de la Huchette**, just east of the place St-Michel, which is largely given over to cheap bars and Greek seafood-and-disco tavernas. At the end of rue de la Huchette, **rue St-Jacques** follows the line of Roman Paris's main thoroughfare. Just west stands the largely fifteenth-century **church of St-Séverin**, with its entrance on rue des Prètres St-Séverin (map 2, G9; Mon–Sat 11am–7.30pm, Sun 9am–8.30pm; Ⓜ St-Michel/Cluny-La Sorbonne). It's one of the city's most intense churches, its interior seemingly focused on the single, twisting central pillar of the Flamboyant Gothic choir.

## The riverside

**Map 2, G9–H9.**

A short way east, the green **square Viviani** faces the cliff-like flank of Notre-Dame across the river. Paris's oldest and most decrepit tree just about lives on here, a false acacia brought over from Guyana in 1680. The church behind is **St-Julien-le-Pauvre** (map 2, G9; daily 9.30am–1pm & 3–6.30pm; Ⓜ St-Michel/Maubert Mutualité), which dates from the same Gothic era as Notre-Dame.

A few steps along, rue de la Bûcherie brings you to the famous American-run bookshop **Shakespeare and Co**. The original shop – as owned by Sylvia Beach, long-suffering publisher of James Joyce's *Ulysses* – was on rue de l'Odéon. The modern successor is staffed by would-be Hemingways who sleep upstairs and pay their rent by manning the tills. More books, postcards and prints are on sale from the **bouquinistes** who display their wares in green padlocked boxes hooked onto the parapet of the **riverside quais**. Upstream, the **Pont de l'Archevêché** – the bridge of the archbishopric – offers fine views of the Ile-St-Louis.

## The Musée National du Moyen Age

**Map 2, F9.** 6 place Paul Painlevé. Wed–Mon 9.15am–5.45pm; €8.50; Ⓦ www.musee-moyenage.fr; Ⓜ Cluny-La Sorbonne.

Heading south down boulevard St-Michel, away from the river, a couple of minutes' walk brings you to the remains of the third-century **Roman baths** and, behind, the **Hôtel de Cluny**, a sixteenth-century mansion built by the abbots of the powerful Cluny monastery in Burgundy as their Paris pied-à-terre. The *hôtel* now houses the rich **Musée National du Moyen Age**, a superb museum of medieval art. The architectural highlight is the **Roman bathhouse**, with its intact vaults arching over the *frigidarium*, or cold room. They shelter two beautifully carved first- and second-century capitals, the *Seine Boatmen's Pillar* and the *Pillar of St-Landry*, which has animated-looking gods and musicians adorning three of its faces. You'll also see the twenty-one thirteenth-century heads of the **Kings of Judea**, lopped off the west front of Notre-Dame during the French Revolution.

The undisputed star of the collection is the exquisite **Lady with the Unicorn**, displayed in a darkened, chapel-like chamber on the first floor. Even if you don't usually like tapestries, it's hard not to be moved and amazed by this one. The richly coloured, detailed and highly allegorical series, which was probably made in Brussels in the late fifteenth century, depicts the five senses. Each tapestry features a beautiful woman flanked by a lion and a unicorn, with a rich red background worked with myriad tiny flowers, birds, plants and animals. The meaning of the sixth and final panel, entitled *A Mon Seul Désir* ("To My Only Desire"), and depicting the woman putting away her necklace into a jewellery box held out by her servant, remains a matter of debate.

The rest of the first floor is an amazing ragbag of carved choir stalls, altarpieces, ivories, stained glass, illuminated Books of Hours, games, brassware and all manner of precious objets d'art. There's also the *hôtel*'s original Flamboyant Gothic **chapel**, its remarkable vault still splaying out from the central pillar.

**Drop-by recitals (€6) of medieval music are usually held at the Musée National du Moyen Age on Friday lunchtimes (12.30pm) and Saturday afternoons (4pm).**

# The Sorbonne

**Map 5, D1.** Place de la Sorbonne. Ⓜ Cluny-La Sorbonne.

In the heart of the Quartier Latin, on the south side of rue des Ecoles, a cluster of lofty buildings belongs to a trio of elite institutions: the **Sorbonne**, Collège de France and Lycée Louis le Grand. Just like the medieval colleges that once huddled here on the top of the Montagne-Ste-Geneviève, they attract some of the finest scholars from all over Europe.

At the head of narrow **rue Champollion**, with its huddle of arty cinemas, stands the traffic-free **place de la Sorbonne**. It's a peaceful place to sit, in a café or just under the lime trees, listening to the play of the fountains and watching students toting their books about. Overshadowing the graceful ensemble is the **Chapelle Ste-Ursule**, built in the 1640s by the great Cardinal Richelieu, whose tomb lies within. The chapel is certainly the most architecturally distinctive part of the modern-day Sorbonne, as the university buildings were entirely rebuilt in the 1880s. Sadly, in the era of anti-terrorism measures, you're no longer able to go inside the Sorbonne's main **courtyard**, one of the flashpoints of the historic student protests of May 1968.

## The Panthéon

**Map 5, D2.** Place du Panthéon. Daily: April–Sept 10am–6.30pm; Oct–March 10am–6pm; €8; Ⓦpantheon.monuments-nationaux.fr; RER Luxembourg/ⓂCardinal-Lemoine.

The most visible of Paris's many domes graces the hulk of the **Panthéon**, the towering mausoleum that tops the Montagne-Ste-Geneviève. It was originally built as a church by Louis XV, on the site of the ruined Ste-Geneviève abbey, to thank the saint for curing him of illness and to emphasize the unity of church and state – not only had the original abbey church entombed Geneviève, Paris's patron saint, but it had been founded by Clovis, France's first Christian king. The building was only completed in 1789, whereupon the Revolution promptly transformed it into a mausoleum, adding the words *Aux grands hommes la patrie reconnaissante* ("The nation honours its great men") to the giant portico. The remains of French heroes such as Voltaire, Rousseau, Hugo and Zola are now preserved in the vast, barrel-vaulted crypt below, along with more recent arrivals: Marie Curie (the only woman), with her husband Pierre (1995), writer and landmark culture minister André Malraux (1996), and the novelist Alexandre Dumas (2002).

The interior is well worth a visit for its unusual, secular decor. You can also see a working model of **Foucault's Pendulum** swinging from the dome. The original experiment, conducted here by the French physicist Léon Foucault in 1851, was the first to clearly demonstrate the rotation of the earth. In summer (April–Sept 10am–5.30pm; free), you can join regular guided tours, which take small groups up into the vertiginous cupola and out onto the high **balcony** running around the outside of the dome.

## St-Etienne-du-Mont

**Map 2, G11.** ⓂCardinal-Lemoine.

Sloping downhill from the main portico of the Panthéon, broad rue Soufflot entices you west towards the Luxembourg gardens (see p.109). On the east side of the Panthéon, however, peeping over the walls of the **Lycée Henri IV**, a lone Gothic tower is all that remains of the earlier church of Ste-Geneviève. Geneviève's mortal remains, and those of two seventeenth-century literary greats who didn't make the Panthéon, Pascal and Racine, lie close at hand in the church of **St-Etienne-du-Mont** on the corner of rue Clovis. The church's facade is a bit of an architectural hotch-potch, but it conceals a stunning interior, where the transition from Flamboyant Gothic choir to sixteenth-century nave is masked by an elaborate, catwalk-like rood screen, which arches across the width of the nave. This last feature is highly unusual in itself; most French rood screens fell victim to Protestant iconoclasts, reformers or revolutionaries.

## Place de la Contrescarpe to Gobelins

**Map 5, E3–F6.** ⓂMonge/Les Gobelins.

East of the Panthéon, the villagey **rue de la Montagne-Ste-Geneviève**, with its cluster of café-bars and restaurants, descends towards place Maubert. Heading uphill, rue Descartes runs into the tiny and attractive **place de la Contrescarpe**, hub of the area's café life. On the sunnier, south-facing side of the square, the swanky *Café Delmas* was once the famous café *La Chope*, as described by Ernest Hemingway in *A Moveable Feast*.





Place de la Contrescarpe once stood at the edges of the medieval city. Leading south, the narrow, ancient incline of **rue Mouffetard** – or "La Mouffe", as it's known to locals – was for generations one of the great **market streets** of Paris. These days, its top half is given over to touristy food stops, but the market traditions still cling on at the southern end, and fascinating traces of the past can be seen adorning the older shop fronts – look out for nos. 6, 12, 69, 122 and 134. Fruit and vegetable stalls do good business in the mornings, while the surrounding shops sell fine cheeses, wines and delicatessen foods. At 118bis is a great old-fashioned market café (see p.216).

At the foot of rue Mouffetard, just beyond the beautiful, painted facade at no. 134, you'll find **St-Médard** (map 5, F4; Tues–Sun 8am–12.30pm & 2.30–7.30pm), once famed as the church that can pardon cannibalism. The simple Gothic nave is offset by a relatively fanciful, late sixteenth-century choir. A short distance south of the church, across the wide boulevard St-Marcel, lies the **Gobelins tapestry works**, at 42 avenue des Gobelins, which has operated here for some four hundred years. The gallery area puts on temporary exhibitions, but come for the fascinating, ninety-minute guided tour (in French only; Tues–Thurs 1pm & 3pm; €10; Ⓦwww.mobiliernational.culture.gouv.fr; ⓂGobelins) and watch the flabbergastingly rich tapestries being woven using traditional, painfully slow methods.

## Val-de-Grâce

**Map 5, C4.** RER Luxembourg/Port-Royal.

West of rue Mouffetard, you penetrate the academic heart of the Quartier Latin. It's a closed world to outsiders, and there's little point in visiting this corner of the city unless it's to see the magnificent Baroque church of **Val-de-Grâce**, set just back from rue St-Jacques. Built by Anne of Austria as an act of pious gratitude following the birth of her first son in 1638, its skyward-thrusting dome and double-pedimented facade make it a suitably awesome monument to the young prince who went on to reign as Louis XIV.

You can only enter via the **Musée du Service de Santé des Armées** (Tues, Wed, Sat & Sun noon–6pm; closed Aug; €5), a history of military medicine occupying the old convent buildings. The church of Val-de-Grâce, properly known as the **Chapelle St-Louis**, is staggeringly impressive in the Roman Baroque manner, with a wonderful trompe l'oeil fresco of Paradise covering the inside of the dome.

## The Paris Mosque

**Map 5, G3.** 2bis place du Puits de l'Ermite. Daily except Fri & Muslim holidays 9am–noon & 2–6pm; €3; Ⓦwww.mosquee-de-paris.net; ⓂMonge.

East of rue Mouffetard, across rue Monge, lie some of the city's most agreeable surprises. Just beyond place du Puits de l'Ermite stand the gate and crenellated walls of the **Paris Mosque**, built by Moroccan craftsmen in the early 1920s. You can wander among the gardens and patios with their geometric tiles and carved ceilings, and Muslims can enter the prayer room. The back gate, on the southeast corner of the complex, on rue Daubenton, leads into a lovely **tearoom** (see p.215), and an atmospheric **hammam** (see p.293).

## Jardin des Plantes

**Map 5, H3.** Daily: April–Aug 7.30am–8pm; Sept–March 8am–dusk; free; Ⓦwww.mnhn.fr; ⓂGare d'Austerlitz/Jussieu/Place Monge. Natural History Museum: Wed–Mon 10am–6pm; €7. Ménagerie: summer Mon–Sat 9am–6pm, Sun 9am–6.30pm; winter daily 9am–5pm; €8, under 26s €6, under 4s free.

Behind the mosque, the **Jardin des Plantes** was founded as a medicinal herb garden in 1626 and gradually evolved into

Paris's botanical gardens. Its splendid (and recently restored) hothouses, shady avenues of trees, lawns, museums and zoo make it a favourite oasis for Parisians. Floral beds make a fine approach to the collection of buildings that form the natural history museum. The most dramatic section is undoubtedly the **Grande Galerie de l'Evolution** (entrance off rue Buffon), where some splendid stuffed animals rescued from the old zoology museum parade around a huge, nineteenth-century glass-vaulted building. Live animals can be seen in the cramped **ménagerie** across the park to the northeast near rue Cuvier. Founded just after the Revolution, this is France's oldest zoo – and it shows.

## Institut du Monde Arabe

**Map 2, I10.** Tues–Sun 10am–6pm; free, museum €5; Ⓦwww.imarabe.org; ⓂJussieu/Cardinal-Lemoine.

By the river, immediately to the north of the uncompromisingly modern and much-loathed Jussieu campus building, stands the **Institut du Monde Arabe**. It's a stunning piece of architecture, designed in part by the celebrated Jean Nouvel. The southern facade comprises thousands of tiny diaphragm-like shutters, which modulate the light levels inside while simultaneously mimicking a *moucharabiyah*, the traditional Arab latticework balcony.

There's a museum of Islamic arts and sciences inside, but the chief reason to visit is for the excellent exhibitions and concerts – or for the views from the ninth-floor terrace over the Seine towards the apse of Notre-Dame. At the adjacent café-restaurant you can sip mint tea and eat cakes.

## Chinatown and the Butte-aux-Cailles

Chinatown: **Map 5, J9.** ⓂTolbiac/Porte d'Ivry. Butte-aux-Cailles: **Map 5, F9.** ⓂCorvisart/Place d'Italie.

Much of the **13$^e$ arrondissement**, in the southeastern corner of Paris, was completely cleared in the 1960s, its crowded slums replaced by tower blocks. The overall architectural gloom is only alleviated by the culinary delights of the **Chinese quarter**. Avenues de Choisy and d'Ivry, in particular, are full of Vietnamese, Thai, Cambodian and Laotian restaurants and food shops, as is **Les Olympiades**, a dingy pedestrian area bizarrely suspended between giant tower blocks, and accessed solely by escalator.

Where the prewar streets were left untouched, however, around the small hillock of the **Butte-aux-Cailles**, a community-spirited neighbourhood flourishes, making this one of the most attractive areas of Paris for low-key nightlife. Alongside the old left-wing establishments – the bar *La Folie en Tête* at no. 33 and the co-operative restaurant *Le Temps des Cerises* at nos. 18–20 – are plenty of relaxed, youthful places to eat and drink till the small hours. The easiest way to arrive is via métro Corvisart, from where you cross the road and head straight through a passageway in the large apartment building opposite, then climb the steps that lead up to rue des Cinq Diamants.

## Paris Rive Gauche

**Map 5, J3–N7.** ⓂBibliothèque François Mitterrand/Quai de la Gare.

From the Gare d'Austerlitz right down to the *périphérique*, at the southernmost end of the 13$^e$ arrondissement, almost every stick of street furniture and every apartment block in the **Paris Rive Gauche** area is shiny and new. The star architectural attraction of this nascent quarter is the **Bibliothèque Nationale de France**, whose four enormous L-shaped towers are supposed to look like open books. Once you mount the giant wooden steps surrounding the library, the perspective changes utterly. From here you can look down into a huge sunken pine grove, with glass walls that filter light into the floors below your feet. There are occasional small-scale exhibitions, and the reading rooms on the "haut-jardin" level – along with their unrivalled collection of foreign newspapers – are open to everyone over 16 (map 5, N7; Mon 2–7pm, Tues–Sat 9am–7pm, Sun 1–7pm; €3.30 for a day pass; Ⓦwww.bnf.fr; ⓂQuai de la Gare/Bibliothèque-François Mitterrand).

Opposite the library, the double-ribbon walkways of the new **Passerelle Simone de Beauvoir** now span the Seine. Between this bridge and the Pont de Tolbiac, a short way upstream, several **barges** have made the area a nightlife attraction in its own right (see p.243). Just downstream of the footbridge, on quai François Mauriac, there's even a floating indoor/outdoor **swimming pool** with a sliding roof, the Piscine Josephine Baker (see p.293).

The most recent development is on the Quai d'Austerlitz, where former warehouses are being transformed into the **Docks en Seine**. The centrepiece is the Cité de la Mode et du Design, a combined fashion institute and retail opportunity whose intrusive design of twisting, lime green tubes is supposed to recall the sinuous shape of the river. Inside, the Institut Français de la Mode (Ⓦwww.ifm-paris.com) is expected to host frequent exhibitions. A café-restaurant complex, with a riverside terrace, was being built at the time of writing.

9

# St-Germain



Picturesque **St-Germain** has all the sophistication of the Right Bank mixed with a certain easy-going chic that makes it uniquely appealing. Encompassing the chichi 6$^{e}$ arrondissement and the eastern fringe of the grandiose 7$^{e}$, it has moved ever further upmarket since it was the natural home of arty trendsetters in the postwar era. Despite gentrification, and a significant expatriate and tourist population, it has retained much of its former offbeat charm.

That said, **shopping** is now king. The streets around the Carrefour de la Croix-Rouge and place St-Sulpice, in particular, swarm with designer boutiques, while towards the river, it's antique shops and art dealers that dominate. Meanwhile, well-heeled foodies now flock to celebrity chefs' gastronomic **restaurants**, and foreign visitors fill the simpler *bistrots* around Mabillon.

Chief among the *quartier*'s many attractions are the **Musée d'Orsay**, loved as much for its stunning railway-station setting as its Impressionist collection, and the notoriously romantic **Jardin du Luxembourg**, one of the largest and loveliest green spaces in the city. There are some fine buildings to take in as you shop or stroll, notably the domed **Collège de France** and the churches of **St-Germain-des-Prés** and **St-Sulpice**. Two small, single-artist museums, the **Musée Maillol** and **Musée Delacroix**, make for an intimate visit, while the art exhibitions at the **Musée du Luxembourg** are regularly among the city's most exciting.

# From the river to the Odéon

ⓂSt-Germain des Prés/Mabillon/Odéon.

From the Right Bank and the Louvre, the pedestrian **Pont des Arts** entices you across the river and into St-Germain. It's a classic place to loiter, especially for couples, who take in the view and, on fair days, bask in the heat that soaks into its wooden planking. Some also fix padlocks to the mesh fencing to signal their commitment – much to the city government's annoyance. The bridge owes its name not to the artists who have long sold their work here but to the institute that sits under the elegant dome on the St-Germain side. This is the **Collège des Quatre-Nations**, seat of the arts and sciences academies of the **Institut de France**. Next door to the institute, at 11 quai de Conti, is the **Hôtel des Monnaies**, redesigned as the Mint in the late eighteenth century and now reduced to housing a nostalgic museum of French coinage.

To the west of the Institut lies the **Ecole des Beaux-Arts** (map 2, D6), the School of Fine Art, whose glory days gave its name to an entire epoch. It's occasionally open for exhibitions of work by its students. West again, at 5bis rue de Verneuil, is the house where pop legend **Serge Gainsbourg** lived until his death in 1991 – now owned by his film star daughter Charlotte. The garden wall is usually adorned with graffitied lyrics.

The riverside chunk of the 6$^{e}$ is defined by **rue St-André-des-Arts** and **rue Jacob**, both lined with bookshops, commercial art galleries, antique shops, cafés and restaurants. If you're looking for lunch, you'll find numerous little *bistrots* on **place** and **rue St-André-des-Arts**. Alternatively, you could make for **rue de Buci**, up towards boulevard St-Germain, which was once a proper street market, but has now been almost completely gentrified.

Towards the end of rue St-André-des-Arts, just short of the main action on rue de Buci, look out for the intriguing little passage of the **Cour du Commerce St André**. Backing onto the street is *Le Procope* – Paris's first coffee house, which opened its doors in 1686 and was frequented by Voltaire and Robespierre.

Sadly, the atmosphere has gone the way of its former clientele. At its southern end, the Cour du Commerce opens out at the **Carrefour de l'Odéon**, named after the recently restored **Théâtre de l'Odéon**, whose proud Doric facade fronts a handsome semi-circular plaza a few steps to the south.

## Jardin du Luxembourg

**Map 2, D11.** RER Luxembourg/Ⓜ Odéon.

The **Palais du Luxembourg**, immediately south of the Odéon theatre, was originally constructed for Marie de Médicis, Henri IV's widow, to remind her of the Palazzo Pitti, in her native Florence. Today it belongs to the French Senate, which may explain why the delightful gardens of the **Jardin du Luxembourg** (open roughly dawn to dusk) are so well tended. The formal lawns, floral parterres and quieter wooded areas are all dotted with sculptures and exotic plants in giant pots. This is the chief lung of the Left Bank: the gardens get fantastically crowded with visitors on summer days, but they're busy pretty much year round with Parisian families and students. Children can rent toy yachts to sail on the central round pond, or head to the more active, western side of the park which boasts **tennis courts**, donkey rides, gentle go-karts, a puppet theatre, a large playground and the inevitable sandy area for boules. There's a pleasant tree-shaded **café** roughly 100m northeast of the pond.

At the northwestern end of the garden, entered via 19 rue de Vaugirard, the **Musée du Luxembourg** (map 2, D10; hours and prices vary for each exhibition; Ⓦwww.museeduluxembourg.fr) puts on some of Paris's biggest and most exciting art exhibitions. Recent successes have included twentieth-century self portraits and artworks by Tiffany.

## Place St-Sulpice

**Map 2, D9.** Ⓜ St-Sulpice.

Broad **place St-Sulpice**, north of the Jardin du Luxembourg, is enchanting, with its lion fountain and chestnut trees, all overlooked by the **church of St-Sulpice** (daily 7.30am–7.30pm). This muscularly classical edifice was erected either side of 1700. It was never quite finished, however: if you look closely you can see uncut masonry blocks at the top, still attending the sculptor's chisel. For decades, the gloomy **interior** was best known for the giant organ (there are frequent concerts) and for three **Delacroix murals** that can be found in the first chapel on the right. Since the publication of *The Da Vinci Code*, however, many visitors come to see its **solar observatory**. A lens in the south transept window, long since removed, once focused the sun's rays on a narrow strip of brass, which still runs right across the floor of the nave to an obelisk on the north side, marking the exact time of the winter and summer solstices. As a printed notice coldly points out, it is an astronomical device, and from it "no mystical notion can be derived".

On the sunny north side of the square, the outside tables at the *Café de la Mairie* hum with conversation on fine days. However, the main attractions here are the fashion boutiques, such as the very elegant **Yves Saint Laurent Rive Gauche**, on the corner of the ancient rue des Canettes.

## Mabillon and St-Germain-des-Prés

**Map 2, D8.** Ⓜ Mabillon/St-Germain-des-Prés.

North of St-Sulpice, pretty rue Mabillon passes the **Marché St-Germain**, a 1990s reconstruction of an ancient covered market. The area around the Marché, on rues Princess, Lobineau, Guisarde and des Canettes, is something of a hub for eating and drinking, though many places suffer from a lack of local regulars to keep standards up.

The **boulevard St-Germain** was bulldozed right through the Left Bank under Baron Haussmann (see p.323). For the greater part of its length, it looks much the same as any of Paris's great avenues, but a short stretch around **place St-Germain-des-Prés** forms the very heart of the quarter. The famous **Deux Magots** café stands on one corner of the square, while the equally celebrated **Flore** lies a few steps further along the boulevard. Both cafés are renowned for the postwar writers and philosophers who drank and debated here – most famously the philosopher-novelist Simone de Beauvoir and her existentialist lover, Jean-Paul Sartre.

The robust tower opposite the *Deux Magots* belongs to the **church of St-Germain-des-Prés**, which is all that remains of an enormous Benedictine monastery whose lands once stretched right across the Left Bank. The church itself is one of twenty-first-century Paris's oldest surviving buildings, parts of it dating back to the late tenth and early eleventh centuries. The choir, however, was rebuilt in the fashionable Gothic style in the mid-twelfth century – work that's just about visible under the heavy greens and golds of nineteenth-century paintwork.

## Place de Furstenberg and the Musée Delacroix

**Map 2, D8.** Ⓜ Mabillon/St-Germain-des-Prés.

Hidden away around the back of St-Germain-des-Prés, off rue Jacob, **place de Furstenberg** is one of Paris's prettiest and quietest squares. Tucked into its northwest corner is the **Musée Delacroix**, 6 rue de Furstenberg (daily except Tues 9.30am–5pm; €5), a charming miniature museum displaying sketches by the artist and various personal effects. Delacroix lived and worked in the house here from 1857 until his death in 1863, watched over by Jenny Le Guillou, who'd been his servant since 1835. You can visit the bedroom where he died, now graced by Jenny's portrait.

## Around Sèvres-Babylone

**Map 2, B9.** Ⓜ Sèvres-Babylone.

The area around Sèvres-Babylone métro station, at the western end of the 6$^{e}$ arrondissement and the eastern fringe of the 7$^{e}$, is one of the best for **shopping**. You might not find the most exclusive Right Bank designers or the more alternative Marais and Montmartre boutiques, but rues Bonaparte, Madame, de Sèvres, de Grenelle, du Vieux-Colombier, du Dragon, du Four and des Saints-Pères are lined with well-known names, from agnès b. on rue du Vieux-Colombier to Zara on rue de Rennes.

On Sunday mornings, the celebrated Raspail **Marché Bio**, or organic food market, lines the boulevard Raspail between the Sèvres-Babylone and Rennes métro stations. Just over the boundary with the 7$^{e}$ arrondissement, at the far side of the green Square Boucicaut, stands the city's oldest department store, **Le Bon Marché** (see p.251), now one of Paris's best and most upmarket.

## Musée Maillol and Deyrolle

Musée Maillol: **Map 2, B8.** 61 rue de Grenelle. Mon, Wed, Thurs, Sat & Sun 10.30am–7pm, Fri 10.30am–9.30pm; €11; Ⓦwww.museemaillol.com. Deyrolle: **Map 2, B7.** Mon–Sat 10am–7pm; free; ⓂRue-du-Bac.

At the **Musée Maillol**, the boundlessly buxom nudes of post-Impressionist sculptor Aristide Maillol are stuffed into a tiny building. Maillol's most famous work, the dumpy *Mediterranean*, sits on the first floor at the top of the stairs. The exhibits all belong to Dina Vierny, Maillol's former model and inspiration. Works by other contemporaries are also collected here, including drawings by Bonnard (for whom Dina also modelled), Dufy and Matisse, and a room full of Poliakoff's jaggedy abstracts on the second floor. The museum also organizes excellent exhibitions of twentieth-century art.

You might not normally go out of your way to visit a taxidermist's, but **Deyrolle**, just north of the Rue-du-Bac métro, should be an exception. On the first floor above an upscale gardening shop is a deeply old-fashioned room packed with fossils, butterflies and scores of stuffed animals, from ducks to bears. Children, in particular, tend to be fascinated by the place.

# The Musée d'Orsay

**Map 6, H2.** 1 rue de la Légion d'Honneur. Tues–Sun 9.30am–6pm, Thurs till 9.45pm; €8, free on first Sun of the month and to under 18s, €12 with the Musée Rodin; Ⓦwww.musee-orsay.fr; ⓂSolférino/RER Musée-d'Orsay.

Facing the Tuileries gardens across the river is one of Paris's most-visited sites, the **Musée d'Orsay**. It houses painting and sculpture created between 1848 and 1914 – which means that it's here you'll find the electrifying works of the French **Impressionists** and **Post-Impressionists**.

The **building** itself was inaugurated as a railway station in 1900 and served southwest France until 1939. It then stood disused until 1986, when the Milanese architect and designer Gae Aulenti set about the rather brilliant conversion job. The **café** on the upper level of the museum – with its summer terrace and wonderful view of Montmartre through the giant railway clock – and the resplendently gilded **restaurant** and tearoom on the middle level, are great spots to recuperate.

## The collection

The **ground floor**, under the great glass arch, is devoted to pre-1870 work, with a double row of sculptures running down the central aisle like railway tracks. On the south side of this level, towards rue de Lille, the first set of rooms is dedicated to **Ingres**, **Delacroix** and the serious-minded, Classically-influenced works of the painters acceptable to the mid-nineteenth-century salons; just beyond are the relatively wacky works of Puvis de Chavannes, Gustave Moreau and the younger Degas.

The influential **Barbizon school** and the **Realists** are showcased on the Seine side, with canvases by Daumier, Corot, Millet and Courbet; these were some of the first to break with the established norms of moralism and idealization of the past. Close alongside are two controversial paintings by **Monet** and **Manet**, both entitled *Déjeuner sur l'herbe*, or *The Picnic* (room 6).

Manet's juxtaposition of nudity and modern dress caused outrage at the 1863 Salon des Refusés – the art show often said to mark the beginning of the **Impressionist** movement.

To continue chronologically, make for the **upper level**, which has been done up like a suite of attic studios. Many visitors experience thrilling feelings of familiarity and recognition as they encounter paintings such as Monet's *Femme à l'ombrelle*, Degas' *L'Absinthe* and Renoir's *Bal du Moulin de la Galette*. Beyond lie the heavyweight masterpieces of Monet and **Renoir** in their middle and late periods, and the experimental, fervid works of **Van Gogh** and **Cézanne**.

Beyond the café, the final suites are devoted to pastels and the various offspring of Impressionism, from **Rousseau**'s dreamy *La Charmeuse de Serpents* (1907) to **Gauguin**'s Tahitian paintings and **Pointillist** works by Seurat, Signac and others. The upper level ends with **Toulouse-Lautrec**'s pastel caricatures of louche Parisian nightlife.

Down on the middle level, the flow of the paintings' chronology continues with **Vuillard** and **Bonnard**. On the far side of this level, overlooking the Seine, you can see a less familiar side of late nineteenth-century painting, featuring large-scale, epic, naturalist works. The collection ends with a troubling handful of international **Symbolist** paintings, including **Klimt**'s *Rosiers sous les Arbres* and some of **Munch**'s lesser-known works.

On the parallel **sculpture** terraces, nineteenth-century marbles on the Seine side face early twentieth-century pieces across the divide, but the **Rodin terrace** bridging the two puts almost everything else to shame.

10

# The Eiffel Tower quarter

The monumental flagpole that is the **Eiffel Tower** surveys the most splendid of all Paris's districts, embracing the palatial heights of the Trocadéro on the west side of the Right Bank, and the wealthy, western swathe of the 7$^{e}$ arrondissement on the Left. Sparsely populated by members of the old and new aristocracies, the area is also home to some compelling **museums**. Newest on the block in the 7$^{e}$ arrondissement is the museum of non-Western art, the **Musée du Quai Branly**. At the other end of the scale, though close at hand, the city's museum of the sewer system is found, appropriately enough, down in the **sewers**. A little further east, the huge military complex of **Les Invalides** is home to a gigantic war museum, while nearby the late sculptor **Rodin** has a beautiful private house entirely devoted to his works. Across the river, in the Trocadéro quarter of the 16$^{e}$ arrondissement, the **Musée Guimet** displays a sumptuous collection of Asian Buddhist art, while the landmark Neoclassical palaces of **Tokyo**, **Chaillot** and **Galliera**, on the elevated north bank of the Seine, house museums devoted to modern and contemporary art, fashion and architecture. For all the pomp and history, corners of neighbourhood life do exist in this quarter – along

**rue de Babylone**, for example, and in the wedge of homely streets between the Invalides and the Champ de Mars, centred on the **rue Cler** market.

## The Eiffel Tower and around

**Map 7, D8.** Daily: mid-June to Aug 9am–12.45am; Sept to mid-June 9.30am–11.45pm; €13.10 (for the top; access closes at 11pm), €8.10 (second level), €4.50 by stairs to second level (access closes 6pm Sept to mid-June); Ⓦwww.tour-eiffel.fr; RER Champ-de-Mars–Tour Eiffel.

It's hard to believe that the **Eiffel Tower**, the quintessential symbol both of Paris and the brilliance of industrial engineering, was designed to be a temporary structure for a world fair. When completed for the 1889 Exposition Universelle, the tower was the tallest structure in the world, at 300m. Outraged critics protested against this "grimy factory chimney" but Eiffel claimed his tower was "formed by the wind itself" – a fitting symbol for a modern, utilitarian age.

Outside daylight hours, distinctive sodium lights illuminate the structure, while a double searchlight has swept the city's skies since the millennium celebrations. For the first ten minutes of every hour thousands of effervescent lights scramble and fizz about, defining the famous silhouette in luminescent champagne.

It's well worth going all the way up: Paris looks surreally microscopic from the top, even if the views are arguably better from the second level, especially on hazier days.

Stretching out from the legs of the Eiffel Tower, the **Champ de Mars** have been open fields ever since they were used as a parading area for royal troops – hence their name "the Martial Fields". At the far southern end lie the eighteenth-century buildings of the **Ecole Militaire**, originally founded in 1751 by Louis XV for the training of aristocratic army officers – including the "little corporal", Napoleon Bonaparte. Behind lies the uninspiring head-quarters of **UNESCO**, built in 1958.

# South of the Eiffel Tower

**Map 1.** ⓂBir Hakeim/RER Champ-de-Mars–Tour Eiffel.

Heading south along the left bank of the Seine, you can watch the métro trains trundling across to Passy on the top level of the two-decker **Pont de Bir-Hakeim**. Up on the adjacent raised walkway, at the beginning of boulevard de Grenelle, a bronze sculptural group commemorates the notorious **rafle du Vel d'Hiv** – the Nazi and French-aided round-up of 13,152 Parisian Jews in July 1942. Leading down from the very middle of the Pont de Bir-Hakeim is the **Allée des Cygnes**, or "swan walk"; a narrow midstream island built up on raised concrete embankments, it offers one of Paris's most curious and satisfying walks. At the downstream end is a scaled-down version of the **Statue of Liberty** – a reminder that the statue, rather like the idea of liberty itself, was originally France's gift to America.

Further south still, on the fringe of the city limits, lies the delightful **Parc André-Citroën** (map 1; Mon–Fri 8am to dusk, Sat & Sun 9am to dusk; ⓂJavel/Balard). It's as much a sight to visit in its own right as a place to lounge around or throw a frisbee. The central grassy area is simple enough, but around it you'll find futuristic terraces, concrete-walled gardens with abstract themes such as "gold", "dark" or "spires", and a massive dancing fountain – a favourite children's play area on hot days. You can't miss the **tethered balloon**, which takes small groups 150m above the ground (fine days only: 9am to roughly one hour before dusk; Mon–Fri €10, Sat & Sun €12; ⓣ01.44.26.20.00).

# Musée du Quai Branly

**Map 7, E7.** 37 quai Branly. Tues, Wed & Sun 11am–7pm, Thurs–Sat 11am–9pm; €8.50; ⓦwww.quaibranly.fr; ⓂIéna/RER Pont de l'Alma.

The new **Musée du Quai Branly** cuts a postmodern swathe along the riverbank, just upstream of the Eiffel Tower. Even if you're not interested in non-European art, it's well worth visiting for Jean Nouvel's exciting building, which unfurls in a long, stilt-supported curve through the middle of an exotic garden. The museum itself brings together stunning folk artefacts from every part of the world except Europe and North America. It's hard not to be moved by the potency and craftsmanship of exhibits such as Papua New Guinean full-body masks, Aboriginal Australian dot-paintings, Indonesian gold jewellery and man-sized wooden statues of the spirits of god-kings from Abomey, in West Africa.

## The sewers

**Map 7, G6.** Place de la Résistance. May–Sept Mon–Wed, Sat & Sun 11am–5pm; Oct–April 11am–4pm; €4.30; RER Pont de l'Alma.

A little way east of the quai Branly site, on the northeast side of the busy junction of place de la Résistance, is the entrance to the **sewers**, or **les égouts**. It's dark, damp and noisy with gushing water, but thankfully not as smelly as you might fear. The main part of the visit runs along a gantry walk perched above a main sewer. Here, displays of photographs, engravings, dredging tools, lamps and other flotsam and jetsam turn the history of the city's water supply and waste management into a surprisingly fascinating topic. What the exhibit doesn't tell you is that around thirty times a year parts of the system become overloaded with rainwater, and the sewer workers have to empty the excess – waste and all – straight into the Seine.

## Quai d'Orsay and rue Cler

**Map 7, H6–H9.** Ⓜ Invalides/La Tour-Maubourg.

A little further upstream from the sewers, the **American Church** on the quai d'Orsay, together with the American College nearby at 31 avenue Bosquet, is a nodal point in the well-organized life of Paris's large American community.

Just to the south, and in stark contrast with the austerity of much of the rest of the 7$^{e}$ arrondissement, is the attractive, village-like wedge of early nineteenth-century streets between avenue Bosquet and the Invalides. The heart of this miniature *quartier* is the lively market street **rue Cler**, whose cross-streets, rue de Grenelle and rue St-Dominique, are full of neighbourhood shops, posh *bistrots* and little hotels.

The **Pont Alexandre III** is surely the most extravagant bridge in the city, its single-span metal arch stretching 109m across the river. It was unveiled in 1900, just in time for the world fair. The nymph stretching out downstream represents the Seine, matched by an upstream nymph symbolizing St Petersburg's River Neva.

On the Left Bank, the green **Esplanade des Invalides** parades down towards the resplendently gilded dome of the **Hôtel des Invalides**. Built as a home for wounded soldiers on the orders of Louis XIV, whose equestrian statue tops the building's giant central arch, it's a kind of barracks version of Versailles, stripped of finer flourishes but crushingly grand nonetheless. The 12kg of gold added to the dome for the bicentennial of the Revolution only accentuates its splendour. A short way further east sits the Palais Bourbon, whose riverfront facade was added by Napoleon to match the pseudo-Greek of the Madeleine. It is now the home of the **Assemblée Nationale**, or French parliament.

## The Musée de l'Armée

**Map 7, J9.** 129 rue de Grenelle. April–Sept Mon–Wed & Fri–Sun 10am–6pm, Thurs 10am–9pm; Oct–March daily 10am–5pm; Oct–June closed first Mon of the month; €8 ticket also valid for Napoleon's tomb; Ⓦwww.invalides.org; ⓂInvalides/Varenne/La Tour-Maubourg.

The Hôtel des Invalides houses the vast **Musée de l'Armée**, the national war museum. Probably its most interesting wings cover the two World Wars. The battles, the resistance and the slow, final liberation are brought to life using memorabilia and stirring contemporary newsreels (most of which have an English-language option). The **Historial Charles de Gaulle** section, in the basement, pays high-tech audiovisual tribute to the Resistance leader and, later, President.

The collection of medieval and Renaissance armour in the west wing of the royal courtyard is also distinctly fabulous. Surprisingly, perhaps, the super-scale three-dimensional maps of French ports and fortified cities in the **Musée des Plans-Reliefs**, under the roof of the east wing, are also well worth a visit. The remainder of the museum is dedicated to the history of the French army from Louis XIV up to the 1870s, and its pedantic collections of uniforms and weaponry are perhaps more for enthusiasts.

At the core of the complex is a double church, built in the 1670s by Jules Hardouin-Mansart. The spartan northern section, known as the **Eglise des Soldats**, or Soldiers' Church, is reached via the main northern courtyard of Les Invalides (no ticket required). It's lined with almost a hundred banners, captured by the French army over the centuries. A glass wall separates it from the stupendously pompous royal church, which has a separate entrance on the south side of the complex. Originally intended for the private worship of Louis XIV and the royal family, it is now the **Eglise du Dôme** (same hours and ticket as Musée de l'Armée), and centres around Napoleon's massive sarcophagus, grandiosely carved in deep red quartzite.

## Musée Rodin

**Map 7, K9.** 79 rue de Varenne. Tues–Sun: April–Sept 9.30am–5.45pm, garden closes at 6.45pm; Oct–March 9.30am–4.45pm, garden closes at 5pm; house and gardens €6 (or €12 with the Musée d'Orsay), garden only €1; Ⓦwww.musee-rodin.fr; ⓂVarenne.

Immediately east of Les Invalides stands the **Musée Rodin.** The museum's setting is superbly elegant, a beautiful eighteenth-century mansion the sculptor leased from the state in return for the gift of all his work upon his death. Bronze versions of major projects like *The Burghers of Calais, The Thinker, The Gates of Hell* and *Ugolino and His Sons* are exhibited in the garden – the latter forming the centrepiece of the ornamental pond.

Inside, the vigorous energy of the sculptures contrasts with the elegantly worn wooden panelling (or "*boisieries*") and the tarnished mirrors and chandeliers. Crowds gather round the marble and bronze versions of Rodin's most famous works, including *The Kiss*, but it's well worth lingering over the museum's smaller, more impressionistic clay works as well, studies that Rodin took from life. Don't miss the ground-floor room devoted to Camille Claudel, Rodin's pupil, model and lover.

## Cité de l'Architecture et du Patrimoine

**Map 7, C6.** 1 place du Trocadéro et 11 novembre. Mon, Wed & Fri–Sun 11am–7pm, Thurs 11am–9pm; €8; Ⓦwww.citechaillot.fr; ⓂTrocadéro.

Facing the Eiffel Tower across the river is the bastardized Modernist-Neoclassical monster that is the **Palais de Chaillot**. Built for the 1937 world fair on the proud, elevated site of the old Trocadéro palace, it wouldn't look out of place in Fascist Rome. Its northern wing has now been turned into the **Cité de l'Architecture et du Patrimoine**, a combined institute, library and museum of architecture. The main gallery displays giant plaster casts taken from the greatest French buildings (chiefly churches) at the end of the nineteenth century, before pollution and erosion dulled their detail. The Galerie des Peintures Murales, with its radiant, full-scale copies of French frescoes and wall-paintings, is equally impressive. The top floor offers a sleek rundown of the modern and contemporary, with models, photographs and a reconstruction of an entire apartment from **Le Corbusier**'s Cité Radieuse, in Marseille.

---

**The broad *terrasse* extending between the two wings of the museum is a popular hangout for in-line skaters and souvenir vendors – and the ideal place to plant yourself for a fine view across to the Eiffel Tower and the Ecole Militaire.**

---

## 10 The Musée Guimet and Musée de la Mode

Musée Guimet: **Map 7, D5.** 6 place d'Iéna. Daily except Tues 10am–6pm; €7.50; ⓦwww.museeguimet.fr; ⓜIéna. Musée de la Mode: **Map 7, E5.** 10 av Pierre 1er de Serbie. Closed until autumn 2011; see ⓦwww.paris.fr for details; ⓜIéna/Alma-Marceau.

The **Musée Guimet** – or Musée National des Arts Asiatiques, to give it its full title – houses a world-renowned collection of **Khmer sculpture** from the civilization that produced Cambodia's Angkor Wat. The museum winds round four floors, groaning under the weight of statues of Buddhas and gods, dramatically lit and imaginatively displayed.

A little further to the east, set in small gardens opposite the Palais de Tokyo, stands the grandiose Palais Galliera, home to the **Musée de la Mode**. The museum's magnificent collection of clothes and fashion accessories from the eighteenth century to the present day is exhibited in temporary, themed shows of which there are usually two or three a year (except during the 2011 closure for works). During changeovers the museum is closed for weeks at a time, so be sure to check what's on and when.

## The Palais de Tokyo

**Map 7, E6.** 13 av du Président-Wilson. ⓜIéna/Alma-Marceau.

Nearby, the **Palais de Tokyo** houses the **Musée d'Art Moderne de la Ville de Paris** (Tues–Sun 10am–6pm; free; ⓦwww.mam.paris.fr). The gallery received unwelcome publicity in May 2010 when a lone thief made off with half a dozen literally priceless canvases by Picasso, Matisse, Modigliani and others, but the museum still has its two marvellous (and entirely untransportable) centrepieces. Facing the stairs as you descend, the chapel-like **salle Matisse** is devoted to the artist's giant triptych, *La Danse de Paris*, its sinuous figures seemingly leaping through colour. Further on, **Raoul Dufy**'s enormous mural *La Fée Electricité* ("The Electricity Fairy") fills an entire, curved room with 250 vivid, cartoon-like panels recounting the story of electricity from Aristotle to the then-modern power station.

The main collection is chronological, starting with Fauvism and Cubism, and progressing through to Dada, the Ecole de Paris and beyond. Most artists working in France – Braque, Chagall, Delaunay, Derain, Dufy, Léger, Modigliani, Picasso and many others – are represented and there is a strong Parisian theme to many of the works. The collection is kept up to the minute by an active buying policy: look out in particular for the works of contemporary lions Annette Messager, Jean-Marc Bustamente, Christian Boltanski and Philippe Parreno.

In the western wing of the palace, the **Site de Création Contemporaine** (Tues–Sun noon–midnight; €6; Ⓦwww.palaisdetokyo.com) is a cutting-edge gallery whose semi-derelict interior focuses exclusively on contemporary and avant-garde art. A constantly changing flow of exhibitions and events – anything from a concept show by Turner Prize winner Jeremy Deller to a temporary "occupation" by squatter-artists – keeps the atmosphere lively, with a genuinely exciting countercultural buzz.

Just beyond the Palais de Tokyo, in **place de l'Alma**, you'll find a full-scale replica of the Statue of Liberty's flame that was given to France in 1987 as a symbol of Franco-American relations. It's now an unofficial memorial to **Princess Diana**, whose car crashed in the adjacent underpass.

# Montparnasse

The swathe of cafés, brasseries and cinemas that runs through the heart of modern **Montparnasse** was long a honey pot for pleasure-seekers, as well as a kind of border town dividing the lands of well-heeled St-Germain from the amorphous populations of the three arrondissements of **southern Paris**. In the nineteenth century, Bohemians and left-leaning intellectuals abandoned the staid city centre for Montparnasse's inexpensive cafés and nightspots, but the *quartier*'s lasting fame rests on the patronage of artists in the 1920s, following the exodus from Montmartre. Picasso, Matisse, Kandinsky, Man Ray, Modigliani, Giacometti and Chagall were all *habitués* of the celebrated **cafés** around place Vavin, and many are buried in **Montparnasse cemetery**. Still more bones lie nearby in the grim **catacombs**. The area is now dominated by the looming **Tour Montparnasse**, which you can ascend for a superb view of the city. In the tower's shadow, a handful of **museums** recall the quarter's artistic traditions.

## Tour Montparnasse and Jardin Atlantique

Tour Montparnasse: **Map 6, G11.** Daily: May–Sept 9.30am–11.30pm; Oct–April 9.30am–10.30pm; €11; Ⓦwww.tourmontparnasse56.com; ⓂMontparnasse-Bienvenüe. Jardin Atlantique: **Map 6, F12.**

Montparnasse's most prominent and least-loved landmark is the brown-glass blade of the **Tour Montparnasse**. At the time of its construction, this was one of Paris's first skyscrapers, and few Parisians have a good word to say for it now. The **view** from the top, however, is arguably better than the one from the Eiffel Tower – it has the Eiffel Tower in it, after all, plus there are no queues and it costs less to ascend. Sunset is the best time to visit.

The interior of the **Gare Montparnasse** is a Modernist confusion of concrete and glass built over one of The city's largest métro interchanges. But behind it lies a hidden jewel: the **Jardin Atlantique**, a public park actually suspended above the tracks. Completed in 1994, between cliff-like glass walls of high-rise blocks, it's a remarkable piece of engineering – and imagination. The lawns rise and fall in waves to better distribute their weight over hidden concrete struts below, while fields of Atlantic-coast grasses wave in the slightest breeze. Access is via lifts on rue Cdt. R. Mouchotte and boulevard Vaugirard, or by the stairs alongside platform #1.

## Musée du Montparnasse and Musée Bourdelle

**Map 6, F10.** Musée du Montparnasse: 21 av du Maine. Tues–Sun 12.30pm–7pm; €6; Ⓦwww.museedumontparnasse.net. Musée Bourdelle: 18 rue Antoine Bourdelle. Tues–Sun 10am–6pm; free, €7 during expos; ⓂMontparnasse-Bienvenüe/Falguière.

Just north of Montparnasse station are two little-visited yet beguiling **museums**. A half-hidden, ivy-clad alley leads to what was once the Russian painter Marie Vassilieff's studio, now converted into the **Musée du Montparnasse**, hosting temporary exhibitions based on Montparnasse artists past and present.

A few steps north of the station, a garden of sculptures invites you into the **Musée Bourdelle**, a museum built around the artist's former studio. As Rodin's pupil and Giacometti's teacher,

Bourdelle bridged the period between naturalism and a more geometrically conceived, Modernist style. His monumental, epic sculptures get pride of place in the chapel-like grand hall, while the sculptor's old **studio** is atmospherically littered with half-complete works.

## Boulevard du Montparnasse

**Map 6, E9–I11.** Ⓜ Vavin.

Most of the bustle in Montparnasse is concentrated on **boulevard du Montparnasse**, particularly the section between the station and Vavin métro. The *quartier*'s most famous cafés are clustered around the Vavin crossroads. If the *Select*, *Coupole*, *Dôme*, *Rotonde* and *Closerie des Lilas* are no longer the wildly social venues they were during the interwar artistic and literary boom, they remain proud Parisian classics. This stretch of the boulevard still stays up late and the relatively simple *Le Select* (best for a coffee; see p.225) and the sumptuous *La Coupole* (best for a meal; see p.225) preserve much of the flavour of the old days, and are as worthy of a visit as any museum.

## The Musée Zadkine and Fondation Cartier pour l'Art Contemporain

Musée Zadkine: **Map 2, D13.** 100bis rue d'Assas. Tues–Sun 10am–6pm; free, or €4 during expos; Ⓜ Vavin/RER Port-Royal. Fondation Cartier: **Map 6, I13.** 261 bd Raspail. Tues 11am–10pm, Wed–Sun 11am–8pm; €7.50; Ⓦ www.fondation.cartier.fr; Ⓜ Raspail.

Just north of the boulevard du Montparnasse, and within a few minutes' walk of the Jardin du Luxembourg (see p.109), is the tiny **Musée Zadkine**. The museum occupies the Russian-born sculptor **Ossip Zadkine**'s studio-house, where he lived and worked from 1928 until his death in 1967. In the garden, enclosed by ivy-covered studios and dwarfed by tall buildings, his angular Cubist bronzes seem to struggle for light. Inside is a collection of his gentler wooden torsos, along with smaller-scale bronze and stone works, notably *Femme à l'éventail*.

Taking a shortcut down rue Campagne-Première leads through to boulevard Raspail and the **Fondation Cartier pour l'Art Contemporain**. The stunning glass-and-steel building was designed by fashionable French architect Jean Nouvel, and has a glass wall following the line of the street, like a false start to the building proper. Inside, temporary exhibitions showcase all kinds of contemporary art – installations, videos, multi-media – often by foreign artists little known in France.

## Montparnasse cemetery and Fondation Cartier-Bresson

Cemetery: **Map 6, H12.** March 16–Nov 5 Mon–Fri 8am–6pm, Sat 8.30am–6pm, Sun 9am–6pm; Nov 6–March 15 closes 5.30pm; free; Ⓜ Raspail/Gaîté/Edgar Quinet. Fondation Cartier-Bresson: **Map 6, G13.** 2 impasse Lebouis. Tues, Thurs, Fri & Sun 1–6.30pm, Wed 1–8.30pm, Sat 11am–6.45pm; closed Aug; €6; Ⓦ www.henricartierbresson.org; Ⓜ Gaîté.

Just east of the station, along boulevard Edgar Quinet, is the main entrance to **Montparnasse cemetery**. It is home to plenty of the illustrious dead, from Baudelaire to Beckett and Sainte-Beuve to Saint-Saëns – you can pick up a leaflet and map from the guardhouse by each entrance. The joint grave of Jean-Paul Sartre and Simone de Beauvoir lies immediately right of the entrance on boulevard Edgar-Quinet. The eastern angle of the cemetery lies across a road; in its far northern corner is a tomb crowned with a version of Brancusi's sculpture *The Kiss* – a poignant statement of grief.

Hidden away a couple of minutes from the cemetery – walk south down rue Raymond Losserand, then turn right on rue Lebouis and right again up the tiny impasse Lebouis – is the **Fondation Henri Cartier-Bresson**. Fascinating shows of the work of the grand old photographer of Paris and his contemporaries alternate with exhibitions promoting younger photographers.



## The catacombs

**Map 6, I14.** 1 place Denfert-Rochereau. Tues–Sun 10am–4pm; €8; Ⓜ Denfert-Rochereau.

The **catacombs** were originally part of the gigantic quarry network underlying southern Paris – there are still some 300km of tunnels. Between 1785 and 1871, some of these quarried-out spaces were stacked with millions of bones cleared from the overcrowded public charnel houses and cemeteries. Today, it's estimated that the remains of six million Parisians are interred here. Lining the passageways, the long thighbones are stacked end-on, forming a bizarre wall behind which heaps of smaller bones can just be seen. Older children often love the whole experience, but be forewarned that there are a good two or three claustrophobic kilometres to walk, and it can be surprisingly cold and damp.

12

# Montmartre and around



Huddled on a hilltop in the northern part of Paris, the buildings of **Montmartre** stand apart from the city. The area's chief landmark, visible from all over the city, is the white church of **Sacré-Coeur**, which crowns the Butte like fairy-tale icing. The slopes below preserve something of the spirit of the little village that once basked here but, unlike most villages, Montmartre has a very diverse and dynamic population, by turns lefty, trendy, arty and sleazy. Some of the city's hippest and most individualistic clothes shops, cafés and restaurants are hidden away in the streets around **Abbesses** métro.

East of Montmartre, you can explore the poor, ethnically mixed **Goutte d'Or** *quartier*; to the south stretch the twin arrondissements of the **9**$^{e}$ and **10**$^{e}$. Where the 10$^{e}$ is rough, boisterous and shabby, the 9$^{e}$ is largely genteel and well-groomed – though the area around **Blanche** and **Pigalle**, just below the Butte Montmartre, is notorious for its cabarets and sex shows.

## Abbesses

**Map 3, F3.** Ⓜ Abbesses.

**Place des Abbesses** is postcard-pretty, centred on one of Guimard's rare, canopied Art Nouveau métro entrances. For

**shopping** and **eating**, the area around Abbesses is one of the most satisfying in Paris. A few peeling, shuttered-up old shops survive from the old Montmartre, but these days most have been turned into restaurants or jazzy little boutiques. Some of the best addresses are listed on pp.251–270, but you can let your eye for fashion guide you round rue des Martyrs, rue des Trois-Frères, rue de la Vieuville, rue Houdon and rue Durantin. Heading west from the métro, **rue des Abbesses** is best for cafés, especially the popular suntrap of *Le Sancerre* (see p.226). On the downhill side of place des Abbesses, the red-brick church of **St-Jean de Montmartre** might be worth sticking your nose in for its reinforced concrete ribs: when the church was built in the early 1900s, this was a daringly radical construction material.

## The southern slopes of the Butte

**Map 3, F2/3–G3.** Ⓜ Abbesses/Anvers.

At 130m, the "Mound" or **Butte Montmartre** is the highest point in Paris. The name is probably a corruption of *Mons Martyrum* ("the Martyrs' hill" – the martyrs being St Denis and his companions), or possibly of *Mons Martis*, after a Roman shrine to Mars. If you're in any doubt about finding your way up the Butte, just keep heading uphill – the area is so charming that there's no such thing as a wrong turn.

Two of the quietest and most attractive **routes** begin at place des Abbesses. The quickest climbs rue de la Vieuville and the stairs in rue Drevet to the minuscule **place du Calvaire**, which offers a lovely view back over the city. For a more leisurely stroll, head up rue Durantin, then right up rue Tholozé, heading towards the looming silhouette of the **Moulin de la Galette**, a lone survivor of Montmartre's forty-odd windmills. The famous dances here were immortalized by Renoir in his painting, *Bal du Moulin de la Galette*. From the windmill, turn right onto rue Lepic, then first left onto place **Marcel Aymé**, home to the sculpture **Le Passe-Muraille**, which celebrates

Aymé's well-loved short story, *The Man Who Could Walk Through Walls*. From here, rue Norvins leads towards the thrum of place du Tertre (see p.131).

A third possible route, up rue Ravignan, would take you past the delightfully tiny place Emile-Goudeau where, in 1904, Picasso took up a studio in an old piano factory known as the **Bateau-Lavoir**. He stayed for the best part of a decade, painting *Les Demoiselles d'Avignon* and sharing loves, quarrels and opium trips with Braque, Juan Gris, Modigliani, Max Jacob, Apollinaire and others. Although the original building burned down some years ago, the modern reconstruction still provides studio space for artists, and the square itself hasn't changed: even the graceful, green **Wallace fountain** is still in place – one of the last surviving of the fifty famous drinking fountains donated to the city in 1872.

The slightly longer alternative would be to head west on Montmartre's version of a high street, rue des Abbesses, then follow the curve of rue Lepic up, following in the traces of the old quarry wagons which once brought plaster of Paris down the hill from the quarries. A resolutely ordinary food market occupies rue Lepic's foot, as it descends towards place Blanche.

If you don't want to walk, you can take the diminutive and determinedly ecological **Montmartrobus** (normal métro/bus tickets are valid), which makes a useful circular route from place Pigalle up to the Sacré-Coeur and back.

## Sacré-Coeur and around

**Map 3, H2.** Church: daily 6.45am–10.30pm. Tower daily: April–Sept 9am–7pm; Oct–March 9am–6pm; €4.50; ⓂAbbesses/Anvers.

The core of Montmartre, the photogenic but bogus **place du Tertre**, is jammed with tourists, overpriced restaurants and "artists" knocking up lurid oils of Paris landmarks. A few steps away, on rue Poulbot, is the **Espace Dalí Montmartre**, at no. 9–11 (map 3, G2; daily 10am–6pm; €10; Ⓦwww.daliparis.com; ⓂAbbesses), more giant souvenir shop than gallery. To lift the spirits, however, you could step off the square into the blessedly serene **church of St-Pierre**. It's one of the oldest in Paris and while much altered, with modern stained glass throughout, it retains its Romanesque and early Gothic bones.

Crowning the Butte, immediately to the east, is the **Sacré-Coeur**, a weird confection of French and Byzantine architecture, whose pimply tower and white ice-cream dome have somehow become a fundamental part of the Paris skyline. Construction began in the 1870s on the initiative of the Catholic Church to atone for the "crimes" of the Commune. The best things about the Sacré-Coeur are its **views** from the top and from the stairs at its foot: both tend to be clearest first and last thing in the day, when the sun isn't full in your face.

## The northern slopes of the Butte

**Map 3, G1/2.** ⓂAbbesses/Lamarck-Caulaincourt.

Rue des Saules tips steeply down the north side of the Butte past the terraces of the tiny **Montmartre vineyard**, which is lovingly tended by an association of local grandees – and produces some 1500 bottles of pretty rough wine every year. To the right, rue Cortot cuts through to the water tower, whose distinctive, white lighthouse-like form is another skyline landmark. The picturesque house standing opposite the lowest corner of the vineyard is the cabaret club **Au Lapin Agile**, made famous by the Montmartre artists who drank here in the 1900s – among them Picasso. The "nimble rabbit" is still alive today, and puts on old-fashioned shows of French *chanson* (map 3, G1; Tues–Sun 9pm–2am; €24; Ⓦwww.au-lapin-agile.com; ⓂLamarck-Caulaincourt); the performances are sincere, the clientiele touristy.

At 12 rue Cortot, a pretty old house with a grassy courtyard was occupied at different times by Renoir, Dufy, Suzanne Valadon and her troubled son, Utrillo. It's now the **Musée de Montmartre** (map 3, G1; Tues–Sun 11am–6pm; €8; Ⓦwww.museedemontmartre.fr; ⓂLamarck-Caulaincourt), which rather half-heartedly attempts to recreate the atmosphere of Montmartre's pioneering heyday via a selection of Toulouse-Lautrec posters, mock-ups of period rooms and painted impressions of how the Butte once looked.



## Southeast of the Butte and the Halle St-Pierre

**Map 3, H3.** Halle St-Pierre: 2 rue Ronsard. Daily 10am–6pm; €7.50; Ⓜ Anvers.

To the south and east of the Sacré-Coeur, the slopes of the Butte drop steeply down towards boulevard Barbès and the Goutte d'Or. Directly below are the gardens of square Willette, overrun with tourists. To avoid the crowds, head down the steeply stepped rue Utrillo, turning right at the pleasant café, *L'Eté en Pente Douce* (see p.226), which has outdoor tables on the corner of rue Paul Albert. From here, more steps lead down along the edge of the gardens to rue Ronsard, where overhanging greenery masks the now-sealed entrances to the original plaster of Paris quarries.

The circular **Halle St-Pierre**, at the bottom of rue Ronsard, was once a market building but is now an exhibition space dedicated to Art Brut, or works by artists that mainstream galleries won't touch. The biannual exhibitions encompass anything from naïve paintings to sci-fi sculptures.

## Montmartre cemetery

**Map 3, D2.** March 16–Nov 5 Mon–Fri 8am–6pm, Sat from 8.30am, Sun from 9am; Nov 6–March 15 closes 5.30pm; Ⓜ Blanche/Place-de-Clichy.

West of the Butte, near the beginning of rue Caulaincourt, **Montmartre cemetery** is an atmospheric tangle of trees and funerary pomposity. Tucked down below street level in the hollow of an old quarry, it's more intimate and somehow less melancholy than Père-Lachaise or Montparnasse cemeteries. The entrance is on avenue Rachel, underneath the bridge section of rue Caulaincourt. The illustrious dead at rest here include Stendhal, Berlioz, Degas, Feydeau, Offenbach, Nijinsky and François Truffaut, as well as La Goulue, the Moulin Rouge dancer immortalized by Toulouse-Lautrec.



## The Goutte d'Or

**Map 3, J2/K2.** ⓂChâteau-Rouge/Barbès-Rochechouart.

Immediately north of the wide, grotty boulevard de la Chapelle, the poetically named *quartier* of the **Goutte d'Or** stretches between **boulevard Barbès** and the **Gare du Nord** rail lines. The setting for Zola's *L'Assommoir*, a classic novel of gritty realism, its name – "Drop of Gold" – is derived from the vineyard that occupied this site in medieval times. For much of the postwar period, this was the North African quarter, but it is now home to a host of vibrant mini-communities, predominantly West African and Congolese, with pockets of South Asian, Haitian, Turkish and other ethnicities.

On rue de la Goutte d'Or itself you'll find one of the city's green ironwork **Wallace fountains** on the corner with rue de Chartres, but the main sight is a few steps north on rue Dejean, where the **Marché Dejean** (map 3, J2; closed Sun afternoon and all day Mon; ⓂChâteau-Rouge) heaves with African groceries and thrums with shoppers. Most of the *quartier*'s cafés and bars tend to be very local in flavour, but there are a couple of friendly cafés and restaurants on **rue Léon**.

## Blanche and Pigalle

**Map 3, E3–F4.** ⓂBlanche/Pigalle.

From place Clichy in the west to Barbès-Rochechouart in the east, the hill of Montmartre is underlined by the sleazy **boulevards de Clichy** and **de Rochechouart**. Between **place Blanche** and **place Pigalle**, sex shows, sex shops and prostitutes – both male and female – vie for the custom of *solitaires* and couples alike. Perfectly placed among all the sex shops and shows is the surprisingly highbrow **Musée de l'Erotisme** (map 3, E3; daily 10am–2am; €8). The ground floor and first floor are awash with model phalluses, fertility symbols and intertwined folk art figurines from all over the world, and there's a fascinating history of Parisian brothels and clips of historic pornography. High-quality exhibitions are held throughout the year. A few steps west, the photogenic **Moulin Rouge** (map 3, D3; ⓣ01.53.09.82.82, ⓦwww.moulinrouge.fr) still thrives on place Blanche. Once Toulouse-Lautrec's inspiration, it trades on its traditional, bare-breasted, can-canning "Doriss Girls", albeit now with a flashy accompanying sound-and-light show and an expensive price tag, at around €100, or half as much again with dinner.

## The 9e arrondissement

The heart of the **9e arrondissement** was first developed in the early nineteenth century as a fashionable suburb. It was soon dubbed the **Nouvelle Athènes**, or New Athens, after the Romantic artists and writers who moved in made it the centre of a minor artistic boom. The handsome centrepiece of the *quartier* is the circular **place St-Georges**. To get the full flavour of the area's nineteenth-century heyday, make for the **Musée de la Vie Romantique**, at 16 rue Chaptal (map 3, E4; daily except Mon 10am–6pm, closed public hols; €4–9 during exhibitions, otherwise free; ⓜSt-Georges/Blanche/Pigalle), which sets out to evoke the Romantic period in a shuttered building at the end of a private alley. The interior preserves the rich colours of a typical bourgeois home of the nineteenth century.

A short way south down rue de la Rochefoucauld, you'll find the curious and little-visited **Musée Moreau** (map 3, E5; daily except Tues 10am–12.45pm & 2–5.15pm; €5; ⓜSt-Georges/Blanche/Pigalle), dedicated to the fantastical, Symbolist paintings of **Gustave Moreau**. The museum's design was conceived by Moreau himself, to be created in the house he shared with his parents for many years; you can visit their stuffy apartment quarters. The paintings get much more room – two huge, studio-like spaces where Moreau's canvases hang cheek-by-jowl, every surface crawling with decadent and weirdly symbolic figures and decorative swirls.





## The 10e arrondissement

The gritty life of the 10e is coloured by the presence of the big **northern railway stations**, the Gare du Nord (map 3, L4) and Gare de l'Est (map 3, M6). The southern end of the arrondissement is its liveliest, a poor but vibrant quarter that has become home to Indian, black African and Near Eastern communities as well as, in recent years, a small vanguard of bourgeois-bohemians – what Parisians call "*les bobos*". At its lower end, the **rue du Faubourg St-Denis** is full of charcuteries, butchers, greengrocers and ethnic delicatessens, as well as a number of restaurants, including the historic brasseries *Julien* (see p.227) and *Flo*.

13

# Eastern Paris

The **Canal St-Martin**, running from Bastille in the south to place de la Bataille de Stalingrad in the north, effectively marks the boundary between central and eastern Paris. Traditionally home to the working classes, eastern Paris is nowadays one of the most diverse and vibrant parts of the city, colonized by sizeable ethnic populations, as well as students and artists, attracted by the area's low rents. The main *quartiers*, **Belleville** and **Ménilmontant**, were once villages on the fringes of the city, and drew migrants from the countryside in the nineteenth century. During this time, the area developed a reputation as a revolutionary hotbed, with the impoverished inhabitants regularly taking to the barricades. Much of the district these days is characterized by high-rise housing developments, though some charming old villagey streets do remain. Of chief interest to visitors are the **Parc de la Villette**, containing a state-of-the-art science museum and a superb music museum; the recently opened **104** contemporary arts space; and the **Père-Lachaise cemetery**, the burial place of numerous well-known artists and writers. The area's current arty, bohemian denizens ensure a cutting-edge arts and nightlife scene, especially around the **Canal St-Martin** and **Ménilmontant**. Ascending the hilly heights of the **Parc de Belleville** and the **Parc des Buttes-Chaumont** reveals the east's other chief asset – fine views of the city below.

# The Canal St-Martin

**Map 4, D1–D4.** Ⓜ République/Jacques-Bonsergent.

Effectively marking the boundary between central Paris and the eastern districts, the **Canal St-Martin** was built in 1825 so that river traffic could shortcut the great western loop of the Seine around Paris. As it happened, it also turned out to be a splendid natural defence for the rebellious quarters of eastern Paris: the canal was spanned by six swing bridges, which could easily be drawn up to halt the advance of government troops. Napoleon III simply got round this by covering over the lower stretch in the latter half of the nineteenth century; the canal now runs underground at the

## Canal cruises

A leisurely way of seeing the Canal St-Martin is to take one of the boat trips operated by **Canauxrama** (reservations Ⓣ01.42.39.15.00, Ⓦwww.canauxrama.com) between the Port de l'Arsenal, opposite 50 boulevard de la Bastille, 12ᵉ (Ⓜ Bastille), and the Bassin de la Villette, 13 quai de la Loire, 19ᵉ (Ⓜ Jaurès), north of the Canal St-Martin. Daily departures are at 9.45am and 2.45pm from La Villette and at 9.45am and 2.30pm from the Port de l'Arsenal. At the Bastille end there's a long, spooky tunnel from which you eventually emerge in the 10ᵉ arrondissement. The ride lasts two and a half hours and costs €16 (students and seniors €11, under 12s €8.50, under 6s free; no concessions weekend afternoons or hols), or slightly less if you book online; in any case booking is essential from October to April and is advisable on weekends the rest of the year. **Paris Canal** (Ⓣ01.42.40.96.97, Ⓦwww.pariscanal.com) also runs trips, usually from March to October, between the Musée d'Orsay, quai Anatole-France, 7ᵉ (RER Musée d'Orsay), and the Parc de la Villette (near the building marked "La Folie des Visites du Parc"; Ⓜ Porte-de-Pantin). Prices are €17 for adults, €14 for students and seniors, €10 for children aged 4 to 11; you'll need to book by phone or online.

Bastille, emerging after 2.5km near the rue du Faubourg-du-Temple, and continuing north to the place de la Bataille de Stalingrad.

The northern reaches of the exposed canal still have a slightly industrial character, but the southern part, along the **quai de Jemmapes** and **quai de Valmy** (ⓂJacques-Bonsergent), has a great deal of charm, with plane trees lining the cobbled *quais*, and elegant high-arched footbridges punctuating the spaces between the locks, from where you can still watch the odd barge slowly rising or sinking to the next level. At 102 quai de Jemmapes is the **Hôtel du Nord**, made famous by Marcel Carné's eponymous film, starring Arletty and Jean Gabin; it's had its facade restored and now thrives as a bar and *bistrot*. The district is popular with an arty crowd, catered to by trendy bars, cafés and boutiques. It's particularly lively on Sundays when the *quais* are closed to traffic, and pedestrians, cyclists and rollerbladers take over the streets, while students hang out along the canal's edge, drinking beer and strumming guitars.

## Place de la Bataille de Stalingrad and Bassin de la Villette

**Map 4, off D1.** ⓂJaurès/Stalingrad.

The Canal St-Martin goes underground again at the busy **place de la Bataille de Stalingrad**, dominated by the Neoclassical **Rotonde de la Villette**, a handsome stone rotunda fronted with a portico. Built in 1784, this was one of the 54 toll houses that surrounded the city in Louis XVI's time. Every road out of Paris had a customs post, or *barrière*, linked by a 6m-high wall – a major irritant in the run-up to the Revolution. Cleaned and restored, the *rotonde*, one of two to survive (the other is at the entrance to Parc Monceau métro station) is currently being turned into an arts/exhibition centre and restaurant.

Beyond here the canal widens out into the **Bassin de la Villette**, built in 1808. The recobbled docks area today bears few traces of its days as France's premier port, its dockside buildings now offering **canal boat trips** (see p.138) and boasting a multiplex cinema, the **MK2**, which has screens on both banks, linked by shuttle boat. It retains a slightly gritty feel, though is rapidly gentrifying: new bars, restaurants, a major contemporary art space, **Le 104** and the hip *St Christopher's* hostel (see p.197), housed in a converted boat hangar, have all opened recently. On Sundays and holidays people stroll along the *quais*, jog, cycle, play boules, fish or take a rowing boat out in the dock. In August, as part of the Paris Plage scheme (see p.285), you can rent canoes and pedaloes, among other activities. At rue de Crimée a hydraulic bridge marks the end of the dock and the beginning of the Canal de l'Ourcq. If you keep to the south bank on quai de la Marne, you can cross directly into the Parc de la Villette.

## Le 104

**Map 1.** 104 rue d'Aubervilliers. Tues–Sat 11am–9pm, Sun 11am–8pm; free entry to the main hall, entry to the artists' studios €5; Ⓦwww.104.fr; ⓂRicquet.

Three blocks west of the Bassin de la Villette, a former, grand funeral parlour, built in the 1870s, has been converted into an impressive multi-media arts space, covering some 39,000 square metres. The ambitious **Le 104** opened in 2008, and thirty-odd established and new artists have now set up studios here. One of the stipulations is that they regularly open their studios to the public, with the aim of stimulating debate and the exchange of ideas. Each week has an artistic theme, and there are regular dance and music performances, lectures, exhibitions and other events, some suitable for children. Also on site are a restaurant, café, bookshop and Emmaüs charity shop.

## Parc de la Villette

**Map 1.** Ⓣ01.40.03.75.75, Ⓦwww.lavillette.com; ⓂPorte-de-Pantin/Porte-de-la-Villette.

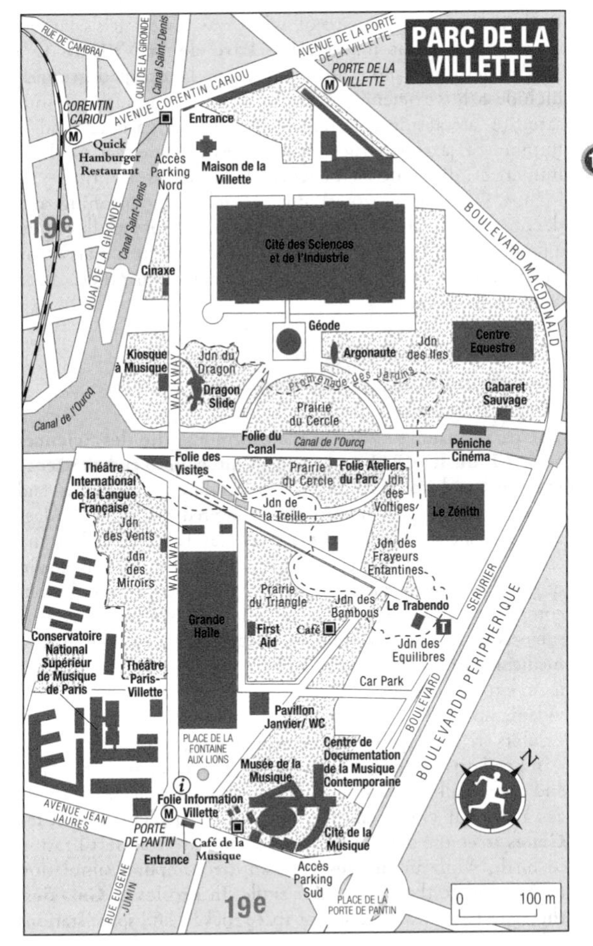
PARC DE LA VILLETTE
RUE DE CAMBRAI
QUAI DE LA GIRONDE
Canal Saint-Denis
AVENUE DE LA PORTE DE LA VILLETTE
PORTE DE LA VILLETTE
AVENUE CORENTIN CARIOU
CORENTIN CARIOU
Entrance
Quick Hamburger Restaurant
Accès Parking Nord
Maison de la Villette
19e
Cité des Sciences et de l'Industrie
BOULEVARD MACDONALD
Cinaxe
Géode
Kiosque à Musique
Jdn du Dragon
Dragon Slide
WALKWAY
Argonaute
Jdn des Iles
Centre Equestre
Promenade des Jardins
Prairie du Cercle
Cabaret Sauvage
Canal de l'Ourcq
Folie du Canal
Péniche Cinéma
Folie des Visites
Théâtre International de la Langue Française
Prairie du Cercle
Folie Ateliers du Parc
Jdn des Voltiges
Le Zénith
Jdn de la Treille
Jdn des Vents
Jdn des Miroirs
Jdn des Frayeurs Enfantines
SERURIER
Grande Halle
Prairie du Triangle
Jdn des Bambous
Le Trabendo
First Aid
Café
Jdn des Equilibres
BOULEVARDD PERIPHERIQUE
Conservatoire National Supérieur de Musique de Paris
Théâtre Paris-Villette
Car Park
BOULEVARD
Pavillon Janvier/ WC
PLACE DE LA FONTAINE AUX LIONS
Centre de Documentation de la Musique Contemporaine
Musée de la Musique
Folie Information Villette
AVENUE JEAN JAURES
PORTE DE PANTIN
Café de la Musique
Cité de la Musique
Entrance
Accès Parking Sud
RUE EUGENE JUMIN
PLACE DE LA PORTE DE PANTIN
0
100 m
N

Built in 1986 on the site of what was once Paris's largest abattoir and meat market, the **Parc de la Villette** is a postmodern arts and science park. The landscaped grounds include a huge science museum, a music museum, various satellite attractions, a series of themed gardens and a number of jarring, bright-red "follies". The effect of these numerous, disparate elements can be quite disorienting – all in line with the creators' aim of eschewing meaning and deconstructing the whole into its parts. All very well, but on a practical level you'll probably want to pick up a map at the information centre at the southern entrance near Ⓜ Porte-de-Pantin.

## Cité des Sciences et de l'Industrie

Tues–Sat 10am–6pm, Sun 10am–7pm; €8; Ⓦ www.cite-sciences.fr; Ⓜ Porte-de-la-Villette.

The park's main attraction is the enormous **Cité des Sciences et de l'Industrie**. This is the science museum to end all science museums, and worth visiting for the building alone: all glass and stainless steel, crow's nests and cantilevered platforms, bridges and suspended walkways, the different levels linked by lifts and escalators around a huge central space open to the full 40m height of the roof. An excellent programme of temporary exhibitions complements the permanent exhibition – **Explora** – covering subjects such as sound, robotics, energy, light, ecology, maths, medicine, space and language. As the name suggests, the emphasis is on exploring, and there are plenty of interactive computers, videos, holograms, animated models and games. Many of the exhibits are accompanied by English-language translation.

In **Les Sons** (sounds), you can watch a video of an x-rayed jaw and throat talking or sit in a cubicle and feel your body tingle as a rainstorm crashes around you. Videos in **L'Homme et les Gènes** trace the development of an embryo from fertilization to birth, while in **Images** you can use computer simulation to manipulate the Mona Lisa's smile. In **Etoiles et Galaxies**, there are large-scale models of space rockets and space stations and a real Mirage jet fighter. Especially popular with children, the **Jeux de Lumière** is a whole series of experiments focusing on colour, optical illusions, refraction and the like. Best of all for children, though, is the **Cité des Enfants** (see below) and they might also enjoy a session in the planetarium (around six shows daily; €3 supplement).

## Cité des Enfants

90min sessions: Tues–Fri 9.45am, 11.30am, 1.30 & 3.15pm; Sat & Sun 10.30am, 12.30, 2.30 & 4.30pm; €6; advance reservations at the Cité des Sciences website or ticket office on ⓣ08.92.69.70.72 are advised; ⓂPorte-de-la-Villette.

The museum's special section for children, the **Cité des Enfants**, with areas for 2- to 7-year-olds and 5- to 12-year-olds, is totally engaging. Children can play about with water, construct buildings on a miniature construction site (complete with cranes, hard hats and barrows), experiment with sound and light, manipulate robots, race their own shadows, and superimpose their image on a landscape. They can listen to different languages by inserting telephones into the appropriate country on a globe, and put together their own television news. The whole area is beautifully organized and managed. If you haven't got a child, it's worth borrowing one to get in here.

## Musée de la Musique

Tues–Sat noon–6pm, Sun 10am–6pm; €8; ⓦwww.citedelamusique.fr; ⓂPorte-de-Pantin.

The **Musée de la Musique**, within the **Cité de la Musique** complex, near the Porte-de-Pantin entrance, presents the history of music from the end of the Renaissance to the present day, both visually, exhibiting some 4500 instruments, and aurally, via headsets (available in English; free). Glass case after glass case holds gleaming, beautiful instruments: jewel-inlaid crystal flutes and a fabulous lyre-guitar are two impressive examples. The instruments are presented in the context of a key work in the history of Western music: as you step past each case, the headphones are programmed to emit a short scholarly narration, followed by a delightful concert.

### The park grounds

Daily 6am–1am; free; ⓂPorte-de-Pantin/Porte-de-la-Villette.

The extensive **park grounds** contain ten landscaped **themed gardens**, featuring mirrors, trampolines, water jets and spooky music. All are linked by a walkway called the Promenade des Jardins. One of the most popular with children is the Jardin du Dragon with its 80m-long slide in the shape of a dragon. Also in the park grounds are two major concert venues, Le Zénith, a large rock and pop stadium, and Le Trabendo, which specializes in the avant-garde.

In front of the Cité des Sciences floats the **Géode** (hourly shows Mon 10.30am–6.30pm, Tues–Sat 10.30am–8.30pm; €10.50; Ⓦwww.lageode.fr), a bubble of reflecting steel, which looks as though it's been dropped from an intergalactic boules game into a pool of water. Inside the bubble, half the sphere is a screen for Imax films, not noted for their plots but a great visual experience. Or there's the **Cinaxe**, between the Cité and the Canal St-Denis (screenings every 15min Tues–Sun; €4.80 with Explora ticket), which shows 3D films. Next to the Géode, you can clamber around a decommissioned 1957 French **submarine**, the **Argonaute** (Mon–Fri 10.30am–5.30pm, Sat & Sun 11am–6.30pm; €3), and view the park through its periscope.

## Père-Lachaise cemetery

**Map 1.** Mon–Fri 8am–5.30pm, Sat 8.30am–5.30pm, Sun 9am–5.30pm; free; ⓂPère-Lachaise/Philippe Auguste.

Final resting place of a host of French and foreign luminaries, **Père-Lachaise** draws around two million visitors a year. Located on a hill commanding grand views of Paris, it extends across some 116 acres, making it one of the world's

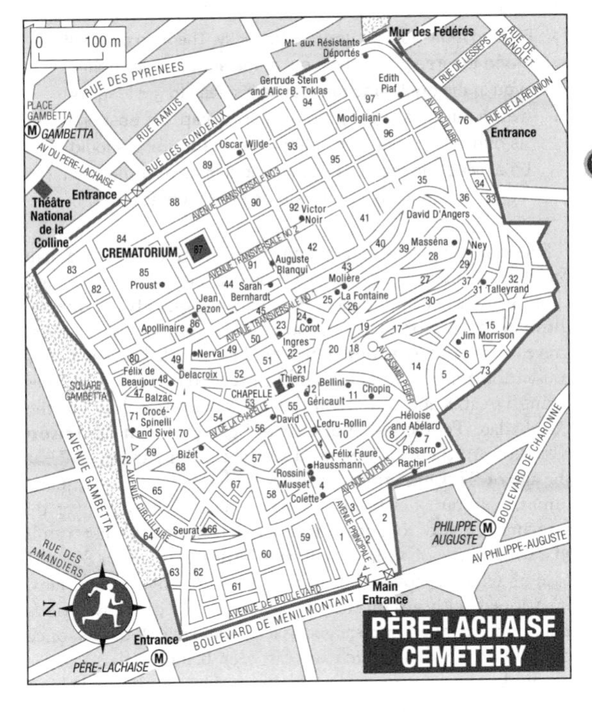


largest cemeteries. In fact, it's rather like a miniature town, with its grid-like layout, cast-iron signposts and neat cobbled lanes – a veritable "city of the dead". Size aside, it's also one of the most atmospheric cemeteries that you're ever likely to visit – an eerily beautiful haven, with terraced slopes and around 6000 magnificent old trees that spread their branches over the moss-grown tombs as though shading them from the outside world.

Finding individual graves can be tricky. The map on p.145 and the free plans given out at the entrance will point you in the right direction, but as it's easy to get lost, it's worth buying a slightly more detailed map; the best one is published by Editions Métropolitain Paris and should be available in the newsagents and florists near the main entrance on boulevard de Ménilmontant.

The cemetery was opened in 1804 in response to a ban on further burials in the overflowing city cemeteries and churchyards; to be interred in Père-Lachaise quickly became the ultimate symbol of riches and success. Among the most visited graves is that of **Chopin** (Division 11), which has a willowy muse mourning his loss and is often attended by groups of Poles laying wreaths and flowers in the red and white colours of the Polish flag. People also flock to the grave of **Jim Morrison** (Division 6); the ex-Doors lead singer died in Paris in 1971 at the age of 27. Once graffiti-covered and wreathed in marijuana fumes, his grave has been cleaned up and is watched over by a security guard to ensure it stays that way. Another tomb that's not short of visitors is **Oscar Wilde**'s (Division 89), the base of which is covered in lipstick kisses left by devoted fans. It's topped with a sculpture by Jacob Epstein of a mysterious Pharaonic winged messenger (sadly vandalized of its once prominent member, which was last seen being used as a paper weight by the director of the cemetery). The inscription behind is a grim verse from *The Ballad of Reading Gaol*.

Most of the celebrated dead have unremarkable tombs. Femme fatale Colette's tomb, close to the main entrance in Division 4, for example, is very plain, though always covered in flowers. The same is true of Sarah Bernhardt's (division 44) and the great chanteuse Edith Piaf's (division 97). Marcel Proust lies in his family's conventional tomb (division 85). Just across the way is the rather incongruous-looking **Colombarium** (Division 87), crudely modelled on the Agia Sophia in Istanbul, with domes and minarets. Here among others of equal or lesser renown lie the ashes of Max Ernst, Georges Pérec, Stéphane Grappelli and American dancer Isadora Duncan, who was strangled when her scarf got tangled in the rear axle of her open-top car.

Among illustrious representatives of the arts, Corot (Division 24) and Balzac (Division 48) both have fine busts. Delacroix lies in a sombre sarcophagus in Division 49, while Jacques-Louis David's heart rests in Division 56 (the rest of him is buried in Belgium, where he died). His pupil Ingres reposes in Division 23. In Division 96 is the grave of Modigliani and his lover Jeanne Herbuterne, who killed herself in crazed grief a few days after he died in agony from meningitis.

It is the monuments to the collective, violent deaths, however, that have the power to change a sunny outing to Père-Lachaise into a much more sombre experience. In Division 97 are the memorials to victims of the Nazi concentration camps, to executed Resistance fighters and to those who were never accounted for in the genocide of World War II. The sculptures are relentless in their images of inhumanity, of people forced to collaborate in their own degradation and death.

Marking one of the bloodiest episodes in French history, the **Mur des Fédérés** (Division 76) is the wall where the last troops of the revolutionary Paris Commune were lined up and shot in the final days of the battle in 1871. A total of 147 were rounded up and killed, after a frenetic chase through the tombstones, and the remains of around a thousand other Communards were brought here and thrown into a grave-pit. The wall soon became a place of pilgrimage for the Left, and remains so today. The man who ordered the execution, Adolphe Thiers, lies in the centre of the cemetery in Division 55.

## Belleville

**Map 4, G3–G4.** Ⓜ Belleville.

Strung out along the western slopes of a ridge that rises from the Seine, the district of **Belleville** is not exactly "belle", but you do glimpse something of the old Paris here. In among the nondescript apartment blocks some characterful streets survive, little changed since the 1930s, especially the cul-de-sacs of terraced houses and gardens **east of rue des Pyrénées**.

The quarter is known for its strong left-wing and community spirit, with organizations such as La Bellevilleuse campaigning to preserve the area from property developers. The availability of affordable and large spaces, ideal for *ateliers*, has attracted many artists to the area. The best opportunity to view their work is during the **Journées portes ouvertes des ateliers d'artistes de Belleville** in mid-May (for exact dates see Ⓦwww.ateliers-artistes-belleville.org), when more than 240 artists living or working in Belleville open their doors to the public. A number of derelict buildings have also been taken over and turned into art squats (or "squarts"), which regularly host exhibitions.

The colourful, if somewhat run-down, main street, **rue de Belleville**, abounds with Vietnamese, Chinese and Turkish shops and restaurants, while adjoining **boulevard de Belleville** is home to Algerian pastry shops, grocers and shisha cafés. A lively market sets up along the whole length of the boulevard on Tuesday and Friday mornings, selling endless arrays of fruit and veg, as well as more exotic produce, spices and fabrics.

## Parc des Buttes-Chaumont

**Map 4, H1.** Daily: May & mid-Aug to end Sept 7am–9pm; June to mid-Aug 7am–10pm; Oct–April 7am–8pm; ⓂButtes-Chaumont/Botzaris.

A short walk from Parc de la Villette is the **Parc des Buttes-Chaumont**, constructed by Haussmann in the 1860s to camouflage what until then had been a desolate warren of disused quarries and miserable shacks. Out of this rather unlikely setting, a romantic, fairy-tale-like fantasy was created – there's a grotto with a cascade and artificial stalactites, and a picturesque lake from which a huge rock rises up, topped with a delicate Corinthian temple. From the temple you can see Sacré-Coeur and beyond.

### Parc de Belleville

**Map 4, I4.** Daily 8/9am till dusk; ⓂCouronnes/Pyrénées.

The **Parc de Belleville**, created in the mid-1990s, tumbles down a slope in a series of terraces and waterfalls. From the top, you get a fantastic view across the city, especially at sunset. A little exhibition/educational centre geared towards children in particular, the **Maison de l'Air** (Tues–Sun 1.30–5pm; free), has lots of information on air quality and meteorology, including live satellite pictures of the weather across Europe.

## Ménilmontant

**Map 4, H1–H6.** ⓂMénilmontant.

Like Belleville, much of **Ménilmontant**, to the south, aligns itself along one long, steep street, the **rue de Ménilmontant** and its lower extension rue Oberkampf. Although seedy and dilapidated in parts, its popularity with students and artists has brought a vitality to the area. Alternative shops and trendy bars and restaurants have sprung up among the grocers and cheap hardware stores, especially along **rue Oberkampf**, which now hosts a thriving bar scene. **Boulevard Ménilmontant**, west of Père-Lachaise, is also prime bar-crawling territory, with places like *La Mère Lachaise* and *Les Lucioles* drawing a young *bobo* (bourgeois-bohemian) crowd. The upper reaches of rue de Ménilmontant, above rue Sorbier, are quieter and, looking back, you find yourself dead in line with the roof-top of the Pompidou Centre, a measure of how high you are above the rest of the city.

For bar listings in Ménilmontant see p.240.

### Musée Edith Piaf

**Map 4, H6.** 5 rue Crespin-du-Gast. Mon–Wed 1–6pm; closed Sept; admission by appointment only on ⓣ01.43.55.52.72; donation; ⓂMénilmontant/St-Maur.

**Edith Piaf**, so the story goes, was abandoned as a baby on the steps of 72 rue de Belleville, and there's a small **museum** dedicated to her nearby in rue Crespin-du-Gast. Piaf was not an acquisitive person: the few clothes (yes, a little black dress), letters, toys, paintings and photographs that she left are almost all here, along with every one of her recordings. The venue is a small flat lived in by her devoted friend Bernard Marchois, who will show you around (he doesn't speak English, but can give you some printed information in English).

14

# Western Paris



Paris's well-manicured western arrondissements, the 16$^{e}$ and 17$^{e}$, commonly referred to as the **Beaux Quartiers**, are mainly residential with few specific sights, the chief exception being the **Musée Marmottan**, with its excellent collection of late Monets. The best area for strolling is around the old villages of **Auteuil** and **Passy**; they exude an almost provincial air, with their tight knot of streets and charming *villas* – leafy lanes of attractive old houses, fronted with English-style gardens full of roses, ivy and wisteria. Auteuil and Passy were only incorporated into the city in 1860, and soon became the capital's most desirable districts. Well-to-do Parisians commissioned new houses here and, as a result, the area is rich in fine examples of **early twentieth-century architecture**: Hector Guimard, designer of the swirly green Art Nouveau métro stations, worked here, and there are some rare Parisian examples of work by interwar architects Le Corbusier and Mallet-Stevens, who created the first "Cubist" buildings. Running all the way down the west side of the 16$^{e}$ is the extensive **Bois de Boulogne**, former playground of the wealthy, while further west, modern architecture comes bang up-to-date with the gleaming, purpose-built business district of **La Défense**, dominated by the enormous **Grande Arche**.

# Auteuil

**Map 1.** ⓂEglise d'Auteuil.

The **Auteuil district** is now an integral part of the city, but there's still a village-like feel about its streets, and it has some attractive little *villas*, not to mention some notable early twentieth-century architecture. The ideal place to start an exploration of the area is the **Eglise d'Auteuil** métro station. Nearby are several of Hector Guimard's **Art Nouveau** buildings: at 8 avenue de la Villa-de-la-Réunion; 41 rue Chardon-Lagache; 142 avenue de Versailles; 39 boulevard Exelmans; and 34 rue Boileau. This last was one of Guimard's first commissions, in 1891. A high fence and wisteria obscure much of the view, but you can see some of the decorative tile-work under the eaves and around the doors and windows. At the end of rue Boileau, beyond boulevard Exelmans, you'll find a series of pretty *villas* backing onto the Auteuil cemetery.

For more Guimard buildings, follow the old village high street, **rue d'Auteuil**, west from the métro exit to **place Jean-Lorrain** and turn right onto rue de la Fontaine where you'll find examples at nos. 14, 17, 19, 21 and 60. Of these, no. 14, the "Castel Béranger" (1898), is the most famous, with exuberant Art Nouveau decoration in the bay windows, roof line and chimney. If you start to tire of the bulgy curves of Art Nouveau, you could head up rue du Dr-Blanche for the cool, rectilinear lines of Cubist architects Le Corbusier and Mallet-Stevens.

## Auteuil bus routes

Handy **bus routes** for exploring Auteuil are the #52 and the #72. The #52 runs between ⓂOpéra in the centre and ⓂBoulogne-Pont-de-St-Cloud near the Parc de Princes, stopping at L'Etoile en route, while the #72's route extends between ⓂHôtel de Ville in the Marais and ⓂBoulogne-Pont-de-St-Cloud, stopping en route by the Exelmans crossroads near some of Guimard's buildings on avenue de Versailles.

## Villa La Roche and around

**Map 1.** Square du Docteur Blanche. Mon 1.30–6pm, Tues–Thurs 10am–6pm, Fri & Sat 10am–5pm; closed Aug; €3; Ⓦwww.fondationlecorbusier.asso.fr; ⓂJasmin.

In a cul-de-sac off rue du Dr-Blanche stand the first private houses built by **Le Corbusier** (1923). One of them, the recently renovated **Villa La Roche**, is in the care of the Fondation Le Corbusier and open to the public. It's built in strictly Cubist style, very plain, with windows in bands, the only extravagances the raising of one wing on piers and a curved frontage. They look commonplace enough now from the outside, but were a radical departure from anything that had gone before, and once you're inside, the spatial play still seems groundbreaking. The interior, appropriately enough, is decorated with Cubist paintings.

Further north along rue du Dr-Blanche and off to the right, the tiny **rue Mallet-Stevens** was built entirely by the architect of the same name, also in Cubist style. No. 12, where Robert Mallet-Stevens had his offices, has been altered, along with other houses in the street, but you can still see the architectural intention of sculpting the entire street space as a cohesive unit.

## Musée Marmottan

**Map 1.** Daily except Mon 11am–6pm, Tues until 9pm; €9; Ⓦwww.marmottan.com; ⓂMuette.

The collection of the **Musée Marmottan** consists largely of works by **Monet**. These were bequeathed, along with the family's former residence – a nineteenth-century *hôtel particulier* – to the Académie des Beaux-Arts by the wealthy industrialist Jules Marmottan and his son, art historian and collector, Paul Marmottan. Among the paintings is Monet's *Impression, Soleil Levant* ("Impression, Sunrise"; 1872), a rendering of a misty sunrise over Le Havre, whose title was borrowed by critics to give the Impressionist movement its name. The painting was stolen from the gallery in October 1985, along with eight other paintings. After a police operation lasting five years, they were discovered in a villa in southern Corsica, and were put back on show with greatly increased security. There's a dazzling selection of works from Monet's last years at Giverny, including several *Nymphéas* (Waterlilies), *Le Pont Japonais*, *L'Allée des Rosiers* and *Le Saule Pleureur*, where rich colours are laid on in thick, excited whorls and lines. These are virtually abstractions, much more advanced than, say, the work of Renoir, Monet's exact contemporary, some of whose paintings are also on display. Two rooms are devoted to another Impressionist, **Berthe Morisot**, who lived most of her life in Passy and is buried in the Cimetière de Passy; her work is characterized by vigorous, almost aggressive, brushwork, seen to best effect in paintings such as *Branches d'oranger* (1889) and *Le Jardin à Bougival* (1884).



# Passy

**Map 1 & map 7, A6–9.** ⓂLa Muette/Passy.

The heart of the Passy *quartier*, northeast of Auteuil, is pleasant little **place de Passy**, with its crowded but leisurely *Le Paris Passy* café. Leading off from here is the old high street, rue de Passy, with its eye-catching parade of boutiques, and the cobbled, pedestrianized **rue de l'Annonciation**, an agreeable blend of genteel affluence and the down-to-earth. At the end of the street you'll find the house that Balzac once lived in, now a museum.

**Trocadéro (see p.121), with its stunning view of the Eiffel Tower, is a leisurely walk from place de Passy.**

## La Maison de Balzac

**Map 7, off A9.** 47 rue Raynouard. Tues–Sun 10am–5.40pm; free; Ⓦwww.balzac.paris.fr; ⓂPassy/Av-du-Prés-Kennedy–Maison-de-Radio-France.

Tucked away down some steps among a tree-filled garden is the **Maison de Balzac**, a delightful, summery little house with pale-green shutters and a decorative iron entrance porch. Balzac moved to this secluded spot in 1840 in the hope of evading his creditors. He lived under a pseudonym, and visitors had to give a special password before being admitted. Should any unwelcome callers manage to get past the door, Balzac would escape through a back door and down to the river via a network of underground cellars. It was here that he wrote some of his best-known works, including *La Cousine Bette* and *Le Cousin Pons*. The museum preserves his study, simple writing desk and monogrammed cafetière – frequent doses of caffeine kept him going during his long writing stints, which could extend for up to eighteen hours a day for weeks on end. Other exhibits include letters to Madame Hanska, whom he eventually married after an eighteen-year courtship, and a highly complex family tree of around a thousand of the four thousand-plus characters that feature in his *Comédie Humaine*.

## Bois de Boulogne

**Map 1.** Ⓜ Porte-Maillot/Porte-Dauphine.

The **Bois de Boulogne** was designed by Baron Haussmann and supposedly modelled on London's Hyde Park – though it's a very French interpretation. The "bois" of the name is somewhat deceptive, though the extensive parklands (just under 900 hectares) do contain some remnants of the once-great Forêt de Rouvray. As its location would suggest, the Bois was once the playground of the wealthy, although it also established a reputation as the site of the sex trade and its associated crime. The same is true today and it's best avoided at night.

By day, however, the park is an extremely pleasant spot, with trees, lakes, cycling trails and the beautiful floral displays of the **Parc de Bagatelle**. The best, and wildest, part for walking is towards the southwest corner. Vélib' bikes are available near the entrance to the **Jardin d'Acclimatation** adventure park, and you

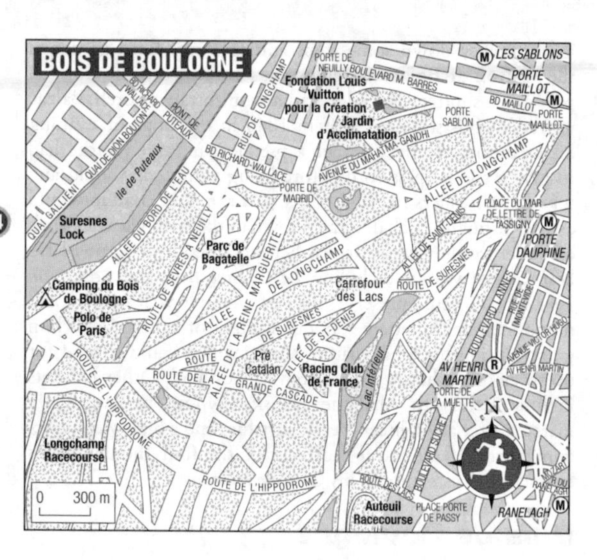


can go boating on the Lac Inférieur. The Jardin d'Acclimatation is also the location for a new contemporary arts space, the **Fondation Louis Vuitton pour la Création**, designed by Frank Gehry and due for completion at the end of 2012.

More information about the Jardin d'Acclimatation and activities for children in the Bois de Boulogne is given on p.298.

## Parc de Bagatelle

Daily 9.30am till dusk; €5; ⓂPorte-Maillot, then bus #244.

Comprising a range of garden styles from French and English to Japanese, the **Parc de Bagatelle** is renowned for its stunning

**rose garden** featuring some 1200 varieties in all, at their best in June. In other parts of the garden there are glorious displays of tulips, hyacinths and daffodils in early April, irises in May, and water lilies in early August. The park's attractive orangerie is the setting for candlelit recitals of Chopin's music during the Festival de Chopin in late June (see p.284).

## La Défense

**Map 1.** Ⓜ/RER Grande-Arche-de-la-Défense.

A futuristic complex of gleaming skyscrapers occupied by Elf, IBM, banks and other big businesses, **La Défense** is Paris's prestige business district and an extraordinary monument to late twentieth-century capitalism. Its most popular attraction is the huge **Grande Arche**, built in 1989 for the bicentenary of the Revolution. It's a beautiful and astounding 112m-high arch, clad in white marble. Standing 6km out and at a slight angle from the Arc de Triomphe, the Grande Arche completes the western axis of a monumental east–west vista. Suspended within the arch's hollow, large enough to enclose Notre-Dame with ease, is a fibreglass "cloud" canopy, which looks like the top half of a circus tent. It's no longer possible to take a lift up to the rooftop, but it's no great loss, as the views from the base of the arch are impressive enough – from here you can see as far as the Louvre on a clear day.

From the Grande Arche to the river extends the main artery of La Défense, the pedestrianized **Esplanade du Général de Gaulle**, bristling with shiny office towers, apartment blocks and modern artworks. It has to be said, however, that some fifty years on from its beginnings, and despite such sleek edifices as the EDF building on place de la Défense, the district is starting to look a little tired – a widely recognized fact that has prompted a major facelift and a new wave of building. Foremost among the projects is the **Tour Phare**, a 300m-high glossy sinuous skyscraper which is due to be completed in 2012 and will rival the Eiffel Tower in height.

SCULPTURES
1 Calder's Stabile
2 La Défense Statue
3 La Fontaine du Parvis
4 La Grenouille
5 Miro's Personnages
6 L'Oiseau Mécanique
7 Takis' Lights Pond

To see the plans for the tower and other new developments call into the little **museum** downstairs at **Info Défense** (April–Oct daily 10am–6pm; Nov–March Mon–Fri 9.30am–5.30pm; free), on the main place de la Défense. Also worth a look are displays of some of the early projects that were put forward for La Défense in the 1930s, such as Le Corbusier's huge *Metropolis*-like high-rises. While here it's worth picking up a map, showing all La Défense's main buildings and outdoor sculptures (of which there are around fifty altogether).

It's best to get off a stop early, at ⓂEsplanade-de-la-Défense, for the most dramatic approach to the Grande Arche and to see the sculptures.

15

# St-Ouen and St-Denis

Few visitors head beyond the official city limits – aside from those on day-trips – thanks in part to the *périphérique* ring-road, which quarantines the centre from its less salubrious suburbs. Just north of Montmartre, however, are two sights that should tempt you that little bit further along the métro lines. The sprawling **St-Ouen market** is a veritable kingdom of antiques and curio shops, while the **basilique St-Denis** is an island beacon of historic grandeur, set in a gritty, post-industrial sea.

## St-Ouen market

**Map 1.** Sat–Mon 9am–6.30pm, varies depending on weather, many stalls closed Mon; Ⓜ Porte-de-Clignancourt/Garibaldi.

The **St-Ouen market**, sometimes called the **Clignancourt** market, is located just outside the northern edge of the 18$^{e}$ arrondissement, in the suburb of St-Ouen. Its popular name of **les puces de St-Ouen** (flea market) dates from the days when secondhand mattresses, clothes and other infested junk was sold here in a free-for-all zone outside the city walls. Nowadays, it's predominantly an expensive **antiques** market selling mainly furniture, plus old zinc café counters, telephones, traffic lights, posters, jukeboxes and so on.

From Porte-de-Clignancourt métro it's a five-minute walk up the avenue de la Porte de Clignancourt. You have to pass through the market's genuinely flea-bitten fringe before you get to the real thing; shaded by the flyover, **rue Jean-Henri-Fabre** is the heart of this light-fingered area, lined with stalls flogging cheap jeans and leather jackets, pirated DVDs and African souvenirs. Watch your wallet, and don't fall for the gangs pulling card scams.

The official market complex lies just beyond rue Jean-Henri-Fabre, with over a dozen separate markets covering some two thousand shops. Most have their entrances on **rue des Rosiers**, the main thoroughfare, but a few lie on **rue Jules-Vallès**. For the chance to buy something you could feasibly carry home by yourself, restrict yourself to one of three markets: Vernaison, Jules-Vallès and Malik. Marché **Vernaison**, the oldest, is the closest thing to a real flea market. Its mazey, creeper-covered alleys are fun to wander along, threading your way between stalls selling all kinds of bric-a-brac. Marché **Jules-Vallès** is smaller but similar, stuffed with books and records, vintage clothing and other curiosities. While you won't find any breathtaking bargains, there's plenty to titillate the eye at both. Marché **Malik** stocks mostly discount and vintage clothes and bags, as well as some high-class couturier stuff. The other markets mostly contain expensive antiques and curios.

There are plenty of **cafés** on rue Paul Bert and rue des Rosiers, or you could brave the rather touristy *buvette* buried at the end of Marché Vernaison's allée 10, *Chez Louisette*.

## St-Denis

**Map 9.** Ⓜ St-Denis-Basilique.

For most of the twentieth century, **St-Denis**, 10km north of the centre of Paris and accessible by métro, was one of the most heavily industrialized communities in France and a bastion of the Communist party. Since those days, however, factories have closed, unemployment has run rife and immigration has radically altered the ethnic mix. The area immediately abutting the historic eponymous **basilica** has been transformed into an extraordinary fortress-like housing and shopping complex, where local youths hang out on mopeds, women shop for African groceries, and men, fresh from the latest conflict zone, beg for a few cents. The centre is at its liveliest during the thrice-weekly **market**, on the main place Jean-Jaurès (Tues, Fri & Sun mornings).

About ten minutes' walk south of the basilica, down rue Gabriel-Péri, is the métro stop St-Denis-Porte-de-Paris. Just beyond it, a broad footbridge crosses the motorway and Canal St-Denis to the dramatic **Stade de France**, scene of France's 1998 World Cup victory.

## The basilica

2 place de la Légion d'Honneur. April–Sept Mon–Sat 10am–6.15pm, Sun noon–6.15pm; Oct–March Mon–Sat 10am–5pm, Sun noon–5.15pm; closed during weddings and funerals; free; necropolis €7 (closed during services); Ⓜ St-Denis-Basilique.

The **Basilique St-Denis**, generally regarded as the birthplace of the Gothic style in European architecture, was built in the first half of the twelfth century by Abbot Suger. Inside, his novel use of rib vaulting made possible the huge, luminous windows that fill the choir with light. Today, the upper storeys of the choir are still airier than they were in Suger's day, having been rebuilt in the mid-thirteenth century, at the same time as the nave.

A much earlier abbey church was probably named after its mid-third-century founder, a Parisian bishop decapitated for his beliefs at Montmartre. Legend has it that **St Denis** picked up his own head and walked all the way to the site of his new church.

The site's **royal history** began with the coronation of Pepin the Short in 754, but it wasn't until the reign of Hugues Capet, in 996, that St-Denis became the customary burial place of the kings of France. Since then, all but three of France's kings have been interred here, and their very fine tombs and effigies are distributed throughout the **necropolis** in the transepts and ambulatory, which is entered separately via the south portal. Note especially the enormous Renaissance memorials to **François I**, **Henri II** and **Catherine de Médicis**, and **Louis XII** and **Anne de Bretagne**. On the south side of the ambulatory, a florid Louis XVI and a busty **Marie-Antoinette** kneel in prayer.

16



# Day-trips

If you're in Paris for any more than a long weekend, taking a day-trip makes sense. The four superb sights described here provide a refreshing balance to Paris's relentless urbanity – and they're all within an hour's easy train ride. The magnificent **château de Versailles** is the apotheosis of French royal self-indulgence, but also has delightful gardens. The Renaissance **château de Fontainebleau** is equally superb, but less overwhelming; you can also take long walks in the ancient forest that surrounds it. **Chartres cathedral** is one of the finest buildings in the world, its twin spires soaring over a pretty provincial town. Lastly, Monet's house at **Giverny** is set among delightful, Japanese-influenced gardens that are a work of Impressionist art in their own right.

## Versailles

**Map 9.** Tues–Sun: April–Sept 9am–6.30pm; Oct–March 9am–5.30pm; all-areas Passeport €18 (April–Oct Sat & Sun €25), château only €15; ⓦwww.chateauversailles.fr; RER line C5 to Versailles-Rive Gauche (frequent; 40min); right out of station, then immediately left to approach palace (5min).

Twenty kilometres southwest of Paris, the **château de Versailles** is France's most staggeringly extravagant palace. It was built for the "sun king", Louis XIV, by the elite design team of architect Le Vau, painter Le Brun and gardener Le Nôtre. Construction began in 1664 and lasted virtually until

Louis' death in 1715. Thereafter, the château remained a royal residence until the Revolution of 1789, when the furniture was sold and the pictures dispatched to the Louvre. Today, the château's management scour the auction houses of the world in search of furnishings from the day of Louis XVI – the last king of the *ancien régime*.

In Louis XIV's heyday, Versailles was the headquarters of every arm of the state, and the entire French court of around 3500 nobles lived in the palace under a rigid code of royal etiquette centred on the king's equally rigid daily schedule. The grand **State Apartments** can be visited without a guide (if you've printed your own e-ticket via the official website, you can walk straight in). The route leads past the grand Baroque royal chapel and a procession of gilded drawing and throne rooms to the dazzling **Galerie des Glaces** (Hall of Mirrors), where the Treaty of Versailles was signed after World War I. If you want to see other, often less crowded areas of the palace, book yourself on one of the excellent English-language **guided tours** (€14.50). Turn up reasonably early in the day to be sure of a place.

## The Park and Trianons

Park: daily dawn to dusk; free. Grand and Petit Trianons: Tues–Sun: April–Oct noon–6.30pm; Nov–March noon–5pm; entry included on Passeport ticket (see opposite), or combined ticket for Trianons and Domaine de Marie Antoinette €10.

You could spend the whole day just exploring the **park** at Versailles, along with its lesser outcrops of royal mania: the Italianate **Grand Trianon**, designed by Hardouin-Mansart in 1687 as a "country retreat" for Louis XIV; and the more modest **Petit Trianon**, built by Gabriel in the 1760s for Louis XV's mistress, Madame de Pompadour. Just beyond these is the **Domaine de Marie Antoinette** and its bizarre **Hameau de la Reine** (closed Nov–March), a play village and thatch-roofed farm built in 1783 for Marie-Antoinette to indulge her fashionable fantasy of returning to the natural life.

The terraces between the château and the park form Le Nôtre's statue-studded **gardens**, with their extravagant **fountains** – which, on summer weekends (April–Oct Sat & Sun; €8 or free with Passeport), are switched on to the accompaniment of piped classical music. Distances in the park are considerable. There's a tourist train, and you can rent **bikes** and **boats** at the Grand Canal, next to a pair of **café-restaurants** – picnics are officially forbidden.

## Fontainebleau

Daily except Tues: April–Sept 9.30am–6pm; Oct–March 9.30am–5pm; €8; Ⓦ www.musee-chateau-fontainebleau.fr; trains from Gare de Lyon to Fontainebleau-Avon (hourly; 50min) then bus #A or #B (15min).

The **château de Fontainebleau**, 60km south of Paris, owes its existence to the magnificent forest that still surrounds it. This vast, tree-filled expanse once made the castle the perfect base for royal hunting expeditions; it still makes Fontainebleau a refreshingly rural excursion from Paris. The transformation of hunting lodge into luxurious palace took place in the sixteenth century, under François I, who imported a colony of Italian artists to carry out the decoration, notably the Mannerists Rosso Fiorentino, Primaticcio and Niccolò dell'Abate. The château enjoyed royal favour well into the nineteenth century and, as a result, has a gloriously chaotic profusion of styles with staircases, wings and towers jostling around hidden courtyards and gardens.

The palace's highlights are the sumptuous Renaissance **interiors**, chiefly the dazzlingly frescoed **Salle de Bal** and the celebrated **Galerie François I**, which is resplendent in gilt, carved, inlaid and polished wood, and adorned down its entire length by intricate stucco work and vibrant Mannerist brushwork. Utterly contrasting in style is the sombre but elegant decor of Napoleon's **Petits Appartements** (guided tour only; €12.50 including château entry), the private rooms of the emperor, his wife, and their intimate entourage.

The **gardens** are equally splendid and in the summer months you can rent boats on the Etang des Carpes. If you want to escape into the relative wilds, head for the **Forest of Fontainebleau**, which is crisscrossed by signposted walking and cycling trails, all marked on the Michelin map *Environs de Paris*.



## Chartres

Cathedral: rue des Acacias. Daily 8.30am–7.30pm; free. North Tower: May–Aug 9.30am–noon & 2–5.40pm, Sun 2–5.30pm; Sept–April Mon–Sat 9.30–noon & 2–4.30pm, Sun 2–4.30pm; free. Trains from Gare du Montparnasse (hourly; 1hr); 5min walk from station to cathedral.

An excursion to **Chartres**, 80km southwest of Paris, can seem a long way to go just to see one building, but then you'd have to go a very long way indeed to find a building to beat it. The sheer size of the cathedral was originally a necessity. In the twelfth century, tens of thousands of pilgrims would have come here each year to venerate Sancta Camisia, supposed to have been the robe Mary wore when she gave birth to Jesus (it still exists, though now rolled up and in storage). But Chartres is famous not for its scale but for its astounding architectural harmony – a result of its unusually fast construction between 1194 and 1260 and the fact that, uniquely, it has stood almost unaltered since its consecration.

The cathedral's most glorious feature, its stunning **stained glass**, is almost entirely original. It's best experienced on a windy day of mixed sunshine and cloud, when the colours pulse and fade with the sunlight, or early or late in the day, when the low sun shines directly through the glass. Even on a cloudy winter's day, however, you can appreciate the amazing artistry of the windows. Particularly superb is the largely twelfth-century "Blue Virgin" window, in the first bay beyond the south transept, which is filled with a primal image of Mary that has been adored by pilgrims for centuries.

The cathedral's stonework is captivating, particularly the **choir screen**, which curves around the ambulatory, and the hosts of sculpted figures that stand like guardians at each entrance portal. On the floor of the nave, the elaborate medieval labyrinth has a diameter exactly the same size as that of the rose window above the main doors. Be sure to climb the **north tower** and take in its bird's-eye view of the sculptures and structure of the cathedral. From the pleasant **gardens** at the back you can contemplate the apse's flying buttresses.

## The Town

Many visitors come just for the cathedral, but the medieval **town** of Chartres is well worth a few hours. There's a peaceful **Musée des Beaux Arts** (May–Oct Mon & Wed–Sat 10am–noon & 2–6pm, Sun 2–6pm; Nov–April Mon & Wed–Sat 10am–noon & 2–5pm, Sun 2–5pm; €3.10) in the former Episcopal palace just north of the cathedral, but the most tempting activity is to walk alongside the river Eure. Behind the museum, rue Chantault leads past old townhouses to the Pont du Massacre, from where you can follow the right bank upstream past ancient wash-houses. A right turn at rue du Bourg, by the Porte Guillaume, will take you straight up into the ancient town centre, situated around place de la Poissonnerie, where a carved salmon decorates what was once a sixteenth-century house. Nearby, a thriving **food market** (Wed & Sat) takes over place Billard and rue des Changes, and there's a **flower market** on place du Cygne (Tues, Thurs & Sat).

Chartres' most eccentric tourist attraction, the rambling **Maison Picassiette** (April Mon & Wed–Sat 10am–noon & 2–5pm, Sun 2–5pm; May–Sept Mon & Wed–Sat 10am–noon & 2–6pm, Sun 2–6pm; Oct Sat 10am–noon & 2–6pm, Sun 2–6pm; €5.10) is entirely coated in mosaics. It is a work of naïve genius created by a local eccentric over a quarter century. It's hidden away in a suburb, at 22 rue du Repos, 1km east of the town centre.

# Giverny

April–Oct Tues–Sun 9.30am–6pm; house and gardens €5.50; Ⓦwww.fondation-monet.com; train from Paris-St-Lazare to Vernon (4–5 daily; 45min); buses meet each train and continue to gardens (6km).

**Claude Monet** considered his **gardens at Giverny** to be his greatest masterpiece. They're 65km from Paris in the direction of Rouen, but well worth the trip. Monet lived in Giverny from 1883 till his death in 1926, painting and repainting the effects of the changing seasonal light on the gardens he laid out between his house and the river. Every month from spring to autumn has its own appeal, but May and June, when the rhododendrons flower around the lily pond and the wisteria bursts into colour over the famous Japanese bridge, are the prettiest months to visit – though you'll have to contend with crowds photographing the waterlilies. Inside **Monet's idyllic green-shuttered house**, the painter's original collection of Japanese prints still hangs on the walls. Picnicking inside the grounds, unfortunately, is forbidden, but there are plentiful tea shops and patisseries in the village.

Just up rue Claude Monet from the gardens, the **Musée des Impressionnismes** (April–Oct daily 10am–6pm; €6.50; Ⓦwww.museedesimpressionnismesgiverny.com) puts on exhibitions of Impressionist work, as well as contemporary art influenced by the movement.

# Disneyland Paris

Children will love **Disneyland Paris** – there are no two ways about it. At just 25km east of the capital, it's easy to visit as a day-trip from Paris, and there are thrilling roller coasters among the Disney-themed rides. There are two separate parks: **Disneyland Park**, which is bigger and has most of the mega-attractions, and **Walt Disney Studios Park**, which offers more technology-based attractions alongside a few thrill rides. There's also **Disney Village**, where most of the hotels and restaurants are found, and the giant shopping extravaganza that is **La Vallée Outlet Shopping Village**.

## Practicalities

**Opening hours** vary depending on the season and whether it's a weekend, but are typically from 10am to 7pm (6pm at Walt Disney Studios) – or as late as 11pm in midsummer. Check when you buy your ticket. The best **time to go** is on an off-season weekday, when you'll probably get round every ride you want, though queuing for and walking between rides is purgatorial in wet or very cold weather.

**Tickets** can be purchased in advance – highly recommended in order to avoid queuing – at Paris tourist offices (see p.24), major métro stations and all RER line A and B stations. You can also buy tickets **online** in your local currency at Ⓦwww.disneylandparis.com. The **one-day one-park pass** allows you to visit either the main Disneyland Park or the Walt

## Admission fees

Children aged 3–11 pay the reduced tariff shown below, while under 3s go free. Prices may drop a few euros in the low season (Oct–March, excluding holidays).

| | |
|---|---|
| 1-day 1-park | €51/43 |
| 1-day Hopper | €62/54 |
| 2-day Hopper | €112/95 |
| 3-day Hopper | €139/118 |

Disney Studios Park, not both; the **Hopper pass** or *passe-partout* lets you move freely between both park areas. If you buy a two- or three-day Hopper you don't have to use the ticket on consecutive days.

## Getting there

**From London**, Eurostar runs trains straight to Disneyland, but it can be less expensive to change onto the TGV at Lille; all these trains arrive at Marne-la-Vallée/Chessy station, right outside the main entrance. Direct shuttle buses connect Charles de Gaulle and Orly **airports** to the park entrance (roughly every 30min; 45min; 8.30am–7.45pm; see Ⓦwww.vea.fr/uk for timetables and pickup points; €17 one-way, under 12s €13, under 3s free).

**From Paris**, take RER line A (from Châtelet-Les Halles/ Gare-de-Lyon/Nation) to Marne-la-Vallée/Chessy station, which is right next to the train terminal. The journey takes around 40 minutes and costs €6.55 per single (under 12s half price, under 3s free).

## Hotels and dining

Disney's six themed **hotels** are only worth staying in as part of a package including park entry, which you can book through Disney or major travel agents. For details look online or call Ⓣ0844/576 5504 in the UK, Ⓣ0825.300.222 from within France, or Ⓣ0033.1.60.30.60.53 from other countries. The

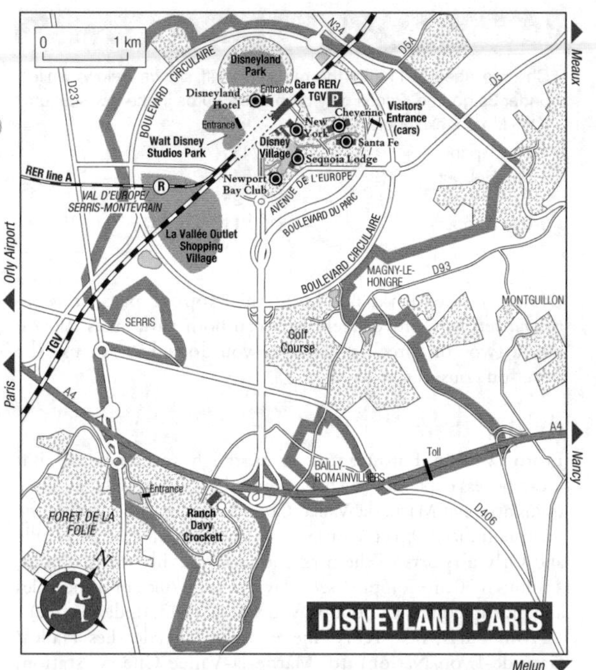


budget alternative, as long as you have a car, is the park's *Davey Crockett Ranch,* a fifteen-minute drive away, with self-catering log cabins. To really economize, you could **camp** at the nearby *Camping du Parc de la Colline*, route de Lagny, 77200 Torcy (Ⓣ01.60.05.42.32, Ⓦwww.camping-de-la-colline.com). Free bright-yellow **shuttle buses** run between the hotels (but not to the ranch) and the park entrance.

**Food** is mostly overpriced American junk – hamburgers and the like. If you want to sit down to a proper meal, the fixed price "all-you-can-eat" buffet restaurants are not a bad deal, with their large salad bars. Officially, you're not supposed to bring any refreshments into the park, but you could always eat a good Parisian breakfast and bring some discreet snacks.



## Disneyland Park

**Main Street USA**, a mythical vision of a 1900s American town with its own **City Hall**, leads up to **Central Plaza**, the hub of the park. Clockwise from Main Street are the four "lands", connected to each other and Main Street Station by a steam-train **railroad** which runs right round the park. **Luggage** can be left in lockers in "Guest Storage" under Main Street Station (€1.50). While there are a few green patches, there is no lawn to loll on: renting a pushchair (from the building opposite City Hall; €7.50) might be a good idea.

Waits for the popular rides are common, so bring sunhats or umbrellas, and make sure your kids have all been to the toilet; keep snacks, drinks and games handy too. The chief rides all use the **Fastpass** scheme, in which you insert your entry card into a ticket machine by the entrance to the ride; the machine then spews out a time at which you should come back and join the much shorter "Fastpass" queue.

### Parades

The all-dancing, all-costumed **Shows** and **Parades** are the ultimate Disney event. Cunning parents will time their visits to the most popular ride to coincide with them, but it's worth catching at least one; pick up a timetable from City Hall. The headline **Once Upon A Dream** parade takes place at 7.15pm in summer, with the **Fantillusion** parade at 10.25pm, followed by fireworks. The best seating is in front of the Fantasyland Castle, one of the points where the floats stop and the characters – all the usual Disney suspects – put on a performance. Characters on foot shake hands with the kids who've managed to get to the front.

## The rides

**Fantasyland**, home of the distinctive castle, is aimed at the youngest kids. There are no height restrictions here, and rides are mostly gentle. Among the more enjoyable are Peter Pan's Flight, a jerky ride over London; Dumbo the Flying Elephant, where you can control the rise and fall of your own pod; and Mad Hatter's Tea Cups, where you slide along a chequered floor. Le Pays des Contes de Fées and It's A Small World are boat rides through fairy-tale scenes, Alice's Curious Labyrinth is a maze with surprises, while Blanche-Neige et les Sept Nains (Snow White and the Seven Dwarves) is a kind of ghost train – potentially frightening for younger children. Sleeping Beauty's Castle is disappointingly small and empty, though a dragon lurks in the dungeon.

### Roller coasters

Each of the park's areas, apart from the toddler-oriented Fantasyland, centres on its roller coasters. The runaway train on Frontierland's **Big Thunder Mountain** and the mine-carts of Adventureland's **Indiana Jones and the Temple of Peril: Backwards!** are fast and exciting, but the emphasis is on thrills rather than sheer terror – you're kept in place by a bar, rather than being fully strapped in. **Space Mountain**, in Discoveryland, and the **Rock 'n' Roller Coaster Starring Aerosmith**, over in the Walt Disney Studios section, are a different matter altogether. Their upside-down loops, corkscrews and terrifying acceleration require a lock-in padded brace. Discoveryland's **Space Mountain Mission 2**, with its weightless drop and head-spinning galactic backdrop, is even more terrifying.

All four rides have different height restrictions, and pregnant women or people with neck or back problems should not risk them. You can avoid queues by using the Fastpass scheme (see p.173); arriving early can also be a good strategy. But be warned: the experience can be so intense that the park's gentler rides may seem disappointing.

**Discoveryland** emphasizes technology and the space age, and is centred on its two extreme indoor, space-themed roller coasters: Space Mountain and Space Mountain Mission 2. Star Tours, a simulated ride in a spacecraft through a *Star Wars*-style set, goes down well with fans, while Orbitron is a relatively sedate aerial ride and Autopia lets you drive a futuristic car (on rails). Buzz Lightyear Laser Blast allows you to shoot at menacing space creatures as you trundle past. Most of the other rides are either high-tech shows presented by actors or walk-through sets, and not especially gripping.

**Adventureland** has the most outlandish, jungly sets, put to good effect in the cave-playground of Adventure Isle (which for once allows children to run around freely) and The Robinsons' Cabin, complete with a 27m mock banyan tree reached by walkways and 170 steps. The two best rides are Indiana Jones and the Temple of Peril: Backwards!, a moderate roller coaster that takes you backwards through a classic Indy landscape; and Pirates of the Caribbean, a satisfyingly long ride that takes you underground, on water and down waterfalls, past scary animated scenes.

The best ride at **Frontierland**, set in the Wild West, is Big Thunder Mountain, a classic (not too excessive) roller coaster mimicking a runaway train round a "mining mountain". In Phantom Manor holographic ghosts appear before cobweb-covered mirrors, but nothing actually jumps out and screams at you, while Thunder Mesa Riverboat Landing takes you on a cruise around the lake on a paddle-boat steamer.

## Walt Disney Studios Park

Other than the Rock 'n' Roller Coaster Starring Aerosmith – a terrifyingly fast, corkscrew-looping, metal-playing white-knuckler – the **Walt Disney Studios Park** complex lacks the big rides offered by its older, larger neighbour. In some ways it's a more satisfying affair, focusing on what Disney was and is still renowned for – animation. At Art of Disney Animation you watch an actor playing a cartoonist having a conversation with an on-screen animated creation, explaining to the creature how it came to look as it did, after which children are taught to draw identical Mickey Mouse faces. Cinémagique is a screening of a century of movie moments, with actors appearing to jump into and out of the on-screen action, helped by special effects, while Walt Disney Television Studios produces a show with the help of a ready-to-hand live audience.

Virtual reality takes centre stage at Cars Race Rally, a (fairly slow) destruction derby-themed ride, and at Armageddon Special Effects, in which a group of fifty or so is ushered into a circular space station which comes under meteor bombardment. There are relatively real thrills on offer at Twilight Zone Tower of Terror, a free-fall elevator drop through a crumbling Hollywood hotel, and at Crush's Coaster, a gentle ride through a virtual underwater world. Studio Tram Tour Featuring Catastrophe Canyon is a sedate circuit of various bits and pieces of film sets, culminating in the halt among the Wild West rocks of Catastrophe Canyon – sit on the left for the scariest ride. Moteurs… Action! Stuntshow Spectacular is a full-on show (listen out for announcements of start times) featuring some spectacular stunts: jumping rally cars, sliding motorbikes, leaping jet skis and so on.

## La Vallée Outlet

3 cours de la Garonne, 77700 Serris. Mon–Fri & Sun 10am–7pm, Sat 10am–8pm; Ⓦ www.lavalleevillage.com; RER Val d'Europe/Serris-Montévrain (line A4) then special shuttle bus.

Just inside the Disney complex's boundaries, **La Vallée Outlet Shopping Village** is a giant outdoor shopping mall, designed to look like a village. It's best for discounted labelled clothing, with the previous season's collections sold at discounts of a third or more. Armani, agnès b., Bonpoint (stunning, pricey French children's clothes), Christian Lacroix, Comptoir des Cotonniers, Maje and Paul Smith are just a few of the hundred-odd French and international brands that have their own discount outlet here.

# Listings

# Listings

18

# Accommodation



**Accommodation** in Paris is often booked up well in advance, particularly in the spring and autumn. It's wise to reserve a place as early as you can, especially if you fancy staying in one of the more characterful places. You can simply call – all receptionists speak some English – but it's also worth bearing in mind that more and more hotels offer online booking as well, sometimes at discounted prices. If you book by phone, many places will ask for a credit card number, others for written or faxed confirmation. If you find yourself stuck on arrival, the main tourist office at rue des Pyramides and the branches at the Gare de Lyon and Eiffel Tower will find you a room in a hotel or hostel free of booking charge.

Compared with other European capitals, hotel prices are not exorbitant, and there is a wide range of comfort, prices and locations. Standards are relatively low, however. Even in well-known three- and four-stars, rooms can be small and service poor. Things are changing, but the most-visited city in the world has tended to be complacent. A double room in an old-fashioned two-star will cost between €60 and €100, though don't expect much in the way of decor at the lower end of the scale. For something with a bit more class – whether that means a touch of design, smooth efficiency or a minibar – you'll pay in the region of €90–200. At the luxury end of the scale the sky's the limit, with prices at €300–400 and upwards not uncommon. It is possible to find a double room in a central location for around €50, though at this level you will probably have to accept a room with just a sink (*lavabo*) and a shared bathroom on the landing (*dans le palier*). Apartment rentals, bed and breakfasts, hostels and campsites are listed separately on pp.194–197.



## Hotels

Our **hotel** recommendations are listed by area, following the same chapter divisions used in the guide. Most hotels have a selection of rooms – singles, doubles, twin-bedded and triples – at different prices. In our listings we give prices for doubles and also cite tariffs for single rooms where these are particularly good value. It's always worth asking for a discount on the advertised rate; in August and from November to March (apart from Christmas) you can often negotiate reductions of ten to twenty percent or more.

### The Islands

**Henri IV Map 2, F7. 25 place Dauphine, 1er ⓣ01.43.54.44.53, ⓦwww.henri4hotel.fr. ⓜPont-Neuf/Cité.** An ancient and well-known cheapie on a beautiful square right in the centre of Paris. A creaking narrow staircase winds its way up to twenty basic rooms spread over five storeys (no lift); a few are available with shared bathrooms (€49). Book well in advance and ring to confirm nearer the time. Doubles €59–78.

**Hôtel de Lutèce Map 2, I9. 65 rue St-Louis-en-l'Ile, 4e ⓣ01.43.26.23.52, ⓦwww.paris-hotel-lutece.com. ⓜPont-Marie.** Twenty-three tiny, but appealing, wood-beamed rooms are eked out of this narrow seventeenth-century townhouse, located on the most desirable island in France. All the rooms have been tastefully renovated in contemporary style and decorated in shades of terracotta and cream, and come with modern, sparkling white bathrooms. Doubles €196.

### The Champs-Elysées and around

**Le 123 Map 7, I2. 123 rue du Faubourg-Saint-Honoré, 8e ⓣ01.53.89.01.23, ⓦwww.astotel.com. ⓜSt-Philippe-du-Roule.** A giant puffball light greets you in the lobby of this above-average mid-range hotel, five minutes' walk from the Champs-Elysées. Rooms are a good size with high ceilings, laminate floors and bathtubs. Each one has at least one antique – a chaise longue, nest of tables or desk – to take the edge off the minimalism. Public rates start at €299, but frequent special offers bring this down to around €200.

**Hôtel Brighton Map 2, C3. 218 rue de Rivoli, 1er ⓣ01.47.03.61.61, ⓦwww.paris-hotel-brighton.com. ⓂTuileries.** An elegant hotel dating back to the late nineteenth century and possessing a certain period charm. The "classic" rooms, with internal views and striped blue-and-white walls, are fine but nothing special; the "superior" rooms are much better, particularly those on the upper floors, with magnificent views of the Tuileries gardens and nice touches such as two sinks in the bathrooms. "Classic" €200–240, "superior" €250–300.

**Hôtel Lancaster Map 7, G3. 7 rue de Berri, 8e ⓣ01.40.76.40.76, ⓦwww.hotel-lancaster.fr. ⓂGeorge-V.** The rooms in this elegantly restored nineteenth-century townhouse retain original features and are chock full of Louis XVI and Rococo antiques, but with a touch of contemporary chic. The hotel was the pied-à-terre for the likes of Garbo, Dietrich and Sir Alec Guinness, and is still a favourite hideout today for those fleeing the paparazzi. A small interior zen-style garden and pleasant service make for a relaxing stay, and there's an excellent restaurant run by Michelin-starred chef Michel Troisgros. It's worth checking their site for special offers, otherwise doubles usually start at €520.

**L'Hôtel Pergolèse Map 7, B1. 3 rue Pergolèse, 16e ⓣ01.53.64.04.04, ⓦwww.hotelpergolese.com. ⓂArgentine.** Owned by the Best Western chain, this is a classy four-star boutique hotel in a tall, slender building on a quiet side street near the Arc de Triomphe. The decor is all contemporary – wood floors, cool colours, chic styling – but without chilliness: sofas and friendly service add a cosy touch. Rooms on six floors (facing the street or the internal courtyard) are comfortable and well appointed, with great designer bathrooms. Doubles from €119.

**Relais St-Honoré Map 2, C3. 308 rue St-Honoré, 1er ⓣ01.42.96.06.06, ⓦrelaissainthonore.com. ⓂTuileries.** A snug little hotel run by friendly and obliging staff, and set in a stylishly renovated seventeenth-century townhouse. The pretty wood-beamed rooms are done out in warm colours and rich fabrics. Facilities include free broadband internet access and flat-screen TVs. Doubles from €208.

**Hôtel de Sers Map 7, F4. 41 av Pierre 1er de Serbie, 8e ⓣ01.53.23.75.75, ⓦwww .hoteldesers.com. ⓜGeorge-V.** A chic and luxurious boutique hotel, just off the Champs-Elysées, offering rooms in minimalist style, with rosewood furnishings and decor in white, grey, deep reds and pinks; facilities include CD/DVD player and huge TV. The two suites on the top floor have fabulous panoramic terraces. Doubles officially start at €450, though there are frequent special offers.

**Hôtel Thérèse Map 2, D3. 5–7 rue Thérèse, 1er ⓣ01.42.96.10.01, ⓦwww .hoteltherese.com. ⓜPalais Royal-Musée du Louvre.** A very attractive boutique hotel, on a quiet street within easy walking distance of the Louvre, offering more expensive "traditional" rooms, which are pared-down and stylish with dark wood fittings, and "classic" rooms, which are small but good value. Book well in advance as it's very popular, especially during the fashion shows. "Classic" doubles from €155, "traditional" from €185.

## The Grands Boulevards and around

**Hôtel Chopin Map 3, H8. 46 passage Jouffroy, 9e; entrance on bd Montmartre, near rue du Faubourg-Montmartre ⓣ01.47.70.58.10, ⓦwww.hotelbretonnerie.com. ⓜGrands-Boulevards.** A charming, quiet hotel set in an atmospheric period building hidden away at the end of a picturesque 1850s passage. Rooms are pleasantly furnished, though the cheaper ones are on the small side and a little dark. Doubles €92–106.

**Hôtel Mansart Map 2, C2. 5 rue des Capucines, 1er ⓣ01.42.61.50.28, ⓦwww .paris-hotel-mansart.com. ⓜOpéra/ Madeleine.** This gracious hotel is situated on the corner of place Vendôme, just a stone's throw from the *Ritz*, but with rooms at a fraction of the price. They're not quite in the luxury bracket but they're attractively decorated in Louis XIV style, with plenty of antique furniture, old prints and quality fabrics – and most are fairly spacious by Parisian standards. The more expensive rooms look out onto the square. Doubles from €120 to €290.

**Hôtel Tiquetonne Map 2, H3. 6 rue Tiquetonne, 2e ⓣ01.42.36.94.58. ⓜEtienne-Marcel.** Located on a pedestrianized street, a block away from Montorgueil street market and around the corner from the rue St-Denis red-light district, the excellent-value, old-fashioned *Tiquetonne* dates back to the 1920s and looks as though it's changed little since. Colour-clash decor and paper-thin walls notwithstanding, the rooms are nice enough and well maintained, many quite spacious by Parisian standards. Rooms without en suites are equipped with a sink and bidet. Breakfast is served in your room. Singles €35, doubles €45–55.

**Hôtel Victoires Opéra Map 2, G3. 56 rue de Montorgueil, 2e ⓣ01.42.36.41.08, ⓦwww.hotelvictoiresopera.com. ⓜLes Halles/Etienne-Marcel.** A stylish boutique hotel on the trendy rue Montorgueil, a pedestrianized market street. The rooms are furnished in contemporary style and warmly decorated in chocolate and coffee tones; the walls are hung with prints of Modigliani drawings. Doubles from €180.

**Hôtel Vivienne Map 3, G8. 40 rue Vivienne, 2e ⓣ01.42.33.13.26, ⓔparis@hotel-vivienne.com. ⓜGrands-Boulevards/Bourse.** A ten-minute walk from the Louvre, this is a friendly, family-run place, with very clean, good-sized, cheery rooms and modern bathrooms. Ten have internet access, and the foyer also has a terminal with free use for guests. Doubles with shower and shared WC €73; doubles with bath €85–112. The single rooms are a decent size and well priced at €58.

## Beaubourg and Les Halles

**Relais du Louvre Map 2, F6. 19 rue des Prêtres St-Germain l'Auxerrois, 1er ⓣ01.40.41.96.42, ⓦwww.relaisdulouvre.com. ⓜPalais Royal-Musée du Louvre.** A discreet hotel with eighteen rooms set on a quiet back street opposite the church of St-Germain l'Auxerrois; you can admire the flying buttresses from the front-facing rooms. The decor is traditional but not stuffy, with rich, quality fabrics, old prints, Turkish rugs and solid furniture. The relaxed atmosphere and charming service attract a faithful clientele. Doubles €170–215.

**Hôtel de Roubaix Map 2, H3. 6 rue Greneta, 3e ⓣ01.42.72.89.91, ⓦwww.hotel-de-roubaix.com. ⓜRéaumur-Sébastopol/Arts-et-Métiers.** An old-fashioned, family-run two-star, with kindly staff and ancient vending machines on the landings. The 53 rooms, with private facilities, are small and decked out with floral wallpaper and rickety furniture, but they're good value when you consider the location, just five minutes' walk from the Pompidou Centre. A basic breakfast – a hunk of bread and a hot drink – is included in the price. Doubles from €77.

**Hôtel Saint-Merry Map 2, H6. 78 rue de la Verrerie, 4e ⓣ01.42.78.14.15, ⓔhotelstmerry@wanadoo.fr. ⓜRambuteau.** "Unique" is a much overused word, but perfectly appropriate when describing this quirky little hotel, where you can indulge your Gothic medieval fantasies in a former presbytery attached to the Eglise St-Merri. There are ten wonderfully atmospheric rooms and two suites, all featuring dark wood furniture, exposed stone walls and wrought iron; room 9, incorporating a flying buttress, is the most popular (and possibly most unusual hotel room in Paris). Possible minus points are the absence of a lift and TVs (apart from in the suite). Breakfast is served in your room. Rooms €160–230, suite €335.

## The Marais

**Hôtel du Bourg Tibourg Map 4, B10. 19 rue du Bourg-Tibourg, 4e ⓣ01.42.78.47.39, ⓦwww .hotelbourgtibourg.com. ⓜHôtel-de-Ville.** Oriental meets medieval, with a dash of Second Empire, at this sumptuously designed boutique hotel. Rooms are tiny, but cosseted with rich velvets, silks and drapes; those on the fifth floor have their own mini balconies, and there's an opulent breakfast area. Doubles €230–260.

**Hôtel de la Bretonnerie Map 4, B10. 22 rue Ste-Croix-de-la-Bretonnerie, 4e ⓣ01.48.87.77.63, ⓦwww .bretonnerie.com. ⓜHôtel-de-Ville.** A charming place on one of the Marais' liveliest streets; the rooms, all different, are exquisitely decorated with quality fabrics, oak furniture and, in some cases, four-poster beds. The location's perfect for exploring the Marais, though front-facing rooms may suffer from street noise at night. Doubles from €135–165.

**Caron de Beaumarchais Map 4, B11. 12 rue Vieille-du-Temple, 4e ⓣ01.42.72.34.12, ⓦwww .carondebeaumarchais.com. ⓜHôtel-de-Ville.** Named after the eighteenth-century French playwright Beaumarchais, who would have felt quite at home here: all the furnishings – the original engravings and Louis XVI furniture, not to mention the pianoforte in the foyer – evoke the refined tastes of high-society pre-Revolution Paris. Rooms overlooking the courtyard are petite, while those on the street are a little more spacious, some with small balconies. Doubles €145–185.

**Hôtel Central Marais Map 4, B10. 33 rue Vieille-du-Temple, 4e; entrance on rue Ste-Croix-de-la-Bretonnerie ⓣ01.48.87.56.08, ⓦwww.hotelcentralmarais.com. ⓂHôtel-de-Ville.** The only self-proclaimed gay hotel in Paris, whose famous and popular gay bar, *Le Central*, is just downstairs. Six small, boxy rooms with shared bathrooms, and only one with en-suite bath and WC. Doubles €89.

**Grand Hôtel Jeanne d'Arc Map 4, C11. 3 rue de Jarente, 4e ⓣ01.48.87.62.11, ⓦwww.hoteljeannedarc.com. ⓂSt-Paul.** A recent makeover has brightened up this old Marais townhouse, just off lovely place du Marché-Ste-Catherine. The en-suite rooms have yellow, orange or mauve walls and often clashing carpets and duvets, but it all seems to work. The triple at the top has good views over the rooftops. Doubles €89–116.

**Grand Hôtel du Loiret Map 4, A11. 8 rue des Mauvais-Garçons, 4e ⓣ01.48.87.77.00, ⓔhotelduloiret@hotmail.com. ⓂHôtel-de-Ville.** A simple budget hotel, grand in name only. The rooms are essentially underwhelming and very small, but acceptable for the price; cheaper ones have washbasin only, all have TV and telephone. Doubles €50 with shared toilet, €70–90 en suite.

**Hôtel de Nice Map 4, B11. 42bis rue de Rivoli, 4e ⓣ01.42.78.55.29, ⓦwww.hoteldenice.com. ⓂHôtel-de-Ville.** A well-run six-storey establishment, with a delightful old-world charm: its small, pretty rooms have Indian-cotton bedspreads, carved wooden wardrobes, elaborate wallpaper and gilded mirrors. The rue de Rivoli is very busy, though, and traffic noise can be a problem despite the double-glazing. Doubles €110–120.

**Hôtel Pavillon de la Reine Map 4, D11. 28 place des Vosges, 4e ⓣ01.40.29.19.19, ⓦwww.pavillon-de-la-reine.com. ⓂBastille.** A perfect honeymoon hideaway in a beautiful ivy-covered mansion secreted away off the adorable place des Vosges. It preserves an intimate ambience, with friendly, personable staff. The rooms mostly have a distinctively 1990s "hip hotel" feel, and could probably use another makeover. Doubles €300–500.

**Hôtel du Petit Moulin Map 4, C8. 29–31 rue du Poitou, 3e ⓣ01.42.74.10.10, ⓦwww.paris-hotel-petitmoulin.com. ⓂSt-Sébastien Froissart/Filles du Calvaire.** A glamorous boutique hotel, set in an old bakery and designed top to bottom by Christian Lacroix. The designer's hallmark *joie de vivre* reigns in the seventeen rooms, each a fusion of different styles, from elegant Baroque to Sixties kitsch: shocking pinks and lime greens give way to toile de Jouy prints, while pod chairs sit alongside antique dressing tables and old-fashioned bathtubs. Doubles €190–350.

**Hôtel St-Louis Marais Map 4, C12. 1 rue Charles-V, 4e ⓣ01.48.87.87.04, ⓦwww.saintlouismarais.com. ⓂSully-Morland.** Formerly part of the seventeenth-century Célestins Convent, this characterful place retains its period feel, with stone walls, exposed beams and tiled floors. Rooms are cosily done out with terracotta-coloured fabrics and old maps of Paris, and have wi-fi access. Standard rooms are very small and have private showers, while superior ones are bigger and have bathtubs; all have flat-screen TVs. There's no lift, but the staff help carry up luggage. A major plus is its location on a very quiet road, just a short walk from all the Marais action further north, and the Left Bank is easily reached over the Pont de Sully. Doubles €115 and €140.

**Hôtel Sévigné Map 4, C11. 2 rue Malher, 4e ⓣ01.42.72.76.17, ⓦwww.le-sevigne.com. ⓂSt-Paul.** A clean, pleasant budget hotel, just off busy rue de Rivoli. The rooms are small and basic but well maintained and double-glazed, and all have either bath or shower. Doubles €84–95.

## Bastille and around

**Nouvel Hôtel Map 4, off I14. 24 av du Bel-Air, 12e ⓣ01.43.43.01.81, ⓦwww.nouvel-hotel-paris.com. ⓂNation.** A quiet, family-run hotel, with a faintly provincial air and small but neat rooms decorated in pastel colours and white-painted furniture, each with private shower or bath, TV and phone. Some overlook the lovely garden (room 9 opens directly onto it), where you can eat breakfast in the shade of a medlar tree. The obliging owners provide a personal touch. It's a bit out of the way, but the nearby RER gets you into the centre in no time. Doubles €86 (shower), €97 (bath).

**Hôtel de la Porte Dorée Map 4, off F14. 273 av Daumesnil, 12e ⓣ01.43.07.56.97, ⓦwww.hoteldelaportedoree.com. ⓂPorte-Dorée.** A good-value hotel, a considerable step above the two-star norm: all rooms have private shower or bath, cable TV, comfy beds and pleasant decor. Traditional features such as ceiling mouldings, fireplaces and the elegant main staircase have been retained and many of the furnishings are antique. Bastille is seven minutes away by métro or a pleasant twenty-minute walk along the Promenade Plantée. Doubles from €57.

**Le Quartier Bercy Square Map 4, off I14. 33 bd de Reuilly, 12e ⓣ01.44.87.09.09, ⓦwww.lequartierhotelbs.com. ⓜDaumesnil/Dugommier.** A worthy addition to Paris's stable of design hotels, *Le Quartier* is located in a cool, untouristy neighbourhood. The sleek en suites are small – some are tiny – but perfectly formed: think lots of smooth curves and subdued lighting, as well as thoughtful features like tea/coffee makers. Staff can be a little haughty, but are generally fine. Doubles from €113.

## The Quartier Latin and the southeast

**Hôtel du Commerce Map 2, G10. 14 rue de la Montagne-Ste-Geneviève, 5e ⓣ01.43.54.89.69, ⓦwww.commerce-paris-hotel.com. ⓜMaubert-Mutualité.** Business-like budget hotel with a range of rooms from washbasin-only cheapies (€49, €39 for one person) up to modern en suites (€99) and family rooms (€69–99). The communal kitchen and dining area are handy, there's free internet access, and the location is excellent. Doubles €49–99.

**Hôtel Degrés de Notre Dame Map 2, H9. 10 rue des Grands Degrés, 5e ⓣ01.55.42.88.88, ⓦwww.lesdegreshotel.com. ⓜSt-Michel/Maubert-Mutualité.** This charming, superbly idiosyncratic hotel has just ten rooms, so book in advance. The building is ancient and the rooms all very different, with prices corresponding to size. Unique, personal touches are everywhere: hand-painted murals, antique mirrors and curious nooks. Perhaps the loveliest room of all is under the roof, with its own stairs. Breakfast included. Doubles €115–170.

**Hôtel Esmeralda Map 2, G9. 4 rue St-Julien-le-Pauvre, 5e ⓣ01.43.54.19.20, ⓔhotel.esmeralda@orange.fr. ⓜSt-Michel/Maubert-Mutualité.** Dozing in an ancient house on square Viviani, this rickety old hotel offers a deeply old-fashioned, faded feel, with resolutely unmodernized en-suite rooms done up in worn red velvet or faded florals. A few rooms have superb views of Notre-Dame (€100–110). Doubles €90.

**Familia Hôtel Map 2, H11. 11 rue des Ecoles, 5e ⓣ01.43.54.55.27, ⓦwww.familiahotel.com.**

**ⓂCardinal-Lemoine/Maubert-Mutualité/Jussieu.** Big, friendly, family-run hotel on a busy road. Rooms are small but attractive, with beams and toile de Jouy wallpaper; some have views of Notre-Dame, others have balconies. Breakfast included. Doubles €70–127.

**Hôtel des Grandes Ecoles Map 2, H12. 75 rue du Cardinal-Lemoine, 5e Ⓣ01.43.26.79.23, Ⓦwww.hotel-grandes-ecoles.com. ⓂCardinal-Lemoine.** Follow the cobbled alleyway to a large, peaceful garden and this tranquil hotel, with its pretty, old-fashioned rooms. Reservations are taken three months in advance, on the 15th of the month; don't be even a day late. Doubles €115–140.

**Hôtel Marignan Map 2, G10. 13 rue du Sommerard, 5e Ⓣ01.43.54.63.81, Ⓦwww.hotel-marignan.com. ⓂMaubert-Mutualité.** Great-value place, totally sympathetic to the needs of rucksack-toting foreigners, with free wi-fi, laundry, ironing and kitchen facilities, a library of guidebooks – and rooms for up to five people. The cheapest share bathrooms with one other room. No credit cards. Doubles €60–90.

**Hôtel Port-Royal Map 5, F5. 8 bd Port-Royal, 5e Ⓣ01.43.31.70.06, Ⓦwww.hotelportroyal.fr. ⓂGobelins.** A friendly, good-value one-star that has been in the same family since the 1930s. Doubles, though small, are attractive and very clean; those with shared bath are considerably cheaper (€52.50, showers €2.50). It's in a quiet, residential area at the rue Mouffetard end of the boulevard, near the métro and the Quartier Latin. No credit cards. Doubles €78.50.

**Hôtel Résidence Henri IV Map 2, H10. 50 rue des Bernardins, 5e Ⓣ01.44.41.31.81, Ⓦwww.residencehenri4.com. ⓂMaubert- Mutualité.** Set back from busy rue des Ecoles on a cul-de-sac, this hotel is discreet and elegant, with classically styled rooms. Some have period features such as fireplaces, and all have miniature kitchenettes. Doubles from €120.

**Select Hôtel Map 2, F10. 51 place de la Sorbonne, 5e Ⓣ01.46.34.14.80, Ⓦwww.selecthotel.fr. ⓂCluny-Sorbonne.** Situated right on the *place*, this hotel has had the full designer makeover, with exposed stone walls, leather and recessed wood trim much in evidence. Doubles from €169.

## St-Germain

**Hôtel de l'Abbaye Map 2, C10. 10 rue Cassette, 6e**

**☎01.45.44.38.11, Ⓦwww.hotelabbayeparis.com. ⓂSt-Sulpice.** An atmosphere of hushed, luxurious calm presides over this four-star hotel. The rooms have swathes of floral fabric and brass fittings, and there's a fair-sized courtyard garden and conservatory out back. Doubles from €240.

**Hôtel du Globe Map 2, E9. 15 rue des Quatre-Vents, 6e ☎01.43.26.35.50, Ⓦwww.hotel-du-globe.fr. ⓂOdéon.** Welcoming hotel in a tall, narrow, seventeenth-century building decked out with four-posters, stone walls, roof beams and the like. Rooms can be small, but aren't expensive for the location. Doubles €125–170.

**L'Hôtel Map 2, D7. 13 rue des Beaux-Arts, 6e ☎01.44.41.99.00, Ⓦwww.l-hotel.com. ⓂMabillon/St-Germain-des-Prés.** Extravagant designer hotel, with twenty sumptuous rooms accessed by a wonderful spiral staircase, and with a tiny pool in the basement. Oscar Wilde died here, "fighting a duel" with his wallpaper, and he's now remembered by a room with a "Wilde" theme. Prices start in the high €200s, but the best rooms can cost double that.

**Hôtel des Maronniers Map 2, D7. 21 rue Jacob, 6e ☎01.43.25.30.60, Ⓦwww.hotel-marronniers.com. ⓂSt-Germain-des-Prés.** A romantic hotel, with small rooms swathed in deep velvet curtains and expensive fabric wall-coverings. The breakfast room gives onto a pleasant courtyard garden, and some attic rooms have views of the church of St-Germain-des-Prés. Doubles from €120.

**Hôtel Michelet-Odéon Map 2, E10. 6 place de l'Odéon, 6e ☎01.53.10.05.60, Ⓦwww.hotelmicheletodeon.com. ⓂOdéon.** A serious bargain for a hotel so close to the Jardin du Luxembourg. Rooms are unusually attractive (especially those facing onto the *place*) and larger than most at this price. Doubles from €110.

**Hôtel de Nesle Map 2, E7. 7 rue de Nesle, 6e ☎01.43.54.62.41, Ⓦwww.hoteldenesleparis.com. ⓂSt-Michel.** Eccentric and sometimes chaotic hotel whose rooms are decorated with cartoon historical murals that you'll either love or hate. Rooms are tiny, but inexpensive for the amazingly central location. Doubles from €75.

**Relais Christine Map 2, E8. 3 rue Christine, 6e ☎01.40.51.60.80, Ⓦwww.relais-christine.com. ⓂOdéon.** Deeply elegant, romantic four-star in a sixteenth-century former convent set around a deliciously hidden courtyard. It's well worth paying

the 20 percent premium for one of the *supérieure* rooms. Doubles from €290.

**Relais Saint-Sulpice Map 2, D9. 3 rue Garancière, 6e ⓣ01.46.33.99.00, ⓦwww.relais-saint-sulpice.com. ⓜSt-Sulpice/St-Germain-des-Prés.** Set in an aristocratic townhouse immediately behind St-Sulpice's apse, this is a discreetly classy small hotel with well-furnished rooms painted in cheerful Provencal colours. The sauna is a nice touch. Doubles from €143.

**Hôtel de l'Université Map 2, C7. 22 rue de l'Université, 7e ⓣ01.42.61.09.39, ⓦwww.hoteluniversite.com. ⓜRue du Bac.** Cosy, quiet boutique three-star with antique details, including beamed ceilings and fireplaces in the larger, slightly pricier rooms. Doubles €140.

## The Eiffel Tower quarter

**Hôtel du Champ-de-Mars Map 6, B4. 7 rue du Champ-de-Mars, 7e ⓣ01.45.51.52.30, ⓦwww.hotelduchampdemars.com. ⓜEcole-Militaire.** Cosy, colourful, excellent-value rooms in a well-run hotel. The location is great, too, in a nice neighbourhood just off the lively rue Cler market. Doubles €98.

**Hôtel du Palais Bourbon Map 6, E4. 49 rue de Bourgogne, 7e ⓣ01.44.11.30.70, ⓦwww.hotel-palais-bourbon.com. ⓜVarenne.** This substantial, handsome old building on a quiet street in the hushed, posh district near the Musée Rodin offers spacious, prettily furnished rooms with parquet floors and plenty of period detail. Homely family rooms (€235) and singles (€110) are also available. Breakfast is included in the price. Doubles from €150.

**Hôtel Saint-Dominique Map 6, C2. 62 rue St-Dominique, 7e ⓣ01.47.05.51.44, ⓦwww.hotelstdominique.com. ⓜInvalides/La Tour-Maubourg.** Welcoming hotel in the heart of this upmarket, villagey neighbourhood near the Eiffel Tower. Smallish but tastefully decorated rooms are arranged around a bright little courtyard where you can sit outside among the greenery. Singles and triples available. Doubles €100–160.

## Montparnasse

**Hôtel de la Loire Map 6, off F14. 39bis rue du Moulin-Vert, 14e ⓣ01.45.40.66.88, ⓦwww.hoteldelaloire-paris.com. ⓜPernety/Alésia.** On a pedestrianized street stands this delightful family hotel. En-suite doubles, with spotless, if tiny, bathrooms, are a bargain. There are cheaper options (with shared WC) in the slightly darker rooms in the annexe, which runs the length of the peaceful garden. Each room is different, and all have charming personal touches. Free wi-fi. Doubles around €75.

**Hôtel Mistral Map 6, G13. 24 rue Cels, 14e ⓣ01.43.20.25.43, ⓦwww.hotel-mistral-paris.com. ⓜPernety/Alésia.** Welcoming, cosy and pleasantly refurbished hotel on a very quiet street, with a little courtyard garden and a shared dining room/kitchen. Some rooms come with showers and shared WC facilities only (€70). Doubles €90.

**Solar Hôtel Map 6, H14. 22 rue Boulard, 14e ⓣ01.43.21.08.20, ⓦwww.solarhotel.fr. ⓜDenfert-Rochereau.** Set on an old-fashioned Montparnasse street, this budget hotel has an original and friendly spirit – there are paintings by local artists on the walls, cultural events in the back garden and the hotel strives to be ecological, with low-energy fittings, organic breakfasts and free bike rental. Don't be put off by the exterior: rooms are basic, but comfortable and bright, with a/c, TV and free wi-fi. Guests have use of a kitchen and living room. Rooms €59.

## Montmartre and around

**Hôtel Amour Map 3, G4. 8 rue Navarin, 9e ⓣ01.48.78.31.80, ⓦwww.hotelamourparis.fr. ⓜPigalle.** Designer hotel for an achingly cool clientele, with old parquet, new paintwork and a deliberately boho Pigalle porn theme. Every room is decorated differently – one is all black with disco balls above the bed – but none has phone or TV, and all have iPod speakers. There's also a spacious dining area and a vodka bar. Doubles from €140.

**Hôtel des Arts Map 3, E2. 5 rue Tholozé, 18e ⓣ01.46.06.30.52, ⓦwww.arts-hotel-paris.com. ⓜBlanche/Abbesses.** Manages that rare combination of homeliness and efficiency, with the family dog lolling by the reception desk and courteous staff. Rooms are fairly small and a little bland, but cosy and well maintained – and the topmost "superior" ones have great views. The location – on a romantically sloping, cobbled street in the heart of the Abbesses quarter, opposite a classic arts cinema – is just fantastic. Doubles €80–140.

**Hôtel Bonséjour Montmartre Map 3, F2. 11 rue Burq, 18e ⓣ01.42.54.22.53, ⓦwww.hotel-bonsejour-montmartre.fr. ⓜAbbesses.** The location on a quiet, untouristy street on the slopes of Montmartre is a dream, and the rooms may be basic and old-fashioned (with shower, but WC down the hall), but it's in a picturesque way. They're a serious bargain, too. Ask for the corner rooms 23, 33, 43 or 53, which have balconies. Doubles from €56.

**Hôtel Eldorado Map 3, B3. 18 rue des Dames, 17e ⓣ01.45.22.35.21, ⓦwww.eldoradohotel.fr. ⓜPlace-de-Clichy.** Idiosyncratic hotel in the bohemian Batignolles village. Characterful rooms with some vintage fittings are brightened up with vivid colour schemes and furnishings, and there's a secluded annexe at the back of the courtyard garden. Rooms with shared bath available for €70. Good onsite *bistrot*. Doubles €73–82.

**Hôtel Ermitage Map 3, H1. 24 rue Lamarck, 18e ⓣ01.42.64.79.22, ⓦwww.ermitagesacrecoeur.fr. ⓜAnvers.** Hushed, family-run hotel set on the lofty heights behind Sacré-Coeur. Rooms are old-fashioned and chintzy; those at the back have views across northern Paris. Complimentary breakfast served in rooms. Approach via the funicular to avoid a steep climb. No credit cards. Doubles €96.

**Hôtel Langlois Map 3, E6. 63 rue St-Lazare, 9e ⓣ01.48.74.78.24, ⓦwww.hotel-langlois.com. ⓜTrinité.** Despite having all the facilities of a two-star, this genteel hotel in an untouristy quarter has barely changed in the last century, with antique furnishings and some spacious, handsome rooms. Doubles €140.

**Hôtel Particulier Montmartre Map 3, F1. 23 av Junot, 18e ⓣ01.53.41.81.40, ⓦwww.hotel-particulier-montmartre.com. ⓜAbbesses/Lamarck-Caulaincourt.** An exceptional hotel for a treat – or perhaps a honeymoon retreat, given its secluded location in a garden off a private passage set back from one of Paris's most exclusive streets. Set in an elegant Neoclassical mansion, this discreet boutique hotel has just five rooms, all large and *très* designer. Doubles €390–590, with discounts during the week in summer.

**Style Hôtel Map 3, C2. 8 rue Ganneron, 18e ⓣ01.45.22.37.59. ⓜPlace-de-Clichy.** An unpromising exterior in Batignolles hides a really lovely budget place, with wooden floors, marble fireplaces and a secluded courtyard. Great value, especially the rooms with shared bathrooms (€40). Doubles €60.

## Eastern Paris

**Hôtel Beaumarchais Map 4, E8. 3 rue Oberkampf, 11e ⓣ01.53.36.86.86, ⓦwww.hotelbeaumarchais.com. ⓜFilles-du-Calvaire/Oberkampf.** A funky, gay-friendly hotel, though the garish Fifties-inspired decor may be a bit much for some: rooms have pink, yellow or orange walls, red bedspreads, swirly carpets and crazy paving-style tiles in the bathrooms. All 31 rooms are en suite with a/c and cable TV, and there's a little patio for breakfast on fine days. Doubles €110–130, suites €150–170.

**Le Général Hôtel Map 4, D6. 5–7 rue Rampon, 11e ⓣ01.47.00.41.57, ⓦwww.legeneralhotel.com. ⓜRépublique.** This cool boutique hotel, run by young, helpful staff and located on a fairly peaceful road, is a lesson in restrained modern design. The bright, airy rooms have spotless bathrooms and rosewood furnishings. Facilities include a sauna and fitness centre, and the breakfast area turns into a bar in the evenings. There are nice touches such as tea- and coffee-making facilities, as well as one or two quirkier features, such as rubber ducks in the bath. Doubles from €185.

**Mama Shelter Map 4, off I11. 109 rue de Bagnolet, 20e ⓣ01.43.48.48.48, ⓦwww.mamashelter.com. ⓜAlexandre-Dumas.** Currently one of the most talked-about hotels in Paris, *Mama Shelter*, owned by Club Med founders the Trigano family, justifies the hype. Philippe Starck-designed, with a hip, industrial-chic theme, it's also extremely good value. The sharp en suites come with an arty graffiti motif on the carpets and ceilings, swanky bathrooms, iMacs and decorative superhero masks. An excellent bar-restaurant, sun terrace and top-notch service complete the package. Doubles from €99; the cheapest deals are available via the website.

**Hôtel de Nevers Map 4, E6. 53 rue de Malte, 11e ⓣ01.47.00.56.18, ⓦwww.hoteldenevers.com. ⓜOberkampf/République.** The entrance to this one-star budget hotel is patrolled by three smoky-grey cats. Needless to say, there's no room to swing one, but otherwise these are for the most part decent, if slightly tatty, cheerfully decorated rooms – the best are the en-suite doubles at the front; courtyard-facing rooms are dark and poky. Doubles €62–69.

## Western Paris

**Hameau de Passy Map 7, off A9. 48 rue Passy, 16e ⓣ01.42.88.47.55,**

Ⓦwww.paris-hotel-hameaudepassy.com. ⓂMuette/Passy. A peaceful modern two-star hotel with a country sensibility, set back from the main street. While the rooms are on the small side, they get lots of natural light and are pleasantly decorated in white, orange and green hues. Faultless service is assured by a charming, polyglot staff. Doubles from €55.

**Hôtel Le Sezz Map 7, A9. 6 av Frémiet, 16e Ⓣ01.56.75.26.26, Ⓦwww.hotelsezz.com. ⓂPassy.** No humble receptionist, but a "personal assistant" welcomes you to this sleek boutique hotel, hidden behind a nineteenth-century facade on a quiet street near the place de Passy. The rooms are decorated with sober minimalism, veering on the austere (slate-grey stone walls, black wooden flooring, glass partitions and chrome furnishings), but with splashes of colour providing a touch of warmth. The standard rooms are smallish; the suites come with huge baths big enough for two, and all rooms have flat-screen TVs, free wi-fi and CD/DVD players. Within easy walking distance of the Eiffel Tower. Doubles from €220.

## Apartments and bed and breakfast

**Rented apartments** are attractive alternatives for families with young children or visitors on an extended visit who want a bit more independence and the option to do their own catering. Staying on a **bed-and-breakfast** basis in a private house is also worth considering if you want to get away from the more impersonal set-up of a hotel, and is a reasonably priced option.

**Alcôve & Agapes Ⓦwww.bed-and-breakfast-in-paris.com.** A family-run bed-and-breakfast referral organization that has an excellent selection of rooms on its books, most accommodating couples, but some able to welcome families. Some hosts offer extras, such as French conversation, wine tasting or cookery classes. Doubles mostly in the €80 to €160 range.

**France Lodge 2 rue Meissonier, 17e Ⓣ01.56.33.85.80, Ⓦwww.apartments-in-paris.com. ⓂWagram.** Offers bed-and-breakfast rooms inside and outside Paris. Prices start at €30 single or €52 double, plus a €15 registration fee.

**Good Morning Paris 43 rue Lacépède, 5e ⓣ01.47.07.28.29, ⓦwww.goodmorningparis.fr.** Bed-and-breakfast accommodation in central Paris, with rates fixed at €56 for a single room and €69 for a double. You have to stay at least two nights but there's no reservation fee – payment in full confirms your booking.

**Lodgis 47 rue de Paradis, 10e ⓣ01.70.39.11.11, ⓦwww.lodgis.com.** A well-run international agency with a large number of furnished flats on its books. A studio flat in the Latin Quarter starts from around €375 a week. Longer-term rentals also available.

**Paris B and B ⓣ1-800/872 2632, ⓦwww.parisbandb.com.** US-based online bed-and-breakfast booking service. The rooms offered are on the luxurious side and start from $90 for a double. Apartments from $120.

## Hostels and campsites

**Hostels** are an obvious choice for a tight budget, but won't necessarily be cheaper than sharing a room in a budget hotel. Many take advance bookings, including the hostel groups FUAJ (ⓦwww.fuaj.fr), which is part of Hostelling International, and MIJE (ⓦwww.mije.com), which runs three excellent hostels in historic buildings in the Marais. (There is a third big hostel group, UCRIF, but it caters largely to groups, so we haven't listed their hostels here; full details can be found online at ⓦwww.ucrif.asso.fr.) Independent hostels tend to be noisier places, often with bars attached. There is no effective age limit at any of these places.

The utterly budget option, of course, is **camping**. Only one site is reasonably close to central Paris, *Camping du Bois de Boulogne* (ⓦwww.campingparis.fr). It's by the Seine and gets booked out in summer; there's a free shuttle bus to the Porte-Maillot métro station. *Camping de la Colline*, in Torcy, on the RER line A4 (ⓦwww.camping-de-la-colline.com) is better for Disneyland, with shuttle buses to the park. Both campsites offer inexpensive bungalow accommodation.

**D'Artagnan Map 4, off I10. 80 rue Vitruve, 20e ⓣ01.40.32.34.56, ⓦwww.fuaj.org. ⓂPorte-de-Bagnolet.** This colourful, modern HI hostel is the largest in France with 440 beds and facilities including a small cinema, restaurant and bar, internet access and a swimming pool nearby. Guests have to vacate the rooms between 11am and 3pm for cleaning. It's very popular, so get here early, book online or book by phone on the central reservations number: ⓣ01.44.89.87.27. Doubles and rooms for three to five are a few euros more per head than the dorm price. Dorm beds from €23.50.

**BVJ Louvre Map 2, F4. 20 rue Jean-Jacques Rousseau, 1er ⓣ01.53.00.90.90, ⓦwww.bvjhotel.com. ⓂLouvre/Châtelet-Les-Halles.** With 200 beds, the *BVJ Louvre* attracts an international studenty crowd, though dorms (sleeping eight) have a slightly institutional feel. Single rooms are available. Restaurant open daily except Sun. Dorm beds €29, twins €62.

**BVJ Paris Quartier Latin Map 2, H10. 44 rue des Bernardins, 5e ⓣ01.43.29.34.80, ⓦwww.bvjhotel.com. ⓂMaubert-Mutualité.** Spick-and-span hostel in a good location. Single rooms (€45) and dorm beds are good value; for double rooms (€66) you can do better elsewhere. Dorm beds €29.

**Le Fauconnier Map 4, C12. 11 rue du Fauconnier, 4e ⓣ01.42.74.23.45, ⓦwww.mije.com. ⓂSt-Paul/Pont Marie.** MIJE hostel in a superbly renovated seventeenth-century building. Dorms sleep three to eight, and there are some single (€49) and double rooms too (€72), with en-suite showers. Dorm beds €30.

**Le Fourcy Map 4, B11. 6 rue de Fourcy, 4e ⓣ01.42.74.23.45. ⓂSt Paul.** Another excellent MIJE hostel (same prices and deal as *Le Fauconnier*, see above). Housed in a beautiful mansion, this place has a small garden and an inexpensive restaurant. Doubles and triples also available.

**Jules Ferry Map 4, E6. 8 bd Jules-Ferry, 11e ⓣ01.43.57.55.60, ⓦwww.fuaj.fr. ⓂRépublique.** Fairly central HI hostel, in a lively area at the foot of the Belleville hill. Difficult to get a place, but they can help find a bed elsewhere. Two to four people in each room. Dorm beds from €23.

**Maubuisson Map 4, A11. 12 rue des Barres, 4e ⓣ01.42.74.23.45. ⓂPont Marie/Hôtel de Ville.** A MIJE hostel in a magnificent medieval building on a quiet street. Shared use of the restaurant at *Le Fourcy* (see above). Dorms only, sleeping four. Dorm beds €30.

**Oops Map 5, G7. 50 av des Gobelins, 5e ⓣ01.47.07.47.00, ⓦwww.oops-paris.com. ⓂGobelins.**

This "design hostel", opened in 2007, is brightly decorated with funky patterns. All dorms are en suite, there's free wi-fi, a/c and a basic breakfast, and it's open 24 hours. Private doubles from €60. Unexceptional location, but it's just a couple of métro stops south of the Quartier Latin. Dorm beds €23–30.

**Plug-inn Boutique Hostel Map 3, E2. 7 rue Aristide Bruant, 18e ⓣ01.42.58.42.58, ⓦwww.plug-inn.fr. ⓜBlanche/Abbesses.** This friendly pocket hostel has a cool designer decor, in parts, and offers free wi-fi and breakfast (and no curfew), but the best thing is the location on the slopes of Montmartre. Dorm beds from €25, double rooms from €60.

**St Christopher's Paris Map 4, off D1. 68–74 quai de la Seine, 19e ⓣ01.40.34.34.40, ⓦwww.st-christophers.co.uk/paris-hostels. ⓜCrimée/Laumière.** Massive new hostel overlooking the waters of the Bassin de la Villette – a long way from the centre. Rooms sleep six to eight and are pleasant in a functional, cabin-like way, but there's a great bar, inexpensive restaurant and free internet access. As well as dorms there are also twins and doubles available (€42–80). Dorm beds €25–30.

**Le Village Hostel Map 3, H3. 20 rue d'Orsel, 18e ⓣ01.42.64.22.02, ⓦwww.villagehostel.fr. ⓜAnvers.** Attractive independent hostel in a handsome building, with good facilities and a view of Sacré-Coeur from the terrace. Doubles €35–45 and triples €32–38 per person, including breakfast. Small discounts in winter. Dorm beds €28.

**Woodstock Hostel Map 3, H5. 48 rue Rodier, 9e ⓣ01.48.78.87.76, ⓦwww.woodstock.fr. ⓜAnvers/St-Georges.** A reliable hostel with its own bar, set in a great location on a pretty street near Montmartre. Twin rooms also available €22–25 per person, breakfast included. Dorm beds €19–22.

**Young and Happy Hostel Map 2, H13. 80 rue Mouffetard, 5e ⓣ01.47.07.47.07, ⓦwww.youngandhappy.fr. ⓜMonge/Censier-Daubenton.** Noisy, basic and studenty independent hostel in a lively, touristy location. Dorms, with shower, sleep four, and there are a few doubles (€26 per person). Curfew 2am; lockout 11am–4pm. Dorm beds from €20.

# 19

# Cafés and restaurants

The French seldom separate the major pleasures of eating and drinking, and there are thousands of establishments in Paris where you can do both. A restaurant may call itself a *brasserie*, *bistrot*, *café*, or indeed *restaurant*; equally, a café can be a place to eat, drink, listen to music or even dance. To simplify matters, we've split our listings for each area into two parts: under **cafés and wine bars**, you'll find venues we recommend primarily for daytime or relaxed evening drinks – though many also serve a *plat du jour* (daily special) or even a full menu; under **restaurants**, you'll find any establishment we recommend specifically for a meal. Alongside cafés, we've listed **wine bars** or *bistrots à vin* which may offer cheeses, cold meats and regional dishes too; also included in this category, you'll find genteel **salons de thé** (tearooms), which typically serve tea, pastries and light meals. If you're looking for cocktails, pints or full-on **nightlife**, you'll find the best venues listed separately in chapter 20, under "**bars**" (see p.233).

Cafés and restaurants often stay **closed** on Sunday or Monday. It's common for cafés to stay open upto 2am, and even extend hours on a Friday and Saturday night, closing

## Breakfast and snacks

Most cafés are able to make you up a filled baguette or a *tartine* on request. This is generally the best way to eat **breakfast**, and works out cheaper than the rate charged by most hotels (typically around €8–12). In the mornings, you may see a basket of croissants or some hard-boiled eggs on the counter. The drill is to help yourself – the waiter will keep an eye on how many you've eaten and bill you accordingly. Brasseries are also possibilities for cups of coffee, eggs, snacks and other breakfast food, while the concept of *le brunch* in a café has taken Paris by storm in recent years, becoming a Sunday institution in areas like the Marais.

In the last few years a range of sophisticated **snack bars** have sprung up as more and more Parisians abandon the traditional sit-down lunch for a quick bite in a trend known as *le snacking*. *Cojean* (17 bd Haussmann and many other branches; ⓦwww.cojean.fr) is one successful example of this sleek breed of contemporary snack bar, serving home-made soups and salads made up of ingredients like quinoa and mangetout. Traditional sandwiches such as the humble *sandwich jambon fromage* (cheese and ham) are of course still widely available at stand-up sandwich bars, while most boulangeries sell quiches and tarts. For **picnic** treats, head for a charcuterie or the delicatessen counter in a good supermarket; some of the city's most specialized or luxurious food shops are listed on pp.264–267 of the "Shopping" chapter. For hot **takeaway food**, crêperies sell *galettes* (wholewheat pancakes) as well as sweet and savoury *crêpes* (flat pancakes). More common are Turkish or North African kebab-and-fries shops, the latter also serving couscous plates with *merguez* (spicy sausage), chicken or lamb, and a spicy, tomatoey vegetable soup.

earlier on Sunday. Restaurants won't usually serve after 10pm, though some **brasseries** serve meals till the early hours. Many restaurants and shops take a **holiday** between the middle of July and the end of August. For the more upmarket or trendy places, and at weekends, it's wise to make **reservations**.

## Paris for vegetarians

Paris's gastronomic reputation is largely lost on **vegetarians**. In most restaurants, aside from the usual salads and cheeses, there is precious little choice for those who don't eat meat, as almost every dish, if not made almost entirely of beef, chicken, or fish, is invariably garnished with *lardons* (bacon), *anchois* (anchovies) or *jambon* (ham). That said, some of the newer, more innovative places will often have one or two vegetarian dishes on offer, and ethnic restaurants are a good bet. *Salons de thé*, too, offer lighter fare such as soups and quiches (*tartes*), which tend to be vegetarian. It's also possible to put together a meal at even the most meat-oriented brasserie by choosing dishes from among the starters (*crudités*, for example, are nearly always available) and soups, or by asking for an omelette. Useful French phrases to help you along are *Je suis végétarien(ne)* ("I'm a vegetarian") and *Il y a quelques plats sans viande*? (Are there any non-meat dishes?).

The few purely vegetarian restaurants that do exist tend to be based on a healthy diet principle rather than haute cuisine, but at least you get a choice. The following list is a good place to start:

**Les Cinq Saveurs d'Anada** 72 rue du Cardinal Lemoine, p.217.

**Au Grain de Folie** 24 rue de La Vieuville, p.227.

**Le Potager du Marais** 22 rue Rambuteau, p.212.

At restaurants, there is often a choice between one or more fixed-price **menus** (or sometimes a budget two-course *formule*), often particularly good value at lunchtime. Eating à la carte, by contrast, gives you access to everything on offer, though you'll pay a fair bit more. House **wines** are usually inexpensive, but a bottle of something interesting will usually add at least €20 to the bill, and potentially much more in a more expensive place. **Service** is legally included in your bill at all restaurants, bars and cafés, but you may want to leave a one- or two-euro coin as a **tip**. **Waiters** answer to monsieur or madame or excusez-moi – never garçon; to ask for the bill, the phrase is *l'addition, s'il vous plaît*.

# The Islands

## Cafés and wine bars

**Berthillon Map 2, I9. 31 rue St-Louis-en-l'Ile, $4^{e}$. ⓂPont-Marie. Wed–Sun 10am–8pm.** As the long queues outside attest, *Berthillon* serves the best ice cream and sorbets in Paris. They come in all sorts of unusual flavours, such as rhubarb, wild strawberry and Earl Grey tea, and are also available at other island sites listed on the door.

**La Charlotte de l'Isle Map 4, C13. 24 rue St-Louis-en-l'Ile, $4^{e}$. ⓂPont-Marie. Thurs–Sun 2–8pm; closed July & Aug.** Imagine the film *Chocolat* reinterpreted by Roald Dahl, and you get a very approximate picture of the enchanting *La Charlotte de l'Isle*. A tiny curiosity shop of a place, packed with chocolate animals, oriental tea boxes, circus-themed mobiles, model elephants and marionettes, it serves the most delicious hot chocolate – smooth and silky, made in a pan over the stove in the kitchen at the back and served in a white porcelain jug.

**Taverne Henri IV Map 2, F7. 13 place du Pont-Neuf, $1^{er}$. ⓂPont-Neuf. Mon–Fri 11.30am–9.30pm, Sat noon–5pm; closed Aug.** An old-style wine bar that's probably changed little since Yves Montand used to come here with Simone Signoret. It's best to drop in at lunchtime when it's at its buzziest, usually full of lawyers from the nearby Palais de Justice tucking into generous ham and cheese platters and toasted sandwiches.

## Restaurants

**Brasserie de l'Ile St-Louis Map 2, I8. 55 quai de Bourbon, $4^{e}$ Ⓣ01.43.54.02.59. ⓂPont-Marie. Thurs–Tues noon–midnight.** A bustling brasserie with a rustic, dark-wood interior and a sunny terrace, and flirty waiters dishing out dollops of sauerkraut with ham and sausage and other brasserie staples (mains around €19).

**Mon Vieil Ami Map 2, I9. 69 rue St-Louis-en-l'Ile, $4^{e}$ Ⓣ01.40.46.01.35. ⓂPont-Marie. Wed–Sun 11.30am–2pm & 7–10.30pm.** Owned by Michelin-starred Alsatian chef Antoine Westermann, this charming little *bistrot* is a firm favourite with locals and those in the know. The cuisine is bold and zesty, using seasonal ingredients, and the wine list includes a fine selection of Alsatian vintages. The minimalist decor of chocolate browns and frosted-glass panels makes for a stylish backdrop. Reckon on around €40 for three courses.

# The Champs-Elysées and around



## Cafés and wine bars

**Angélina Map 2, B3. 226 rue de Rivoli, 1er. ⓂTuileries. Mon–Fri 8am–7pm, Sat & Sun 9.15am–7pm; closed Tues in July & Aug.** This elegant old *salon de thé*, with its murals, gilded stucco work and comfy leather armchairs, does the best hot chocolate in town – a generous jugful with whipped cream on the side is enough for two. The other house speciality is the Mont Blanc, a chestnut cream, meringue and whipped cream dessert.

**Café Jacquemart-André Map 7, I1. 158 bd Haussmann, 8e. ⓂSt-Philippe-du-Roule/Miromesnil. Daily 11.45am–5.30pm.** Part of the Musée Jacquemart-André, but with independent access, this is the most sumptuously appointed *salon de thé* in the city. Admire the ceiling frescoes by Tiepolo while savouring the fine pastries or salads. €9 for tea and pastry, set lunch €16.50.

**Café Véry (also known as Dame Tartine) Map 7, N6. Jardin des Tuileries, 1er. ⓂConcorde. Daily noon–11pm.** The best of a number of café-restaurants in the gardens, with tables outside under shady horse chestnuts, frequented by Louvre curators and other aesthetes. Snacks and more substantial meals available.

**Le Fouquet's Map 7, F3. 99 av des Champs-Elysées, 8e ⓣ01.47.23.70.60. ⓂGeorge-V. Daily 8am–1.30am.** Dating from 1899, *Le Fouquet's* is the favourite venue for celebrations after the annual César film awards. You can just enjoy a drink on the terrace, a prime spot for people-watching on the Champs, or sink into a red velvet banquette in the plush café-brasserie. You do pay well over the odds (coffee €8, mains €32–56), but then this is the Champs-Elysées.

## Restaurants

**La Maison de l'Aubrac Map 7, H4. 37 rue Marbeuf, 8e ⓣ01.42.89.66.09. ⓂFranklin-D.-Roosevelt. Daily 24hr.** Large photographs of prize-winning cattle from the restaurant's own farm in the Auvergne leave you in little doubt as to what to expect at this all-night restaurant, with its cosy, ranch-style wooden cubicles: very meaty country cuisine, such as *pot-au-feu* and sausage with *aligot* (creamy mashed potato and cheese). The most carnivorous of cravings should

## Gourmet restaurants

With its plethora of top **haute cuisine restaurants**, Paris is the perfect place to splash out on the meal of a lifetime. Among the most talked-about haute cuisine chefs at the moment are young Pascal Barbot at *L'Astrance* (see p.230) and Yannick Alléno at *Le Meurice* (see p.204), both known for their bold and innovative cuisine. Also highly rated is Alain Ducasse at the *Plaza-Athénée* hotel (see p.204); the first-ever chef to have been awarded six Michelin stars (shared between two restaurants), Ducasse swept like a tidal wave through the world of French cuisine in the early 1990s and hasn't looked back. Other greats include *Pierre Gagnaire* (see p.204), known for his experimental "molecular cuisine"; and more traditional *Taillevent* (see p.205). Over on the Left Bank, you'll find featured two relatively unusual establishments: the *Restaurant d'Hélène* (see p.221) stands out in having a female chef, the Ducasse-trained Hélène Darroze, while Alain Passard's *L'Arpège* (see p.223) eschews most meat in favour of superb fish and vegetable dishes.

Prices at most of these restaurants are often cheaper if you go at midday during the week, and some offer a set lunch *menu* for around €80–95 per person. In the evening, prices average at about €150, and there's no limit on the amount you can pay for top wines. Recently, some of the star chefs have made their fine cuisine more accessible to a wider range of customers by opening up less expensive, more casual, but still high-quality establishments. In addition to presiding over the *Plaza-Athénée*, for example, Alain Ducasse runs the *Aux Lyonnais bistrot* (see p.207). Hélène Darroze has her tapas-style *Salon d'Hélène* (see p.221) underneath the main restaurant, Pierre Gagnaire oversees the seafood restaurant *Gaya Rive Gauche* (see p.221), and Guy Savoy has his rôtisserie, *L'Atelier Maître Albert* (see p.216).

be satisfied by the *trilogie de viande* (*salade de boeuf*, *steak tartare* and *faux filet grillé sauce béarnaise*). There's also an impressive thousand-plus wines to choose from, with several available by the glass. Mains cost around €20.

**Le Meurice Map 2, B3.** ***Hôtel Meurice*****, 228 rue de Rivoli, 1er ⓣ01.44.58.10.55, ⓦwww.meuricehotel.com. ⓂTuileries/Concorde. Mon–Fri 12.30–2pm & 7.30–10pm; closed July & Aug for dinner.** This sumptuous three Michelin-starred restaurant, decorated by Philippe Starck in Louis XVI style, complete with ornate gildings and marble, wows diners with chef Yannick Alléno's adventurous cuisine. You might start with foie gras "iodized" in sugar bread, followed by veal sweetbreads with chestnuts, and finish with melted meringue with pink grapefruit and green apple jelly. *Menu dégustation* €220, à la carte around €200; drinks are extra. A set lunch menu is available at €78. Male diners are requested to wear a jacket at dinner.

**Pierre Gagnaire Map 7, G1.** ***Hôtel Balzac*****, 6 rue Balzac, 8e ⓣ01.58.36.12.50, ⓦwww.pierre-gagnaire.com. ⓂGeorge-V. Mon–Fri noon–1.30pm & 7.30–9.30pm, Sun 7.30–9.30pm.** Regularly judged among the top ten restaurants in the world by *Restaurant* magazine, *Pierre Gagnaire* is a gastronomic adventure. The tasting menu (€265) has nine courses, featuring such treats as sea bass with Breton prawns, pomegranate, lychee, white cabbage and passion fruit (and that's just one course). À la carte around €300, set lunch *menu* for €105.

**Plaza-Athénée Map 7, G5.** ***Hôtel Plaza-Athénée*****, 25 av Montaigne, 8e ⓣ01.53.67.65.00. ⓂAlma-Marceau. Mon–Wed 7.45–10.15pm, Thurs & Fri 12.45–2.15pm & 7.45–10.15pm; closed mid-July to end Aug.** One of Paris's top haute cuisine temples, run by Alain Ducasse, whose sublime and inventive offerings are likely to revive even the most jaded palate. The menu might include Bresse chicken with truffle sauce or prawns with Iranian caviar. The decor is Louis XV with a modern gloss and the service is exceptional. From about €200 per head.

**Le Relais de l'Entrecôte Map 7, G4. 15 rue Marbeuf, 8e ⓣ01.49.52.07.17. ⓂFranklin-D.-Roosevelt. Daily noon–2.30pm & 7–11.30pm.** Don't worry if a menu isn't forthcoming here – there isn't one. The only dish is *steak frites*, arguably the best in town and served with a delicious sauce, the ingredients of which are a closely kept secret. Make sure you leave room for seconds. Reckon on around €25 a head, including a salad first course, or a little extra with dessert (and these are well worth investigating). No reservations are taken so you may have to queue, or arrive early. Second branch at 20bis rue St-Benoit, 6e (ⓂSt-Germain-des-Prés).

**Taillevent Map 7, G2. 15 rue Lamennais, 8e ⓣ01.44.95.15.01, ⓦwww.taillevent.com. ⓂGeorge-V. Mon–Fri noon–2.15pm & 7.15–11pm; closed Aug.** One of Paris's finest gourmet restaurants. Alain Solivérès' Provencal-influenced cuisine is outstanding, with the emphasis on the classic rather than the experimental; sample dishes include spelt risotto with frogs' legs, and saddle of lamb with braised artichokes in wine. The main dining room is wood-panelled and decorated in soothing colours, and the attentive and charming waiting staff manage to make you feel like VIPs. Set menus are €140 and €190, and there's also a special set lunch for €80.

# The Grands Boulevards and around

## Cafés and wine bars

**A Priori Thé Map 2, E2. 35 Galerie Vivienne, 2e. ⓂBourse. Mon–Sat 9am–6pm, Sun 12.30–6.30pm.** An attractive little *salon de thé* in a charming *passage*, with some tables spilling into the arcade itself. You can get crumbly home-made scones and tea, plus more substantial dishes at lunch.

**L'Arbre à Cannelle Map 3, G8. 57 passage des Panoramas, 2e. ⓂGrands-Boulevards. Mon–Sat 11.30am–6pm.** Tucked away in an attractive *passage*, between an autograph dealer and a stamp shop, this early twentieth-century *salon de thé* with its exquisite wood panelling, frescoes and painted ceilings makes an excellent spot to treat yourself to salads and quiches, and desserts such as pear and chocolate tart.

**Le Dénicheur Map 2, H3. 4 rue Tiquetonne, 2e ⓣ01.42.21.31.03. ⓂEtienne-Marcel. Tues–Sat 12.30–3.30pm & 7pm–midnight, Sun noon–4pm. Closed 2 weeks in Aug.** This chic, gay-friendly café-restaurant is a hodgepodge of wacky decor: bright-blue globes above, garden gnomes and bin-shaped lampshades all about. Salads are the main event here, though you can find lasagne, ravioli, gazpacho and *tartines* too, all at reasonable prices. Big, popular weekend brunches.

**Juvéniles Map 2, E3. 47 rue de Richelieu, 1er. Ⓜ Palais Royal-Musée du Louvre. Mon 7.30–11pm, Tues–Sat 11am–11pm, Sun noon–2pm.** A very popular, tiny wine *bistrot* run by a Scot. Wine costs from €15 a bottle and there are usually around ten varieties available by the glass (from €4); *plats du jour* cost around €16, and cheese platters and tapas-style dishes are also available.

**Ladurée Map 7, M4. 16 rue Royal, 8e. Ⓜ Madeleine. Mon–Sat 8.30am–7pm.** Lavishly decorated with gilt-edged mirrors and ceiling frescoes, this classy tearoom is renowned for its melt-in-your-mouth macaroons. The light-as-air meringues and *millefeuilles* are almost as good.

**Verlet Map 2, D4. 256 rue St-Honoré, 1er. Ⓜ Palais Royal-Musée du Louvre. Mon–Sat 9.30am–6.30pm.** The intoxicating aroma of more than 30 types of coffee from all over the world, including gourmet options like Jamaican Blue Mountain, greet you inside this long-established coffee merchant and café, with its wood furnishings, green leather benches and stacks of tea caddies. If you're having trouble deciding, opt for one of the house's own rich and smoky blends; there's a good selection of teas and light snacks too.

## Restaurants

**Bistrot des Victoires Map 2, E3. 6 rue de la Vrillère, 1er ☎ 01.42.61.43.78. Ⓜ Bourse. Daily 9am–11pm.** Located just behind the chic place des Victoires, but very reasonably priced for the area, this charming, old-fashioned *bistrot* with zinc bar, mustard-coloured walls, globe lamps and dark-purple banquettes serves good old standbys such as *confit de canard* and *poulet rôti* for around €11, as well as huge salads and hearty *tartines* such as the *savoyarde* (with bacon, potatoes and Gruyère). Sun brunch for €15.50.

**Dilan Map 2, G3. 13 rue Mandar, 2e ☎ 01.40.26.81.04. Ⓜ Les Halles/Sentier. Mon–Sat noon–3pm & 7.30–11.30pm.** An excellent-value Kurdish restaurant, with a cosy, kilim-strewn interior. You could do worse than start with the delicious *babaqunuc* (stuffed aubergines), followed by *beyti* (spiced minced beef wrapped in pastry, with yoghurt, tomato sauce and bulgar wheat). Mains cost from €12; around €11 for half a litre of Kurdish Yakut wine.

**Drouant Map 2, D2. 16–18 place Gaillon, 2e ☎ 01.42.65.15.16. Daily noon–3pm & 7pm–midnight. Ⓜ Opéra.** Legendary restaurant

*Drouant*, the setting for the annual Goncourt prize, has renowned Alsatian chef Antoine Westermann at the helm. The main courses are well prepared and fairly traditional, but it's really the starters and desserts that steal the show – you get four of each served in small portions and grouped around a theme, such as "four corners of the world". Starters cost €25, mains €30 (€20 at lunch), desserts €13, and there's a lunchtime *menu* for €43 and a €17.50 *plat du jour.*

**Gallopin Map 2, F2. 40 rue Notre-Dame-des-Victoires, 2e ⓣ01.42.36.45.38. ⓜBourse. Daily noon–midnight.** An utterly endearing old brasserie, with all its original brass and mahogany fittings and a beautiful painted glass roof in the back room. The place heaves at lunchtime with journalists, business people and glamorous Parisiennes. The classic French dishes, especially the *foie gras maison*, are well above par; *menus* range from €24.50 to €36.

**Higuma Map 2, D3. 32bis rue Ste Anne, 1er ⓣ01.47.03.38.59. ⓜPyramides. Daily 11.30am–10pm.** The pick of the numerous Japanese canteens in this area, *Higuma* serves up cheap and filling staples like pork *katsu* curry, *yaki udon* and *gyosa*. Sit at the counter and watch the chefs at work from close quarters, or cram onto one of the tiny tables further back. It's very popular and you may have to queue at lunchtime. *Menus* €11–12.

**Aux Lyonnais Map 3, F8. 32 rue St-Marc, 2e ⓣ01.42.96.65.04. ⓜBourse/ Richelieu-Drouot. Tues–Fri noon–2pm & 7.30–11pm, Sat 7.30–11pm.** This old *bistrot*, with its *belle époque* tiles and mirrored walls, has been taken over by star chefs Alain Ducasse and Thierry de la Brosse. They've preserved the old-fashioned ambience and done wonders with the cuisine, serving up delicious Lyonnais fare – try the *quenelles* (light and delicate fish dumplings) followed by the heavenly Cointreau soufflé for dessert. Service is friendly and there's a buzzy atmosphere. Three-course set *menu* €34.

**Le Vaudeville Map 3, G9. 29 rue Vivienne, 2e ⓣ01.40.20.04.62. ⓜBourse. Daily noon–3pm & 7pm–1am; breakfast Mon–Sat 7–11am.** There's often a queue to get a table at this lively, late-night Art Deco brasserie, attractively decorated with marble and mosaics. Dishes include tuna steak with chorizo, and lamb with *boulangère* potatoes. Set *menus* €24–32, main course and a coffee €18.50.

# Beaubourg and Les Halles

## Cafés and wine bars

**Café Beaubourg Map 2, H5. 43 rue St-Merri, 4e. ⓂRambuteau/Hôtel-de-Ville. Mon–Thurs & Sun 8am–1am, Sat 8am–2am.** A seat under the expansive awnings of this stylish café, bearing the trademark sweeping lines of designer Christian de Portzamparc, is one of the best places for people-watching on the Pompidou Centre's piazza. It's also a good place for a lazy Sunday brunch – €24 for the full works (hash browns, sausage, scrambled eggs, bread and jams, and drinks).

**Le Café des Initiés Map 2, F4. 3 place des Deux-Ecus, 1er. ⓂChâtelet-Les-Halles/Louvre. Mon–Sat 7.30am–1am.** A smart yet intimate and comfortable café, with dark-red leather banquettes, wood floor and arty photos on the wall. Locals knock back a quick espresso at the zinc bar or linger on the terrace with an aperitif. Salads and dishes such as grilled king prawns, steak *tartare* (around €15) and home-made apple crumble are available from noon till late evening.

**A la Cloche des Halles Map 2, F4. 28 rue Coquillière, 1er. ⓂChâtelet-Les Halles/Louvre. Mon–Fri noon–10pm, Sat noon–4pm.** The bell hanging over this little wine bar is the one that used to mark the end of trading in the market halls, and the great ambience is owed to the local vendors who spend their off-hours here. You are assured of some very fine wines, best sided with the *jambon d'Auvergne* or one of their delectable cheeses, all very reasonably priced.

## Restaurants

**Georges Map 2, H5. Centre Georges Pompidou, 4e ☎01.44.78.47.99. ⓂRambuteau/Hôtel-de-Ville. Wed–Mon noon–1am.** On the top floor of the Pompidou Centre, this trendy, ultra-minimalist restaurant commands stunning views over the rooftops of Paris and makes a stylish place for lunch or dinner; the fluid aluminium-swathed interior calls to mind a Frank Gehry museum. The fusion cuisine is passable, though overpriced (main courses from €30), but then that's not the main reason you come. Reservations are advisable for lunch and dinner.

**La Robe et le Palais Map 2, G6. 13 rue des Lavandières Ste-Opportune, 1er ☎01.45.08.07.41. ⓂChâtelet. Mon–Sat noon–2.30pm &**

**7.30–11pm.** Small, busy *restaurant à vins* serving traditional cuisine and a *tête*-boggling selection of 250 wines *au compteur* (priced according to how much you consume). Although the food here can be rough on your cholesterol level, it is excellently prepared. Reckon on around €40 a head for three courses without wine.

**La Tour de Montlhéry (Chez Denise) Map 2, F5. 5 rue des Prouvaires, 1er ⓣ01.42.36.21.82. ⓜLouvre-Rivoli/ Châtelet. Mon–Fri noon–3pm & 7.30pm–5am; closed mid-July to mid-Aug.** An old-style, late-night Les Halles *bistrot*, packed with diners sitting elbow to elbow at long tables and tucking into substantial meaty French dishes, such as *daube* of beef, *andouillette* (tripe sausages) and haddock in a *beurre blanc* sauce with perfectly cooked chips. Mains cost €20–25.

# The Marais

## Cafés and wine bars

**L'Apparemment Café Map 4, C9. 18 rue des Coutures-St-Gervais, 3e. ⓜSt-Sébastien-Froissart. Mon–Fri noon–2am, Sat 4pm–2am, Sun 12.30pm–midnight.** Chic, cosy café resembling a series of comfortable sitting rooms, with quiet corners and deep sofas. Recommended are the salads, which you compose yourself by ticking off your chosen ingredients and handing your order to the waiter. The popular Sunday brunch (until 4pm) costs €21.

**L'As du Falafel Map 4, B10. 34 rue des Rosiers, 4e. ⓜSt-Paul. Sun–Thurs noon–midnight.** The sign above the doorway of this falafel shop in the Jewish quarter reads "Toujours imité, jamais égalé" ("Always copied, but never equalled"), a boast that few would challenge, given the quality of the food and the queues outside. Falafels to take away cost only €5, or pay a bit more and sit in the buzzy little dining room.

**Café Charlot Map 4, C7. 38 rue de Bretagne, 3e. ⓜFilles-du-Calvaire. Daily 7am–2am.** You'll need to fight for a seat on the terrace of this smart, white-tiled café, a former boulangerie, which bursts at the seams on weekends with local hipsters and in-the-know tourists. The food – a mix of French and American standards – is not that special, but it's a great place for a drink and a spot of people-watching.

**Café Martini Map 4, D11. 11 rue du Pas de la Mule, 4e. ⓂSt-Paul. Daily 8.30am–2am. Happy hour 7–10pm.** Just off place des Vosges, but much more down-to-earth and patronized mostly by locals, this relaxing little café with low, wood-beamed ceiling, stone walls and jazz in the background is run by friendly staff and offers very reasonably priced food. €4–5 for sandwiches, cakes or a hot chocolate with kirsch; a small beer is €3.20.

**Le Loir dans la Théière Map 4, C11. 3 rue des Rosiers, 4e. ⓂSt-Paul. Mon–Fri 11am–7pm, Sat & Sun 10am–7pm.** Comfy, battered sofas and *Alice in Wonderland* murals create a homely atmosphere at this laid-back *salon de thé*, serving enormous portions of home-made cakes and excellent vegetarian quiches. Sunday brunch (€20) is particularly busy and queues for a table often stretch out the door.

**Mariage Frères Map 4, B10. 30 rue du Bourg-Tibourg, 4e. ⓂHôtel de Ville. Tues–Sun 3–7pm.** The ultimate tearoom, serving over five hundred varieties, and with no shortage of tempting pastries. The decor is elegant and faintly colonial while service is assured by handsome white-suited waiters. Reckon on around €18 for tea and pastries. Brunch is also available at weekends, though is steeply priced at €30–42.

**Le Petit Fer à Cheval Map 4, B10. 30 rue Vieille-du-Temple, 4e. ⓂSt-Paul. Mon–Fri 9am–2am, Sat & Sun 11am–2am; food served noon–midnight.** Very attractive, small *bistrot*/bar with original fin-de-siècle decor, including a marble-topped bar in the shape of a horseshoe (*fer à cheval*). It's a popular drinking spot, with agreeable wine, and you can have a snack in the little back room furnished with old wooden métro seats.

## Restaurants

**404 Map 4, A7. 69 rue des Gravilliers, 3e ⓣ01.42.74.57.81. ⓂArts-et-Métiers. Daily noon–midnight.** Very popular, trendy Moroccan restaurant, with a lanterned, dimly lit interior that screams colonialist romance. The standard North African fare here is good enough, but it's the Casbah fetish ambience you're paying for. Reckon on around €38 for three courses exclusive of drinks. Their famed weekend Berber Brunch requires reservations (Sat & Sun noon–4pm).

**Ambassade d'Auvergne Map 4, A8. 22 rue du Grenier St-Lazare, 3e ⓣ01.42.72.31.22. ⓂRambuteau. Daily noon–2pm &**

**7.30–11pm; closed last 2 weeks in Aug.** Suited, moustachioed waiters serve scrumptious Auvergnat cuisine that would have made Vercingétorix proud. There's a set menu for €38, but you may well be tempted by some of the house specialities, such as the roast *Marvejols* lamb. Among the after-dinner treats are a cheese platter and divine profiteroles.

**Au Bourguignon du Marais Map 4, B12. 52 rue François-Miron, 4e ⓣ01.48.87.15.40. ⓜSt-Paul. Tues–Sat noon–11pm; closed 2 weeks in Aug.** A warm, relaxed restaurant and *cave à vins* with attractive contemporary decor and tables outside in summer, serving excellent Burgundian cuisine (snails with parsley and garlic, *boeuf bourguignon*, pike perch with pinot noir), with carefully selected wines to match. Mains €15–25.

**Chez Marianne Map 4, B10. 2 rue des Hospitalières-Saint-Gervais, 4e ⓣ01.42.72.18.86. ⓜSt-Paul. Daily noon–10.30pm.** A Marais institution, this homely place with cheery red awnings specializes in Middle Eastern and Jewish delicacies. A platter of mezze for two (from €26) might include tabbouleh, aubergine purée, chopped liver and hummus, and there's a good selection of wines. You can sit outside in fine weather, and the place stays open throughout the summer.

**Chez Omar Map 4, C7. 47 rue de Bretagne, 3e ⓣ01.42.72.36.26. ⓜArts-et-Métiers. Daily except Sun lunch noon–2.30pm & 7–11.30pm.** No reservations are taken at this popular North African couscous restaurant, but it's no hardship to wait for a table at the bar, taking in the handsome old brasserie decor, fashionable crowd and spirited atmosphere. Portions are copious and the couscous light and fluffy. The delicious *merguez* (spicy sausage) costs €13, or go all out for the royal (€24). No credit cards.

**Le Dôme du Marais Map 4, B10. 53 rue des Francs-Bourgeois, 4e ⓣ01.42.74.54.17. ⓜRambuteau. Tues 7–10.30pm, Wed–Sat noon–2pm & 7–10.30pm; closed 3 weeks in Aug.** A charming, romantic restaurant in an unusual setting: a high-ceilinged Neoclassical glass-domed room decorated with red and gold leaf, formerly part of a bank. The refined French cuisine rises to the occasion, and there are unexpected extras like *amuse-bouches* and palette-cleansers. Perfect for a special meal without paying over the odds, but make sure you book a seat under the dome, otherwise you might end up in the less interesting ante-room. Around €45 for three courses.

**L'Enoteca Map 4, C12. 25 rue Charles-V, 4e ⓣ01.42.78.91.44. ⓜSt-Paul. Daily noon–11.30pm; closed for a week in Aug.** Situated in an old Marais building, this fashionable Italian *bistrot à vins* boasts an impressive wine list (22 pages). Food doesn't take a back seat either: choose from an array of *antipasti*, fresh pasta or more substantial dishes like stuffed courgettes or *cochon de lait* (spit-roasted pork) for €15–20.

**Le Pamphlet Map 4, D8. 38 rue Debelleyme, 3e ⓣ01.42.72.39.24. ⓜFilles du Calvaire. Mon & Sat 8–10.30pm, Tues–Fri noon–2pm & 8–10.30pm; closed 2 weeks in mid-Aug.** One of the Marais' best offerings, where the cuisine is *haute*, but the prices aren't. The excellent-value three-course menu at €35 might include such delights as duck croquettes followed by a main course of pork fillet with chorizo, prunes and a lentil salad. Although billed as a *bistrot*, it's more like a comfy restaurant, with upholstered chairs, and soothing taupe and rust-red decor.

**Le Potager du Marais Map 4, A9. 22 rue Rambuteau, 4e ⓣ01.42.74.24.66. ⓜRambuteau. Mon–Fri noon–3pm & 6–10.30pm, Sat & Sun noon–10.30pm.** Come early or book in advance for a place at this tiny vegetarian restaurant, with only 25 covers at a long communal table. The ingredients are all organic and there's plenty for vegans and those with gluten allergies, too. Dishes include goat's cheese with honey, "crusty" quinoa burger and ravioli with basil. Set menu €25.

**Robert et Louise Map 4, B10. 64 rue Vieille du Temple, 4e. ⓜHôtel-de-Ville/Rambuteau. Tues & Wed 7–11pm, Thurs–Sun noon–2.30pm & 7–11pm.** This gem has an open kitchen, smoky wood fire, copper cooking utensils hanging from the walls, and hearty, good-value fare like coarse country pâté and lamb shank, all of which gives it the feel of a rustic rural inn from the 1950s magically transferred to the centre of contemporary Paris. Lunchtime *formule* €12, mains around €18.

**Le Rouge Gorge Map 4, C12. 8 rue St-Paul, 4e ⓣ01.48.04.75.89. ⓜSt-Paul. Mon–Sat noon–3pm & 7–11pm; closed last fortnight in Aug.** A small, charming *restaurant à vins* with bare stone walls and wood beams, and jazz or classical music playing in the background. It's devoted to exploring a wide range of wines: one week it might be Corsica, the next Spain or the Loire, and the theme is taken up in the frequently changing menu. Mains around €18. If you're taken with a particular wine you can buy a bottle from the downstairs cellar to take home.

# Bastille and around

## Cafés and wine bars

**Le Baron Rouge Map 4, G14. 1 rue Théophile-Roussel, corner place d'Aligre market, 12e. ⓂLedru-Rollin. Tues–Fri 10am–2pm & 5–10pm, Sat 10am–10pm, Sun 10.30am–3.30pm.** This popular and inexpensive *bar à vins* is as close as you'll find to the spit-on-the-floor, saloon stereotype of the old movies. If it's crowded inside you can join the locals on the pavement and stand around the wine barrels lunching on *saucisson*, mussels or Cap Ferret oysters washed down with a glass of Muscadet.

**Café des Anges Map 4, F11. 66 rue de la Roquette, 11e. ⓂBastille. Mon–Sat 8am–2am.** A friendly, low-key corner café hung with old photos, great for cheap and filling dishes – burgers, veggie lasagne, salads and quiches – and a popular place for evening drinks.

**Café de l'Industrie Map 4, F11. 16 rue St-Sabin, 11e. ⓂBastille. Daily 10am–2am. Food served noon till late evening.** One of the best Bastille cafés (actually two cafés, across the road from each other), packed out at lunch and every evening. There are rugs on the floor around solid old wooden tables, mounted rhinoceros heads, old black-and-white photos on the walls and a young, unpretentious crowd enjoying the comfortable absence of minimalism. Simple *plats du jour* such as sausage and mash and pasta dishes cost around €9. The waitresses are charming, though service can be slow.

**Pause Café Map 4, G12. 41 rue de Charonne, corner rue Keller, 11e. ⓂLedru-Rollin. Mon–Sat 8am–2am, Sun 8.45am–8pm.** This place could be called "Pose Café", given its popularity with the *quartier*'s young and fashionable (sunglasses are worn at all times) who bag the pavement tables at lunch and apéritif time. Service is predictably insouciant. *Plats du jour* around €13.

## Restaurants

**A la Biche au Bois Map 4, off F14. 45 av Ledru-Rollin, 11e ☎01.43.43.34.38. ⓂGare de Lyon.**

**Mon 7–11pm, Tues–Fri noon–2pm & 7–11pm; closed 4 weeks July–Aug.** The queues leading out through the conservatory at the front are a strong indicator of the popularity of this restaurant, which mixes charming service with keenly priced, well-produced food. The house speciality is a huge and rich *coq au vin*, and you can start off with a pâté or *terrine*. Mains around €18.

**Bistrot Paul Bert Map 4, I13. 18 rue Paul Bert, 11e ⓣ01.43.72.24.01. ⓂFaidherbe-Chaligny. Tues–Sat noon–2pm & 7.30–11pm; closed 3 weeks in Aug.** A quintessential Parisian *bistrot*, with the menu chalked up on the board, little wooden tables and white tablecloths, tobacco-stained ceiling, and old posters and paintings on the mustard-coloured walls. A mix of locals and visitors flock here for the cosy, friendly ambience and high-quality simple fare such as *poulet rôti* as well as more sophisticated dishes such as guinea fowl with morel mushrooms. Reckon on around €35 a head for dinner; the wine list is reasonably priced, with an excellent selection of familiar and rarer vintages.

**Le Bistrot du Peintre Map 4, G12. 116 av Ledru-Rollin, 11e ⓣ01.47.00.34.39. ⓂLedru-Rollin. Mon–Sat 7am–2am, Sun 10am–8pm.** A charming, traditional *bistrot*, with small tables jammed together beneath faded Art Nouveau frescoes and wood panelling. The emphasis is on hearty Auvergne cuisine, with *plats* for around €15.

**L'Encrier Map 4, off F14. 55 rue Traversière, 11e ⓣ01.44.68.08.16. ⓂLedru-Rollin. Mon–Fri noon–2.15pm & 7.30–11pm, Sat 7.30–11pm.** The simple interior of exposed brick walls and wood beams complements the inexpensive (under €30 a head), homely fare served up by pleasant, helpful staff in this little restaurant near the Viaduc des Arts. The food has a slight south-western influence and might include goose breast in honey or steak and morel mushrooms.

**Le Train Bleu Map 5, M2. Gare de Lyon, 12e ⓣ01.43.43.09.06. ⓂGare de Lyon. Daily 11.30am–3pm & 7–11pm.** *Le Train Bleu*'s opulent decor is straight out of a bygone golden era – everything drips with gilt, and chandeliers hang from frescoed ceilings. The traditional French cuisine has a hard time living up to all this, but is more than acceptable, if a tad overpriced. The set menu is €52, including half a bottle of wine; for *à la carte* reckon on €70.

**Au Vieux Chêne Map 4, I13. 7 rue du Dahomey, 11e ⓣ01.43.71.67.69. ⓂFaidherbe-Chaligny. Mon–Fri noon–2pm & 8–10.30pm, Sat 8–10.30pm; closed**

**for a week in July and 2 weeks in Aug.** An excellent *bistrot* with fresh flowers, shelves heaving with books and charming staff. The kitchen shows considerable flair: you could try smoked haddock on a bed of carrots and lentils with a lemon-butter sauce, followed by a perfect *tarte tartin*. The *menus* – lunchtime €13.50/17 for two/three courses, dinner €28/33 – are a steal considering the quality of the food.

**Waly Fay Map 4, H12. 6 rue Godefroy-Cavaignac, 11ᵉ ⓣ01.40.24.17.79. ⓜCharonne/ Faidherbe-Chaligny. Mon–Sat noon–2pm & 7.30–11pm; closed last 2 weeks of Aug.** A West African restaurant with a cosy, stylish atmosphere. Smart, young Parisians come here to dine on perfumed, richly spiced stews and other West African delicacies at a moderate price (mains around €13).

# The Quartier Latin and the southeast

## Cafés and wine bars

**Café de la Mosquée Map 2, I13. 39 rue Geoffroy-St-Hilaire, 5ᵉ. ⓜMonge. Daily 9am–midnight.** Drink mint tea and eat sweet cakes in the courtyard of the Paris mosque – a haven of calm. The indoor salon has a beautiful Arabic interior, where meals are served for around €15 upwards. There's even a hammam-massage-meal option.

**Café de la Nouvelle Mairie Map 2, F12. 19 rue des Fossés-St-Jacques, 5ᵉ. ⓜCluny-La Sorbonne/RER Luxembourg. Mon, Wed & Fri 9am–8pm, Tues & Thurs 9am–midnight.** Sleek café-wine bar with a relaxed feel and a university clientele (note it's shut at weekends). Serves good food like lamb curry or linguine, as well as *assiettes* of cheese or charcuterie (all around €10). On warm days there are outside tables on the picturesque square.

**L'Ecritoire Map 2, F10. 3 place de la Sorbonne, 5ᵉ. ⓜCluny-La Sorbonne/RER Luxembourg. Daily 7am–midnight.** This classic university café has outside tables right beside the Sorbonne.

**La Fourmi Ailée Map 2, G9. 8 rue du Fouarre, 5ᵉ. ⓜMaubert-Mutualité. Daily noon–11pm.** Simple, filling fare is served in this relaxed *salon de thé*. A high, mural-painted ceiling and background jazz contribute to the atmosphere. Around €12 for a *plat*.

**Les Pipos Map 2, G11. 2 rue de l'Ecole-Polytechnique, 5e. Ⓜ Maubert-Mutualité/Cardinal-Lemoine. Mon–Sat 8.30am–1am; closed 2 weeks in Aug.** This antique bar has a decor that's heavy on old wood, and a local clientele. Serves wines from €5 a glass along with simple plates of Auvergnat charcuterie, cheese and the like (€10–15).

**Le Reflet Map 2, F10. 6 rue Champollion, 5e. Ⓜ Cluny-La Sorbonne. Daily 10am–2am.** This cinema café has a strong flavour of the *nouvelle vague*, with its scruffy black decor and rickety tables packed with artsy film-goers. Perfect for a drink, perhaps accompanied by a steak or quiche from the blackboard specials, either side of a film at one of the arts cinemas on rue Champollion.

**Le Verre à Pied Map 2, H14. 118bis rue Mouffetard, 5e. Ⓜ Monge. Tues–Sat 9am–8.30pm, Sun 9am–3.30pm.** Deeply old-fashioned market bar where traders take their morning *vin rouge*, or sit down to eat a *plat du jour* for €11. Some have been doing it so long they've got little plaques on their tables.

## Restaurants

**L'Atelier Maître Albert Map 2, H9. 1 rue Maitre Albert, 5e ⓣ 01.56.81.30.01. Ⓜ Maubert-Mutualité. Mon–Wed noon–2.30pm & 6.30–11.30pm, Thurs & Fri noon–2.30pm & 6.30pm–1am, Sat 6.30pm–1am, Sun 6.30–11.30pm.** One of celebrity chef Guy Savoy's ventures, this rôtisserie looks like a contemporary designer's take on a medieval château, and the speciality is spit-roast meat. You can find lighter dishes, however: perhaps marinated tuna with carrot and seafood jelly followed by spit-roast sole with a herb risotto then grapefruit terrine with a tea sauce. There's a lunch *menu* at €28, or €35 at dinner but you'll pay double that for dining à la carte.

**L'Avant Goût Map 5, G9. 37 rue Bobillot, 13e ⓣ 01.45.81.14.06. Ⓜ Place d'Italie. Tues–Sat 12.30–2pm & 7.45–10.45pm.** Small neighbourhood restaurant with a big reputation for exciting modern French cuisine (think classic ingredients with some spices and surprises) and wines to match. Cool contemporary decor, bright red leather banquettes, and superb value *menus* (lunch €14, dinner €31).

**Le Bambou Map 5, off K9. 70 rue Baudricourt, 13e ⓣ 01.45.70.91.75. Ⓜ Tolbiac. Tues–Sun 11.45am–3.30pm & 6.45–10.30pm.** Tiny Asian-quarter restaurant crammed with punters, French and Vietnamese alike, tucking into sublime, inexpensive Vietnamese food. Serves giant portions of powerful pho soups, and a full menu of delicious specialities. Last orders at 10.30pm, but you can stay till midnight.

**Brasserie Balzar Map 2, F10. 49 rue des Ecoles, 5e ⓣ01.43.54.13.67. ⓂMaubert-Mutualité. Daily 8am–11.30pm.** This classic, high-ceilinged brasserie with its attentive, suited watiers feels almost intimidatingly Parisian – though if you're unlucky, or eat early, the tourist clientele can spoil the Left Bank mood. À la carte is around €40.

**Le Buisson Ardent Map 2, I11. 25 rue Jussieu, 5e ⓣ01.43.54.93.02. ⓂJussieu. Mon–Fri noon–2pm & 7.30–10pm, Sat 5.30–10pm; closed 2 weeks in Aug.** Generous helpings of first-class cooking with vivacious touches: think *velouté* of watermelon followed by a perfectly cooked sea bream. The dining room is high-ceilinged, panelled and muralled but the atmosphere is never less than convivial. Lunch *menu* €15, dinner €29. Reservations recommended.

**Chez Gladines Map 5, F9. 30 rue des Cinq-Diamants, 13e ⓣ01.45.80.70.10. ⓂCorvisart. Mon & Tues noon–3pm & 7pm–midnight; Wed–Sun noon–3pm & 7pm–1am.** This tiny, Basque-run corner *bistrot* is always warm, welcoming and packed with young people. Serves excellent wines and rich Basque and southwest dishes such as *magret de canard*. Giant salads cost under €10, and you'll pay less than €20 for a (very) full meal.

**Les Cinq Saveurs d'Anada Map 2, H12. 72 rue du Cardinal-Lemoine, 5e ⓣ01.43.29.58.54. ⓂCardinal-Lemoine. Tues–Sun noon–2.30pm & 7.30–10.30pm.** Airy and informal restaurant serving delicious organic vegetarian food. Salads (€8) are good, as are more robust dishes such as tofu soufflé or *confit* of tempeh with ginger (around €14–18).

**L'Ecurie Map 2, G11. 58 rue de la Montagne-Ste-Geneviève, cnr rue Laplace, 5e ⓣ01.46.33.68.49. ⓂMaubert-Mutualité/Cardinal-Lemoine. Mon–Sat noon–3pm & 7pm–midnight, Sun 7pm–midnight.** Shoe-horned into a former stables, this family-run restaurant is bustling and very lovable. Outside tables provide a few extra seats, but not many, so book ahead. Expect well-cooked meat dishes served without flourishes – grilled with *frites*, mostly – for less than €20.

**Perraudin Map 2, F11. 157 rue St-Jacques, 5e ⓣ01.46.33.15.75. RER Luxembourg. Mon–Fri noon–2pm & 7.30–10.15pm; closed**

**last 2 weeks in Aug.** One of the classic *bistrots* of the Left Bank, featuring enjoyable homely cooking. The place is brightly lit, packed and thick with Parisian chatter. Lunch *menu* at €18, evening *menu* at €28.

**Le Petit Pontoise Map 2, H10. 9 rue de Pontoise, 5e ⓣ01.43.29.25.20. ⓜMaubert-Mutualité. Daily noon–2.30pm & 7-10.30pm.** This relaxed, young *bistrot* is as authentically Parisian as you can get this close to the river: lace café-curtains, little wooden tables, a bar in one corner and specials on the black-board – salad of haricot beans with prawns, lamb steak and duck breast. Good, reasonably priced wines; outstanding puddings. Expect to pay around €35 a head.

**Le Pré-Verre Map 2, G10. 8 rue Thénard, 5e ⓣ01.43.54.59.47. ⓜMaubert-Mutualité. Tues–Sat noon–2pm & 7.30–10.30pm; closed 3 weeks in Aug.** This sleek *bistrot à vins* has a great wine list, and interesting modern French food with a few judiciously oriental touches – you might find swordfish on blue poppy seeds and artichoke, or chicken with avocado and ginger. *Menus* at €28.50, or just €13.50 at lunch.

**Le Reminet Map 2, H9. 3 rue des Grands-Degrés, 5e ⓣ01.44.07.04.24. ⓜMaubert-Mutualité. Mon & Thurs–Sun noon–3pm & 7.30–11pm; closed 2 weeks in Aug.** This artful little *bistrot*-restaurant shows its class through small touches such as snowy-white tablecloths and fancy chandeliers. Imaginative sauces grace high-quality traditional French ingredients. Gastronomic *menu* at around €50, but you can get à la carte for about half that, and the lunch *menu* is a bargain at €14.

# St-Germain

## Cafés and wine bars

**Bar du Marché Map 2, E8. 75 rue de Seine, 6e. ⓜMabillon. Daily 7am–2am.** A thrumming café where the *serveurs* are cutely kitted out in flat caps and aprons. It's a fashionable place for a *kir* or a coffee but you do pay a little extra for the colours and smells of the rue de Buci market on the doorstep.

**Bistrot des Augustins Map 2, F8. 39 quai de Grands-Augustins, 6e. ⓜSt-Michel. Daily 10am–midnight.** That a wine bar this friendly and traditional should be found on the riverbank between the Pont Neuf and place St-Michel is quite incredible. Serves good charcuterie, salads and hot *gratins*, all for around €10, and filling *tartines* – perfect with a glass of wine.

**Café de la Mairie Map 2, D9. 8 place St-Sulpice, 6e. ⓂSt-Sulpice. Mon–Sat 7am–2am.** A peaceful, pleasant café on the sunny north side of this gorgeous square, right opposite the church of St-Sulpice. Perfect for basking at an outdoor table with a coffee or an apéritif, and admiring the neighbourhood's beautiful people.

**Café du Musée d'Orsay Map 2, B5. 1 rue de Bellechasse, 7e. RER Musée-d'Orsay/ⓂSolférino. Tues–Sun 9.30am–5pm.** The Musée d'Orsay's rooftop café offers one of the city's quirkier views – over the Seine and towards Montmartre – seen through the giant clock face dominating the room. Serves snacks and drinks, with a wonderful outdoor terrace for sunny days.

**Le Flore Map 2, D8. 172 bd St-Germain, 6e. ⓂSt-Germain-des-Prés. Daily 7am–1.30am.** The great rival and immediate neighbour of the equally famous (and rather similar) *Les Deux Magots*, with a trendier and distinctly more local clientele. There's a unique hierarchy: tourists on the *terrasse*, beautiful people inside, intellectuals upstairs. Sartre, de Beauvoir, Camus and Marcel Carné used to hang out here. Serves an especially good hot chocolate.

**La Palette Map 2, E7. 43 rue de Seine, 6e. ⓂOdéon. Mon–Sat 9am–2am.** This once-famous Beaux-Arts student hangout is now frequented by art dealers, though it's still very relaxed, and attracts a trendy young crowd in the evenings. The decor is superb, including, of course, a large selection of paint-spattered palettes hanging on the walls. There's a roomy *terrasse* outside, and some good daily specials on the menu.

**Au Petit Suisse Map 2, E10. 16 rue de Vaugirard, 6e. RER Luxembourg/ⓂCluny-La Sorbonne. Mon–Sat 7am–midnight, Sun 7am–11.30pm.** The perfect retreat from the Jardin du Luxembourg, with everything you'd need from a café: an outdoor terrace; an in-house *tabac*; a two-hundred-year history; an Art Deco interior; a menu of sandwiches and *plats du jour*; and a mezzanine level that's made for people-watching.

**Veggie Map 2, C6. 38 rue de Verneuil, 7e. ⓂSolférino. Mon–Fri**

**9.30am–3pm, summer also open 5–7.30pm.** This chichi deli near the Musée d'Orsay offers a small selection of organic vegetarian foods to eat in or take away – think fresh salads and *tartes*, as well as more refined grocery goods. Pricey, but very tempting.

## Restaurants

**Allard Map 2, F8. 41 rue St-André-des-Arts, 6e ☎01.43.26.48.23. Ⓜ Odéon. Daily noon–2.30pm & 7.30–11pm; closed Mon & Sun in Aug.** Expect the menu at this proudly unreconstructed Parisian restaurant to be meaty and rich rather than sophisticated or imaginative – and you'll be very satisfied. The atmosphere is unimpeachably antique – apart from the international clientele. From around €35.

**L'Atlas Map 2, E8. 11 rue de Buci, 6e ☎01.40.51.26.30. Ⓜ Mabillon. Daily 6.30am–1am.** Despite a few Art Deco details, the decor at *L'Atlas* is functional rather than classic, but that's half the charm of this unpretentious market brasserie. Good seafood, and simple, meaty main dishes from €14.

**Brasserie Lipp Map 2, D8. 151 bd St-Germain, 6e ☎01.45.48.53.91. Ⓜ St-Germain-des-Prés. Daily noon–12.45am.** One of the most celebrated of all the classic Paris brasseries; the haunt of the very successful and very famous, with a wonderful 1900s wood-and-glass interior. There are decent *plats du jour*, including the famous *choucroute* (sauerkraut), for under €20, but exploring à la carte gets expensive.

**Le Christine Map 2, E8. 1 rue Christine, 6e ☎01.40.51.71.64. Ⓜ St-Germain-des-Prés. Mon–Fri noon–2.30pm & 6.30pm–midnight, Sat & Sun 6.30pm–midnight.** *Le Christine* is a cut above the usual *bistrot*. Yes, there are old beams and stone walls, but there are fresh flowers and contemporary paintings too. Yes, there's duck leg and *filet de boeuf* on the list of mains, but the veal liver comes with lemon spaghetti, and you might find something like poached eggs with violet artichokes among the starters. Menus from €34–58.

**L'Epigramme Map 2, E8. 9 rue de l'Eperon, 6e ☎01.44.41.00.09. Ⓜ Odéon. Tues–Sun noon–2.30pm & 7.30–11.30pm.** Rough stone walls, a terracotta floor, mirrors with the menu written on them and a window onto the kitchen indicate the emphasis here: quality French cooking, stripped bare of pretensions. The dining room is tiny, the reputation high and the prices reasonable (around €30, plus wine), so book well ahead.

**La Ferrandaise Map 2, E10. 8 rue de Vaugirard, 6e ⓣ01.43.26.36.36. ⓂSt-Germain-des-Prés. Mon–Thurs noon–2pm & 7.30–10.30pm, Fri noon–2pm & 7.30–11pm, Sat 7.30pm–midnight.** Don't be fooled by the arty photos of Ferrandaise-breed cows on the walls: it's about more than beef at this relaxed, airy restaurant near the Jardin du Luxembourg. You might have crab ravioli, oven-steamed pike-perch or the richest shoulder of lamb, followed by spiced strawberries in red wine. Evening *menu* €32.

**Gaya Rive Gauche Map 2, B7. 44 rue du Bac, 6e ⓣ01.45.44.73.73. ⓂRue du Bac. Mon–Sat noon–2.30pm & 7.30–11pm.** This hyper-designed, upscale mini-restaurant is the fishy satellite of celebrity chef Pierre Gagnaire's empire. There's plenty of his trademark inventiveness: *pressé* of skate with a bloody mary sauce; grilled swordfish on a bed of caramel, soya and Asian mushrooms. Prices are lowish for gastro-cuisine: around €90 a head with wine.

**Polidor Map 2, E10. 41 rue Monsieur-le-Prince, 6e ⓣ01.43.26.95.34. ⓂOdéon. Mon–Sat noon–2.30pm & 7pm–12.30am, Sun noon–11pm.** Eating at *Polidor* is a classic of Left Bank life. Open since 1845, it's bright and bustling with aproned waitresses and packed with noisy regulars until late in the evening. The menu features solid French classics, with mains like *confit de canard* or guinea fowl with *lardons* from around €13.

**Le Salon d'Hélène Map 2, B10. 4 rue d'Assas, 6e ⓣ01.42.22.00.11. ⓂSt-Sulpice/ Sèvres-Babylone. Tues–Sat 12.30–2.15pm & 7.30–10.15pm; closed Aug.** Celebrated chef Hélène Darroze's gastronomic, Michelin starred *Restaurant d'Hélène* (lunch *menus* from €52, evenings from €125) has a more relaxed ground-floor "salon", where you can find similarly imaginative, southern-European tinged dishes, in tapas portions. Don't let the lack of windows put you off: this is some of the most interesting cooking in Paris, at low prices for the quality – from €28 up to €105 for the tasting menu with wine. Book well in advance.

**La Tourelle Map 2, F9. 5 rue Hautefeuille, 6e ⓣ01.46.33.12.47. ⓂSt-Michel. Mon–Fri noon–3pm & 7–10.30pm, Sat 7–11.30pm; closed Aug.** This splendidly medieval little *bistrot* is packed into a low, stone-walled, convivial room. The meaty cuisine is fresh, simple and very traditional. Service is

particularly considerate and the three-course *menu* good value at €19. No reservations, so turn up and wait.

**Vagenende Map 2, E8. 142 bd St-Germain, 6e ⓣ01.43.26.68.18. ⓂMabillon. Daily noon–1am.** This Art Nouveau marvel is registered as a historic monument, all mirrors, marble pillars, chandeliers and dark wood that has been polished for decades to a lustrous glow. Worthwhile if you go for the ambience rather than the food – stick to the straightforward brasserie dishes (mains at €16–26) or seafood specials.

**Ze Kitchen Galerie Map 2, F8. 4 rue des Grands-Augustins, 6e ⓣ01.44.32.00.32. ⓂSt-Michel. Mon–Fri noon–2.30pm & 7–11pm, Sat 7–11pm.** Hovering halfway between restaurant and trendy art gallery in atmosphere, the food is equally studied, mixing Asian influences with contemporary Mediterranean cuisine – try gnochetti with squid and *nori*, or pork croquettes with Thai herbs. At dinner, expect to pay upwards of €60 for three courses, without wine.

# The Eiffel Tower quarter

## Cafés and wine bars

**Café Carlu Map 7, B7. Palais de Chaillot, 16e. ⓂIéna/Alma-Marceau. Mon, Wed & Fri–Sun 11am–7pm, Thurs 11am–9pm.** From its outdoor terrace, this museum café has phenomenal views across the river to the Eiffel Tower, opposite. Prices are only slightly inflated.

**Café du Marché Map 6, B4. 38 rue Cler, 7e. ⓂLa Tour-Maubourg. Mon–Sat 7am–midnight.** Big, busy café-brasserie in the middle of the rue Cler market, serving reasonably priced meals and chunky salads. There's outdoor seating, or a covered *terrasse* in winter.

**Tokyo Eat/Tokyo Self Map 7, E6. Palais de Tokyo, 16e ⓣ01.47.20.00.29. ⓂIéna/Alma-Marceau. Tues–Sun noon–1am, bar till 2am.** The restaurant inside the Site de Création Contemporaine is a self-consciously cool place to eat, with its futuristic, colourful decor, arty clientele and Mediterranean fusion menu. The quality is a bit patchy, however, and the prices somewhat inflated. The *Tokyo Self* café is a reliable bet for a drink and a snack, and has a more dressed-down vibe.

## Restaurants

**L'Arpège Map 6, E4. 84 rue de Varenne, 7e ⓣ01.45.05.09.06. ⓜVarenne. Mon–Fri noon–2.30pm & 8–11pm.** Alain Passard is one of France's great chefs – and he really pushes boundaries here by giving vegetables the spotlight. Dishes such as grilled turnips with chestnuts or duck with black sesame and orange brandy are astounding. The lunch *menu* costs €130 and the incredible *menu dégustation* an outrageous €320; you'll pay €200–300 à la carte. Reserve well in advance and dress up.

**Au Bon Accueil Map 7, F8. 14 rue de Monttessuy, 7e ⓣ01.47.05.46.11. ⓜDuroc/Vaneau. Mon–Fri noon–2.30pm & 7–10.30pm, Sat 7–10.30pm.** Set on something of a gastro-street in the shadow of the Eiffel Tower, this relaxed, modern wine-*bistrot* offers refined, well-turned-out dishes like a delicate salad of prawns, salmon and lemon verbena, and veal liver with Jerusalem artichoke purée. There are a few coveted outside tables. *Menus* at around €30, or expect to pay around €50 à la carte, with wine.

**Le Café du Commerce Map 6, off A8. 51 rue du Commerce, 15e ⓣ01.45.75.03.27. ⓜEmile-Zola. Daily noon–3pm & 7pm–midnight.** This classic restaurant dates from 1922, when it was a kind of workers' canteen, and it's still a buzzing place to eat, with the tables set on three storeys of galleries running round a central patio. Honest, high-quality meat is the speciality, with steaks from Limousin cows bought whole, and there's always a fish and vegetarian dish too. Expect to pay €15–20 for a *plat*, or a little under €30 for the *menu*, though the lunch *menu* is a bargain €15.

**La Fontaine de Mars Map 7, G8. 129 rue St-Dominique, 7e ⓣ01.47.05.46.44. ⓜLa Tour-Maubourg. Daily noon–2.30pm & 7.30–11pm.** Heavy, pink-checked tablecloths, leather banquettes, tiled floor, attentive service: this restaurant offers a quintessentially French atmosphere. The food is reliable, meaty southwestern French fare: think snails, *magret de canard* and delicious Basque *boudin* sausages. There are lovely outside tables opposite the old stone fountain, too – no wonder President Obama chose to eat here. Starters at €11–15, *plat du jour* €20, carafe of Beaujolais €12.

**Le Jules Verne Map 7, D8. Pilier Sud, Eiffel Tower, 7e ⓣ01.45.55.61.44. ⓜBir-Hakeim.**

**Daily noon–2pm & 7–10pm.** Dining halfway up the Eiffel Tower is enough of a draw in itself, but since Alain Ducasse's team took over in 2007, the ultra-luxe (but not overly heavy) gastronomic food and smart decor now match the setting. Best at dinner (€200), but cheaper for a weekday lunch (a mere €85). Reserve months in advance, and don't expect a window table.

**Aux Marchés du Palais Map 7, E6. 5 rue de la Manutention, 16e ⓣ01.47.23.52.80. Ⓜléna. Mon–Fri noon–2pm & 7.30–10.30pm, Sat 7.30–10.30pm.** Simple, traditionally styled *bistrot*, with sunny tables on the pavement opposite the side wall of the Palais de Tokyo. There's always a good *entrée* and *plat du jour* – you might find a creamy broccoli *velouté* followed by sturgeon fillet, Charolais steak or prawn risotto. You can eat very well for around €35, and there's nothing half as satifsying anywhere nearby.

**L'Os à Moelle 3 rue Vasco-de-Gama, 15e ⓣ01.45.57.27.27. ⓂLourmel. Tues–Sun noon–3pm & 7pm–midnight; closed 3 weeks in Aug.** The highlight of this relaxed *bistrot* is the €35 four-course *menu*, which brings you everything from Jerusalem artichoke and black truffle soup to fine steaks, via scallops and giant snails. There's an inexpensive lunch menu, or you could make your way across the road to *La Cave de l'Os à Moelle* (ⓣ01.45.57.28.88/28): at this no-frills offshoot you sit at communal tables, cut your own slice of *terrine* and help yourself to a steaming pot of stew (*menu* €22.50). Reserve well in advance at either.

**Au Petit Tonneau Map 6, C2. 20 rue Surcouf, 7e ⓣ01.47.05.09.01. ⓂInvalides. Daily noon–3pm & 7–11.30pm.** Madame Boyer runs this tiny, welcoming, *bistrot*-style restaurant with panache, cooking delicious traditional French cuisine with few concessions to modern fads. Wild mushrooms are a speciality, along with a free-range *coq-au-vin*. All prices are à la carte: under €10 for starters, around €25 for mains.

**Thoumieux Map 6, C2. 79 rue St-Dominique, 7e ⓣ01.47.05.49.75. ⓂLa Tour-Maubourg. Daily noon–2.30pm & 7–11pm.** This classic brasserie was recently taken over by the fashionable Costes-Pièges team and given a gastronomic makeover – while mostly leaving the much be-mirrored and banquetted Art

Deco interior blessedly intact. The food adds fancy flavours to big-hearted brasserie classics – imagine pork belly with Asian spices, or squid carbonara. Around €50 à la carte.

# Montparnasse

## Cafés and wine bars

**L'Entrepôt Map 6, E14. 7–9 rue Francis-de-Pressensé, 14^e^. Ⓜ Pernety. Mon–Sat noon–2am.** A spacious, relaxed café – part of an arty cinema – with particularly lovely outside seating in its green courtyard. Serves a great Sunday brunch (€25), has *plats du jour* for around €15–25, and holds occasional concerts in the evening.

**Le Select Map 6, H10. 99 bd du Montparnasse, 6^e^. Ⓜ Vavin. Daily 7am–2am, Fri & Sat till 4am.** If you want to visit one of the great Montparnasse cafés, as frequented by Picasso, Matisse, Henry Miller and F. Scott Fitzgerald, make it this one. It's the most traditional of them all and the prices aren't over-inflated. Only the brasserie-style food is disappointing.

## Restaurants

**La Coupole Map 6, H10. 102 bd du Montparnasse, 14^e^ Ⓣ 01.43.20.14.20. Ⓜ Vavin. Daily 8am–1am.** The largest and most enduring arty-chic Parisian brasserie, *La Coupole* remains a genuine institution, buzzing with conversation and clatter from the diners packed in tightly under the high, chandeliered roof. The menu runs from oysters to Welsh rarebit, with plenty of fishy and meaty classics in between. Evening *menu* at €30.50, but you can have two courses for €23.50 before 6pm and after 10pm.

**La Régalade 49 av Jean-Moulin, 14^e^ Ⓣ 01.45.45.68.58. Ⓜ Alésia. Mon 7.30–11.30pm, Tues–Fri noon–2.30pm & 7.30–11.30pm; closed Aug.** Diners at this renowned *bistrot* are packed cheek-by-jowl onto banquettes and café chairs, and the service can be slow, but that's all part of the joy of this quintessentially old-fashioned place, with its tiled floor and old pictures on the walls. Chef Bruno Doucet's dishes sound deceptively simple – beautifully sauced meats, for the most part – but the standard €32 *menu prix fixe* delivers a memorable meal. Well worth the trek out from the centre.

**La Rotonde Map 6, H10. 105 bd du Montparnasse, 6e ⓣ01.43.26.68.84. ⓜVavin. Daily 7.15am–2am.** One of the grand old Montparnasse establishments, frequented in its time by the full roll-call of pre-world war I artists and writers. Since those days it has moved upmarket, gaining a plush decor of red velvet and brass, and is now best visited for a reliable meal, served at almost any time of day or night. Mains cost around €30.

# Montmartre and around

## Cafés and wine bars

**Café des Deux Moulins Map 3, E3. 15 rue Lepic, 18e ⓣ01.42.54.90.50. ⓜBlanche. Mon–Sat 7am–2am, Sun 9am–2am.** Having seen its early-2000s heyday of fans on the trawl of *Amélie* lore (she waited tables here in the film), this diner-style café is back to what it always was: a down-to-earth neighbourhood hangout, preserved in a bright, charming 1950s interior. Sunday brunch is popular.

**L'Eté en Pente Douce Map 3, I2. 23 rue Muller, 18e (cnr rue Paul-Albert) ⓣ01.42.64.02.67. ⓜChâteau-Rouge. Daily noon–midnight.** The food is unspectacular (big salads and *plats* around €14), but the main reason for coming is to soak up the atmosphere: chairs and tables are set out on a terrace alongside the steps leading up to Sacré-Cœur.

**Le Progrès Map 3, G3. 1 rue Yvonne-Le Tac, 18e. ⓜAbbesses/Anvers. Daily 9am–2am.** Generous glazed windows overlook this crossroads at the heart of Abbesses, making this café something of a lighthouse for the young *bobos* of Montmartre. By day, a simple, relaxed café – serving reasonably priced meals and salads (€12–15) – by night, a pub-like venue.

**Le Relais de la Butte Map 3, G2. 12 rue Ravignan, 18e. ⓜAbbesses. Daily 8.30am–midnight.** Come for the outdoor café tables on the expansive terrace, with its amazing views over Paris. The food is unexceptional and only slightly overpriced: salads and *plats* for around €15.

**Le Sancerre Map 3, F3. 35 rue des Abbesses, 18e. ⓜAbbesses. Daily 7am–2am.** A much-loved and always thrumming Montmartre hangout under the southern slope of Montmartre, with a row of outside tables perfect for watching the world go by. The food can be disappointing.

## Restaurants

**Café Burq Map 3, F2. 6 rue Burq, 10e ☎01.42.52.81.27. Ⓜ Abbesses. Mon–Sat 7pm–2am.** Ultra-relaxed bar-restaurant offering (from 8pm to midnight) zesty-flavoured dishes such as an asparagus *velouté*, veal with lime cream sauce, or honey-roast camembert. You'll jostle elbows with a trendy young clientele, whose noisy conversation competes with the DJ soundtrack.

**Chez Casimir Map 3, K5. 6 rue de Belzunce, 10e ☎01.48.78.28.80. Ⓜ Gare du Nord. Mon 7.30–10.30pm, Tues–Fri noon–2pm & 7.30–10.30pm.** It's astonishing that so good a restaurant can exist this close to the Gare du Nord. In basic, unrenovated *bistrot* surroundings you can enjoy inexpensive but well-cooked dishes. You might be brought an entire *terrine de porc*, from which to help yourself, then enjoy succulent wild-boar steaks – all for €22 at lunch, or €29 in the evening. The Sunday "brunch" (€25) is an adventure – think scallops and cod casserole, not eggs and ham. At the sister restaurant *Chez Michel*, next door but one (☎01.44.53.06.20), you'll pay around €40 for cosier decor and a more adventurous, occasionally Breton-flavoured menu.

**Au Grain de Folie Map 3, G3. 24 rue de La Vieuville, 18e ☎01.42.58.15.57. Ⓜ Abbesses. Tues–Sat 12.30–2.30pm & 7.30–10.30pm, Sun 12.30–10.30pm.** A tiny, simple and colourfully dilapidated vegetarian place where all the food is inexpensive and organic and there's always a vegan option.

**Julien Map 3, K9. 16 rue du Faubourg-St-Denis, 10e ☎01.47.70.12.06. Ⓜ Strasbourg-St-Denis. Daily noon–3pm & 7pm–1am.** Here, it's all globe lamps, hat stands, white linen, brass and polished wood, with frescoes of flowery Art Deco maidens surveying the scene. This brasserie is so handsome, in fact, that even the poor service and crammed-in clientele can't spoil it. Waiters in ankle-length aprons bring satisfying if unsophisticated fish and seafood dishes, along with brasserie classics like salt pork with lentils. *Menus* from €30 and up.

**Le Mono Map 3, F3. 40 rue Véron, 18e ☎01.46.06.99.20. Ⓜ Abbesses. Thurs–Tues 7.30–11pm.** Welcoming, family-run Togolese restaurant. Mains (around €12) are mostly grilled fish or meat served with sour, hot sauces, with rice or cassava on the side. Enjoyable atmosphere, with soukous on the stereo, Afro-print tablecloths and Togolese carvings on the walls.

**Le Moulin de la Galette Map 3, F2. 83 rue Lepic, 18e ⓣ01.46.06.84.77. ⓜBlanche/Abbesses. Daily noon–11.30pm.** Eating in one of the last surviving Montmartre windmills might seem irresistible – never mind that the real, famous Moulin de la Galette is just down the street! It's spacious and welcoming inside, with wooden tables jostling together and a delightful garden arbour out back. The food is classic French with a few modestly ambitious touches: duck with honey and Sauternes, roast bream with leeks and ginger. Two-course lunch at €17, or expect to pay around €45 a head at dinner.

**A la Pomponnette Map 3, F2. 42 rue Lepic, 18e ⓣ01.46.06.08.36. ⓜBlanche/Abbesses. Tues–Thurs noon–2.30pm & 7–11pm, Fri & Sat noon–2.30pm & 7pm–midnight.** A genuine old Montmartre *bistrot*, with posters, drawings and a zinc-top bar. The traditional French food is just as it should be, with an evening *menu* at €34.

**Refuge des Fondus Map 3, G3. 17 rue des Trois-Frères, 18e ⓣ01.42.55.22.65. ⓜAbbesses. Daily 7pm–2am.** The €16 *menu* here gets you a pretty basic but filling fondue – Bourguignonne (meat) or Savoyarde (cheese) – and your personal *biberon*, or baby bottle, full of wine. This idea is unflaggingly popular with a raucous, studenty crowd, who squeeze onto the banquette tables between the zanily graffitied walls.

**Le Relais Gascon Map 3, G3. 6 rue des Abbesses, 18e ⓣ01.42.58.58.22. ⓜAbbesses. Daily 10am–2am.** Serving hearty, filling meals all day, this two-storey restaurant provides a welcome blast of straightforward Gascon heartiness in this touristy part of town. The enormous warm salads cost €11.50, and there are equally tasty *plats* for around €12.

**Wepler Map 3, C3. 14 place de Clichy, 18e ⓣ01.45.22.53.24. ⓜPlace-de-Clichy. Daily noon–1am, café from 8am.** Now over a hundred years old, and still a beacon of conviviality amid the hustle of place de Clichy. Its clientele has moved upmarket since it was depicted in Truffaut's *Les 400 Coups*, but as palatial brasseries go, *Wepler* has remained unashamedly *populaire*. Serves honest brasserie fare and classic seafood platters (€40–45 à la carte).

# Eastern Paris

## Cafés and wine bars

**L'Atmosphère Map 4, C3. 49 rue Lucien-Sampaix, 10e. ⓂGare-de-l'Est. Tues–Fri 11am–2am, Sat 5.30pm–2am.** Lively café-bar with decent evening *plats*, on a pleasant corner beside the Canal St-Martin. Tables on the towpath on sunny days, and occasional live music on Sun, with an alternative flavour. Beer, coffee and fresh lemonade from €2.50.

**Chez Prune Map 4, D4. 36 rue Beaurepaire, 10e ⓣ01.42.41.30.47. ⓂJacques-Bonsergent. Mon–Sat 8am–2am, Sun 10am–2am.** Named after the owner's grandmother (a bust of whom is inside), *Chez Prune* is popular with an arty and media crowd, but remains friendly and laid-back, with pleasant outdoor seating overlooking the canal. Lunchtime dishes around €13; evening snacks like platters of cheese or charcuterie around €10; beer €3.

**Aux Folies Map 4, G3. 8 rue de Belleville, 20e. ⓂBelleville. Daily 6.30am–1am.** Scruffy *Aux Folies* offers a real slice of Belleville life, its clientele reflecting the area's diversity; its outside terrace and long brass bar, with mirrored tiles, pinball machine and broken window panes held together with sticking tape, are packed day and night. Beer from €2, cocktails from €3.50.

**La Mère Lachaise Map 4, I7. 78 bd Ménilmontant, 20e ⓣ01.47.97.61.60. ⓂPère-Lachaise. Mon–Sat 8am–2am, Sun 9am–1am.** The sunny terrace of this bar-restaurant, popular with students and a young, trendy crowd, makes a good place for a drink after a visit to Père-Lachaise. Also check out its cosy interior bar, with retro-chic decor of painted wood and wrought-iron lamps.

## Restaurants

**L'Auberge Pyrénées Cévennes Map 4, E5. 106 rue de la Folie-Méricourt, 11e ⓣ01.43.57.33.78. ⓂRépublique. Mon–Fri noon–2pm & 7–11pm, Sat 7–11pm.** Make sure you come hungry to this homely little place serving hearty portions of country cuisine. Highly recommended are the garlicky *moules marinières* for starters and the superb *cassoulet*, served in its own copper pot. Around €30 a head.

**Le Baratin Map 4, I3. 3 rue Jouye-Rouve, 20e ⓣ01.43.49.39.70. ⓂPyrénées/Belleville. Tues–Fri noon–1am, Sat 8pm–1am; closed first week of Jan & 3 weeks in Aug.** At first glance there's little to distinguish *Le Baratin* from any other local *bistrot à vins*: the chalkboard menu, tiled floor and black-and-white photos are all in place. But the stellar cooking and fine selection of organic wines elevate it above the competition. The three-course *menu* (€35–40) might include a thick bean soup, a melt-in-the-mouth *daube* of beef and a quivering crème caramel. It's best to book for both lunch and dinner.

**Chez Imogène Map 4, E7. Cnr rue Jean-Pierre-Timbaud and rue du Grand-Prieuré, 11e ⓣ01.48.07.14.59. ⓂOberkampf. Mon noon–2.30pm, Tues–Sat noon–2.30pm & 7–11pm.** A great little crêperie, tucked away on a side street: you could start with a home-made blini with smoked salmon, followed by a *crêpe savoyarde* (with a cheese, potato, onion and ham filling) and finish with a sweet version, with flambéed apple in Calvados, for example. A *kir breton* (cider with cassis) is the perfect accompaniment. It's best to book for dinner. Lunch *menus* €9.50–13.50, dinner €16.

**Lao Siam Map 4, off I2. 49 rue de Belleville, 19e ⓣ01.40.40.09.68. ⓂBelleville. Mon–Fri noon–3pm & 6–11.30pm, Sat & Sun noon–12.30am.** The surroundings are nothing special, but the excellent Thai and Lao food, popular with locals, makes up for it. Dishes from €8. Best to book in advance.

**Le Sporting Map 4, C2. 3 rue des Récollets, 10e ⓣ01.46.07.02.00. ⓂGare-de-l'Est. Daily noon–11.30pm.** Modern, pan-European dishes like *tartare* of turbot, pesto ravioli and osso bucco are served to young cosmopolites at this bar-restaurant on the Canal St-Martin. The food is comforting rather than special, but it's a good, dark spot for dates – be sure to try out their large cocktail menu. Count on around €35 without wine.

# Western Paris

## Restaurants

**Astrance Map 7, B8. 4 rue Beethoven, 16e ⓣ01.40.50.84.40. ⓂPassy. Tues–Fri noon–1.45pm & 8–9.45pm; closed Aug.** Young chef Pascal Barbot's triple-Michelin-starred *Astrance* produces some of the city's most exciting cuisine. The €190 "surprise" *menu* might include avocado and crab ravioli with almond oil; foie gras and mushroom *millefeuille* with lemon confit and hazelnut oil; or lemon-grass and pepper sorbet. The pleasantly contemporary dining room seats only 26 and bookings are notoriously hard to get: try at least a month in advance. Lunch *menus* €70 and €120, evening €120, €190 and €290.

**La Gare 19 Chaussée de la Muette, 16e ⓣ01.42.15.15.31. ⓂMuette. Restaurant: daily noon–3pm & 7pm–midnight. Bar: daily noon–2am.** The focus is firmly on French classics at this renovated former train station turned elegant restaurant-bar, which boasts a huge, sunny dining room and serves, among other things, a popular €21–23 lunch *menu*. You can sit out on the attractive terrace on sunny days, and the bar upstairs (which often has samba, soul and house music DJs in the evenings) is well worth a look.

**La Table Lauriston Map 7, A5. 129 rue Lauriston, 16e ⓣ01.47.27.00.07. ⓂTrocadéro. Mon–Fri noon–2.30pm & 7.15–10pm, Sat 7.30–10.30pm.** A slightly older, well-off crowd from the neighbourhood usually dines at this traditional *bistrot* run by chef-to-the-stars Serge Rabey. Game *terrine* with chanterelle mushrooms and *poularde fondante au vin jaune* (chicken croquettes with Arbois wine) are indicative of the upscale dishes here, and be sure to taste their famed Baba au Rhum. You'll easily spend around €50 per person, but the *cuisine bourgeoise* is excellent.

20

# Bars, clubs and live music

Paris's fame as the quintessential home of decadent, hedonistic **nightlife** has endured for centuries. That reputation seems only to grow stronger, fuelled by a vibrant **bar and club scene** and a world-class **live music** programme, from rock and world music to jazz and electro-lounge.

To find out **what's on** you need to get hold of one of the city's weekly **listings magazines** – *Pariscope* is the traditional first port of call, though for nightlife you'll do better with *Nova* magazine (ⓦwww.novaplanet.com); both are available from all newsstands. To seek out the latest club nights you'll need to pick up flyers – or word-of-mouth tips – in one of the city's trendier bars, or check out sites such as Die Nacht (ⓦwww.die-nacht.fr) and Trisélectif (ⓦwww.triselectif.net). The easiest places to get **tickets** for concerts, whether rock, jazz, Parisian *chanson* or classical, are at one of Paris's many FNAC stores – the main branch is in the Forum des Halles, 1–5 rue Pierre-Lescot, 1er (Mon–Sat 10am–7.30pm; ⓣ08.25.02.00.20, ⓦwww.fnac.fr; ⓂChâtelet-Les Halles).

# Bars

If you're looking for the city's liveliest venues for **night-time drinking**, from late-opening **cafés** to **beer cellars**, Irish **pubs** and **cocktail bars**, we've collected them all here, under "**bars**". You'll find more relaxed, daytime-oriented cafés listed in the "Cafés and restaurants" chapter (see pp.198–231), while full-on clubs, with entry fees and proper sound systems, are reviewed separately on p.242.

## The Champs-Elysées and around

**Buddha Bar Map 7, M4. 8 rue Boissy d'Anglas, 8e. Ⓜ Concorde. Bar daily 4pm–2am; restaurant 7pm–12.30am.** This is where the *Buddha Bar* phenomenon all began, and while this particular locale no longer profits from the "it" status it once enjoyed, it's still well worth a stop, either for well-priced cocktails at the beautifully designed bar or a meal in the pan-Asian restaurant, presided over by a giant Buddha.

**Costes Map 2, B2. *Hôtel Costes*, 239 rue St-Honoré, 1er. Ⓜ Concorde/Tuileries. Daily 7pm–2am.** A favourite haunt of fashionistas and film and media stars, this is a decadently romantic place for an aperitif or late-night drinks amid an opulent nineteenth-century decor of red velvet, swags and columns, set around an Italianate courtyard draped in ivy. Don't expect much deference from the ridiculously good-looking staff, though. Cocktails around €16.

**Impala Lounge Map 7, G3. 2 rue de Berri, 8e. Ⓜ George-V. Daily 9.30am–4am.** A trendy, *Out of Africa*-themed bar, with great atmosphere and music – mostly remixed reggae, funk and afro-jazz beats. In the evenings a youngish intellectual crowd settles in to talk shop.

**Mini Palais Map 7, J5. Pont Alexandre III, av Winston Churchill, 8e. Ⓜ Champs-Elysées. Mon–Fri 8.30am–1am, Sat & Sun 10.30am–1am.** The Grand Palais' slick bar/restaurant is small in name only, with high ceilings, large windows (the inward-facing ones overlook the exhibition space), giant lampshades and an ample terrace. While the food is so-so, the cocktails (around €15) are great.

**Pershing Lounge Map 7, G4. Pershing Hall, 49 rue Pierre-Charron, 8e. Ⓜ George-V. Daily**

**6pm–2am.** The lounge bar of the hip, minimalist hotel, *Pershing Hall*, is a delightful retreat from the bustle of the city, with its 30m-high vertical garden, planted with exotic vegetation. It's a bit of a jetsetters' hangout, with cocktails priced to match.

## The Grands Boulevards and around

**Bar Hemingway Map 2, C2. *Ritz Hôtel*, 15 place Vendôme, 1$^{er}$. Ⓜ Tuileries/Opéra. Tues–Sat 6.30pm–2am.** Hemingway first came here with F. Scott Fitzgerald in the 1920s at a time when he was too poor to buy his own drinks. Once he'd made his money, he returned here frequently to spend it; with a classic, authentic decor of warm wood panelling, stately leather chairs and deferential suited barmen, it's easy to see why. Sip the famed dry martinis or choose from a large selection of malt whiskies. There's very little on the drinks list under €20.

**Le Café Noir Map 2, F3. 65 rue Montmartre, 2$^{e}$. Ⓜ Les Halles/ Sentier. Mon–Fri 8.30am–2am, Sat 4pm–2am.** Despite the name, it's the colour red that predominates in this cool little corner café-bar, with papier-mâché globes and other bits of eccentric decor. It's great for an aperitif or late-night drinks, when the music and ambience hot up and it's standing room only at the bar.
DJ Thurs & Fri.

**Kitty O'Shea's Map 2, C1. 10 rue des Capucines, 2$^{e}$. Ⓜ Opéra. Daily noon–1.30am.** A favourite haunt of expats, and a decent stab at an Irish bar, with excellent Guinness, Magners and reasonably priced meals like Irish stew and fish and chips. Anglo-Irish football and rugby matches are shown on the big screens, and there's live music on Sun evenings.

**Le Tambour Map 2, F3. 41 rue Montmartre, 2$^{e}$. Ⓜ Sentier. Daily 6pm–6am.** A dusty local habitués' bar, eccentrically furnished with recycled street signs, old paving stones and the like. It's a throwback to the old Les Halles market days and still keeps long hours. Hearty salads and snacks available, as well as fuller meals, with mains like pigs' trotters around €14; beer from €3.50.

**De La Ville Café Map 3, J8. 34 bd de la Bonne Nouvelle, 10$^{e}$. Ⓜ Bonne-Nouvelle. Daily 11am–2am.** The grand staircase, gilded mosaics and marble columns hint at this bar's former incarnation as a bordello. It draws in crowds of hip pre-clubbers, who sling back a mojito or two under the multicoloured awning before moving on to one of the area's clubs; tellingly, absinthe is listed as an aperitif. On weekends, well-known DJs play till the early hours.

## Beaubourg and Les Halles

**Le Cochon à l'Oreille Map 2, G4. 15 rue Montmartre, 1er. Ⓜ Châtelet-Les Halles/Etienne-Marcel. Mon–Sat 6pm–2am.** This classic little café-bar, with raffia chairs outside and scenes of fruit and veg stalls on ceramic tiles inside, dates from Les Halles' days as a market. The intellectual conversation is accompanied by Coltrane and other jazz greats.

**Le Fumoir Map 2, E5. 6 rue de l'Amiral-Coligny, 1er. Ⓜ Louvre-Rivoli. Daily 11am–2am.** Animated chatter rises above a mellow jazz soundtrack and the sound of cocktail shakers in this coolly designed bar, popular with a fashionable, thirty-something crowd. You can browse the international press and there's also a restaurant at the back, walled with books. Cocktails around €10.

**Kong Map 2, F6. 1 rue du Pont Neuf, 5th floor, 1er ⓣ 01.40.39.09.00. Ⓜ Pont-Neuf. Bar daily 12.30pm–2am; restaurant 10.30am–2am.** This über-cool, Philippe Starck-fashioned bar/restaurant atop the flagship Kenzo building is very swanky; while the gorgeous *demoiselles* meeting the lift will let you in, you might get ignored by the bartenders – and everyone else – if you can't claim the right pedigree. The decor is new Japan meets old, so think geisha girls and manga cartoons. Booths eerily beam holograms of heads of models who glare at you as you sip your €15 cocktail. The separate restaurant upstairs is under an impressive glass roof, with views over the Seine. The Asian-influenced food (€50–65 per head) includes dishes such as black cod with miso. Happy hour daily 6–8pm.

**Au Trappiste Map 2, G6. 4 rue St-Denis, 1er. Ⓜ Châtelet. Mon–Thurs noon–2.30am, Fri–Sun noon–4.30am.** Over 140 draught beers here include Jenlain, France's best-known *bière de garde*, Belgian Blanche Riva and Kriek from the Mort Subite (Sudden Death) brewery – ask for a taster if you can't decide – plus very good *moules frites* and various *tartines*. Or, if you've come on a full stomach, go all out for the giraffe – a three-litre tube filled with beer, with a tap at the bottom.

## The Marais

**Andy Wahloo Map 4, A7. 69 rue des Gravilliers, 3e. Ⓜ Arts-et-Métiers. Mon–Sat 11am–2am.** This very popular bar, decked out in original

Pop Art-inspired Arabic decor, with outdoor seating in a leafy courtyard, gets packed to the gills at weekends. Delicious mezze appetizers are served until midnight and the bar boasts a few original cocktails, including the Wahloo Special (rum, lime, ginger, banana and cinnamon; €10). DJs play a wide range of dance music, Moroccan rock and Algerian raï.

**L'Attirail Map 4, B7. 9 rue au Maire, 3e. ⓂArts-et-Métiers. Daily 10am till around 2am.** An intimate little *café-concerts* buried away in the Haut Marais' Chinatown district. The tiny back room is the venue for a varied programme of live music – anything from Balkan gypsy music to jazz rock – lapped up by an enthusiastic and slightly alternative studenty crowd. Music starts around 8 or 9pm.

**La Belle Hortense Map 4, B10. 31 rue Vieille du Temple, 4e ⓣ01.48.04.71.60. ⓂSt-Paul. Mon–Wed 5pm–2am, Thurs & Fri 4pm–2am, Sat 1pm–2am, Sun 1pm–midnight.** Named after a Jacques Roubaud novel, this cross between a bookshop and a wine bar predictably attracts literary types. It also publishes its own magazine and hosts regular readings, book signings and other events, which are well worth attending if your French is up to it.

**La Perle Map 4, C9. 78 rue Vieille-du-Temple, 3e. ⓂSt-Paul. Daily 6am–2am.** An Emperor's New Clothes kind of place, which, despite its nondescript decor and generic dance music, maintains a *très cool* reputation and is always packed with an arty, indie crowd knocking back cheap beer.

**Stolly's Map 4, B11. 16 rue Cloche-Perce, 4e. ⓂSt-Paul. Daily 4.30pm–2am.** Tiny, no-nonsense, almost exclusively Anglo bar with a very friendly atmosphere and broadcasts of all major sporting events. It's all washed down with pints of Guinness, Grolsch and Kilkenny, plus a wide selection of spirits and cocktails (from €6.50).

## Bastille and around

**Bar des Ferrailleurs Map 4, F12. 18 rue de Lappe, 11e. ⓂBastille. Mon–Fri 5pm–2am, Sat & Sun 3pm–2am.** Dark and stylishly sinister, with rusting metal decor, an eccentric owner, fun wig-wearing bar staff and a relaxed and friendly crowd.

**Café de l'Industrie Map 4, F11. 16 rue St-Sabin, 11e. ⓂBastille. Daily 10am–2am.** An enduringly popular café, packed out every evening. See p.213.

**Le Fanfaron Map 4, G13. 6 rue de la Main d'Or, 11e. ⓂLedru-Rollin.**

**Tues–Sat 6pm–2am; closed 2 weeks in Aug.** On a tiny back street north of rue du Faubourg St-Antoine, this little retro bar, with its old film posters and Sixties rock music (and much expert discussion on both topics), is appealingly nostalgic, and the beer is cheap, too.

**Le Lèche-Vin Map 4, F12. 13 rue Daval, 11e. ⓂBastille. Daily 6pm–2am.** The owners of this kitsch bar appear to have ransacked a church for the decor. The statue of Mary with a cross (and an AIDS ribbon) in the window is certainly eye-catching; the pics in the toilet, on the other hand, are far from pious. Gets packed very quickly in the evenings with a young, cosmopolitan crowd.

**Les Marcheurs de Planète Map 4, G11. 73 rue de la Roquette, 11e. ⓂVoltaire. Tues–Sat 5.30pm–2am, Sun 8.30pm–2am.** Good old-fashioned Parisian atmosphere, with an effortlessly cool, vaguely retro vibe: chess tables, a hat stand, various musical instruments, posters covering the walls and a wild-haired owner are all present and correct. More than 50 wines (from €2.70 a glass) are on offer, plus excellent cheeses and charcuterie dishes.

**SanZSanS Map 4, F13. 49 rue du Faubourg-St-Antoine, 11e. ⓂBastille. Mon 9am–2am, Tues–Sat 9am–5am, Sun 6pm–midnight.** This gothic get-up of red velvet, oil paintings and chandeliers is popular with a young crowd, especially on Friday and Saturday evenings, when DJs play rare groove and funky/Brazilian house. Drinks are reasonably priced.

## The Quartier Latin and the southeast

**Curio Parlor Map 2, H9. 16 rue des Bernardins, 5e. ⓂMaubert-Mutualité. Tues–Thurs & Sun 6pm–2am, Fri & Sat 6pm–4am.** This secretive – spot the entrance if you can – pocket cocktail bar is much patronized by Paris's gilded youth, who loll fashionably on the comfy velvet sofas, while DJs play in the designer-dressed basement. Expensive and glossy.

**Le Pantalon Bar Map 2, F12. 7 rue Royer-Collard, 5e. RER Luxembourg. Daily 5.30pm–2am.** This archetypal student dive sports weathered mirrors and graffiti-covered walls, and serves very cheap drinks, especially in the pre-evening happy hour – often a happy two hours, starting at 5.30pm.

**Le Piano Vache Map 2, G11. 8 rue Laplace, 5e. ⓂCardinal-Lemoine. Mon–Fri noon–2am, Sat & Sun 9pm–2am.** Venerable bar crammed with students drinking

at little tables. Cool music and a laid-back, grungy atmosphere.

**Le Violon Dingue Map 2, G11. 46 rue de la Montagne-Ste-Geneviève, 5e. Ⓜ Maubert-Mutualité. Daily 6pm–2.30am.** Long, dark student pub that's also popular with young travellers. Noisy and friendly, with English-speaking bar staff and cheap drinks. The cellar bar stays open until 4.30am on busy nights.

## St-Germain

**Le 10 Map 2, E9. 10 rue de l'Odéon, 6e. Ⓜ Odéon. Daily 6pm–2am.** Classic Art Deco-era posters line the walls of this small, dark, studenty bar. The atmospheric vaulted cellar bar gets noisy in the small hours.

**Bar du Marché Map 2, E8. 75 rue de Seine, 6e. Ⓜ Mabillon. Daily 7am–2am.** This former market café is just as satisfying and just as busy at night as by day. Expect animated conversation rather than banging techno.

**Chez Georges Map 2, D9. 11 rue des Canettes, 6e. Ⓜ Mabillon. Tues–Sat noon–2am; closed Aug.** This dilapidated wine bar is one of the few authentic addresses in an area dominated by big, noisy theme pubs (you'll find plenty in the vicinity if you're in the market). The young, studenty crowd gets good-naturedly rowdy later on in the cellar bar.

**L'Echelle de Jacob Map 2, D7. 12 rue Jacob, 6e. Ⓜ St-Germain-des-Prés. Mon–Sat 10am–5am.** Named the "Jacob's ladder" for the staircase leading up to the intimate mezzanine bar, this is one for the exceptionally well-styled and well-heeled "Germainopratins" of the area, who squeeze onto velour loungers for flavoured Martinis and pre-club sounds.

**Les Etages St-Germain Map 2, E8. 5 rue de Buci, 6e. Ⓜ Mabillon. Daily 11am–2am.** Fashionably distressed café-bar, with a downstairs level open to the street. Upstairs you can lounge around on dog-eared armchairs, chilling out with a reasonably priced cocktail.

**La Mezzanine de l'Alcazar Map 2, E8. 62 rue Mazarine, 6e. Ⓜ Odéon. Daily 7pm–2am.** Both decor and clientele are *très design* at this über-cool cocktail bar, set on a mezzanine level overlooking Conran's *Alcazar* restaurant. Expensive (€10 for a drink) but exquisite – again, much like the clientele. Most nights start off relaxed and finish with feverish dancing, with hardcore types moving on to the *WAGG* club, p.244. DJs Wed–Sat.

## Montparnasse

**Café Tournesol Map 6, G11. 9 rue de la Gâité, 14e. Ⓜ Edgar Quinet. Daily 7am–2am.** This corner café-bar attracts bohemian twenty-somethings for its distressed chic, outside tables and cool playlists. Fashionable yet welcoming – a rare combination.

**La Folie en Tête Map 5, E9. 33 rue Butte-aux-Cailles, 13e. Ⓜ Place-d'Italie/Corvisart. Mon–Sat 6pm–2am.** Surveying the Butte-aux-Cailles from its prime corner spot, this vibrant, friendly and distinctly lefty café-bar is a classic. The walls are littered with bric-a-brac and musical instruments and there's usually something cool playing on the system – laid-back underground beats, perhaps, or a young singer-songwriter's latest album.

**Le Merle Moqueur Map 5, F9. 11 rue Butte-aux-Cailles, 13e. Ⓜ Place-d'Italie/Corvisart. Daily 5pm–2am.** Classic narrow, shop-front-style Butte-aux-Cailles bar, which once saw the Paris debut of Mano Negra and Manu Chao. It maintains an alternative edge, though most days serves up 1980s French rock CDs and home-made flavoured rums to young Parisians. If you don't fancy the playlist when you arrive, you can always try the very similar *Le Diapason*, two doors along.

## Montmartre and around

**Chez Camille Map 3, F3. 8 rue Ravignan, 18e. Ⓜ Abbesses. Tues–Sat 9am–2am, Sun 9am–8pm.** *Très chouette* (very cool) is how locals have been describing this little bar for years. In a great location on the slopes of the Butte, it has a stylish interior of old mirrors, ceiling fans and mismatched seating and a clientele typical of the location – young and trendy in a well-to-do kind of way.

**La Fourmi Map 3, G4. 74 rue des Martyrs, 18e. Ⓜ Pigalle/Abbesses. Mon–Thurs 8am–2am, Fri & Sat 8am–4am, Sun 10am–2am.** Artfully distressed, high-ceilinged place with a long bar, drawing the locals and discerning *bobos* of Abbesses and the 10e for cocktails, wine and chatter.

**Olympic Café Map 3, K1. 20 rue Léon, 10e Ⓦ www.rueleon.net. Ⓜ Château-Rouge. Tues–Sun 11am–2am.** In the heart of the poor and peeling Goutte d'Or, this boho café-restaurant pumps out life and energy like a lighthouse. The big rainbow peace banner and faded 1930s Art Deco interior say it all, but the main draw is the basement venue featuring six gigs a week, from African rock to klezmer, Bulgarian folk and French *chanson*.

**Au Rendez-Vous des Amis Map 3, G2. 23 rue Gabrielle, 18e. Ⓜ Abbesses. Daily 8.30am–2am.** Halfway up the Butte, this small, ramshackle, smoky and community-spirited hangout is a magnet for Montmartre locals, especially the young, artsy and alternative-leaning.

## Eastern Paris

### Canal St-Martin

**L'Abracadabar Map 4, off E1. 123 av Jean-Jaurès, 19e ⓦwww.abracadabar.fr. ⓂLaumière. Daily 6pm–2am, Fri & Sat till 5am.** This popular little music bar pulsates with live rock, ragga, funk, blues, jazz and techno most evenings, drawing a mixed crowd of students and thirty-somethings. Hundreds of photos of past guests are pegged up on washing lines and strung across the bar. Music usually starts at 8.30pm and there's sometimes a small entry fee of €2/3. Drinks are very reasonably priced.

**Bar Ourcq Map 4, off E1. 68 quai de la Loire, 19e. ⓂLaumière. Summer Wed & Thurs 3pm–midnight, Fri & Sat 3pm–2am, Sun 3–10pm; winter Wed–Fri 5–9.30pm, Sat 3pm–2am, Sun 3–9.30pm.** This popular bar, with its turquoise facade and large windows looking out onto the canal *quai*, really comes into its own in the warmer months when you can sit out on the quayside, or borrow the bar's set of *pétanques*. It also has a cosy interior with sofas and cushions. Drinks are reasonably priced, and there are DJs on Fri, Sat & Sun.

**Favela Chic Map 4, D5. 18 rue du Faubourg-du-Temple, 11e. ⓂRépublique. Tues–Fri 7.30pm–2am, Sat 7.30pm–4am.** Eclectic music nights and kitsch furnishings bring twenty-somethings of all creeds and persuasions to this Brazilian bar known for its ribald DJ evenings. Table-dancing and dirty dancing are *de rigueur*.

**Le Jemmapes Map 4, D3. 82 quai de Jemmapes, 10e. ⓂJacques Bonsergent. Daily 11am–2am.** In the summer this neighbourhood resto-bar and boho hangout is well known for letting its patrons cross the road to sip at their drinks along the banks of the canal. The standard French cuisine is good, but the lure here is the hipster atmosphere.

### Ménilmontant and Oberkampf

**L'Alimentation Générale Map 4, F6. 64 rue Jean-Pierre Timbaud, 11e. ⓂParmentier. Wed–Sun 5pm–2am.** A vibrant bar, restaurant and music venue rolled into one, the "Grocer's Store" puts on consistently good live music acts, often world music, but also hip-hop, rock and jazz, sometimes free or no more than €5, and there are also frequent DJ nights. Check out the cocktails, containing unusual ingredients such as herbs and figs.

**Café Charbon Map 4, H6. 109 rue Oberkampf, 11$^{e}$. ⓂSt-Maur/Parmentier. Daily 9am–2am.** The place that pioneered the rise of the Oberkampf bar scene in the mid-90s is still going strong and continues to draw in a young, fashionable, mixed crowd day and night. Part of its allure is the attractively restored *belle époque* decor. Happy hour daily 5–7pm and a DJ Thurs, Fri & Sat nights 10pm–2am.

**Café Chéri Map 4, G2. 44 bd de la Villette, 19$^{e}$. ⓂBelleville. Daily 8am–2am.** A DJ and live music bar, with appealingly scruffy red interior and popular terrace, where local hipsters sit at their laptop or read during the day, or drop in for drinks after work and stay long into the night. Drinks are reasonably priced; try one of the fruit cocktails, such as the *plateau* (pineapple, mango, rum and cinnamon). Music, from hip-hop to indie, Thurs–Sat nights.

**La Caravane Map 4, F5. 35 rue de la Fontaine-au-Roi, 11$^{e}$. ⓂGoncourt. Daily 11am–2am.** A colourful, fun place, with Chinese lanterns, bright-red curtains and mismatched tables and chairs. Handsome bar staff serve a bohemian, arty crowd. It's equally popular at lunch, when you can get a plate of pad thai or a quiche and salad for around €10. DJs most Fridays and Saturdays.

**La Flèche d'Or Map 4, off I11. 102bis rue de Bagnolet, cnr of rue des Pyrénées, 20$^{e}$ Ⓣ01.44.64.01.02, Ⓦwww.flechedor.fr. ⓂPorte-de-Bagnolet/Alexandre-Dumas – 10min walk from either. Mon–Thurs 8pm–2am, Fri & Sat 8pm–6am; closed Aug.** Housed in the old Bagnolet station on the *petite ceinture* railway that encircled the city until around thirty years ago, this bar and live music venue has a punkish atmosphere, with throngs of bikers, clubbers, musos, students and aspiring trend-setters. They are drawn by an eclectic music programme – indie-pop, ska, rock, *chanson* and punk regularly feature – which has made it one of the hottest tickets in town (gigs up to €10).

**L'International Map 4, H6. 5/7 rue Moret, 11$^{e}$. ⓂMénilmontant. Tues–Sat 2pm–2am, Sun 6pm–midnight.** This live music bar is a great deal for a night out: two or three bands, a mix of well-established and up-and-coming, play each night for free, and there's a happy hour until 9pm, with drinks from €2.

**Lou Pascalou Map 4, I7. 14 rue des Panoyaux, 20$^{e}$. ⓂMénilmontant. Daily 9am–2am.** Trendy but friendly place with a zinc bar, this local *bobo* hangout is a great weekend find for the area, especially if you're interested in leaving with your eardrums intact. Be sure to try some of their delicious mint tea – over a ponderous game of chess if you fancy it. Wide range of beers bottled and on tap from €3.

**Les Lucioles Map 4, I7. 102 bd Ménilmontant, 20e. Ⓜ Père-Lachaise. Daily 9am–2am.** This relaxed and friendly neighbourhood bar/restaurant, with an inviting outside terrace in warmer weather, is popular with a youngish crowd. They hold poetry readings on Tues and have live music on weekends in a fun, party atmosphere.

**Piston Pelican Map 4, off I11. 15 rue de Bagnolet, 20e Ⓦ www.pistonpelican.com. Ⓜ Alexandre-Dumas. Mon–Fri 8.30am–2am, Sat 10am–2am (food: Mon noon–3pm, Tues–Sat noon–3pm & 7–11.30pm); closed Aug.** This friendly local joint, with its assortment of chipped mirrors, posters and pop culture memorabilia, has an appealingly eclectic soundtrack, featuring rock, Eighties pop and the odd drum'n'bass anthem. DJ sets and live bands on weekends. Happy hour daily 6–8pm.

## Clubs

Paris's **club** scene is moving ever further away from monster-clubs; and where deep house and techno once ruled, you can now find hip-hop, r'n'b, electro-lounge, tech-funk and even rock nights. The clubs listed here support good programmes and attract interesting crowds, but the general vibe really depends on who's running the individual *soirée*, and some places also showcase occasional live acts. It's worth checking the listings for **live music** venues (see p.245), which often hold DJ-led sessions after hours, as well as the **gay and lesbian** club listings (see pp.305–308). Note too that lots of **bars** bring in DJs at the weekend.

Most clubs **open** between 11pm and midnight, but venues rarely warm up before 1 or 2am. It's worth dressing up, especially for trendier venues; groups of men are especially likely to get turned away, but being an English-speaking tourist tends to make you more popular with the bouncers. Booking online in advance can also prevent problems. Most **entry prices** include one free drink (*consommation*), and may vary from night to night. Given the difficulty of finding a **taxi after hours** (see p.22), many Parisian clubbers aim to keep going until the métro starts up at around 5.30am, or even later, moving on to one of the city's famous *after* events.

## Nightclubs

**Le Baron Map 7, F5. Av Marceau, 8e Ⓦwww.clublebaron.com. ⓂAlma-Marceau. Daily 11.30pm–5am.** *Le Baron* is quite deliberately both expensive and exclusive – you'll have to not only look good but look as if you're in with the right crowd to be allowed the privilege of entry. There's no door charge, but carry a fat wallet for drinks. The result is a small and posey bar-club packed out with well-connected, wealthy and well-dressed Parisians schmoozing, flirting and dancing till dawn.

**Bâteau Concorde Atlantique Map 6, G1. Port de Solférino, 23 quai Anatole France, 7e Ⓣ01.40.56.02.82. ⓂAssemblée Nationale/RER Musée d'Orsay. Daily 11pm–5am.** Summer-only club (roughly late June to mid-Sept), which takes over this two-level boat for hedonistic parties in the hot months. The boat doesn't actually go anywhere, but a drink on the deck is an unusually pleasant way to chill out before heading back down to the dancefloor – *soirées* vary, but it's mostly house or techno. Entry around €15.

**Batofar Map 5, N7. Opposite 11 quai François Mauriac, 13e Ⓣ01.56.29.10.33, Ⓦwww.batofar.org. ⓂEtienne-Marcel. Tues–Thurs 8pm–2am, Fri 11pm–dawn, Sat 11pm–noon.** This old lighthouse boat moored at the foot of the Bibliothèque Nationale is a small but classic address. The programme is mostly electro, house, techno, hip-hop, whatever – with the odd experimental funk night or the like thrown in to mix it up a bit. Entry €8–12.

**Le Cab Map 2, E4. Place du Palais-Royal, 1er Ⓣ01.58.62.56.25. ⓂPalais-Royal. Mon–Sat 11.30pm–5am.** This is a smallish, upmarket venue – on weekend nights you'll need to look good to get in. Designer retro-meets-futuristic lounge decor, with a similar music policy. Entry €20.

**Le Nouveau Casino Map 4, G6. 109 rue Oberkampf, 11e**

**Ⓣ01.43.57.57.40, Ⓦwww .nouveaucasino.net. ⓂParmentier. Tues & Wed 9pm–2am, Thurs–Sat midnight–5am.** Right behind *Café Charbon* (see p.241) lies this excellent venue. An interesting, experimental line-up of live gigs makes way for a relaxed, dancey crowd later on, with music ranging from electro-pop or house to rock and world music. There's a good sound system and ventilation, but not all that much space. Entry price ranges from free up to around €15, depending on who's playing and when you arrive.

**Rex Club Map 3, I8. 5 bd Poissonnière, 2e Ⓣ01.42.36.10.96. ⓂBonne-Nouvelle. Wed–Sat 11.30pm–5am.** The clubbers' club: spacious but not intimidatingly so, and serious about its music, which is strictly electronic, notably techno. Attracts big-name DJs. Entry €10–13.

**La Scène Bastille Map 4, G12. 2bis rue des Taillandiers, 11e Ⓣ01.48.06.50.70 (restaurant reservations: Ⓣ01.48.06.12.13), Ⓦwww.la-scene.com. ⓂBastille. Mon–Thurs & Sun till 2am, Fri & Sat till 5am.** A club, concert venue and restaurant all rolled into one, in a converted warehouse luxuriously refurbished in plush colours. The eclectic music policy embraces rock, electro and funk, with frequent, popular gay nights. Entry €12.

**Showcase Map 7, J6. Pont Alexandre III, 8e Ⓣ01.45.61.25.43, Ⓦwww .showcase.fr. ⓂChamps-Elysées-Clemenceau/Invalides.** This big club occupies a former boatyard underneath the Alexandre III bridge, and with its stone arches it's both spacious and atmospheric. Its not as ragingly fashionable with Paris's posher crowd as it was a couple of years ago, but it's still committed to showcasing good electronic music, and you'll still need to dress up to get in. Entry €10–15.

**Social Club Map 2, F1. 142 rue Montmartre, 2e Ⓣ01.40.28.05.55, Ⓦwww.parissocialclub.com. ⓂPalais de la Bourse. Daily till 6am.** *Les physios* (the bouncers) won't turn you away at this unpretentious, excitable, music-loving club, but you might struggle to get in when the big-name DJs are guesting, as it's not huge. The mad futuristic interior, with skeletal grid and strip lights tells the story: this is electro-land, albeit with forays into stranger territory. Entry costs vary.

**WAGG Map 2, E8. 62 rue Mazarine, 6e Ⓣ01.55.42.22.00. ⓂOdéon. Fri & Sat midnight–6am, Sun**

**5pm–midnight.** Adjoining Terence Conran's flashy *Alcazar* restaurant and bar, the *WAGG* offers glossy good times, with Seventies-themed "Carwash" nights on Fri, Eighties grooves on Sat, and Latino/salsa on Sun. Entry €12, Sun free.

## Rock and world music

Most of the **venues** listed here are primarily concert venues, though some double up as clubs on certain nights, or after hours. A few of them will have live music all week, but the majority host bands on just a couple of nights. Admission **prices** vary depending on who's playing. Note that the most interesting clubs tend to host gigs earlier on in the evening; jazz venues (see p.246) often branch out into other genres such as world music and folk.

### Rock and world music venues

**Le Bataclan Map 4, E8. 50 bd Voltaire, 11e ⓣ01.43.14.00.30, ⓦwww.myspace.com/bataclanparis. ⓜOberkampf.** Classic pagoda-style ex-theatre venue (seats 1200) with one of the best and most eclectic line-ups covering anything from international and local dance and rock acts – Francis Cabrel, Chemical Brothers, Khaled, Hole – to *chanson*, opera, comedy and techno nights.

**Café de la Danse Map 4, F12. 5 passage Louis-Philippe, 11e ⓣ01.47.00.57.59, ⓦwww.cafedeladanse.com. ⓜBastille.** Rock, pop, world, folk and jazz music played in an intimate and attractive space. Open nights of concerts only.

**La Cigale Map 3, G4. 120 bd de Rochechouart, 18e ⓣ01.49.25.81.75, ⓦwww.lacigale.fr. ⓜPigalle.** Formerly playing host to the likes of Mistinguett and Maurice Chevalier, since 1987 and a Philippe Starck renovation this historic 1400-seat Pigalle theatre has become a leading venue for cutting-edge rock, world music and indie acts, especially French bands. You might see anything from Rock dinosaur Marc Lavoine to electro superstars Beat Torrent, or from actress/*chanteuse* Charlotte Gainsbourg to Ivory Coast reggae star Tiken Jah Fakoly – or maybe the Divine Comedy and Dandy Warhols.

**Le Divan du Monde** Map 3, G4. 75 rue des Martyrs, 18e ⓣ01.40.05.06.99, ⓦwww.divandumonde.com. ⓂAnvers. A youthful venue in a café whose regulars once included Toulouse-Lautrec. One of the city's most diverse and exciting programmes, ranging from techno to Congolese rumba, with dancing till dawn on weekend nights.

**Elysée Montmartre** Map 3, H3. 72 bd de Rochechouart, 18e ⓣ01.55.07.06.00, ⓦwww.elyseemontmartre.com. ⓂAnvers. A cavernous historic Montmartre nightspot that pulls in a young, excitable crowd with its rock, soul, r'n'b and hip-hop acts – the Pharcyde, the Hives, Public Enemy. Also hosts up-tempo Latin and club nights.

**Maroquinerie** Map 4, off I5. 23 rue Boyer, 20e ⓣ01.40.33.35.05, ⓦwww.lamaroquinerie.fr. ⓂGambetta. This smallish concert venue is the downstairs part of a trendy arts centre. The line-up is rock, folk and jazz, with a particularly good selection of French musicians.

**Point Ephemère** Map 4, D1. 200 quai de Valmy, 10e ⓣ01.40.34.02.48, ⓦwww.pointephemere.org. ⓂJaurès. Run by an arts collective in a disused warehouse, this superbly dilapidated venue lives up to its reputation as a nexus for alternative and underground performers of all kinds. There are gigs most nights, covering anything from electro to Afro-jazz via folk-rock, as well as dance studios, rehearsal spaces and the like.

## Jazz, blues and *chanson*

**Jazz** has long enjoyed an appreciative audience in France, especially since the end of World War II, when the intellectual rigour and agonized musings of bebop struck an immediate chord of sympathy in the existentialist hearts of the *après-guerre*.

Gypsy guitarist Django Reinhardt and his partner, violinist Stéphane Grappelli, whose work represents the distinctive and undisputed French contribution to the jazz canon, had much to do with the genre's popularity. But it was also greatly enhanced by the presence of many front-rank black American musicians, such as soprano sax player Sidney Bechet, for whom Paris was a haven of freedom and culture after the racial prejudice of the States.

Jazz is still alive and well in the city, with a good selection of clubs playing all styles from New Orleans to current experimental. Frequent festivals are also a good source of concerts, particularly in the summer (see p.283). *Bistrots* and bars are decent places to catch musicians carrying on the tradition of Django Reinhardt – Romane and the Ferré brothers are just some of musicians doing the rounds – as well as French traditional *chanson*. Gigs aren't usually advertised in the press, but you'll see posters in the *bistrots* themselves.

## Mainly jazz

**Le Baiser Salé Map 2, G6. 58 rue des Lombards, 1er ⓣ01.42.33.37.71, ⓦwww.lebaisersale.com. ⓜChâtelet. Daily 5pm–6am.** A small, crowded upstairs room with live music every night from 10pm – usually jazz, rhythm and blues, fusion, reggae or Brazilian. There are free jam sessions on Mon and the downstairs bar is great for just chilling out. Admission €12–20.

**Caveau de la Huchette Map 2, G8. 5 rue de la Huchette, 5e ⓣ01.43.26.65.05, ⓦwww.caveaudelahuchette.fr. ⓜSt-Michel. Sun–Wed 9.30pm–2.30am, Thurs–Fri 9.30pm–dawn.** A wonderful slice of old Parisian life in an otherwise touristy area. Both Lionel Hampton and Art Blakey played here. Live jazz, usually trad and big band, to dance to on a floor surrounded by tiers of benches, and a bar decorated with caricatures of the barman drawn on any material to hand. Sun–Thurs €12, Fri & Sat €14; drinks from €8.

**Le Duc des Lombards Map 2, G6. 42 rue des Lombards, 1er ⓣ01.42.33.22.88, ⓦwww.ducdeslombards.com. ⓜChâtelet/Les-Halles. Daily until 3am.** Modern, stylish club with performances every night from 9pm. Numerous TV screens stream images from the stage if your view is obscured. This is the place to hear gypsy jazz, as well as jazz piano, blues, ballads and fusion, often played by big names. Daily until 3am. Most gigs €23 or €25.

**Jazz Club Lionel Hampton *Hôtel Méridien*, 81 bd Gouvion-St-Cyr, 17e ⓣ01.40.68.30.42, ⓦwww.jazzclub-paris.com. ⓜPorte-Maillot. Daily 7pm–2am, with concerts at 10.30pm.** Inaugurated by Himself, this is a first-rate jazz venue, with big-name musicians. There's no entry fee but your first drink will cost from €26 (refills €15).

**New Morning Map 3, K7. 7–9 rue des Petites-Ecuries, 10e ⓣ01.45.23.51.41, ⓦwww.newmorning.com. ⓂChâteau-d'Eau. Usually Mon–Sat 8pm–1.30am, concerts 9pm.** The decor's somewhat spartan, a bit like an underground garage, but this is the place where the big international names in jazz come to play, and it attracts true aficionados. It's often standing room only unless you get here early. Blues and Latin, too. Admission is €15–21.

**Le Petit Journal Map 2, E11. 71 bd St-Michel, 5e ⓣ01.43.26.28.59. RER Luxembourg. Mon–Sat 9pm–2am; closed Aug.** Small, smoky bar, with good, mainly French, traditional and mainstream sounds. These days it's rather middle-aged and tourist-prone. Admission with first drink from €17, subsequent drinks from €6.50; from €44 including meal.

**Le Petit Journal Montparnasse Map 6, F12. 13 rue du Commandant-Mouchotte, 14e ⓣ01.43.21.56.70, ⓦwww.petitjournal-montparnasse.com. ⓂMontparnasse-Bienvenüe. Mon–Sat 8.30pm–2am, concerts 10pm.** Under the *Hôtel Montparnasse*, and sister establishment to *Le Petit Journal* (see above), with bigger visiting names, both French and international. Admission with first drink from €25; from €55 including meal.

**Le Sunset/Le Sunside Map 2, G6. 60 rue des Lombards, 1er ⓣ01.40.26.46.20, ⓦwww.sunset-sunside.com. ⓂChâtelet/Les-Halles. Daily 9pm–2.30am.** Two clubs in one: *Le Sunside* on the ground floor features mostly traditional jazz, whereas the downstairs *Sunset* is a venue for electric and fusion jazz. The *Sunside* concert usually starts at 9pm and the *Sunset* at 10pm, so you can sample a bit of both. Admission is €20–25.

## Mainly *chanson*

**Casino de Paris Map 3, D5. 16 rue de Clichy, 9e ⓣ01.49.95.99.99, ⓦwww.casinodeparis.fr. ⓂTrinité. Most performances 8.30pm.** This decaying, once-plush casino in one of the seediest streets in Paris is a venue for all sorts of performances – *chanson*, poetry combined with flamenco guitar, cabaret. Check the listings magazines under "Variétés" and "Chanson". Tickets from €25.

**Au Limonaire Map 3, I8. 18 Cité Bergère, 9e ⓣ01.45.23.33.33, ⓦlimonaire.free.fr. ⓂGrands-Boulevards. Daily, performances at 10pm on weekends, 7pm during**

**the week; closed Sun & Mon in July & Aug.** Tiny backstreet venue, perfect for Parisian *chanson* nights showcasing young singers and zany music/poetry/performance acts. Dinner beforehand – traditional, inexpensive, and fairly good – guarantees a seat for the show at 10pm – otherwise you'll be crammed up against the bar, if you can get in at all.

**Les Trois Baudets Map 3, E3. 64 bd de Clichy, 18e ⓣ01.42.62.33.33, ⓦwww.lestroisbaudets.com. ⓜBlanche/Pigalle. Tues–Sat 6.30pm–1.30am.** Thanks to the government of the city of Paris, this historic theatre was refitted in 2009 as a venue dedicated to the "young, sexy, playful, moving and provocative" art of *chanson*, and has already found a proud place on the Pigalle nightlife scene. It specializes in developing young, upcoming French musicians, so concerts are something of a lucky dip, but tickets are inexpensive at around €10–15. The venue is pleasingly intimate (250 seats), and there are often *after* events with DJs at the lively bar/restaurant.

# 21 Shops and markets

When it comes to **shopping**, Paris is an epicurean wonderland. Despite pressures to concentrate consumption, Parisians, for the most part, remain fiercely loyal to their small local traders; some of the most entertaining and memorable experiences of a trip to Paris are to be had just browsing in small shops.

The most distinctive and unusual shopping options are in the nineteenth-century arcades, or *passages,* in the **2e and 9e arrondissements**, almost all now smartly renovated. On the streets proper, the square kilometre around **place St-Germain-des-Prés** is hard to beat: to the north of the square lie rows of antique shops and arts and interior design boutiques, while to the south you'll find every designer clothing brand you can think of.

The **Les Halles** and **Sentier** districts are also well-stocked, good for everything from records through to designer clothes. The hip *quartiers* of the **Marais**, **Bastille** and north-eastern Paris (**Oberkampf** and the **Canal St-Martin**) are full of dinky little boutiques, interior design, arty and specialist shops and galleries. For Parisian **haute couture** – Hermès and the like – the traditional bastions are avenue Montaigne, rue François 1er and the upper end of **rue du Faubourg-St-Honoré** in the 8e.

**Markets**, too, are a grand spectacle. Though food is perhaps the best offering of the Paris markets, there are also street markets dedicated to secondhand goods (the *marchés aux puces*), clothes and textiles, flowers, birds, books and stamps.

## Clothes and accessories

Paris is a fabulous place to buy clothes, and you can snap up some excellent bargains if you're able to time your visit to coincide with the **sales**, officially held twice a year, beginning in mid-January and mid-July and lasting a month.

### Department stores and hypermarkets

**Bazar de l'Hôtel de Ville (BHV) Map 4, A10. 52–64 rue de Rivoli, 4e. Ⓜ Hôtel-de-Ville. Mon–Sat 9.30am–7pm, Wed & Thurs till 8.30pm.** Only two years younger than the Bon Marché and noted in particular for its DIY department, artists' materials, new menswear department and cheap self-service restaurant overlooking the Seine. For light refreshment, hunt out the cosy *Bricolo Café* in the DIY section (near the rue de Rivoli entrance), done out like an old-fashioned workshop complete with workbenches and lamps. The store is less elegant in appearance than some of its rivals, but it's pretty good value for money.

**Le Bon Marché Map 2, B9. 38 rue de Sèvres, 7e. Ⓜ Sèvres-Babylone. Mon–Wed & Sat 10am–8pm, Thurs & Fri 10am–9pm.** Paris's oldest department store, founded in 1852. It's calmer and classier than its Right Bank rivals, Galeries Lafayette and Printemps, but there's still plenty of high-end Paris fashion. Excellent kids' department and a legendary food hall (see p.265).

**Galeries Lafayette Map 3, D7. 40 bd Haussmann, 9e Ⓦ www.galerieslafayette.com. Ⓜ Havre-Caumartin. Mon–Sat 9.30am–7.30pm, Thurs till 9pm.** The store's forte is high fashion, with two floors given over to the latest creations by leading designers; the third floor is dedicated almost entirely to lingerie, plus there's a large section devoted to clothes for

## Where to shop for clothes in Paris

For designer prêt-à-porter, the department stores **Galeries Lafayette** and **Printemps**, just behind the Opéra Garnier on boulevard Haussmann, have unrivalled selections: if you're looking for a one-stop hit of Paris fashion, this is probably the place to come. Alternatively, the streets around St-Sulpice métro, on the Left Bank, are lined with clothing shops of all kinds. You'll find rich pickings if you wander down rues du Vieux Colombier, de Rennes, Madame and du Cherche-Midi, and the relatively compact size and relaxed, Left Bank atmosphere makes this one of the most appealing of Paris's shopping quarters. The historic **Bon Marché** department store, on rue de Sèvres, is another good reason to begin your shopping trip in this part of the Left Bank, while rues du Cherche-Midi and de Grenelle are particularly good for shoes, and rue des Saints-Pères is known for its underwear shops.

For couture and seriously expensive designer wear, make for the wealthy, manicured streets around the **Champs-Elysées**, especially rue François 1er, avenue Montaigne and rue du Faubourg-St-Honoré. Younger designers have colonized the lower reaches of the latter street, between rue Cambon and rue des Pyramides. In the heart of this area, luxurious place Vendôme is the place to find serious jewellery.

On the eastern side of the city, around the **Marais**, **Canal St-Martin** and **Bastille**, the clothes, like the residents, are younger, cooler and more relaxed. Chic boutiques cluster on rue Charlot, rue du Poitou and rue Saintonge in the Haut Marais, and young, trendy designers and hippy outfits congregate on Bastille streets rue de Charonne and rue Keller.

At the more alternative and avant-garde end of the spectrum, there's a good concentration of one-off designer boutiques around Abbesses métro, at the foot of **Montmartre** – try rues des Martyrs, des Trois-Frères, de la Vieuville, Houdon and Durantin. For more streetwise clothing, the **Forum des Halles** and surrounding streets are a good place to browse – though you'll have to sift through a fair few shops selling cheap leather jackets and clubbing gear. **Rue Etienne Marcel** and pedestrianized **rue Tiquetonne** are good for young, trendy fashion boutiques.

children on the fourth floor. Then there's a host of big names in men's and women's accessories and a huge parfumerie – all under a striking 1900 dome. Just down the road at no. 35 is Lafayette Maison, five floors of quality kitchenware, linen and furniture.

**Printemps Map 3, C7. 64 bd Haussmann, 9e ⓦwww.printemps .com. ⓂHavre-Caumartin. Mon–Sat 9.35am–8pm, Thurs till 10pm.** The main store has an excellent women's fashion department spread over three floors, plus a whole floor devoted to shoes and one to accessories. The sixth-floor brasserie is right underneath the beautiful Art Nouveau glass dome. Next door is a huge men's store, stocking a wide range of labels; the Paul Smith-designed *World Bar* on the top floor is a perfect spot for a shopping break.

**Tati Map 3, J3. 4 bd de Rochechouart, 18e ⓦwww.tati.fr. ⓂBarbès. Mon–Fri 10am–7pm, Sat 9.15am–7pm. Map 6, G12. Galerie Gaîté Montparnasse, 68 av du Maine, 14e. ⓂGaîté.** Budget department store chain with a distinctive pink gingham logo that sells reliable and utterly cheap clothing, among a host of other items.

## Classic style

**agnès b. 2, 3 & 6 rue du Jour, 1er (Map 2 F4; ⓂChâtelet-Les-Halles); 6 & 10 rue du Vieux-Colombier, 6e (Map 2, C9; ⓂSt-Sulpice). April–Sept Mon–Sat 10.30am–7.30pm, Oct–March Mon–Sat 10am–7pm.** The queen of Gallic understatement rebels against heavily styled and elaborate garments, favouring sleek, chic staples.

**APC 38 rue Madame, 6e (Map 2, C10; Mon–Sat 11am–7.30pm; ⓂSt-Sulpice); 112 rue Vieille-du-Temple, 3e (Map 4, D8; daily 11.30am–8pm; ⓂSt-Sébastien Froissart).** The clothes here are young and urban, but still effortlessly classic in that beautifully cut Parisian way. The men's and women's shops face each other across the road. The same gear, but discounted over-stock fare, can be found at Surplus APC, 20 rue André del Sarte, 18e (Map 3, I2; Tues–Sun 1–7.30pm; ⓂAnvers).

**Comptoir des Cotonniers Map 2, D8/9. 30 rue de Buci & 12 place St-Sulpice, 6e. ⓂMabillon. Map 2, F4. 10 rue du Jour, 1er. ⓂLes Halles. Map 4, B10. 33 rue des Francs-Bourgeois 4e. ⓂSt-Paul. Mon 11am–7pm, Tues–Sat 10am–7.30pm.** Utterly reliable chain (there are some thirty shops in Paris) stocking comfortable, well-cut women's basics displaying concessions to contemporary fashions without being modish. Trousers, shirts and dresses for around €100.

**Isabel Marant Map 4, F12. 16 rue de Charonne, 11e. Ⓜ Bastille. Mon–Sat 10.30am–7.30pm.** Marant excels in feminine and flattering clothes in quality fabrics such as silk and cashmere. Prices are €90 upwards for skirts, around €250–300 for coats.

**Kabuki Map 2, G3. 25 rue Etienne-Marcel, 1er. Ⓜ Etienne-Marcel. Mon–Sat 10.30am–7.30pm.** A one-stop store for all your Prada, Issey Miyake and Calvin Klein needs.

**Sabbia Rosa Map 2, C8. 71–73 rue des Saints-Pères, 6e. Ⓜ St-Germain-des-Prés. Mon–Sat 10am–7pm.** Supermodels' knickers – literally, they all shop here – at supermodel prices. Beautiful lingerie creations in silk, fine cotton and Calais lace. An ensemble will cost around €150, and you could pay three times that.

**Vanessa Bruno Map 2, D9. 25 rue St-Sulpice, 6e. Ⓜ Odéon. Map 4, D8. 100 rue Vieille du Temple, 3e. Mon–Sat 10.30am–9.30pm. Ⓜ St-Sébastien Froissart.** Bright, breezy and effortlessly beautiful women's fashions – trainers/sneakers, dresses and bags – with a hint of updated hippy chic, and some gracefully sexy touches.

**Zadig & Voltaire Map 2, C9. 1 & 3 rue du Vieux-Colombier, 6e. Ⓜ St-Sulpice. Map 2, F4. 15 rue du Jour, 1er. Ⓜ Les Halles. Map 2, C3. 9 rue du 29-Juillet, 1er. Ⓜ Tuileries. Map 2, G4. 11 rue Montmartre, 1er. Ⓜ Les Halles. Map 4, C11. 3 rue des Rosiers, 4e. Ⓜ St-Paul. Mon–Sat 10am–7pm.** The women's clothes at this small, moderately expensive Parisian chain (there are a dozen branches) are pretty and feminine. In style it's not a million miles from agnès b. (see p.253), only with a more wayward flair.

## Trendy and avant-garde

**Anne Willi Map 4, G12. 13 rue Keller, 11e. Ⓜ Ledru-Rollin/Voltaire. Mon 2–8pm, Tues–Sat 11.30am–8pm.** Completely original pieces of clothing which nonetheless respect classic French sartorial design. The works are done in gorgeous, luxurious fabrics and run the gamut from layered casual-chic sets to one-piece geometric studies of the body. Prices from €60.

**Cancan Map 3, F4. 30 rue Henry Monnier, 9e. Ⓜ Pigalle. Tues–Sat 11am–7.30pm.** In the last couple of years a handful of boutiques have sprung up on rue Monnier, all stocking choice selections of women's clothes by French *créateurs* – Cancan usually has some quirky, stylish dresses that you won't see back home, and that won't break the bank either.

**No Good Store Map 3, G5. 52 rue des Martyrs, 9e. Ⓜ Pigalle. Mon noon–7pm, Tues–Sat 11am–8pm.**

Long known for gourmet food shops, rue des Martyrs is now possibly the trendiest shopping street in Paris – and No Good Store is the most celebrated of its boutiques. It stocks mostly lesser known, younger designers with a boho or urban edge, catering for men and women, with prices generally in the €100–200 range. In the women's vintage section downstairs you might find a 1980s Thierry Mugler dress for around €400. See also Roxan at 34 rue des Martyrs and Annabel at no.36.

**Paul & Joe Map 2, C8. 62–66 rue des Saints-Pères, 7e. Ⓜ Sèvres-Babylone. Mon–Sat 10.30am–7.30pm. Map 2, F3. 46 rue Etienne-Marcel, 2e. Ⓜ Sentier.** The clothes here are quintessentially French – classic but quirky, cool but not overly radical, feminine but with an edge. As long as they've got slim, French-style figures to match, Paul & Joe can magically transform men and women into chic young Parisians.

**Spree Map 3, G3. 16 rue de La Vieuville, 18e. Ⓜ Abbesses. Mon–Sat 11am–7pm, sometimes also open Sun.** So fashionable it actually looks like an art gallery. The hip, feminine clothing collection is led by individual designers such as Vanessa Bruno, Isabel Marant and Christian Wijnants, and there are often a few vintage pieces too, as well as accessories. Clothing mostly falls in the €100–250 range.

**Swildens Map 4, C8. 22 rue de Poitou, 3e. Ⓜ St-Sébastien Froissart. Mon-Sat 10am–7.30pm.** Womenswear designer Juliette Swildens makes well-cut, affordable clothes, with a hint of rock'n'roll. Typical pieces are off-the-shoulder smocks, slouchy sweatshirts, baggy harem pants and layered knits.

**Vincent Jalbert et Yves Andrieux Map 4, C7. 55 rue Charlot, 3e. Ⓜ Filles-du-Calvaire. Mon–Fri 10am–1pm & 2–7pm, Sat 11am–7pm.** It's hard to believe these elegant and beautiful clothes (each piece is unique, and costs from around €400) were made from something so utilitarian as recycled army uniforms from the 1950s. The tailored jackets and long coats are particularly stylish, and there are flouncy skirts made from recycled parachutes and tents. A more affordable range of attractive bags, made out of floral vintage fabrics, is also available, as well as some jaunty panama hats fashioned out of psychedelic 1960s fabrics.

## The big designer names

Below is a selection of the main or most conveniently located outlets of Paris's

**top designers.** Nearly all the shops below operate normal French boutique **opening hours** of Mon–Sat 10am–7pm.

**Balenciaga Map 7, F5. 10 av George V, 8e. ⓂAlma Marceau/ George V.** The Spanish fashion house (now owned by a French multinational and led by Nicolas Ghesquière), once famed for its bubble skirts, is currently producing some of the most exciting designs in Paris.

**Chanel Map 7, H4. 42 av Montaigne, 8e. ⓂFranklin-D. Roosevelt.** Born in 1883, Gabrielle "Coco" Chanel engendered a way of life that epitomized elegance, class and refined taste. Her most famous signatures are the legendary No. 5 perfume, the black evening dress and the once-omnipresent tweed suit.

**Chloé Map 7, M4. 54 rue du Faubourg-St-Honoré, 8e. ⓂMadeleine.** Dark, tweed wool trousers, light knit tops and lovely semi-formal prêt-à-porter dresses.

**Christian Lacroix Map 7, L3. 73 rue du Faubourg-St-Honoré, 8e. ⓂConcorde. Map 2, B2. 366 rue St-Honoré, 1er. ⓂMadeleine.** Best known for his flamboyant, Zorro-inspired vests and cloaks, this baroque, theatrical designer now does everything from just-woke-up rumpled trousers to sequined and laméd miniskirts.

**Comme des Garçons Map 7, L3. 54 rue du Faubourg-St-Honoré, 8e. ⓂConcorde.** Led by Tokyo-born Rei Kawakubo, this very popular label favours novel tints and youthful, asymmetric cuts that defamiliarize the body. Exceptional lace sweaters.

**Jean-Paul Gaultier Map 7, F3. 44 av George V, 8e. ⓂGeorge V. Map 2, E2. 6 rue Vivienne, 2e. ⓂBourse.** The primordial young turk of Paris fashion, his current sets are very industrial-meets-Second Empire. Colouring is quite eclectic, with lots of greys and blacks and the odd chartreuse or fuchsia thrown in to unbalance you. The denim collection at the stores is well within reach of those not being chased by paparazzi.

**Lagerfeld Gallery Map 2, D7. 40 rue de Seine, 6e. ⓂMabillon.** Though he still designs for Chanel and Fendi, Karl Lagerfeld's life as an *intellectuel* and *auteur* clearly shows in his own ready-to-wear line, typified by stalwart tailoring, bold colours and comfy-fitting tops and jackets that make a lasting first impression.

**Pierre Cardin Map 7, K4. 27 av Marigny, 8e. ⓂPlace-Clemenceau.** Famous early on for his futuristic body suits, Cardin's current label uses irregular cuts in outspoken, brash prints and fabrics.

**Sonia Rykiel Map 2, C8. Women: 175 bd St-Germain, 6e. Ⓜ St-Germain-des-Prés.** Unmistakably Parisian designer who threw out her first line when the *soixante-huitards* threw Europe into social revolution. Her multicoloured designs – especially sweaters – are all the rage, as is Sonia, her daugher Nathalie's younger, funkier clothing offshoot (61 rue des Saints-Pères, 6e; Ⓜ Sèvres-Babylone).

**YSL Rive Gauche Map 2, D9. Women: 6 place St-Sulpice, 6e. Ⓜ St-Sulpice/ Mabillon. Map 7, M4. Men & women: 32–38 rue du Faubourg-St-Honoré, 8e. Ⓜ Concorde.** When Yves Saint Laurent retired in 2002, he closed shop on his revered couture line and passed the baton over to Tom Ford, who initially designed this prêt-à-porter spin-off. The inspiration remains very YSL, however: classic monochrome chic, especially for men.

## Discount clothing

A number of dedicated "stock" shops (short for *déstockage*) sell end-of-line and last year's models at thirty- to fifty-percent **reductions**. Before you get too excited, however, remember that thirty percent off €750 still leaves a hefty bill – not that all items are this expensive. The best times of year to join the scrums are after the new collections have come out in January and October.

**La Clef des Marques Map 6, H10. 124 bd Raspail, 7e. Ⓜ Vavin. Mon 12.30–7pm, Tues–Sat 10.30am–7pm.** Huge store with a wide choice of inexpensive brand-name clothes for men and women – also lots of lingerie and children's clothes.

**Défilé de Marques Map 6, B3. 171 rue de Grenelle, 7e. Ⓜ La Tour-Maubourg. Tues–Sat noon–8pm.** *Dépôt-vente* shop selling a wide choice of designer clothes for women – as returned unsold from the big-name boutiques. Labels from Prada to Paco Rabanne discounted to around €200–300.

**Le Mouton à Cinq Pattes Map 2, E9. 138 bd St-Germain, 6e. Ⓜ Odéon/Mabillon. Mon–Sat 10.30am–7.30pm. Map 2, B10. 18 rue St-Placide. Women only: 8 rue St-Placide, 6e. Both Ⓜ Sèvres-Babylone. Mon–Sat 10am–7pm.** Names such as Helmut Lang and Gaultier can be found among the racks of smart, discounted end-of-line and last-season's clothes for men and women, though often enough the labels are cut out so you'll have to trust your judgement.

## Secondhand and retro clothes

**Alternatives Map 4, B11. 18 rue du Roi-de-Sicile, 4e. Ⓜ St-Paul. Tues–Sat 1–7pm.** Vintage meets designer at this fantastic shop where you can perfect *le look parisien* both with fashionable labels and lesser-known brands. The clothes here are often straight off the bodies of runway models.

**Kiliwatch Map 2, G3. 64 rue Tiquetonne, 2e. Ⓜ Etienne-Marcel. Mon 2–7pm, Tues–Sun 10am–7pm.** A clubbers' mecca, where rails of new cheap 'n' chic streetwear and a slew of trainers/sneakers meet the best range of unusual secondhand clothes and accessories in Paris. This is the place in Paris to buy jeans for men, with no fewer than fifteen well-displayed brands.

**L'Occaserie 30 rue de la Pompe, 16e Ⓦ www.occaserie.com. Ⓜ Muette/Passy. Mon–Sat 11am–7pm. All branches Map 1, B4. 16 & 21 rue de l'Annonciation; 14 rue Jean Bologne; 19 rue de la Pompe, all 16e. Ⓜ Muette/Passy.** Specialists in secondhand haute couture – Dior, Prada, Cartier and the like. "Secondhand" doesn't mean cheap though: Chanel suits are around €720 and Louis Vuitton handbags €300.

**Réciproque 89, 92, 93–97, 101 & 123 rue de la Pompe, 16e Ⓦ www.reciproque.fr. Ⓜ Pompe. Tues–Sat 11am–7pm.** A series of shops akin to L'Occaserie, this one is slightly more chichi and better for couture labels, with expensive finds like Christian Lacroix, Moschino and Manolo Blahnik. Women's design at no. 93–95; accessories and coats for men at no. 101; more accessories and coats for women at no.123.

## Shoes, accessories and perfumes

Some of the best streets for shoe shopping are rue de Grenelle and rue du Cherche-Midi in the 6e and rue du Meslay in the 3e.

**Annick Goutal Map 2, B3. 14 rue de Castiglione, 1er. Ⓜ Tuileries. Mon–Sat 10am–7pm.** Though Goutal herself has passed on, the business is still in the family, continuing to produce her exquisite perfumes, all made from natural essences. Her best-selling fragrance is Eau d'Hadrien, a heady blend of citrus fruits and cypress, and there's also a range for men.

**Autour du Monde Map 4, C10. 8 rue des Francs-Bourgeois, 4e. Ⓜ Saint-Paul. Mon–Sat 11am–7.30pm, Sun 2–7pm.** Stocks cute canvas pumps by Bensimon in colours such as lime green, orange and pink, though the classic white is hard to beat.

**Biberon & Fils Map 2, D4. 334 rue St-Honoré, 1er. ⓂPyramides/Tuileries. Mon–Sat 10.30am–6.30pm.** An unexpected find on one of the city's most exclusive shopping streets, this bargain shop sells very stylish French-made leather handbags in citrus colours as well as classic shades (€60–80).

**Cécile et Jeanne Map 4, off F14. 49 av Daumesnil, 12e. ⓂGare-de-Lyon. Mon–Fri 10am–7pm, Sat & Sun 2–7pm.** Innovative jewellery design from local artisans in one of the Viaduc des Arts showrooms. Many pieces under €100.

**Editions de Parfums Frédéric Malle Map 2, B8. 37 rue de Grenelle, 7e. ⓂRue-du-Bac. Mon–Sat 11am–7pm; closed 2 weeks in Aug.** All the perfumes at this deliciously serious boutique have been created by "authors", which means professional parfumeurs working under their own name through this "publishing house". A 50ml bottle costs upwards of €50, or you could spend a fortune having a perfume individually designed for you.

**Galerie Hélène Porée Map 2, E9. 1 rue de l'Odéon, 6e. ⓂOdéon. Tues–Sat 11am–7pm.** Original jewellery from a number of artisan jewellers, as well as ceramics. Prices range from €200 to several thousand euros.

**Hermès Map 7, M4. 24 rue du Faubourg-St-Honoré, 8e. ⓂConcorde. Mon–Sat 10am–6.30pm.** Luxury clothing and accessory store; come here for the ultimate silk scarf – at a price.

**Jamin-Puech Map 3, J7. 61 rue d'Hauteville, 10e. ⓂPoissonière. Tues–Sat 10.30am–7pm. Map 4, B10. 68 rue Vieille-du-Temple, 4e. ⓂHôtel de Ville. Tues noon–7pm, Wed–Sat 11am–7pm.** An exquisite range of beautifully crafted bags (around €200) in brightly coloured leather, crepe silk and other luxury fabrics.

**Marie Mercié Map 2, D9. 23 rue St-Sulpice, 6e. ⓂOdéon. Mon–Sat 11am–7pm.** This grande dame of *chapellerie* sells a glamorous collection of plaid, felt and fur hats for all occasions, for €180 and up.

**Repetto Map 3, D9. 22 rue de la Paix, 2e. ⓂOpéra. Mon–Sat 9.30am–7.30pm.** This long-established supplier of ballet shoes, which has shod ballet stars from Margot Fonteyn to Sylvie Guillem, has branched out to produce attractive pumps in assorted colours, much coveted by the fashion crowd.

**Séphora Map 7, H3. 70 av des Champs-Elysées, 8e. ⓂFranklin-D. Roosevelt. Mon–Sat 10am–midnight, Sun 11am–midnight.** A huge perfume and cosmetics emporium, stocking every conceivable brand, including Séphora's own line of fun, girly and reasonably priced cosmetics and accessories. There are lots of testers, and you can get free makeovers, pampering and beauty consultations from the solicitous sales staff. It's also open till midnight, and handy if you're out on the town without your lipstick.

## Art

The commercial **art galleries** are concentrated in the Haut Marais, on rue Charlot and others; in the 8$^{e}$, especially in and around avenue Matignon; on rue Quincampoix, near the Pompidou Centre; and in St-Germain. There are literally hundreds of galleries and, for an idea of who is being exhibited where, look up details in *Pariscope* under "Expositions". Entry to commercial galleries is free.

**Comptoir des Ecritures Map 2, H5. 35 rue Quincampoix, 4$^{e}$. Ⓜ Rambuteau. Tues–Sat 11am–7pm.** A delightful shop entirely devoted to the art of calligraphy, with an extensive collection of paper, pens, brushes and inks.

**Dubois Map 2, F11. 20 rue Soufflot, 5$^{e}$. RER Luxembourg. Tues–Sat 9am–7pm.** In the same great apothecary-style building since the mid-1800s, the Dubois family still offers an excellent selection of art supplies and paints alongside very knowledgeable service.

**Papier Plus Map 4, A11. 9 rue du Pont-Louis-Philippe, 4$^{e}$. Ⓜ St-Paul. Mon–Sat noon–7pm.** Fine-quality, colourful stationery, including notebooks, travel journals, photo albums and artists' portfolios.

## Design

A small selection of places where contemporary and the best of twentieth-century **design** can be seen is listed below. Also worth checking out are the shops in the art and design museums.

**Colette Map 2, C3. 213 rue St-Honoré, 1er. Ⓜ Tuileries. Mon–Sat 10.30am–7.30pm.** This cutting-edge concept store, combining high fashion and design, complete with photo gallery and exhibition space, has become something of a tourist attraction. When you've finished sizing up the Pucci underwear, Stella McCartney womenswear and Sonia Rykiel handbags, you could head for the cool *Water Bar*, with its 80 different kinds of H2O.

**CSAO (Compagnie du Sénégal et de l'Afrique de l'Ouest) Map 4, C10. 9 rue Elzévir, 3e Ⓦ www.csao.fr. Ⓜ St-Paul. Mon–Sat 11am–7pm, Sun 2–7pm.** Fair-trade crafts and artwork from West Africa, including quilts, cushion covers and Malian cotton scarves in rich, earthy tones and painted glass from Senegal.

**Fiesta Galerie Map 4, B11. 24 rue du Pont Louis Philippe, 4e. Ⓜ Pont Marie. Mon–Sat noon–7pm, Sun 2–7pm.** A big selection of twentieth-century kitsch and retro objects.

**Galerie Patrick Séguin Map 4, G12. 5 rue des Taillandiers, 11e. Ⓜ Bastille. Tues–Sat noon–7pm.** A fine collection of furniture and objects from the 1950s, including pieces by Le Corbusier and Jean Prouvé, though not everything is for sale.

**Louvre des Antiquaires Map 2, D4. 2 place du Palais-Royal, 1er. Ⓜ Palais-Royal/Musée-du-Louvre. Tues–Sun 11am–7pm; closed Sun in July & Aug.** An enormous antiques and furniture hypermarket where you can pick up anything from a Mycenaean seal ring to an Art Nouveau vase – for a price.

**Lulu Berlu Map 4, E7. 2 rue du Grand Prieuré, 11e. Ⓜ Oberkampf. Mon–Sat 11.30am–7.30pm.** This shop is crammed with twentieth-century toys and curios, most with their original packaging. There's a particularly good collection of 1970–90s favourites, including Doctor Who, Star Wars, Planet of the Apes and Batman toys, and they also do a good range of new toys.

**Résonances Map 7, M3. 3–5 bd Malesherbes, 8e. Ⓜ Madeleine. Mon–Sat 10am–8pm.** Stylish kitchen and bathroom accessories, with an emphasis on French design. Covetable items include elegant wine decanters and a white porcelain hot-chocolate maker.

**Le Viaduc des Arts Map 4, F14. 9–129 av Daumesnil, 12e. Ⓜ Bastille/Gare de Lyon. Most shops Mon–Sat 10.30am–7.30pm.** Practically the entire north side of the street is dedicated to an extremely high standard of skilled workmanship and craft. Each arch of this old railway viaduct houses a shop front and workspace for the artists within, who produce contemporary metalwork, ceramics, tapestry, sculpture and much more.



# Books

The most atmospheric areas for **book** shopping are the Seine *quais*, with their rows of new and secondhand bookstalls perched against the river parapet, and the narrow streets of the Quartier Latin. **English-language bookshops** function as home-away-from-home for expats, often with readings from visiting writers, and the occasional handy noticeboards for flat-shares, language lessons and work.

For a general French-language bookshop, the classic is **Gibert Jeune**, with various branches around place St-Michel, in the Quartier Latin.

## English-language books

**Galignani Map 2, C3. 224 rue de Rivoli, 1er. Ⓜ Concorde. Mon–Sat 10am–7pm.** Claims to be the first English bookshop established on the Continent way back in 1802. Stocks a good range, including fine art and children's books.

**Red Wheelbarrow Map 4, C12. 22 rue Saint Paul, 4e Ⓦ www.theredwheelbarrow.com. Ⓜ Saint Paul. Mon 10am–6pm, Tues–Sat 10am–7pm, Sun 2–6pm.** A small, friendly, Canadian-run bookshop, stocking a good selection of general fiction, history and children's books, as well as English-language books set in Paris. Check the website for occasional readings and musical *soirées*.

**Shakespeare & Co Map 2, G9. 37 rue de la Bûcherie, 5e Ⓦ www.shakespeareco.org. Ⓜ Maubert-Mutualité. Daily noon–midnight.** A cosy and very famous literary haunt (see p.98). Has the biggest selection of secondhand English books in town and runs lots of events. Every Mon at 8pm there are readings in the library upstairs (where you can sit and read for as long as you like at other times).

**Tea and Tattered Pages Map 6, F9. 24 rue Mayet, 6e. Ⓜ Duroc. Mon–Sat 11am–7pm, Sun noon–6pm.** A secondhand bookshop with more than 15,000 titles in English, mostly tatty fiction. You can munch on cheesecake, bagels and the like in the small, attached tearoom.

**Village Voice Map 2, D9. 6 rue Princesse, 6e. ⓂMabillon. Mon 2.30–7pm, Tues–Sat 10am–7.30pm, Sun 1–6pm.** A welcoming recreation of a neighbour-hood bookstore, with a good, two-floor selection of fiction and non-fiction. Also runs frequent readings and author signings.

**W. H. Smith Map 2, B3. 248 rue de Rivoli, 1er. ⓂConcorde. Daily 9.30am–7pm.** A Parisian outlet of the British chain with a wide range of new books, newspapers and magazines.

## Art, architecture and cookery

**Artcurial Map 7, I4. 7 Rond-Point des Champs-Elysées, 8e ⓦwww.artcurial.com. ⓂFranklin-D. Roosevelt. Mon–Fri 10.30am–7pm; closed 2 weeks in Aug.** The best art bookshop in Paris, set in an elegant townhouse. Sells French and foreign editions, and there's also a gallery, which puts on interesting exhibitions, and an attractive café.

**FNAC Map 2, G5. Forum des Halles, niveau 2, Porte Pierre-Lescot, 1er. Ⓜ/RER Châtelet-Les Halles. Map 2, B11. 136 rue de Rennes, 6e. ⓂSt-Placide. Map 7, H3. 74 av des Champs-Elysées, 8e. ⓂFranklin-D. Roosevelt. Map 1, A2. CNIT, 2 place de la Défense. ⓂLa Défense. ⓦwww.fnac.com. Mon–Sat 10am–7.30pm.** Lots of comics, guidebooks, maps, fiction, and more.

**La Hune Map 2, C8. 170 bd St-Germain, 6e. ⓂSt-Germain-des-Prés. Mon–Sat 10am–11.45pm, Sun 11am–7.45pm.** A good general French range, but the main selling point – apart from its fifty-year history as a Left Bank arts institution – is the art, design, fashion and photography "image" collection on the first floor.

**Librairie des Archives Map 4, A9. 83 rue du Temple, 3e ⓦwww.librairiedesarchives.com. ⓂRambuteau/Hôtel de Ville. Tues–Sat noon–7pm.** An extensive selection of fine and decorative arts and fashion, plus a large number of out-of-print books.

**Librairie Gourmande Map 2, F2. 90 rue Montmartre, 2e ⓦwww.librairie-gourmande.fr. ⓂSentier. Mon–Sat 11am–7pm.** The very last word in books about cooking.

**Librairie le Moniteur Map 2, E10. 7 place de l'Odéon, 6e. ⓂOdéon. Mon–Sat 10.30am–7pm.** Entirely dedicated to architecture, both contemporary and historical, with books in English as well as French. There's even an in-house magazine devoted to public building projects.

**Librairie du Musée d'Art Moderne de la Ville de Paris Map 7, E6. Palais de Tokyo, 11 av du Président-Wilson, 16e. Ⓜléna.** Specialist publications on modern art, including foreign works. For museum opening hours, see p.122.

**Librairie du Musée des Arts Décoratifs Map 2, D4. 107 rue de Rivoli, 1er. ⓂPalais-Royal. Daily 10am–7pm.** Design, posters, architecture, graphics and the like.

## Comics (Bandes Dessinées)

**Album Map 2, G9. 6–8 rue Dante, 5e. ⓂMaubert-Mutualité. Map 2, E10. 60 rue Monsieur-le-Prince, 6e. ⓂOdéon. Ⓦwww.album.fr. Mon–Sat 10am–8pm.** Serious collection of French *BD*s, some of them rare editions with original artwork. This block of rue Dante houses no fewer than five separate comic book shops.

**Editions Déesse Map 2, H10. 8 rue Cochin, 5e. ⓂMaubert-Mutualité. Mon 2.30–7pm, Tues–Fri 11am–1pm & 2.30–7pm, Sun 11am–7pm.** Specializes in older, rarer comics. The well-informed owner speaks excellent English and should be able to help you locate whatever you need.

**Thé-Troc Map 4, F6. 52 rue Jean-Pierre Timbaud, 11e. ⓂParmentier. Mon–Fri 9.30am–8pm, Sat 11am–8pm.** The friendly owner publishes *The Fabulous Furry Freak Brothers* in French and English (he is a friend of the author of the famous 1970s comics, who lives nearby). There are other comic books and memorabilia on sale, too, as well as a wide selection of teas and teapots, secondhand records, jewellery and assorted junk. The attached *salon de thé* (until 7pm) is comfy, colourful and restful, and has board games.

# Food and drink

Paris has resisted the march of megastores with admirable resilience. Almost every *quartier* still has its charcuterie, boulangerie and **weekly market**, while some streets, such as rue Cler, in the 7e and rue des Martyrs, in the 9e, are literally lined with groceries, butchers' shops, delicatessens, pâtisseries, cheese shops and wine merchants. Shopping at these places is an aesthetic experience.

As for buying food with a view to economical eating, you will be best off shopping at the street markets or supermarkets

– though save your bread-buying at least for the local boulangerie. Useful **supermarkets** with branches throughout Paris are Monoprix, Franprix and Ed l'Epicier, with Leader Price at the bottom end of the market. Naturalia is the big chain of organic grocery shops.

## Gourmet food shops

Any list of food shops in Paris has to have at its head these three palaces.

**Fauchon Map 7, N3. 24–30 place de la Madeleine, 8e. Ⓜ Madeleine. Mon–Sat 9am–8pm.** An amazing range of extravagantly beautiful groceries, exotic fruit and vegetables, charcuterie, wines, both French and foreign – almost anything you can think of, all at exorbitant prices. The quality is assured by blind testing, which all suppliers have to submit to. There's also a *traiteur* and a restaurant.

**La Grande Epicerie Map 2, A10. 38 rue de Sèvres, 7e. Ⓜ Sèvres-Babylone. Mon–Sat 8.30am–9pm.** This edible offshoot of the famous Bon Marché department store may not be quite as nakedly epicurean as Fauchon and Hédiard, but it's a fabulous emporium of fresh and packed foods. Popular among choosy Parisians, moneyed expats (for its country-specific favourites) and gastro-tourists alike.

**Hédiard Map 7, N3. 21 place de la Madeleine, 8e. Ⓜ Madeleine. Mon–Sat 8am–10pm.** The aristocrat's grocer since the 1850s. Superlative-quality coffees, spices and confitures. There's also an upstairs restaurant.

## Bread, cheese and charcuterie

**Barthélémy Map 2, B8. 51 rue de Grenelle, 7e. Ⓜ Rue du Bac. Tues–Sat 8.30am–1pm & 4–7.15pm; closed Aug.** Purveyors of carefully ripened and meticulously stored seasonal cheeses to the rich and powerful.

**Aux Ducs de Gascogne Map 4, C11. 111 rue St-Antoine, 4e. Ⓜ St-Paul. Mon–Sat 10am–8pm.** Excellent range of high-quality charcuterie, as well as enticing – and expensive – deli goods ranging from little salads to caviar.

**Flo Prestige Map 2, C2. 42 place du Marché-St-Honoré, 1er. Ⓜ Pyramides. Daily 8am–11pm.** Stocks all sorts of super delicacies, plus wines, champagne and exquisite ready-made dishes.

**Labeyrie Map 2, G4. 6 rue Montmartre, 1er. Ⓜ Châtelet-Les**

**Halles. Tues–Fri 11am–2pm & 3–7pm.** Specialist in products from the Landes region, pâtés in particular: Bayonne hams, goose and duck pâtés, conserves, etc.

**La Maison du Fromage Map 2, H14. 118 rue Mouffetard, 5e. Ⓜ Censier-Daubenton. Map 6, F8. 62 rue de Sèvres, 6e. Ⓜ Duroc. Tues–Sat 9am–1pm & 4–7.30pm, Sun 9am–1pm.** Offers a wonderful selection, beautifully displayed. Specializes in goat, sheep and mountain cheeses.

**Petrossian Map 6, C2. 18 bd de Latour-Maubourg, 7e. Ⓜ Latour-Maubourg. Mon–Sat 9.30am–8pm.** Not just gilt-edged fish eggs, but other Russian and French delicacies too. You can try delights such as smoked salmon sorbet at the restaurant next door.

**Poilâne Map 2, C9. 8 rue du Cherche-Midi, 6e. Ⓜ Sèvres-Babylone. Mon–Sat 7.15am–8.15pm.** The source of the famous *pain poilâne* – a type of bread baked using traditional methods (albeit ramped up on an industrial scale) as conceived by the late and legendary Monsieur Poilâne himself.

## Chocolates and pâtisseries

**Debauve et Gallais Map 2, C7. 30 rue des Saints-Pères, 7e. Ⓜ St-Germain-des-Prés/Sèvres-Babylone. Mon–Sat 9.30am–7pm.** A beautiful shop specializing in chocolate and elaborate sweets that's been around since chocolate was taken as a medicine – and an aphrodisiac.

**Jean-Paul Hévin Map 2, C3. 231 rue Saint-Honoré, 8e. Ⓜ Tuileries. Mon–Sat 10am–7.30pm.** One of the best chocolatiers in Paris, with a sleek shop displaying an array of elegantly presented tablets of chocolate, all bearing little descriptions of their aroma and characteristics, as if they were fine wines. Upstairs is a cosy *salon de thé* serving delicious chocolate cakes.

**Pâtisserie Stohrer Map 2, G3. 51 rue Montorgueil, 2e. Ⓜ Sentier. Daily 7.30am–8pm; closed first 2 weeks in Aug.** Bread, pâtisserie and chocolate have been prepared here since 1730. Discover what *pain aux raisins* should really taste like.

## Tea and coffee

**Mariage Frères Map 4, B10. 30 rue du Bourg-Tibourg, 4e. Ⓜ Hôtel-de-Ville. Daily 10.30am–7.30pm.** Hundreds of teas, neatly packed in tins, line the floor-to-ceiling shelves of this 100-year-old tea emporium. There's also a classy *salon de thé* (see p.210).

**Verlet Map 2, D4. 256 rue St-Honoré, 1er. Ⓜ Palais Royal-Musée du Louvre. Mon–Sat 9am–7pm.** A café and old-fashioned *torréfacteur* (coffee merchant), one of the best known in Paris, selling both familiar and less common varieties of coffee and tea from around the world.

### Wine

**Les Caves Augé Map 7, L2. 116 bd Haussmann, 8e. Ⓜ St-Augustin. Mon 1–7.30pm, Tues–Sat 9am–7.30pm.** This old-fashioned, wood-panelled shop is the oldest *cave* in Paris and not only sells fine wines, but also a wide selection of port, armagnac, cognac and champagne.

**La Crèmerie Map 2, E9. 9 rue des Quatre-Vents, 6e. Tues–Sat 10.30am–10pm; closed Aug. Ⓜ Odéon.** Excellent wine shop set behind an attractive old dairy shop front. The Miard family, who run it, can recommend some fine lesser-known wines, especially from the Loire and Burgundy.

Like an Italian *enoteca*, they offer wines by the glass, with plates of hams and cheeses (€6–11) to aid tasting.

**Lavinia Map 2, B1. 3–5 bd de la Madeleine, 8e. Ⓜ Madeleine. Mon–Fri 10am–8pm, Sat 9am–8pm.** The largest wine and spirits store in Europe. The gorgeous, modern interior displays thousands of bottles from over 43 countries, and the wine cellar holds some of the rarest in the world. The attached wine library and bar entices you to read up, then drink up.

**De Vinis Illustribus Map 2, G11. 48 rue de la Montagne-Ste-Geneviève, 5e. Ⓜ Maubert-Mutualité. Tues–Sat 11am–8pm.** International wine dealer Lionel Michelin has set up shop in the ancient cellar where Hemingway used to buy his wine. Specializes in old and rare vintages, but will happily sell you a recherché €10 bottle of good *vin de pays*.

## A miscellany

**Abdon Map 4, E11. 6 bd Beaumarchais, 11e. Ⓜ Chemin-Vert. Tues–Sat 9.30am–12.30pm & 1.30–6.30pm.** New and secondhand photographic equipment. If they don't have what you're looking for, try the half-dozen other camera shops on the same street.

**Archives de la Presse Map 4, B9. 51 rue des Archives, 3e. Ⓜ Rambuteau. Mon–Sat 10.30am–7pm.** A fascinating shop for a browse, trading in old French newspapers and magazines, with vintage *Vogues* giving a good insight into the changing fashion scene.

**Boîte à Musique Anna Joliet Map 2, E3. Jardin du Palais-Royal, 9 rue de Beaujolais, 1er. ⓂPalais Royal-Musée du Louvre. Mon–Sat 10am–7pm.** A delightful, minuscule boutique selling every style of music box, from inexpensive self-winding toy models to grand cabinets costing thousands of euros. Prices begin at around €10 and quickly go up from there.

**De Bouche à Oreille Map 4, B11. 26 rue du Roi-de-Sicile, 4e. ⓂSt-Paul. Tues–Sat 11.30am–7pm.** Attractive *objets* for the home, such as Baroque-style candelabras, lamps, embroidered teacloths, glass carafes and reproductions of Robert de Vaugandy's globe (1745) – just the thing for the study.

**Ciné-Images Map 6, E6. 68 rue de Babylone, 7e ⓦwww.cine-images.com. ⓂSèvres-Babylone. Tues–Fri 10am–1pm & 2–7pm, Sat 2–7pm.** Suitably located right opposite the famous La Pagode cinema, this classy shop sells original and mainly French film posters. Prices range from €30 for something small and recent to tens of thousands of euros for the historic advert for the Lumière brothers' *L'Arroseur Arrosé*.

**Le Pot à Tabac Map 7, M1. 28 rue de la Pépinière, 8e. ⓂSt-Augustin. Daily 7.30am–7.30pm.** Classy selection of pipes, cigars, tobacco and thermidors, plus an enormous choice of international cigarettes.

**Trousselier Map 7, M2. 73 bd Haussmann, 8e. ⓂSt-Augustin. Mon–Sat 10am–7pm.** Described in French *Vogue* as *the* artificial flower shop. Every conceivable species of flora fashioned from man-made fibre, from a simple basket of roses to more decadent and pricey arrangements.

# Markets

Many of Paris's biggest and most historic **markets**, such as those on rue Mouffetard (5e) and rue des Martyrs (9e) are now lined with food shops, but it's still remarkably easy to find fresh fruit, vegetables and even meat, fish and cheese on the city's streets. There are also a number of specialist markets, from those selling books and art to the famous "flea markets" – which nowadays are really giant antiques emporia.

## Books, stamps and art

For books and old posters, don't forget the **bouquinistes**, who hook their green, padlocked boxes onto the riverside *quais* of the Left Bank.

**Marché du Livre Ancien et d'Occasion Pavillon Baltard, Parc Georges-Brassens, rue Brancion, 15e. Ⓜ Porte-de-Vanves. Sat & Sun 9am–6pm.** Secondhand and antiquarian books; best in the morning.

**Marché aux Timbres Map 7, K4. Junction of avs Marigny & Gabriel, on the north side of place Clemenceau in the 8e. Ⓜ Champs-Elysées–Clemenceau. Thurs, Sat, Sun & hols 10am–7pm.** Around twenty stalls selling common and rare stamps, as well as postcards and phonecards.

## Clothes and flea markets

Paris has three main **flea markets** (*marchés aux puces*) of ancient descent gathered about the old gates of the city. No longer the haunts of the flamboyant gypsies and petty crooks of literary tradition, they are nonetheless good entertainment.

**Porte de Montreuil Av de Porte de Montreuil, 20e. Ⓜ Porte-de-Montreuil. Sat, Sun & Mon 7.30am–5pm.** Cheap new clothes have begun to dominate what was the best of Paris's flea markets for second-hand clothes – still cheapest on Mon when leftovers from the weekend are sold off. Also old furniture, household goods and assorted junk.

**Puces de Vanves Map 1. Av Georges-Lafenestre/av Marc-Sangnier, 14e. Ⓜ Porte-de-Vanves. Sat & Sun 7am–1.30pm.** The best choice for bric-a-brac and little Parisian knick-knacks. Professionals deal alongside weekend amateurs.

**St-Ouen/Porte de Clignancourt Map 1. 18e. Ⓜ Porte-de-Clignancourt. Mon, Sat & Sun 7.30am–7pm.** The biggest and most touristy flea market, with nearly a thousand stalls selling new and secondhand clothes, shoes, records, books and junk of all sorts. The majority of the covered market, however, is now given over to expensive antiques. For a full description, see pp.160–162.

## Food markets

For a full list of Paris's many street food markets, search Ⓦ www.paris.fr under "marchés". The most historic markets – the rue Mouffetard (5e), rue Cler (7e), rue des Martyrs (9e), rue Lévis (17e) and rue Montorgueil (2e) – are now more market street than street market, with their stalls mostly metamorphosed into permanent, often fairly luxurious shops. For real **street markets** the Left Bank offers a tempting scattering in the 5e – notably on place Maubert (Tues, Thurs & Sat) and place Monge (Wed, Fri & Sun). The larger Left Bank markets are found alongside the cemetery on boulevard Edgar-Quinet, 14e (Wed & Sat, with a flea market on Sun); opposite Val-de-Grâce hospital on boulevard Port-Royal, 5e (Tues, Thurs & Sat); and on rue de la Convention, in the 15e (Tues, Thurs & Sun). On the Right Bank, the rue Lepic market (Tues–Sun), in Montmartre is satisfyingly authentic. On Sunday mornings a very fancy organic market takes over boulevard Raspail, 7e, in the vicinity of rue du Cherche-Midi; there's more organic produce on Saturday mornings, at place Brancusi, 14e. For a different feel and more exotic **foreign produce**, take a look at the Mediterranean, Oriental and African displays in boulevard de Belleville, 20e (Tues & Fri); place d'Aligre, 12e (Tues–Sun); and rue Dejean, 18e (Tues–Sun)

Food markets are traditionally **morning** affairs, usually starting between 7 and 8am and tailing off sometime between 1 and 2.30pm. However, in a break with Parisian tradition, there are a few afternoon-only markets – very well received by those who prefer to sleep in.

22

# Film, theatre and dance

Movie-goers have a choice of around three hundred **films** showing in Paris in any one week, covering every country and era. The city also has a vibrant **theatre** scene and several superstar directors are based here, including Peter Brook and Ariane Mnouchkine, known for their highly innovative, cutting-edge productions. **Dance** enjoys a high profile, enhanced by the opening in 2004 of the Centre National de la Danse, Europe's largest dance academy.

---

Listings for all films and stage productions are detailed in *Pariscope* and other weekly listing magazines (see p.24). The leading film listings website ⓦ www.allocine.fr is in French only, but pretty much navigable even if you only speak a few words.

---

# Film

Despite the success of the multiscreen cinema chains, Paris's smaller and more historic **cinemas** continue to screen splendidly varied programmes of art-house and international cinema. Aside from new and recent film releases, the repertoires of outstanding directors from the world over are regularly shown as part of retrospective seasons. These will be listed along with other cinema-clubs and museum screenings under "Séances exceptionnelles" or "Ciné-clubs", and are usually cheaper than ordinary cinemas.

**To watch foreign films in the original language (with subtitles in French) look for version originale or "v.o." in the listings, and avoid version française or "v.f.", which means it's dubbed into French.**

For the seriously committed film-freak, the best movie venue in Paris is the **Cinémathèque Française**, 51 rue de Bercy (Ⓜ Bercy; ⓣ 01.71.19.33.33, ⓦ www.cinemathequefrancaise.com). Along with a dedicated museum of cinema (see p.93), you get a choice of around two dozen different films and shorts every week, many of which would never be shown commercially – and it's all packaged in an incredible building designed by Frank Gehry. Tickets are only €6.50. At the newly restored **Forum des Images**, 2 Grande Galerie, Porte St-Eustache, Forum des Halles (ⓣ 01.44.76.63.00, ⓦ www.forumdesimages.net), several films (or projected videos) are screened daily, with tickets at just €5. The forum also offers a large library of newsreel footage, film clips, adverts and documentaries. Cultural institutions and embassies also have their own cinema programmes and screenings: one with particularly good programmes is the **Pompidou Centre**, place Georges-Pompidou (Ⓜ Rambuteau; ⓣ 01.44.78.12.33, ⓦ www.centrepompidou.fr).

## Cinemas

**L'Arlequin Map 2, C9. 76 rue de Rennes, 6e. ⓂSt-Sulpice.** Owned by Jacques Tati in the 1950s, L'Arlequin has now been renovated and is once again *the* cinephiles' palace in the Latin Quarter. There are special screenings of classics every Sun at 11am, followed by debates in the café opposite.

**L'Entrepôt Map 6, E14. 7–9 rue Francis-de-Pressensé, 14e Ⓦwww.lentrepot.fr. ⓂPernety.** One of the best alternative Paris cinemas, with a great bookshop and bar/restaurant.

**L'Escurial Map 5, F5. 11 bd de Port-Royal, 13e. ⓂGobelins.** Combines plush seats, a big screen, and more art than commerce in its programming policy – and no dubbing.

**Grand Action and Action Ecoles Grand Action and Action Ecoles: Map 2, F10. 5 & 23 rue des Ecoles, 5e. ⓂCardinal-Lemoine/Maubert-Mutualité. Action Christine Odéon: Map 2, E8. 4 rue Christine, 6e. ⓂOdéon/St-Michel.** The Action chain specializes in new prints of old classics and screens contemporary films from around the world.

**Le Grand Rex Map 3, I8. 1 bd Poissonnière, 2e. ⓂBonne-Nouvelle.** The ultimate 1930s public movie-watching experience, though you're most likely to be watching a blockbuster and, if foreign, it'll be dubbed. Still, the Big Rex has an Art Deco facade, a ceiling of glowing stars and a kitsch, Hollywood-meets-Baroque cityscape inside its 2750-seater, three-storey Grande Salle.

**MK2 Bibliothèque Map 5, N7. 128–162 av de France, 13e. ⓂBibliothèque/Quai de la Gare.** Architecturally cutting-edge cinema with a very cool café and fourteen screens showing a varied range of French films – mostly new, some classic – and *v.o.* foreign movies.

**La Pagode Map 6, E6. 57bis rue de Babylone, 7e. ⓂFrançois-Xavier.** The most beautiful of the city's cinemas, built in Japanese style. The wall panels of the Salle Japonaise auditorium are embroidered in silk; golden dragons and elephants hold up the candelabra; and a battle between warriors rages on the ceiling. Shows a mix of arts films and documentaries, and commercial movies in *v.o.*

**Reflet Medicis/Filmothèque du Quartier Latin Map 2, F10. 3, 5, 7 & 9 rue Champollion, 5e. ⓂCluny-La-Sorbonne/Odéon.** A cluster of inventive little cinemas, tirelessly offering up rare screenings and classics, including frequent retrospective cycles covering great directors (always in *v.o.*). The small cinema café *Le Reflet*, on the other side of the street, is a little-known cult classic in itself.

**Le Studio 28 Map 3, F2. 10 rue de Tholozé, 18e. Ⓜ Blanche/Abbesses.** This historic art-house cinema still hosts avant-garde premieres as well as regular festivals.

**Le Studio des Ursulines Map 2, F13. 10 rue des Ursulines, 5e. RER Luxembourg.** Screens and sometimes premieres avant-garde movies, arts films and documentaries, often followed by in-house debates with the directors and actors.

**Cinema tickets rarely need to be purchased in advance, and they're cheap by European standards. Prices are mostly €8–10; and some cinemas have lower rates on Monday or Wednesday, as well as reductions for students from Monday to Thursday. Some matinée showings also have discounts.**

## Theatre

Looking at the scores of métro posters advertising **theatre** in Paris, you might think bourgeois farces starring gurning celebrities you've never heard of form the backbone of French theatre. To an extent, that's true, though the classics – Molière, Corneille and Racine – are also staple fare, and well worth a try if your French is up to it. You can easily get by with quite basic French, however, at one of the frequent performances of plays by the great postwar generation of Francophone dramatists: Anouilh, Genet, Camus, Sartre, Adamov, Ionesco, Cocteau and Beckett. The **Huchette** theatre has been playing Ionesco's *La Cantatrice Chauve* every night since October 1952, and the **Comédie Française**, the national theatre for the classics, is as likely to put on Genet's *Les Paravents*, which set off riots on its opening night, as Racine.

## Buying theatre tickets

**Booking** well in advance is essential for new productions and all shows by the superstar directors. Prices are mostly in the range of €15–40, though inexpensive previews are advertised in *Pariscope*, etc, and there are weekday discounts at some places for students. Most theatres are closed on Sunday and Monday, and during August.

The easiest place to get tickets to see a stage performance in Paris is from one of the FNAC shops (see p.263) or Virgin Megastores (main branch at 52 av des Champs-Elysées; Ⓜ Franklin-D. Roosevelt; map 7, H3). If you buy online at Ⓦ www.fnac.com or Ⓦ www.virginmega.fr you can pick up tickets from a branch or get them sent; FNAC also lets you print them out at home. At Ⓦ www.theatreonline.com you're given a reference number which you present to the box office half an hour before the performance to claim your tickets. Same-day tickets with a fifty-percent discount and a small commission are available from the **half-price ticket kiosks** (Ⓦ www.kiosquetheatre.com) on place de la Madeleine, opposite no. 15, and on the Esplanade de la Gare du Montparnasse, 14e (Tues–Sat 12.30–8pm, Sun 12.30–4pm), but queues can be long and the tickets are likely to be for the more commercial plays.

For monolingual visitors, the most rewarding theatre in Paris is likely to be the genre-busting, avant-garde, highly styled and radical kind best represented by **Ariane Mnouchkine** and her Théâtre du Soleil, based at the Cartoucherie in Vincennes, and **Peter Brook**, the British director of the Bouffes du Nord theatre. Brook is due to retire in 2011, but any show by either of these two should not be missed.

The best time of all for theatre lovers to come to Paris is for the **Festival d'Automne** from mid-September to late December (see p.286), an international celebration of all the performing arts, which attracts stage directors of the calibre of the American Robert Wilson and Canadian Robert Lepage.

## Theatres

**Bouffes du Nord Map 3, M3. 37bis bd de la Chapelle, 10e ☎01.46.07.34.50. Ⓜ La Chapelle.** Peter Brook resurrected the derelict Bouffes du Nord in 1974 and has been based there ever since, mounting innovative, unconventional and controversial works. The theatre also invites renowned international directors and hosts top-notch chamber music recitals.

**Cartoucherie Rte du Champ-de-Manoeuvre, 12e ☎01.43.74.24.08, Ⓦwww.theatre-du-soleil.fr. Ⓜ Château-de-Vincennes.** This ex-army munitions dump is home to several cutting-edge theatre companies, most notably the Théâtre du Soleil.

**Comédie Française Map 2, D4. 2 rue de Richelieu, 1er ☎01.44.58.15.15, Ⓦwww.comedie-francaise.fr. Ⓜ Palais-Royal.** This venerable national theatre is a longstanding venue for the classics – Molière, Racine, Corneille – as well as twentieth-century greats, such as Anouilh and Genet.

**Odéon Théâtre de l'Europe Map 2, E10. 1 place Paul-Claudel, off place de l'Odéon, 6e ☎01.44.41.36.36. Ⓜ Odéon.** This gorgeous, Neoclassical state-funded theatre puts on contemporary plays by top directors such as Robert Wilson, as well as *version originale* productions by well-known foreign companies. During May 1968, the theatre was occupied by students and became an open parliament with the backing of its directors, Jean-Louis Barrault (of Baptiste fame in *Les Enfants du Paradis*) and Madeleine Renaud, one of the great French stage actresses. Since then it has been splendidly restored.

**Opéra Comique Map 3, F8. Rue Favart, 2e ☎01.42.44.45.46. Ⓜ Richelieu-Drouot.** Artistic director Jérôme Savary blends all forms of stage arts: modern and classical opera, musicals, comedy, dance and pop music, creating a bold and exciting programme.

**Théâtre de la Huchette Map 2, G8. 23 rue de la Huchette, 5e ☎01.43.26.38.99. Ⓜ St-Michel.** Almost sixty years on, this intimate little theatre, seating ninety, is still showing Ionesco's *La Cantatrice Chauve* (*The Bald Prima Donna*; 7pm) and *La Leçon* (8pm), two classics of the Theatre of the Absurd.

**Théâtre National de Chaillot Map 7, B7. Palais de Chaillot, place du Trocadéro, 16e ☎01.53.65.30.00, Ⓦwww.theatre-chaillot.fr. Ⓜ Trocadéro.** Puts on an exciting programme and regularly hosts foreign productions; Deborah Warner and Robert Lepage are regular visitors.

**Théâtre National de la Colline**
**15 rue Malte-Brun, 20$^{e}$.** **ⓣ01.44.62.52.52, ⓦwww.colline.fr. ⓜGambetta.** Known for its modern and cutting-edge productions under director Alain Françon.



## Dance

The status of **dance** in the capital received a major boost with the inauguration in 2004 of the Centre National de la Danse, a long overdue recognition of the importance of the art in a nation that boasts six hundred dance companies. A huge complex on the scale of the Pompidou, the CND is committed to promoting every possible dance form from classical to contemporary and including ethnic traditions. Its creation also reflects an increased interest in dance in the capital, especially in contemporary styles, and while Paris itself has few homegrown companies (government subsidies go to regional companies expressly to decentralize the arts) it makes up for this by regularly hosting all the best contemporary practitioners. Names to look out for are **Régine Chopinot**'s troupe from La Rochelle, **Maguy Marin**'s from Rillieux-le-Pape and **Angelin Preljocaj**'s from Aix-en-Provence. Creative choreographers based in or around Paris include José Montalvo, Karine Saporta and the Californian Carolyn Carlson.

Many of the **theatres** listed above include dance in their programmes. Plenty of space and critical attention are also given to **tango**, **folk** and to visiting **traditional dance** troupes from all over the world. As for **ballet**, the principal stage is at the Palais Garnier, home to the Ballet de l'Opéra National de Paris, and directed by Brigitte Lefèvre. It still bears the influence of Rudolf Nureyev, its charismatic, if controversial, director from 1983 to 1989, and frequently revives his productions, such as *Swan Lake* and *La Bayadère*.

Festivals combining theatre, dance and classical music include the Festival Exit in Créteil in late March, the Paris Quartier d'Eté from mid-July to mid-August and the Festival d'Automne from mid-September to late December (see "Festivals", p.286).



## Dance venues

**Centre Mandapa Map 5, D9. 6 rue Wurtz, 13e ⓣ01.45.89.01.60. ⓂGlacière.** Mainly hosts (and gives lessons in) classical Indian dance, but also showcases other Asian music and dance traditions.

**Centre National de la Danse 1 rue Victor Hugo, Pantin ⓣ01.41.83.27.27, ⓦwww.cnd.fr. ⓂHoche/RER Pantin.** The capital's major new dance centre occupies an impressively large building, ingeniously converted from a disused 1970s monolith into an airy and light high-tech space. Though several of its eleven studios are used for performances, the main emphasis of the centre is to promote dance through training, workshops and exhibitions.

**Opéra Bastille Map 4, E13. Place de la Bastille, 12e ⓣ08.36.69.78.68, ⓦwww.opera-de-paris.fr. ⓂBastille.** Stages some productions by the Ballet de l'Opéra National de Paris, usually large-scale or contemporary works.

**Palais Garnier Map 3, D8. Place de l'Opéra, 9e ⓣ08.36.69.78.68, ⓦwww.opera-de-paris.fr. ⓂOpéra.** Main home of the Ballet de l'Opéra National de Paris and *the* place to see ballet classics.

**Théâtre des Abbesses Map 3, F3. 31 rue des Abbesses, 18e. ⓂAbbesses.** Sister company to the Théâtre de la Ville, with a slightly more risk-taking programme – including Indian and other international forms of dance.

**Théâtre des Champs-Elysées Map 7, G5. 15 av Montaigne, 8e ⓣ01.49.52.50.50. ⓂAlma-Marceau.** This prestigious venue occasionally hosts stars, such as Sylvie Guillem, and foreign troupes, like the Tokyo Ballet.

**Théâtre de la Ville Map 2, G6. 2 place du Châtelet, 4e ⓣ01.42.74.22.77, ⓦwww.theatredelaville-paris.com. ⓂChâtelet.** Specializes in avant-garde dance by top European choreographers such as Anne Teresa de Keersmaeker.

23

# Classical music and opera



**Classical music**, as you might expect in this Neoclassical city, is alive and well. Some ten to twenty concerts take place every day of the week: not just in the big venues but in the fine settings of churches and museums such as the Louvre and Musée d'Orsay. The Paris Opéra, with its two homes – the Palais Garnier and Opéra Bastille – puts on a fine selection of **opera and ballet**. The capital's two main **orchestras** are the renowned Orchestre de Paris, directed by Paavo Järvi, and the Orchestre National de France, under the baton of Daniele Gatti.

The city hosts a good number of music **festivals**; the major ones are listed on pp.283–287. One of the most popular is the Festival de Chopin, a series of Chopin's piano recitals given in the romantic setting of the Orangeries of the Parc de Bagatelle in the Bois de Boulogne, from mid-June to mid-July. For details of this and other festivals pick up the current year's festival schedule from one of the tourist offices or the Hôtel de Ville.

**Tickets** for classical concerts in the auditoriums and theatres listed below are best bought at the box offices or branches of FNAC (see p.263) or Virgin Megastore (main branch at

52 avenue des Champs-Elysées; ⓂFranklin-D. Roosevelt; map 7, H3), though for big names you may find overnight queues, and a large number of seats are always booked by subscribers. The price range is very reasonable. There's often no admission fee for recitals in churches and you can sometimes get free tickets for live broadcasts at the Maison de la Radio, 166 avenue du Président-Kennedy (Ⓣ01.56.40.15.16, Ⓦwww.radiofrance.fr; ⓂPassy). Turn up half an hour in advance at the Salle Olivier Messiaen to secure a yellow *carton d'invitation*. *Pariscope* (see p.24) has concert **listings**, and you can check the programmes of hundreds of Parisian venues online at Ⓦwww.viparis.com. Note that, as of 2012, there will be another, major new venue, Jean Nouvel's state-of-the-art, 2400-seat **Philharmonie de Paris** auditorium in La Villette, on the city's northeastern outskirts (see Ⓦwww.philharmoniedeparis.com).

## Classical music venues

**Cité de la Musique 221 av Jean-Jaurès, 19e Ⓣ01.44.84.44.84, Ⓦwww.cite-musique.fr. ⓂPorte-de-Pantin.** Adjustable concert hall with seating for 800–1200 listeners depending on the programme, which can cover anything from traditional Korean music to the contemporary sounds of the centre's own *Ensemble Intercontemporain*. Performances also take place in the museum amphitheatre. Tickets from €17.

**Conservatoire National Supérieur de Musique et de Danse de Paris 209 av Jean-Jaurès, 19e Ⓣ01.40.40.46.46, Ⓦwww.cite-musique.fr. ⓂPorte-de-Pantin.** Debates, masterclasses and free recitals from the Conservatoire's students. Free entry.

**Eglise de la Madeleine Map 2, A1. Place de la Madeleine, 8e Ⓣ01.42.64.83.16. ⓂMadeleine.** Organ recitals and choral concerts. Tickets €20–40.

**IRCAM (Institut de Recherche et Coordination Acoustique/Musique) Map 2, H5. 1 place Igor Stravinsky, 4e Ⓣ01.44.78.48.16, Ⓦwww.ircam.fr. ⓂHôtel-de-Ville.** IRCAM, the experimental music laboratory set up by Pierre Boulez, hosts regular concerts and also performs in the main hall (Grande Salle) of the nearby Pompidou Centre and at the Théâtre des Bouffes du Nord. Ticket prices vary.

**Musée Carnavalet Map 4, C10. 23 rue de Sévigné, 3e ⓣ01.48.04.85.94. ⓜSaint-Paul.** Mainly chamber music from the Baroque period, held in one of the museum's elegant salons. Tickets around €15.

**Musée du Louvre Map 2, D5. Palais du Louvre, 1er (Pyramid entrance) ⓣ01.40.20.84.00, ⓦwww.louvre.fr. ⓜLouvre-Rivoli & ⓜPalais-Royal-Musée-du-Louvre.** Midday and evening concerts of chamber music in the auditorium. Tickets €12–30.

**Musée d'Orsay Map 2, B5. 1 rue de Bellechasse, 7e ⓣ01.40.49.47.17, ⓦwww.musee-orsay.fr. ⓜSolférino & RER Musée-d'Orsay.** Varied programme of midday and evening concerts in the auditorium. Tickets €15–25.

**St-Julien-le-Pauvre Map 2, G9. 23 quai de Montebello, 5e ⓣ01.42.08.49.00. ⓜSt-Michel.** Mostly chamber music and choral recitals. Tickets €15–23.

**St-Séverin Map 2, G9. 1 rue des Prêtres-St-Séverin, 5e ⓣ01.48.24.16.97. ⓜSt-Michel.** Organ recitals and concerts of sacred music. Varied programmes. Tickets from €15.

**Sainte-Chapelle Map 2, F7. 4 bd du Palais, 1er ⓣ01.42.77.65.65. ⓜCité.** A fabulous setting for mainly Mozart, Bach and Vivaldi classics. Tickets €16–30.

**Salle Gaveau Map 7, J2. 45 rue de la Boétie, 8e ⓣ01.49.53.05.07, ⓦwww.sallegaveau.com. ⓜMiromesnil.** This atmospheric and intimate concert hall, built in 1907, is a major venue for piano recitals by world-class players, as well as chamber music recitals and full-scale orchestral works. Tickets from €15.

**Salle Pleyel Map 7, G1. 252 rue du Faubourg-St-Honoré, 8e ⓣ01.45.61.53.00, ⓦwww.sallepleyel.fr. ⓜTernes.** This distinguished concert hall, with Art Deco reception hall, has been restored to full splendour. The Orchestre de Paris (ⓦwww.orchestredeparis.com), the city's top orchestra, performs here most frequently, along with visiting international performers such as Martha Argerich and Jessye Norman. Tickets from €10.

**Théâtre des Champs-Elysées Map 7, G5. 15 av Montaigne, 8e ⓣ01.49.52.50.50, ⓦwww.theatrechampselysees.fr. ⓜAlma-Marceau.** A two-thousand-seat capacity in this historic theatre built in 1913. Home to the Orchestre National de France and the Orchestre Lamoureux, but also welcomes international superstar conductors, ballet troupes and opera companies.

Buying the lowest-priced tickets will mean you won't have a view, but on average you can reckon on €30 for a decent seat.

**Théâtre Musical de Paris Map 2, G6. Théâtre du Châtelet, 1 place du Châtelet, 1er ⓣ01.40.28.28.00, ⓦwww.chatelet-theatre.com. ⓜChâtelet.** A prestigious concert hall with a varied programme of high-profile operas, ballets, concerts and solo recitals. Tickets from €8.

# Opera

The **Opéra National de Paris** has two homes: the original **Palais Garnier**; and the newer **Opéra Bastille**, Mitterrand's most extravagant legacy to the city. In addition to these main venues, operas are regularly hosted by the **Théâtre des Champs-Elysées** (see p.281) and the **Théâtre Musical de Paris** (see above). The **Opéra Comique** (see p.276) gives a platform to solo singers and also puts on opéra bouffe and operettas.

**Tickets** (€5–172) for both venues can be booked online at ⓦwww.opera-de-paris.fr or on ⓣ08.92.89.90.90; the more popular productions sell out within days of tickets becoming available – which happens online first. For last-minute tickets it's worth joining the queue early in the day at the venues themselves; unfilled seats are also sold at a discount to students five minutes before the curtain goes up.

**Palais Garnier Map 3, D8. Place de l'Opéra, 9e. ⓜOpéra.** The lavishly refurbished old Palais Garnier tends to concentrate on smaller-scale operatic and ballet productions. The programme for 2011 includes Mozart's *Così Fan Tutte* and Anne Teresa De Keersmaeker's *Rain*.

**Opéra Bastille Map 4, E13–F14. 120 rue de Lyon, 12e. ⓜBastille.** Critics are divided over the quality of the acoustics of the new opera house, but there's no disputing the high calibre of the Bastille orchestra, and nearly every performance is a sell-out. Its new director, Nicolas Joel, concentrates on the mainstream repertoire with A-list performers, in contrast to his notoriously radical predecessor, Gérard Mortier.

24

# Festivals and events



Paris hosts an impressive roster of **festivals** and events. The city's most colourful jamborees are Bastille Day, on July 14, and the summer-long beach spectacle, Paris Plage, but throughout the year there's invariably something on. The tourist office produces a biannual "Saisons de Paris – Calendrier des Manifestations", which gives details of all the mainstream events, but the following listings give a selection of the most important and entertaining highlights of the Paris calendar.

## February

**Chinese New Year** Paris's Chinese community brings in the New Year in the 13e around avenue d'Ivry.

## March

**Paris Fashion Week First week of March (and also first week of Oct) ⓦ www.modeaparis.com.** Alongside Milan and London, the fashion event of the year. Technically for professionals only, but surely there's a door left ajar somewhere.

**Banlieues Bleus Early March to early April ⓦ www.banlieuesbleues.org.** International jazz festival in the Seine-St-Denis *département*, with venues at Le Blanc-Mesnil, Aubervilliers, Pantin, St-Ouen, St-Denis and Bobigny.

**Festival Exit Late March ⓦ www.maccreteil.com.** International festival of contemporary dance, performance and theatre at Créteil.

**Festival de Films de Femmes End of March to beginning of April ⓦ www.filmsdefemmes.com.** Major women's film festival at Créteil.

## April

**Poisson d'Avril April 1.** April Fools' Day, with spoofs in the media and children traditionally sticking paper fishes on the backs of the unsuspecting.

**Foire du Trône April to May ⓦ www.foiredutrone.com.** Centuries-old funfair located in the Pelouse de Reuilly, Bois de Vincennes, 12ᵉ.

**Festival de St-Denis April to early July ⓦ www.metis-plainecommune.com.** Classical and world music festival with opportunities to hear music in the Gothic St-Denis basilica.

**Foire de Paris End of April to beginning of May ⓦ www.foiredeparis.fr.** Food, wine, house and home fair at the Parc des Expositions, Porte de Versailles.

## May

**Fête du Travail May Day (May 1).** Everything closes and there are marches and festivities in eastern Paris and around place de la Bastille.

**Printemps des Rues Early May ⓦ www.leprintempsdesrues.com.** Free street performances in the areas of La Villette, Gambetta, Nation and République.

## June

**Festival Agora First week of June ⓦ www.ircam.fr.** Contemporary theatre/dance/music festival organized by IRCAM and the Pompidou Centre.

**Paris Jazz Festival Mid-June to end July ⓦ www.parisjazzfestival.fr.** Big jazz names give free afternoon concerts at weekends, in the Parc Floral at the Bois de Vincennes.

**Fête de la Musique June 21 ⓦ www.fetedelamusique.culture.fr.** Live bands play at mini sound-stages throughout the city – mostly enjoyed by teenagers.

**Foire St-Germain June to July ⓦ www.foiresaintgermain.org.** Concerts, antique fairs, poetry and exhibitions in a mini tent city on place St-Sulpice, 6ᵉ.

**Festival de Chopin Mid-June to mid-July ⓦ www.frederic-chopin.com.** Free afternoon Chopin recitals, then concerts by candlelight, held in the Orangerie de Bagatelle, in the Bois de Boulogne; lots of other associated events too.

**Pride March Last Sat in June** ⓦ **www.marche.inter-lgbt.org.** The Lesbian, Gay, Bisexual and Trans Pride march parades extravagantly from Montparnasse to Bastille on the last Saturday in June; wild parties and club *soirées* ensue.

**La Goutte d'Or en Fête Week around late June/early July** ⓦ **www.gouttedorenfete.org.** Music festival of rap, reggae and raï with local and international performers in the Goutte d'Or district, 18e.

## July

**Bastille Day July 14 & evening before.** The 1789 surrender of the Bastille is celebrated in official pomp, with parades of tanks down the Champs-Elysées, firework displays and concerts. On the evening of the 13th, there's dancing in the streets around place de la Bastille to good French bands, and "Bals Pompiers" parties rage inside every fire station in Paris – rue Blanche and rue des Vieux-Colombiers host some of the best.

**Arrivée du Tour de France Cycliste Third or fourth Sunday** ⓦ **www.letour.fr.** The Tour de France cyclists cross the finishing line on the avenue des Champs-Elysées.

**Festival de Cinéma en Plein Air Mid-July to end Aug** ⓦ **www.villette.com** or **www.cinema.arbo.com.** Thousands turn up at dusk every night for free, open-air classic cinema at the Parc de la Villette.

**Paris Plage 20 July to 20 Aug** ⓦ **www.paris.fr.** The Seine *quais* – at various points between the Pont de Sully and the Tuileries – are closed to traffic and transformed into mini-beaches, complete with imported sand, palm trees, parasols, sun-loungers and beach games. Free concerts on Fri and Sat evenings. There's also a beach on the Bassin de la Villette (19e).

## August

**Cinéma au Clair de Lune Throughout August** ⓦ **www.forumdesimages.fr.** Open-air screenings of films shot in Paris on a giant screen that tours the arrondissements.

**Fête de l'Assomption Aug 15.** A procession from Notre-Dame around the Ile de la Cité.

**Rock en Seine End Aug** ⓦ **www.rockenseine.fr.** Major three-day rock festival featuring the biggest acts, set in the lovely gardens of the Domaine National de Saint-Cloud, 9km southwest of central Paris.

## September

**Fête de l'Humanité Second weekend** ⓦ **www.humanite.fr.** Three-day Communist-sponsored event just north of Paris at La Courneuve, attracting people in their tens of thousands and of every political persuasion. Food and drink (all very cheap), and music and crafts from every corner of the globe, are the predominant features. Ends on Sun night with an impressive firework display.

**Biennale des Antiquaires Last two weeks ⓦ www.bdafrance.eu.** The city's largest antiques show, held at the Carrousel du Louvre every even-numbered year, with everything from coins to stamps, and art to furniture and jewellery.

**Journées du Patrimoine Third weekend ⓦ www.journeesdu patrimoine.culture.fr.** The France-wide "heritage day" sees normally off-limits buildings – like the Palais de l'Elysée where the President resides – opened up to a curious public.

**Villette Jazz Festival Mid-Sept ⓦ www.villette.com.** One of the city's best jazz festivals, with music played by legendary greats and local conservatory students, held in the park and Grande Halle at la Villette.

**Festival d'Automne Mid-Sept to late Dec ⓦ www.festival-automne.com.** Major festival of contemporary theatre, music, dance and avant-garde arts. Companies from all over the world descend on the city for three months.

**Techno Parade Late Sept ⓦ www .technopol.net.** One of the highlights of the Rendez-vous Electroniques festival, attracting hundreds of thousands. Floats with sound systems parade from place de la République to Pelouse de Reuilly, where a big party kicks off.

## October

**Prix de l'Arc de Triomphe First weekend ⓦ www.prixarcdetriomphe .com.** Horse flat-racing with high stakes at Longchamp.

**Fêtes des Vendanges First or second Sat ⓦ www.fetedesvendan-gesdemontmartre.com.** Bacchanalian grape harvest festival in the Montmartre vineyard, at the corner of rue des Saules and rue St-Vincent.

**Nuit Blanche First or second Sat ⓦ www.paris.fr.** All-night cultural events at unusual venues.

## November

**Paris Photo Mid-Nov ⓦ www .parisphoto.fr.** Photographic exhibitions held in museums, galleries and cultural centres throughout the city.

**Le Beaujolais Nouveau Third Thurs.** Numerous cafés and wine bars celebrate the new vintage with special menus and events.

## December

**Noël Dec 24–25.** Christmas Eve is a huge affair all across France, and of much more importance than the following day. Both Notre-Dame and the Eglise de la Madeleine hold midnight mass services, though you'll need to arrive early to avoid standing (doors open at 10pm, ceremony begins at 10.30pm).

**Le Nouvel An Dec 31.** New Year's Eve means dense crowds of out-of-towners on the Champs-Elysées, fireworks at the Champs de Mars and super-elevated restaurant prices everywhere.

25

# Activities

If you've had enough of following crowds through museums, shopping or just wandering through the city, Paris has saunas to soak in, ice-skating rinks to fall on and swimming pools to dive into. You can also rent a bike, go on a boat trip or view the city from a helicopter.

*Pariscope* has useful listings of **sports** facilities, pools, hammams and so on (under "Sport et bien-être"). **Information** on municipal facilities is available from the town hall, the Mairie de Paris; check the comprehensive website Ⓦwww.paris.fr.

## Boat trips

Seeing Paris by **boat** is one of the city's most popular and durable tourist experiences – and a lot of fun. The best-known boats are the **Bateaux-Mouches**; you may not be able to escape the running commentary, but the rides certainly give a close-up view of the classic, glamorous buildings along the Seine. Trips start from the Embarcadère du Pont de l'Alma, on the Right Bank (information and reservations Ⓣ01.42.25.96.10, Ⓦwww.bateaux-mouches.fr; ⓂAlma-Marceau). The rides, which usually last an hour, run roughly hourly to every half hour, depending on the season. Summer departures are 10.15am–11pm, winter 10.15am–9pm. Tickets cost €10, or €5 for under 12s and over 65s.

## Views of the city

Few cities present such a uniform skyscape as Paris. Looking down on the ranks of seven-storey apartment buildings from above, it's easy to imagine the city as a lead-roofed plateau split by the leafy canyons of the boulevards and avenues. Spires, towers and parks – not to mention multicoloured art museums and glass pyramids – stand out all the more against the solemn grey backdrop. Here are some of the best vistas in town:

**Arc de Triomphe** (see p.52): look out on an ocean of traffic and enjoy impressive vistas of the Voie Triomphale.

**Grande Arche de la Défense** (see p.157): take the long view.

**Eiffel Tower** (see p.116): the classic, best at night.

**Institut du Monde Arabe** (see p.104): sip mint tea on the rooftop overlooking the Seine.

**Musée d'Orsay** (see p.113): peer through the old station clock towards Montmartre.

**Notre-Dame** (see p.33): perch among the gargoyles.

**Parc André-Citroën** (see p.117): a tethered balloon rises 150m above this quirky park.

**Parc de Belleville** (see p.149): watch the sun set over the city.

**Pompidou Centre** (see p.69): a stunning backdrop to modern art.

**Sacré-Coeur** (see p.132): this puffball dome soars over Montmartre.

**Tour Montparnasse** (see p.124): stand eye to eye with the Eiffel Tower.

The main **competitors** to the Bateaux-Mouches can all be found detailed in *Pariscope* under "Croisières" in the "Visites-Promenades" section. An alternative way of riding on the Seine – one in which you are mercifully spared the commentary – is the **Batobus**, the city's own river transport system; see "City transport" (p.19) for more details.

### Canal trips

Less overtly touristy than the Bateaux-Mouches and their clones are the **canal-boat trips**. Canauxrama services (reservations required Oct–April ⓣ01.42.39.15.00, ⓦwww.canauxrama.com) chug up and down between the Port de l'Arsenal (opposite 50 bd de la Bastille; ⓂBastille) and the Bassin de la Villette (13 quai de la Loire; ⓂJaurès) on the Canal St-Martin (see p.138). There are daily departures at 9.45am and 2.45pm from La Villette and at 9.45am and 2.30pm from the Port de l'Arsenal. At the Bastille end is a long, spooky tunnel from which you surface in the 10e arrondissement. The ride lasts around two and a half hours – not bad for €16 (students €11, under 12s €8.50, under 6s free).

**Paris Canal** (ⓦwww.pariscanal.com) also runs canal trips (reservations online) between the Musée d'Orsay (quai Anatole-France by the Pont Solférino; ⓂSolférino) and the Parc de la Villette ("La Folie des Visites du Parc", on the canal by the bridge between the Grande Salle and the Cité des Sciences; ⓂPorte-de-Pantin), which last nearly three hours. Boats depart from the Musée d'Orsay at 9.30am and at 2.25pm. Parc de la Villette departures are at 10am and 2.30pm. Trips take place daily from mid-March to mid-November and cost €18, 12–25s and over 60s €15, 2–11s €11.

## Guinguettes

For the ultimate Parisian retro experience, head for a traditional riverbank **guinguette** or open-air dance hall. You can usually eat good, homely French food, but the real draw is the orchestra. Families, older couples and trendy young things from the city sway with varying degrees of skill to foxtrots, tangos and lots of well-loved accordion numbers – especially good for a Sunday afternoon.

**Chalet du Lac Facing the lac de St-Mandé, Bois de Vincennes, 11e ⓣ01.43.28.09.89, ⓦwww.chaletdulac.fr. ⓜSt-Mandé-Tourelles.** Afternoon dancing on Mon, Thurs, Fri and Sat (€3–10), but it's best to save yourself for the elegant Sun Grand Bal (3pm–2am; €14), when a live band helps smooth out your footwork. The restaurant serves good brasserie classics.

**Chez Gégène 162bis quai de Polangis, Joinville-le-Pont ⓣ01.48.83.29.43, ⓦwww.chez-gegene.fr. RER Joinville-le-Pont. Open April–Oct.** Just the other side of the Bois de Vincennes, this original *guinguette* was established in the 1900s, though the band now mixes in pop anthems with the accordion classics. There's a decent restaurant, and the time to come is on Sat nights (April–Dec 8pm–2am) and Sun afternoons (April–Dec 3–7pm), when a live band plays ballroom classics and traditional French numbers. Admission €16 for non-diners.

**Guinguette de l'Ile du Martin-Pêcheur 41 quai Victor-Hugo, Champigny-sur-Marne ⓣ01.49.83.03.02, ⓦwww.guinguette.fr. RER A2 to Champigny-sur-Marne. Dancing mid-March to Dec Thurs–Sat 7.30pm–2am, Sun 2–6pm.** Traditional and charming *guinguette* situated on an island in the River Marne. You don't have to dine – or pay – to dance.



## Swimming pools and gyms

For €3, you can go swimming in most of Paris's **municipal pools**. If you plan to swim a lot, the €24 carnet of ten tickets (each good for one entrance) is good value. **Privately run pools**, whether owned by the city or not, are usually more expensive. As for **gyms**, you'll find any number of aerobics classes, dance workouts and anti-stress fitness programmes offered, along with yoga, t'ai chi and martial arts.

### Gyms and fitness

**Aquaboulevard 4 rue Louis-Armand, 15e ⓣ01.40.60.10.00, ⓦwww.aquaboulevard.com. ⓜBalard/Porte de Versailles/RER Bd-Victor.** The biggest in town, with a state-of-the-art fitness centre, squash and tennis courts, a climbing wall, driving range, aquatic diversions, hammams, dancefloors, shops and restaurants. To gain access to the full range of facilities, most importantly the gym, you're supposed to be accompanied by a member, but exceptions are sometimes made. €20 for a day pass.

**Club Quartier Latin Map 2, H10. 19 rue de Pontoise, 5e ⓣ01.55.42.77.88, ⓦwww.clubquartierlatin.com. ⓜMaubert-Mutualité. Mon–Fri 9am to midnight, Sat & Sun 9.30am–7pm.** Dance, gym, swimming and squash; €20 day pass for the pool and gym.

**Espace Vit'Halles Map 2, H5. 48 rue Rambuteau, 3e ⓣ01.42.77.21.71, ⓦwww.vithalles.fr. ⓜRambuteau. Mon–Fri 8am–10.30pm, Sat 9am–7pm, Sun 10am–7pm.** One of the flashier fitness clubs in the city, with endless classes of every kind, weight rooms, various gyms, a sauna and hammam, and everything else you'd expect. For €20, the day pass gives access to all of the above.

## Swimming pools

At weekends, most municipal pools are open something like Saturday 10am–6pm, Sunday 8am–6pm; on weekdays, they typically open for an hour in the early morning and at lunch, then close for the morning and afternoon school sessions and reopen in the early evening until about 6–8pm. It's best to ring in advance, or check under "loisirs" then "sport", then "piscines" on the Mairie's website (ⓦwww.paris.fr). Otherwise just choose a pool nearby and consult their timetable. Many municipal pools are also closed on Monday in school terms.

**Les Amiraux Map 3, off J1. 6 rue Hermann-Lachapelle, 18e ⓣ01.46.06.46.47. ⓜSimplon.** Handsome 1920s pool – as featured in the film *Amélie* – surrounded by tiers of changing cabins.

**Aquaboulevard 4 rue Louis-Armand, 15e ⓣ0800.803.813, ⓦwww.aquaboulevard.com. ⓜBalard/Porte de Versailles/RER Bd-Victor.** The big, landscaped private pool has wave machines and some incredible water slides, and there are jacuzzis and grassy and sandy outdoor sunning areas. €25 (€12 for children aged 3–11).

**Butte aux Cailles Map 5, G9. 5 place Paul-Verlaine, 13e ⓣ01.45.89.60.05. ⓜPlace-d'Italie.** Housed in a spruced-up 1920s brick building with an Art Deco ceiling, this is one of the most pleasant municipal pools in the city. There's a children's pool inside and, in summer, a 25m heated outdoor pool.

**Les Halles Suzanne Berlioux Map 2, G5. 10 place de la Rotonde, niveau 3, Porte du Jour, Forum des Halles, 1er ⓣ01.42.36.98.44. ⓜChâtelet/ RER Châtelet-Les Halles.** Very centrally located, this private 50m pool with vaulted concrete ceiling sports a glass wall looking through to a tropical garden. Often open as late as 11pm. €4.

**Henry-de-Montherlant 32 bd Lannes, 16e ⓣ01.40.72.28.30. ⓜPorte-Dauphine.** This municipal facility has two pools, one 25m and one 15m, plus a terrace for sunbathing, a solarium – and the Bois de Boulogne close by.

**Jean Taris Map 2, G12. 16 rue Thouin, 5e ⓣ01.55.42.81.90. ⓜCardinal-Lemoine.** A 25m unchlorinated municipal pool in the centre of the Latin Quarter. A student favourite, with a small pool for children.

**Josephine Baker Map 5, N6. 32 quai François Mauriac, 13e ⓣ01.56.61.93.50. ⓜQuai de la Gare.** Eye-catching floating 25m pool, moored on the Seine by the Bibliothèque Nationale.

**Pailleron Map 4, off G1. 32 rue Edouard-Pailleron, 5e ⓣ01.40.40.27.70. ⓜBolivar. Mon–Thurs 8am–10.30pm, Fri & Sat 9am–midnight, Sun 9am–6pm.** One of the coolest and best-kept pools in the city – a 1930s Art Deco marvel surrounded by tiers of changing rooms and arched over by a gantry roof. The Parc des Buttes-Chaumont is close at hand, and during school holidays it's open late.

**Pontoise-Quartier Latin Map 2, H10. 19 rue de Pontoise, 5e ⓣ01.55.42.77.88. ⓜMaubert-Mutualité.** Art Deco architecture, beautiful blue mosaic interior and a 33m pool. Juliette Binoche memorably swam here in the Kieslowski film *Three Colours Blue*. On weekdays outside school terms, this privately run pool features weekday night sessions until 11.45pm. Pool €4.20, or €10 at night.

# Hammams

**Hammams**, or Turkish baths, are one of the unexpected delights of Paris. Much more luxurious than the standard Swedish sauna, these are places to linger and chat, and you can usually pay extra for a massage and a *gommage* – a rub-down with a rubber glove – followed by mint tea to recover. Don't let modesty get the better of you; all are quite restrained in terms of nudity and the staff are consummate professionals. You're provided with a strip of linen, but swimsuits are almost always required for mixed men-and-women sessions.



**Les Bains du Marais Map 4, B10. 31–33 rue des Blancs-Manteaux, 4e ⓣ01.44.61.02.02, ⓦwww.lesbainsdumarais.com. ⓜRambuteau/St-Paul.** As much a posh health club as a hammam, with a rather chichi clientele and glorious interior. Offers facials, massage and haircuts, and you can lounge about in a robe with mint tea and a newspaper. Sauna and steam room entry costs €35, massage/*gommage* is around €70 for 50min. There are exclusive sessions for women (Mon 10am–8pm, Tues 10am–11pm, Wed 10am–7pm) and men (Thurs 10am–11pm, Fri 10am–8pm), as well as mixed sessions (Wed 7–11pm, Sat 10am–8pm, Sun 10am–11pm) for which you have to bring a swimsuit.

**Hammam de la Mosquée Map 2, I13. 39 rue Geoffroy-St-Hilaire, 5e ⓣ01.43.31.38.20. ⓜCensier-Daubenton.** One of the most atmospheric baths in the city, with its vaulted cooling-off room and marble-lined steam chamber. The clientele is very mixed – lots of Muslims, gay guys and older men are regulars at the men-only sessions, but all are welcome. It's very good value for €15, though towels are extra, and you can also have a reasonably priced massage and *gommage* (30min massage costs €30). After your bath you can order mint tea and honey cakes around a fountain in the little courtyard café. Women only: Mon, Wed, Thurs & Sat 10am–9pm, Fri 2–9pm; men only: Tues 2–9pm, Sun 10am–9pm.

## Rollerblading

**Rollerblading** has become so popular in Paris that it takes over entire streets most Friday nights from 9.30pm, when thousands of expert skaters meet on the esplanade of the Gare Montparnasse in the 14e (ⓜMontparnasse) for a demanding three-hour circuit of the city; check out ⓦwww.pari-roller.com for details. A more sedate outing – and a better choice for families – takes place on Sundays, departing at 2.30pm from place de la Bastille and returning at 5.30pm (Ⓦwww.rollers-coquillages.org). A good place to find more information and hire blades (around €10 for a half-day) is Nomades, 37 boulevard Bourdon, 4e (Ⓣ01.44.54.07.44, Ⓦwww.nomadeshop.com; ⓂBastille).



## Ice skating

In winter, a big **outdoor rink** is set up on place de l'Hôtel de Ville, 3e; you can hire skates (*patins*) for around €5 (bring your passport) and there's a small section cordoned off for children under 6. From early December to February, another seasonal rink can be found on place Raoul-Dautry, 15e (ⓂMontparnasse-Bienvenüe). Entrance is free, though skate hire is €5.

You can get on the ice **year-round** at the Patinoire de Bercy, at the Palais Omnisports, 8 boulevard de Bercy, 12e (Wed 3–6pm, Fri 9.30pm–12.30am, Sat 3–6pm & 9.30pm–12.30am, Sun 10am–noon & 3–6pm; Ⓣ01.40.02.60.60; ⓂBercy). The Patinoire Pailleron, 32 rue Edouard-Pailleron, 19e (school holidays: Mon–Thurs noon–10pm, Fri noon–midnight, Sat 9am–midnight, Sun 10am–6pm; times vary during term time; Ⓣ01.40.40.27.70; ⓂBolivar) is big and newly refurbished.

## Cycling

In the last few years, the Mairie de Paris has installed thousands of dedicated **cycle lanes** all over the city, and you can pick up free Vélib' bikes all over town. "Paris Respire", another town hall-sponsored scheme, closes off numerous roads, including parts of the Seine-side *quais*, on Sundays and public holidays year-round (9am–7pm), making them popular places for cyclists and rollerbladers to meet up. The two *quais* are voie Georges-Pompidou, on the right bank of the Seine, in the 8e and 12e arrondissements; and the left bank stretch from quai Anatole-France to quai Branly, in the 7e. Other car-free Sunday roads include the *quais* alongside the Canal St-Martin (10e), and the neighbourhoods around rue Mouffetard (5e) and rue des Rosiers, in the Marais (3e and 4e).

If you prefer cycling in a more natural environment, the Bois de Boulogne and the Bois de Vincennes have extensive bike tracks, and you can pick up Vélib' bikes by the park entrances. If you want a more rideable, enjoyable bike, consider a specialist rental outlet, or a bike tour.

**Paris a Vélo C'est Sympa Map 4, E9. 22 rue Alphonse Baudin, 11e ⓣ01.48.87.60.01, ⓦwww.parisvelosympa.com. Mon & Wed–Fri 9.30am–1pm & 2–6pm, Sat & Sun 9am–7pm. ⓂSt-Sébastien-Froissart/Richard Lenoir.** One of the least expensive (from €25 for the weekend) and most helpful for bike rental. Their excellent three-hour tours of Paris – including one at night and another at dawn – all cost €34.

**Paris Bike Tour Map 4, C8. 38 rue de Saintonge, 3e ⓣ01.42.74.22.14, ⓦwww.parisbiketour.net. Daily 9.30am–6.30pm. ⓂFilles du Calvaire.** Offers 21-speed and mountain bikes, and morning bike delivery to your address. €15 per day, weekend €26.

# 26

# Kids' Paris



The French are extremely welcoming to **children** and Paris's vibrant atmosphere, with its street performers and musicians, lively pavement cafés and brightly lit carousels is certainly family friendly. The obvious pull of Disneyland aside (covered in Chapter 17), there are plenty of other attractions and activities to keep kids happy, from circuses to rollerblading. As you'd expect, museum-hopping with youngsters in Paris can be as tedious as in any other big city, but while the Louvre and Musée d'Orsay cater to more acquired tastes, the Musée des Arts et Métiers, the Pompidou Centre, Parc de la Villette and some of the other attractions listed below will interest children and adults alike. Travelling with a child also provides the perfect excuse to enjoy some of the simpler pleasures of city life – the playgrounds, ice-cream cones, toy shops and pastries that Paris seems to offer in endless abundance.

In terms of **practicalities**, many cafés, bars or restaurants offer *menus enfants* (special children's set menus) or are often willing to cook simpler food on request, and hotels tack only a small supplement for an additional bed or cot onto the regular room rate. You should have no difficulty finding disposable nappies/diapers, baby foods and milk powders for infants. Throughout the city the RATP transport system charges half-fares for 4- to 10-year-olds; under 4s travel free. It's worth remembering that **Wednesday afternoons**, when primary school children have free time, and **Saturdays** are the peak times for children's activities and entertainment;

Wednesdays continue to be child-centred even during the school holidays.



## Parks and gardens

Children are well catered for by the **parks and gardens** within the city. There's even a park designed especially for kids, the **Jardin d'Acclimatation**, in the Bois de Boulogne, with an impressive array of activities and attractions. On the other side of the city in the Bois de Vincennes, the **Parc Floral** also offers a host of treats, and the high-tech **Parc de la Villette** (described on pp.140–144), in the northeast, will keep children entertained for hours. Most of the city's other parks have some activities for children, usually an enclosed playground with swings, climbing frames and often a sandpit. Many also have **guignol** (puppet) shows, the French equivalent of Punch and Judy.

**Jardin d'Acclimatation Map 1. Bois de Boulogne. €2.70, under 3s free; rides €2.50, or buy a *carnet* of 15 tickets for €30; Ⓦwww.jardindacclimatation.fr. ⓂLes Sablons/Porte-Maillot. A little train takes you there from ⓂPorte-Maillot (behind *L'Orée du Bois* restaurant) 11am–6pm (every 15min); €5.40 return, includes admission. Daily: April–Sept 10am–7pm, Oct–March 10am–6pm; special attractions Wed, Sat, Sun & all week during school hols.** The Jardin d'Acclimatation is a cross between a funfair, zoo and amusement park, with temptations ranging from bumper cars, go-karts, pony and camel rides, sea lions, birds, bears and monkeys, to a magical mini-canal ride ("la rivière enchantée"), distorting mirrors, a huge trampoline, scaled-down farm buildings and a puppet theatre. The park also has its own theatre, the Théâtre du Jardin, which puts on musicals, ballets and poetry readings. Outside the *jardin*, in the Bois de Boulogne (see p.155), older children can amuse themselves with mini-golf and bowling, boating on the Lac Inférieur or roaming the wood's 14km of cycle trails (there are a number of Vélib' stands in the area, including one at ⓂLes Sablons and one at ⓂPorte-Maillot).

**Parc Floral Map 1. Bois de Vincennes, on rte de la Pyramide**

**Ⓦwww.parcfloraldeparis.com. ⓂChâteau-de-Vincennes, then bus #112 or a 15min walk through the grounds of the Château de Vincennes. Daily: Nov–Jan 9.30am–5pm; Feb & Oct 9.30am–6pm; March & April 9.30am–7pm; May–Sept 9.30am–8pm. Free, except Wed, Sat & Sun June–Sept when entry is €5; under 7s free; supplements for some activities.** Much to the delight of visiting kids, the Parc Floral has much more than just flowers. It's known for its excellent playground, with slides, swings, ping-pong and pedal carts (from 2pm), mini-golf (from 2pm), an electric car circuit, and a little train touring all the gardens (April–Oct daily 1–5pm). Tickets for the paying activities are sold at the playground between 2 and 5.30pm weekdays and until 7pm on weekends; activities stop fifteen minutes after closing. Note that many of these activities are available from March/April to Aug only and on Wed and weekends only in Sept and Oct. On Wed at 2.30pm (May–Sept) there are free performances by clowns, puppets and magicians. A further programme of mime and other shows is put on at the Théâtre Astral (Wed & Sun 3pm, school hols Mon–Fri & Sun 3pm; Ⓣ01.43.71.31.10, Ⓦwww.theatreastral.com), for which you're best off calling ahead and making reservations as they're popular with school groups. Another hit with kids is the wonderful butterfly garden (mid-May to mid-Oct Mon–Fri 1.30–5.15pm, Sat & Sun 1.30–6pm).



## Funfairs

Three big **funfairs** (*fête foraines*) take place in Paris each year. The season kicks off in late March with the Fête du Trône in the Bois de Vincennes (running until late May), followed by the funfair in the Tuileries gardens in mid-June to late August, with more than forty rides including a giant ferris wheel, and ending up with the Fête à Neu Neu, held near the Bois de Boulogne from early September to the beginning of October. Look up "Fêtes Populaires" under "Agendas" in *Pariscope* for details if you're in town at these times.

Out of season, rue de Rivoli around ⓂSt-Paul occasionally hosts a mini-fairground, and there's usually a merry-go-round at the Forum des Halles and beneath Tour St-Jacques at Châtelet. Merry-go-rounds for smaller children are to be found on place de la République, at the Rond-Point des Champs-Elysées by avenue Matignon, at place de la Nation, and at the base of the Montmartre funicular in place St-Pierre.



## Circuses

**Circuses** (*cirques*) are taken seriously in France and come under the heading of culture as performance art (and there are no qualms about performing animals). As circuses tend to travel, you'll find details of the seasonal ones under "Cirques" in the "Jeunes" section of *L'Officiel des Spectacles* and under the same heading in the "Enfants" section of *Pariscope*. The Cirque Diana Moreno Bormann, 112 rue de la Haie-Coq, 19e (Ⓣ01.48.39.04.47, Ⓦwww.cirque-diana-moreno.com; bus #65, direction Mairie d' Aubervilliers) is a perennial favourite; admission prices start at €10.

## Museums

One of the city's best treats for children of every age from 3 upwards is the **Cité des Sciences** (see p.142) in the Parc de la Villette. Most children will also enjoy the **Grande Galerie de l'Evolution** (see p.104), which has a children's discovery room on the first floor with child-level microscopes, glass cases with live caterpillars and moths and a burrow of Mongolian rodents. The **Pompidou Centre** (see p.69) has a special children's gallery with fun exhibits. Paris has two excellent **planetariums**, in the Palais de la Découverte (see p.52) and the Cité des Sciences. Two entertaining ways for children to find out about Paris itself and its history are the **Paris-Story** (see p.62), an enjoyable, if highly romanticized, 45-minute, wide-screen film on the history of Paris; and the **Musée Grévin** (see p.61), with its mock-ups of key events in French history, especially the more grisly ones.

For a more earthy experience, you could visit **les égouts** – the sewers – at place de la Résistance, in the 7e. Dank, damp, dripping, claustrophobic and filled with echoes, this is just the sort of place pre-teens love; for further details, see p.118. Another underground experience popular with youngsters is the **catacombs** at 1 place Denfert-Rochereau, 14e, described on p.128.



## Shops

The fact that Paris is filled with beautiful, enticing, delicious and expensive things all artfully displayed is not lost on most modern youngsters. Below is a small selection of shops to seek out, be dragged into or to avoid at all costs.

### Books

**Chantelivre Map 2, B9.13 rue de Sèvres, 6e. Ⓜ Sèvres-Babylone. Mon 1–6.50pm, Tues–Sat 10am–6.50pm; closed mid-Aug.** A huge selection of everything to do with and for children, including good picture books for the younger ones, an English section and a play area.

### Toys and games

In addition to the shops below, be sure to check out the superb selection of toys at the Le Bon Marché department store.

**Le Bonhomme de Bois 141 rue d'Alésia, 14e Ⓦ www.bonhommedebois.com. Ⓜ Alésia. Mon–Sat 10am–7.30pm.** Perfect little shop with classic wooden cars and dolls, and plush, colourful, floppy-eared stuffed animals.

**JouéClub Map 3, G8. Passage des Princes, 2e. Ⓜ Richelieu-Drouot. Mon–Sat 10am–8pm.** This toy emporium is the largest in Paris and takes up the whole of the renovated passage des Princes. This is the place to buy French Trivial Pursuit or two-thousand-piece jigsaws of French paintings such as Renoir's *Moulin de la Galette*.

**Au Nain Bleu Map 7, M3. 5 bd Malesherbes, 8e Ⓦ boutique.aunainbleu.com. Ⓜ St-Augustin. Mon–Sat 10am–6.30pm; closed Mon in Aug.** Since opening in the 1830s, Au Nain Bleu has become expert at delighting children with wooden toys, dolls and faux-china tea-sets.

**Pain d'Epices Map 3, H8. 29 passage Jouffroy, 9e ⓦwww.paindepices.fr. ⓂGrands-Boulevards. Mon 12.30–7pm, Tues–Sat 10am–7pm, Thurs till 9pm.** Fabulous dolls' house necessities from furniture to wine glasses, and puppets.

**Puzzles Michèle Wilson Map 6, F14. 116 rue du Château, 14e ⓦwww.pmw.fr. ⓂPernety. Tues–Fri 10am–8pm, Sat 10am–7pm.** Puzzles galore and a workshop on the premises.

**Si Tu Veux Map 2, E2. 68 galerie Vivienne, 2e ⓣ01.42.60.59.97. ⓂBourse. Mon–Sat 10.30am–7pm.** Well-made traditional toys, plus do-it-yourself and ready-made costumes.

## Clothes

Besides the specialist shops listed here, most of the big department stores and discount shops have children's sections.

**agnès b. Map 2, F4. 2 rue du Jour, 1er. Ⓜ/RER Châtelet-Les Halles. Mon–Sat 10am–7pm.** Very fashionable and desirable clothes as you'd expect from this chic Parisian designer. Just opposite is Le Petit B for babies, selling lots of very French-looking outfits in navy blue and white.

**Du Pareil au Même Map 4, G13. 122 rue du Faubourg-St-Antoine, 12e ⓦwww.dpam.fr. ⓂLedru-Rollin. Mon–Sat 10am–7pm.** Beautiful kids' clothing at very good prices. Gorgeous, inexpensive floral dresses, cute jogging suits and brightly coloured basics. Branches all over Paris.

**Petit Bateau Map 7, F3. 116 av des Champs-Elysées, 8e ⓦwww.petit-bateau.fr. ⓂCharles-de-Gaulle-Etoile. Mon–Sat 10am–7.30pm.** Stylish and comfortable cotton T-shirts, vests and pyjamas. Dozens of branches all over France.

**Pom d'Api Map 2, F4. 13 rue du Jour, 1er. Ⓜ/RER Châtelet-Les Halles. Mon–Sat 10.30am–7pm.** The most colourful, imaginative and well-made kids shoes in Paris, up to size 40/UK 7, and from around €40.

**See Chapter 21 for listings of department stores and other clothes shops.**

# Gay and lesbian Paris



It's perhaps not as exuberantly queer as, say, Berlin or San Francisco, but the historic French notion that sexuality is a private matter – a courtesy extended to everyone from the city's mayor down to the most casual day-tripper – makes it a rewardingly relaxed place for gay and lesbian visitors. It has a gay history to match either Berlin's or San Francisco's, along with plentiful bars, clubs, restaurants and shops catering to a gay clientele. The focal point of the scene is the **Marais**, whose central street, rue Ste-Croix-de-la-Bretonnerie, has visibly gay-oriented businesses at almost every other address. **Lesbians** are less well served commercially.

The high points on the calendar are the huge annual **Marche des Fiertés LGBT**, or gay pride march, which normally takes place on the last Saturday in June, and the **Bastille Day Ball** (July 13, 10pm–dawn), a wild open-air dance on the quai de la Tournelle, 5e (Ⓜ Pont-Marie), which is free for all to join in.

# Information and contacts

The gay and lesbian community is well catered for by the **media**, and there are plentiful voluntary information and support organizations. Listed below are a handful of the most useful contacts.



## Useful contacts and organizations

**Centre Gai et Lesbien de Paris Map 2, I4. 63 rue Beaubourg, 3e ⓣ01.43.57.21.47, ⓦcglparis.org. ⓂBastille/Ledru-Rollin/Voltaire. Mon 6–8pm, Tues–Thurs 3–8pm, Fri & Sat 12.30–8pm, Sun 4–7pm.** The first port of call for information and advice – legal, social, psychological and medical. Also has a good library and puts on small exhibitions.

**MAG Map 1, H5. 106 rue de Montreuil, 11e ⓣ01.43.73.31.63, ⓦwww.mag-paris.org. ⓂAvron.** The Mouvement d'Affirmation des Jeunes Gais et Lesbiennes is a group aimed at young people: it publishes an online magazine, the *Magazette*, and organizes a drop-in welcome service on Friday and Saturday evenings, as well as occasional tea dances, picnics, and cinema and theatre nights.

**Maison des Femmes Map 1, G5. 163 rue de Charenton, 12e ⓣ01.43.43.41.13, ⓦmaisondes-femmes.free.fr. ⓂReuilly-Diderot. Daily 9am–7pm.** The main women's centre in Paris and home to a number of lesbian groups who organize workshops and meetings. Frequent gay/straight lunches and parties, too.

**Paris Gai Village ⓦwww.parisgaivillage.com.** Voluntary association that acts as an alternative tourist office, with guided walks and museum visits ("gay Louvre", for example) and a one-hour welcome-to-gay-Paris service.

**Pharmacie du Village Map 2, I6. 26 rue du Temple, 4e ⓣ01.42.72.60.71. ⓂHôtel-de-Ville. Mon–Sat 8.30am–9.30pm, Sun 9am–8pm.** This gay-run pharmacy is sympathetic to most needs.

## The media and websites

**2X ⓦwww.2xparis.fr.** "Deux Fois" aka "Two Weeks" is the city's premier free gay paper for cultural and nightlife listings, small ads, lonely hearts, services, etc. Out every other Thurs.

**Citegay ⓦwww.citegay.fr.** One of the best websites, with lots of links, features and contacts.

**Les Mots à la Bouche Map 4, B10. 6 rue Ste-Croix-de-la-Bretonnerie, 4e ⓣ01.42.78.88.30, ⓦwww.motsbouche.com. ⓂHôtel-de-Ville. Mon–Sat 11am–11pm, Sun 1–9pm.** The main gay and lesbian bookshop, with exhibition space and meeting rooms; a selection of literature in English, too. Lots of free listings maps and club flyers to pick up, and one of the helpful assistants usually speaks English.

**Paris Gay ⓦwww.paris-gay.com.** Major portal for gay tourists visiting Paris. The online *Guide Gay* has lots of reviews of bars, restaurants, clubs, saunas and the like, though the English translations tend to be rather brief.

**Têtu ⓦwww.tetu.com.** The glossiest and most readable of France's gay monthlies – the name means "headstrong". The pull-out section, "Agenda", is full of contact details, addresses and reviews, though it's not restricted to Paris.



## Nightlife

Parisians like to complain about the bar scene in Paris relative to rival cities like London or New York, but in truth there's a fair range of gay and lesbian **bars**, especially in the "pink triangle" of the Marais. Straights are welcome in some gay establishments.

A few classic **club** addresses are given here, but many, if not most, mainstream clubs run gay *soirées*, so check also the listings on pp.242–245. The best option with clubs, however, is to keep an eye on flyers or ask around in bars to find out what the latest flavour of the month is. Club **opening hours** are largely irrelevant: they're all pretty empty before at least 1am and keep going till at least dawn – some continue into *after* events well into weekend mornings. Club **entry prices** are generally around €10–20, depending on the size of the venue and the popularity of the individual *soirée*. The entry cost usually entitles you to a *conso*, or "free" drink.

### Mainly women – bars

**3W-Kafé Map 4, B11. 8 rue des Ecouffes, 4e ⓣ01.48.87.39.26. ⓂHôtel-de-Ville. Daily 5.30pm–2am.** Swish lipstick-lesbian lounge-café, full of sophisticated professionals earlier on, but warming up considerably at weekends, when the cellar bar gets moving. The owners also run *Les Jacasses*, immediately opposite, a lower-key wine bar which does decent tapas, bruschetta and the like.

**La Champmeslé Map 2, E2. 4 rue Chabanais, 3e ⓣ01.42.96.85.20. ⓜSt-Paul. Daily 4pm–4am.** Long-established lesbian address in a handsome old building. Popular among thirty-somethings, though packs everyone in for the live music or cabaret nights from Thursday to Saturday. It holds frequent exhibitions and has a definite community atmosphere – a good place to begin exploring the scene.

**Le Troisième Lieu Map 2, H5. 62 rue Quincampoix, 4e ⓣ01.48.04.85.64. ⓜRambuteau. Daily 6pm–2am.** Buzzy, upbeat new disco-diner offering all things: (inexpensive) cocktail bar, restaurant (with excellent "big salads") and dancing later on at weekends. In all, a welcoming and fairly mixed space, though mainly frequented by *les filles*, and mostly younger ones at that.

**L'Unity Bar Map 2, H4. 176 rue St-Martin, 3e. ⓜRambuteau. Daily 4pm–2am.** Predominantly butch bar where life is centred on the beer tap and the pool table.

## Mainly men – bars

**Café Cox Map 4, A10. 15 rue des Archives, 3e ⓣ01.42.72.08.00. ⓜHôtel-de-Ville. Mon–Thurs 12.30pm–2am, Fri–Sun 1.30pm–2am.** Muscular types up for a seriously good time pack out this loud, riotous neon-coloured bar. Friendly – if your face fits – with DJs at weekends.

**Le Carré Map 4, A10. 18 rue du Temple, 4e ⓣ01.44.59.38.57. ⓜHôtel-de-Ville. Mon–Thurs & Sun 11am–2am, Fri & Sat 11am–4am.** Stylish, designer café with good food, comfortable chairs, cool lighting, an excellent *terrasse* on the street, and occasional video projects or fashion shows on the side. Mostly full of sophisticated Parisians, but occasional clued-up tourists find their way here too.

**Le Duplex Map 4, A8. 25 rue Michel-le-Comte, 3e ⓣ01.42.72.80.86. ⓜRambuteau. Mon–Thurs & Sun 8pm–2am, Fri & Sat 8pm–4am.** Arty little bar that's popular with intellectual or media types for its relatively relaxed and chatty atmosphere. Friendly rather than cruisy – the barmen know all the regulars by name. Puts on art exhibitions.

**Le Free DJ Map 4, A10. 35 rue Ste-Croix de la Bretonnerie, 4e ⓣ01.42.78.26.20. ⓜHôtel-de-Ville. Mon–Wed & Sun 6pm–3am, Fri &**

**Sat 6pm–4am.** This stylish, fairly recent addition to the scene draws the young and *très looké* – beautiful – types. It's friendly, though, and features some big sounds (house, disco-funk) in the basement club.

**L'Open Café Map 4, A10. 17 rue des Archives, 3e ⓣ01.48.87.80.25. ⓂArts-et-Métiers. Mon–Thurs & Sun 11am–2am, Fri & Sat 11am–4am.** The first gay café-bar to have tables out on the pavement, and they're still there, with overhead heaters in winter. *L'Open* is *the* most famous gay bar in Paris and, as such, it's expensive and quite touristy, but still good fun.

**Le Raidd Map 4, A10. 23 rue du Temple, 4e. ⓂHôtel-de-Ville. Daily 5pm–2am.** One of the city's biggest, glossiest (and most expensive) bars, famous for its beautiful staff, topless waiters and go-go boys' shower shows every hour.

## Clubs

**Les Bains Douches Map 2, H4. 7 rue du Bourg l'Abbé, 3e ⓦwww.lesbainsdouches.net. ⓂEtienne Marcel.** This classic and distinctly upmarket club has long been the choice of the style-conscious gay clubber, especially on hedonistic Saturday nights. Expensive restaurant upstairs.

**CUD Map 4, B8. 12 rue des Haudriettes, 3e. ⓂRambuteau.** The "Classic Up and Down" is just that: bar upstairs, club below. A great, miniature venue for low-key, relaxed dancing with no queues, door policies or overpriced drinks. More for bears than boys, though it's pretty mixed.

**Queen Map 7, G3. 102 av des Champs-Elysées, 8e ⓦwww.queen.fr. ⓂGeorge V.** The legendary gay club of the 1980s has bounced back from its inevitable fall, though it's still a bit packed out with eager provincials – except on the friendly (and somewhat kitsch), gay-leaning Sunday nights.

**Le Rive Gauche Map 2, C8. 1 rue du Sabot, 6e ⓦwww.lerivegauche.com. ⓂSt-Germain-des-Près.** Currently very fashionable among gorgeous young *gamines*, this pocket club is a historic 1970s address (preserving some of its gold mirror-mosaic decor), and fast becoming a lesbian classic.

**Le Tango Map 4, B7. 13 rue au-Maire, 3e ⓣ01.42.72.17.78. ⓂArts-et-Métiers.** Relaxed, unpretentious (and inexpensive) gay and lesbian club with a traditional Sunday-afternoon *bal* from 7pm, featuring proper slow dances as well as tangos and camp 1970s and 1980s disco classics. Turns into a full-on club later on, and on Fri and Sat nights.

## Hotels

Although gay and lesbian visitors aren't likely to come across any anti-social behaviour in **hotels** and **restaurants**, there is a choice of gay-oriented places to stay. You don't need to look any further than the Marais.

**Hôtel Beaumarchais Map 4, E8. 3 rue Oberkampf, 11<sup>e</sup> Ⓣ01.53.36.86.86, Ⓦwww.hotelbeaumarchais.com. ⓂFilles-du-Calvaire/Oberkampf.** See p.193.

**Hôtel Central Marais Map 4, B10. 33 rue Vieille-du-Temple, 4<sup>e</sup> Ⓣ01.48.87.56.08, Ⓦwww.hotelcentralmarais.com. ⓂHôtel-de-Ville.** See p.185.

# 28

# Directory



**Addresses** Paris is divided into twenty districts, or arrondissements. The first arrondissement, or 1$^{er}$, is centred on the Louvre, in the heart of the city. The rest wind outwards in a clockwise direction like a snail's shell: the 2$^{e}$, 3$^{e}$ and 4$^{e}$ are in the centre; the 5$^{e}$, 6$^{e}$ and 7$^{e}$ lie on the inner part of the Left (south) Bank; while the 8$^{e}$–20$^{e}$ make up the outer districts. Parisian addresses often quote the arrondissement, along with the nearest métro station or stations.

**Airport information** see pp.15–17.

**Banks and exchange** On the whole, the best exchange deals are to be found online before you go; once in Paris, banks tend to offer the best rates, though there's always a commission charge on top. Be wary of bureaux de change, which cluster around arrival points and tourist spots, as they can really rip you off. Standard banking hours are Mon to Fri from 9am to 4 or 5pm, though some may close for lunch. A few are open on Sat from 9am to noon; all are closed on Sun and bank holidays. Money-exchange bureaux stay open until 6 or 7pm, tend not to close for lunch and may even open on Sun in the more touristy areas.

**Crime** Petty theft is fairly rare, but sometimes occurs on the métro and at train stations – particularly at the Gare du Nord, the RER lines from the airport and métro line 1 – and at tourist hotspots, including restaurants and clubs. Serious crime against tourists is rare. If you need to report a theft, go to the commissariat de police of the arrondissement in which the theft took place, or to the central Préfecture de Police de Paris, 7 boulevard du Palais (Ⓣ01.53.73.53.73).

**Disabilities, travellers with** Paris's narrow pavements are notoriously difficult for people with limited mobility or wheelchair-users, and the métro is hopeless. Buses, however, are now equipped with platforms and wheelchair spaces, and museums are finally equipping themselves with disabled facilities. A new edition of the extremely handy publication *Access in Paris* (Ⓦwww.accessinparis.org) came out in 2008 and the text can be downloaded from the website. Otherwise, up-to-date information can be obtained from the French tourist board (Ⓦwww.franceguide.com) or from organizations including Ⓦwww.apf.asso.fr and Ⓦwww.jaccede.com.

**Doctors** Doctors can be found under "Médecins" in the yellow pages of phone directories; to call one out you can use SOS Médecins Ⓣ01.47.07.77.77.

**Electricity** 220V out of double, round-pin wall sockets.

**Embassies/Consulates**
Australia: 4 rue Jean-Rey, 15e Ⓣ01.40.59.33.00, Ⓦwww.france.embassy.gov.au (ⓂBir-Hakeim); Canada: 35 av Montaigne, 8e Ⓣ01.44.43.29.00, Ⓦwww.amb-canada.fr (ⓂFranklin-D. Roosevelt); Ireland: 4 rue Rude, 16e Ⓣ01.44.17.67.00, Ⓦwww.embassyofirelandparis.com (ⓂCharles-de-Gaulle–Etoile); New Zealand: 7ter rue Léonardo-de-Vinci, 16e Ⓣ01.45.00.24.11, Ⓦwww.nzembassy.com/france (ⓂVictor-Hugo); South Africa: 59 quai d'Orsay, 7e Ⓣ01.53.59.23.23, Ⓦwww.afriquesud.net (ⓂInvalides); UK 35 rue du Faubourg-St-Honoré, 8e; ⓂConcorde Ⓣ01.44.51.31.00, Ⓦukinfrance.fco.gov.uk;
USA: rue St-Florentin, 1er Ⓣ01.43.12.22.22, Ⓦfrance.usembassy.gov (ⓂConcorde).

**Emergencies** Fire brigade/paramedics (Sapeurs-Pompiers) Ⓣ18; Ambulance Ⓣ15; Rape crisis (SOS Viol; Mon–Fri 10am–6pm) Ⓣ08.00.05.95.95.

**Health** British citizens with a European Health Insurance Card (from post offices or online at Ⓦwww.dh.gov.uk/travellers) can take advantage of French health services. Non-EU citizens are strongly advised to take out travel insurance. See also "Pharmacies" see opposite.

**Internet access** Internet access is everywhere in Paris. If it's not in your hotel there will likely be a café nearby. Most post offices, too, have a computer geared up for public internet access.

**Left luggage** Located at all the main train stations. You cannot leave luggage at the airports.

**Lost baggage** Airports: Orly Ⓣ01.49.75.04.53; Charles de Gaulle Ⓣ01.48.62.10.86.

**Lost property** Bureau des Objets Trouvés, Préfecture de Police,

36 rue des Morillons, 15e (Ⓣ08.21.00.25.25; Mon & Wed 8.30am–5pm, Thurs 8.30am–8pm, Fri 8.30am–5.30pm; ⓂConvention). For property lost on public transport, phone the RATP on Ⓣ08.92.68.77.14. If you lose your passport, report it to a police station and then to your embassy.

**Pharmacies** All pharmacies, signalled by an illuminated green cross, can give good advice on minor complaints, offer appropriate medicines and recommend a doctor. They are also equipped to give first aid on request (for a fee). They keep normal shop hours (roughly 9am–7pm), and some stay open all night: details of the nearest one open are posted in all pharmacy windows. You can find a good English-speaking chemist at Swann, 6 rue Castiglione, 1er (Ⓣ01.42.60.72.96). Night pharmacies include Dérhy/Pharmacie des Champs-Elysées, 84 av des Champs-Elysées, 8e (Ⓣ01.45.62.02.41; 24hr; ⓂGeorge-V); and Pharmacie des Halles, 10 bd Sébastopol, 4e (Ⓣ01.42.72.03.23; Mon–Sat 9am–midnight, Sun 9am–10pm; ⓂChâtelet).

**Post office** Post offices are located in every neighbourhood – look for the bright yellow signs and the words "la Poste" or "le PTT" – and are generally open Mon–Fri 8am–7pm, Sat 8am–noon. The main office at 52 rue du Louvre, 1er (ⓂEtienne-Marcel) is open 24hr daily for all postal services (except banking). Stamps (*timbres*) are sold at tobacconists (*tabacs*).

**Public holidays** January 1, New Year's Day; Easter Sunday; Easter Monday; Ascension Day (40 days after Easter); Pentecost or Whitsun (seventh Sunday after Easter, plus the Monday); May 1, May Day/Labour Day; May 8, Victory in Europe Day; July 14, Bastille Day; August 15, Assumption of the Virgin Mary; November 1, All Saints' Day; November 11, Armistice Day; December 25, Christmas Day.

**Public toilets** Ask for *les toilettes* or look for signs for the WC (pronounced "vay say"); when reading the details of facilities outside hotels, don't confuse *lavabo*, which means washbasin, with lavatory. Some French toilets in bars are still of the hole-in-the-ground squatting variety, and tend to lack toilet paper. Standards of cleanliness aren't always high. Toilets in railway stations and department stores are commonly staffed by attendants who will expect a bit of spare change. Some have coin-operated locks, so you might want to keep some loose change to hand. The tardis-like automatic public toilets on the streets, known as "sanisettes", are free.

**Radio** The BBC World Service (Ⓦwww.bbc.co.uk/worldservice) can be found on 648kHz or 198kHz long wave from midnight to 5am (and Radio 4 during the day). The Voice of America (Ⓦwww.voa.gov) transmits on 90.5, 98.8 and 102.4FM. You can listen to the news in English on Radio France International (RFI; Ⓦwww.rfi.fr) at 7am, 2.30pm and 4.30pm on 738KHz AM. For radio news in French, there's the state-run France Inter (87.8FM), Europe 1 (104.7FM), or round-the-clock news on France Info (105.5FM).

**Safer sex** A warning: Paris has the highest incidence of AIDS of any city in Europe and people who are HIV positive are just as likely to be heterosexual as homosexual. Condoms (*préservatifs*) are readily available at supermarkets, clubs, from dispensers on the street – often outside pharmacies – and in the métro. From pharmacies you can also get spermicidal cream and jelly (*dose contraceptive*), suppositories (*ovules, suppositoires*), and (with a prescription) the pill (*la pilule*), a diaphragm or IUD (*le stérilet*). Pregnancy test kits (*tests de grossesse*) are sold at pharmacies; the morning-after pill (*la pilule du lendemain*) is available from pharmacies without prescription.

**Sales tax** VAT (Value Added Tax) is referred to as TVA in France (*taxe sur la valeur ajoutée*). The standard rate in France is 19.6 percent; it's higher for luxury items and lower for essentials, but there are no exemptions (children's clothes, for example, are more expensive than in the UK). However, non-EU residents who have been in the country for less than six months are entitled to a refund (*détaxe*) of some, or all, of this amount (but usually around 14 percent) if you spend at least €175 in a single trip to one shop. Not all stores participate in this scheme though, so you'll have to ask. The procedure is rather complicated: present your passport to the shop while paying and ask for the three-paged *bordereau de vente à l'exportation* form. They should help you fill it in and provide you with a self-addressed envelope. When you leave the EU, get customs to stamp the filled-in form; you will then need to send two of the pages back to the shop in the envelope within three months;

the shop will then transfer the refund through your credit card or bank. The Centre de Renseignements des Douanes (ⓣ08.25.30.82.63, ⓦwww.douane.gouv.fr) can answer any customs-related questions.

**Smoking** Smoking in public places in France has been banned since 2008. Restaurants, cafés, bars and clubs are still allowed to have smoking rooms, but these now have to be strictly supervised and staff are not obliged to enter or serve them.

**Student information (CROUS)** 39 av Georges-Bernanos, 5e (ⓣ01.40.51.36.00, ⓦwww.crous.fr; RER Port-Royal).

**Telephones** For calls within France – local or long-distance – dial all ten digits of the number. Paris and Ile-de-France numbers start with ⓣ01. Numbers beginning with ⓣ08.00 are free numbers; ⓣ08.10 is charged at local rates, no matter where you're calling from; all other ⓣ08 numbers are premium rate (from €0.34 per minute) and can't be accessed from outside France. Numbers beginning with ⓣ06 are mobile and therefore expensive to call (usually around €0.40 per minute). Local calls are timed in France. Off-peak times (30 percent less than the peak rate, for local, long-distance and international calls) are weekdays between 7pm and 8am, and all day Saturday and Sunday, as well as holidays. France operates on the European GSM standard, so US cellphones won't work in France unless you've got a tri-band phone. If you're making a lot of calls on your mobile, consider buying a local sim card or a pre-pay (*mobicarte*) package once in Paris. These are sold in mobile phone shops, FNAC stores (see p.263) and some supermarkets. Expect to pay around €30 for a sim card. You can make international phone calls from any telephone box (*cabine*) and can receive calls where there's a blue logo of a ringing bell. You'll need to buy a phonecard (*télécarte*), or, if you're making a lot of calls, it's worth buying a card with a PIN (*une carte à code*), which can be used from a public or private telephone; just dial the toll-free number on the card, followed by your PIN (given on the card) and then the number you want to reach. All phonecards are available from *tabacs* and newsagents.

**Television** TNT (*télévision numérique terrestre*), or digital terrestrial TV, accesses fourteen free French TV channels, if the viewer has a decoder or is hooked up to satellite or cable. The five most popular channels are the public channels France 2, Arte/La Cinquième and France 3, and the commercial channels TF1 and M6. Also widely watched is the subscription channel, Canal Plus. In addition, there are the cable networks, which include CNN, the BBC World Service, BBC Prime (*Eastenders*, etc) and France's own rolling news station, France 24, which broadcasts in French, English and Arabic. The main French news broadcasts are at 8pm on F2 and TF1.

**Time** France is one hour ahead of Britain (Greenwich Mean Time), six hours ahead of Eastern Standard Time (eg New York), and nine hours ahead of Pacific Standard Time (eg Los Angeles). Australia is eight to ten hours ahead of France, depending on which part of the continent you're in. Remember also that France uses a 24hr clock, with, for example, 2am written as 2h and 2.30pm written as 14h30. The most confusing are noon and midnight – respectively 12h and 00h. Talking clock Ⓣ36.99.

**Tours** The best walking tours of Paris in English are those offered by Paris Walks (Ⓣ01.48.09.21.40, Ⓦwww.paris-walks.com; 2hr; €12, children under 15 €8), with subjects ranging from "Hemingway's Paris" to "Historic Marais". If you want to save your feet, try the popular Paris L'Open Tour bus (Ⓦwww.pariscityrama.com), which operates a hop-on, hop-off service; a one-day pass costs €29, two days €32 (4- to 11-year-olds €15 for one or two days). For bike tours, see p.23, for boat tours p.288.

**Trafffic and road conditions** For news on Paris traffic listen to 105.1 FM (FIP) on the radio; for the *boulevard périphérique* and main routes in and out of the city, ring Ⓣ08.26.02.20.22, or log onto Ⓦwww.securiteroutiere.gouv.fr.

**Weather** Paris and Ile-de-France Ⓣ08.92.68.02.75, or online at Ⓦwww.meteofrance.com.

# Contexts

# Contexts

# A brief history of Paris

## Beginnings

When the **Gauls** or **Celts** began to settle in the Paris region, probably in the third century BC, they called their settlement Lutetia or Lucotetia, from a Celtic root word for "marshland". Back then, the Seine was broader, flowing past a miniature archipelago of five islets. The modern name for the city comes from the local Quarisii or **Parisii** tribe, who built an iron-age fort on the largest island, at the eastern end of what is now the Ile de la Cité. This fort commanded a perfect site: defensible and astride the most practicable north–south crossing point of an eminently navigable river.

When Julius Caesar's conquering armies arrived in 52 BC, they found a thriving settlement. Romanized Lutetia prospered too, even if the town was fairly insignificant by **Gallo-Roman** standards, with a population of some eight thousand. The Romans established their basilica on the Ile de la Cité, but the town lay almost entirely on the Left Bank, on the slopes of the Montagne Ste-Geneviève.

Although Roman rule in Gaul disintegrated under the impact of **Germanic invasions** around 275 AD, Lutetia itself held out for almost two hundred years. The marauding bands of Attila the Hun were repulsed in 451, supposedly thanks to the prayerful intervention of Geneviève, who became the city's patron saint. The city finally fell to **Clovis the Frank** in 486; the first, and by no means the last, time the city would fall to German troops. Clovis's descendants founded the Christianized but endlessly warring **Merovingian** dynasty, whose bodies were buried in the great basilica at St-Denis.

In the early ninth century, the king **Charlemagne** conquered half of Europe and sparked a mini-Renaissance, but Paris's good fortune plummeted after the break-up of his empire as the city was repeatedly sacked and pillaged by the **Vikings** from the mid-840s onwards. Thereafter Paris lay largely in ruins, a provincial backwater without power, influence, or even a significant population.



## The medieval heyday

In the eleventh century, the Paris region was ruled by the **Capetian dynasty**, but as the royal family did not deign to base itself in the miserable capital, regeneration was slow. By 1100, the city's population was only around three thousand. One hundred years later, however, Paris had become the largest city in the Christian world (which it would remain until overtaken by London in the eighteenth century), as well as its intellectual and cultural hub. By the **1320s**, the city's population had swollen even further reaching almost a quarter of a million inhabitants. This rapid expansion was owed to Paris's valuable river-borne trade and the associated growth of the **merchant classes**, coupled with thriving **agriculture** in the wider Paris region. The economic boom was matched by the growth of the city's university on the Left Bank – notably the **Sorbonne** college. Meanwhile, the capital was protected by the novelty of a relatively strong – and largely Paris-based – monarchy.

To defend his burgeoning metropolis, **Philippe-Auguste** (1180–1223), built the **Louvre fortress** and a vast **city wall**, which enclosed an area now roughly traced by the inner ring of modern Paris's 1$^{er}$–6$^{e}$ arrondissements. The administration of the city remained in the hands of the monarchy until 1260, when **Louis IX** (St Louis) ceded a measure of responsibility to the *échevins* or leaders of the Paris watermen's guild, whose power was based on their monopoly control of all river traffic and taxes thereon. The city's government, when it has been allowed one, has been conducted ever since from the place de Grève/place de l'Hôtel-de-Ville.

## A city adrift

From the mid-fourteenth to mid-fifteenth centuries Paris shared the same unhappy fate as the rest of France, embroiled in the long and destructive **Hundred Years' War**, which pitted the French and English nobility against each other in a power struggle whose results were misery for the French peasant classes, and penury for Paris. A break in the Capetian line led to the accession of Philippe VI, the first of the **Valois dynasty**, but the legitimacy of his claim to the throne was contested by Edward III of England. Harried by war, the Valois monarchs spent much of their troubled reigns outside the capital, whose loyalty was often questionable. Infuriated by the lack of political representation for merchant classes, the city mayor, or Prévôt des Marchands, **Etienne Marcel**, even let the enemy into Paris in 1357.

**Charles V**, who ruled from 1364, built a new Louvre and a new city wall that increased Paris's area by more than half again (roughly incorporating what are now the modern 9$^{e}$–11$^{e}$ arrondissements, on the Right Bank), but the population within his walls was plummeting due to disease and a harsh climate in Europe generally, as well as warfare and political instability. The **Black Death**, which arrived in the summer of 1348, killed around eight hundred Parisians a day, and over the next 140 years, one year in four was a plague year. Harvests repeatedly failed – icebergs even floated on the Seine in 1407 – and, politically, things were no better.

In 1422 the Duke of Bedford set up his government of northern France in Paris. **Joan of Arc** made an unsuccessful attempt to drive the English out in 1429, but the following year the English king, Henry VI, had the cheek to have himself crowned king of France in Notre-Dame. Meanwhile, the Valois kings fled the city altogether for a life of pleasure-seeking irrelevance in the gentle Loire Valley.

## Renaissance and rebirth

It was only when the English were expelled – from Paris in 1437 and from France in 1453 – that the city had the chance to recover. When, in 1528, **François I** decided to bring the royal court back to the capital, Paris's fortunes improved further. Work began on reconstructing the Louvre and building the Tuileries palace for Catherine de Médicis and an economic boom brought peasants in from the countryside in droves, enlarging the city's population well past its medieval peak. Although centralized planning coughed into life to cope with the influx, Paris remained, as Henri II put it, a city of "mire, muck and filth".

In the second half of the century, war interrupted early efforts at civic improvement – this time **civil war** between Catholics and Protestants. Paris swung fanatically behind the Catholic cause, leading to the infamous **St Bartholomew's Day massacre**, on August 25, 1572, when some two thousand Protestants were murdered in the streets. After years of outright war, and the death of about forty thousand Parisians from disease or starvation, the Protestant leader Henri of Navarre entered the city as the Catholic king **Henri IV**. "Paris is worth a Mass", he is reputed to have said, to justify renouncing his Protestantism in order to soothe the Catholic sensibilities.

The Paris Henri IV inherited was filthy and overcrowded, and he quickly set out to revive its fortunes. He instituted tight building regulations and created the splendid place des Vosges and place Dauphine, as well as building the **Pont Neuf**, the first of the Paris bridges not to be cluttered with medieval houses. The tradition of grandiose public building was to continue, reaching its apogee in the seventeenth century under **Louis XIV** – even when the entire court moved outside Paris to the vast palace of **Versailles** in 1671. But civic works also continued, as Paris's old fortifications were cleared to make way for the new **boulevards** and **avenues**, notably the Champs-Elysées. The aristocratic *hôtels*, or private mansions, of the **Marais** were largely erected during the seventeenth century, only to be superseded early in the **eighteenth century** by the **Faubourg St-Germain** as the fashionable quarter of the rich and powerful. Towards the end of the century, coffee-houses or "cafés" were opening by the hundreds to serve the needs of the burgeoning **bourgeoisie**. Obscured by all the glitter, however, were the **poor living conditions** of the ordinary citizens – the centre of the city remained a densely packed and unsanitary warren of medieval lanes and tenements.

## Revolution and empire

In 1789, Louis XVI summoned a meeting of the "Estates General" – a parliament of representatives of the clergy (the First Estate), the nobility (the Second) and the middle classes (the Third) – to help sort out his disastrous finances. When the Estates duly met, however, the bourgeois representatives of the Third Estate proved troublesome. When Louis posted troops around Versailles and Paris, the city's deputies entered the Hôtel de Ville and declared a municipal government or **Commune**, setting up a militia – the National Guard – and preparing to defend Paris against attack. When a band of ordinary Parisians stormed the **Bastille** prison on July 14 looking for weapons with which to arm themselves, the National Guard joined in. From this moment on, the ordinary people of Paris – known as the **sans-culottes**, or "people without breeches" – became the shock troops of the Revolution.

At this point the king bowed to pressure and legalized a new National Assembly, which in August 1789 passed the **Declaration of the Rights of Man**, sweeping away the feudal privileges of the old order. In 1791 Louis attempted to flee abroad, but was forced to return to Paris; by August 1792, he was a virtual prisoner of the *sans-culottes*. In September, the monarchy was abolished, the Republic declared, and the king put on trial for treason; Louis was convicted and guillotined on place de la Concorde in January 1793.

The Republican Convention, however, was wracked with infighting and the moderate Girondin faction lost out to the radical **Jacobins**. Under the ruthless Maximilien **Robespierre**, the Committee of Public Safety began the extermination of "enemies of the people", a period known as the **Grande Terreur** – among the first casualties was **Marie-Antoinette**.

The revolutionary chaos ended only after Robespierre himself was sent to the Guillotine, in July 1794, and a new leader emerged. **Napoleon Bonaparte** officially overthrew the Directory in a **coup d'état** in November 1799, subsequently appointing himself first consul for life in 1802 and then **emperor** in 1804.

Although Napoleon took France into numerous costly and bloody **wars**, his rule brought relative prosperity and stability to Paris, making it the heart of an efficient and highly centralized bureaucracy, and beginning many grandiose building schemes. He lined the Seine with 4km of stone *quais*, provided Paris with its modern water supply, and built the Arcs de Triomphe and Carrousel as well as a further extension for the Louvre. After the disastrous **invasion of Russia** in 1812, however, Napoleon was forced to abdicate and **Louis XVIII**, brother of the decapitated Louis XVI, was installed as king. In a last desperate attempt to regain power, Napoleon escaped from exile on the Italian island of Elba and reorganized his armies, only to meet final defeat at **Waterloo** on June 18, 1815.

## The nineteenth century

France's glorious and powerful rulers, from Philippe-Auguste to Napoleon, may have created Paris's great landmark buildings but Paris's distinctive cityscape only took shape thanks to the bourgeoisie, in the **nineteenth century**. This was the century of the middle classes, punctuated by brief and often bloody revolts led by Paris's poor.

The first rebellion, however, was bourgeois. When King Charles X refused to accept the result of the 1830 National Assembly elections, **Adolphe Thiers** led the opposition in revolt; barricades were erected in Paris and there followed three days of bitter street fighting, known as *les trois glorieuses*. The outcome of this **July Revolution** was the election of **Louis-Philippe** as a constitutional "bourgeois monarch".

For the **poor**, living and working conditions in Paris only deteriorated, with twenty thousand deaths from cholera in Paris in 1832 alone. Smaller expressions of discontent occurred in Paris in 1832 and 1834, but the major eruption came on June 23, 1848, when working-class Paris – Poissonnière, Temple, St-Antoine, the Marais, Quartier Latin, Montmartre – rose, united, in revolt. In this **1848 Revolution**, men, women and children fought fifty thousand troops in three days of fighting. Nine hundred soldiers were killed; no-one knows how many of the insurgents died.

In November 1848, the anxious middle classes elected **Louis Napoleon Bonaparte**, nephew of the Emperor Napoleon, as President. Within three years he brought the tottering republic to an end by announcing a coup d'état. Twelve months later, he had himself crowned Emperor Napoleon III. There followed a period of laissez-faire capitalism, which greatly increased the **economic wealth** of France. Napoleon III's great legacy to Paris, however, was the appointment of **Baron Haussmann** as Prefect of the Seine department. He undertook a total **transformation of the city**, driving 135km of broad new streets and boulevards through the cramped quarters of the medieval city. Haussmann's taste also dictated the uniform grey stone facades, mansard roofs and six to seven storeys – some with elegant ironwork balconies – that are still the architectural hallmark of the Paris street today.

The downside of this urban redesign was that some 350,000 poor Parisians were simply displaced, many moving out to the ever-growing **banlieue**, the city beyond the old walls. These suburbs tripled in population between 1860 and the outbreak of World War I, becoming the home of one and a half million almost-Parisians. Inside the city proper, the working classes were coralled into ever-smaller islands of poverty, where sanitation was nonexistent, and cholera and TB rife.

Haussmann's scheme was at least in part designed to keep the workers under control, the broad boulevards facilitating cavalry manoeuvres and artillery fire. The system was soon tested. In September 1870, Napoleon III surrendered to Bismarck at the border town of Sedan, less than two months after France had declared war on the superior forces of the **Prussian** state. The humiliation was enough for a Republican government to be instantly proclaimed in Paris. The Prussians advanced and by September 19 were laying **siege** to the capital. Daring balloonists kept the city in contact with the outside world, but meanwhile, Parisians starved. Finally, a newly elected Assembly surrendered the city to the Prussians and, on March 1, enemy troops marched down the Champs-Elysées.

Less than three weeks later, working-class Paris rose up in revolt, and the **Commune** was proclaimed from the Hôtel de Ville; it lasted all of 72 days – a festival of the oppressed, Lenin called it. Socialist in inspiration, the Commune had no time to implement lasting reforms, succumbing to the army of Adolphe Thiers' conservative government on May 28, 1871, after a week of street-by-street warfare – the so-called *semaine sanglante*, or "Bloody Week" – during which several of the city's landmark buildings were destroyed, including the Tuileries palace and the original Hôtel de Ville.

## Paris at play and at war

Within six or seven years of the Commune, few signs of the fighting remained. Visitors remarked admiringly on Paris's teeming streets, the expensive shops and energetic nightlife: this was the start of the capital's decadent heyday. In 1889 the **Eiffel Tower** stole the show at the great Exposition, and for the 1900 repeat, the **métro** was unveiled. Paris now emerged as the supremely inspiring environment for artists and writers – the so-called Bohemians – both French and foreign. **Impressionism**, **Fauvism** and **Cubism** were all born in Paris in this period, while French **poets** like Apollinaire, Laforgue, Max

Jacob, Blaise Cendrars and André Breton were preparing the way for Surrealism, concrete poetry and Symbolism. **Cinema**, too, first saw the light in Paris, with the jerky documentaries of the Lumière brothers and George Méliès' fantastical features both appearing in the mid-1890s. It was a constellation of talents that Western culture has rarely seen.

As a city, Paris escaped **World War I** relatively lightly. The human cost was rather higher: one in ten Parisian conscripts failed to return. But Paris remained the world's art – and party – capital after the war, with an injection of foreign blood and a shift of venue from Montmartre to Montparnasse. Indeed, the **années folles** (or "mad years") of the 1920s were some of Paris's most decadent and scintillating, consolidating a longstanding international reputation for hedonistic, often erotic, abandon that has sustained its tourism industry for the best part of a century.

As **Depression** deepened in the 1930s and Nazi power across the Rhine became more menacing, the mood changed, and attention turned to politics. The Left won the **1936 elections** but the brave new government soon foundered and returned to opposition, where it remained, with the exception of coalition governments, until 1981. After the outbreak of **World War II** and the fall of France, Paris suffered the humiliation of a four-year Nazi **occupation**. Food, fuel for heating and petrol were short, and many Parisians were forced to make compromises in order to survive. In 1942, Parisian Jews were rounded up – by other Frenchmen – and shipped off to Auschwitz. The **Resistance**, however, was also very active in the city. As Allied forces drew near to Paris in 1944, the FFI (armed Resistance units) called their troops onto the streets – some said, in a leftist attempt to seize political power. On August 23, Hitler famously gave orders that Paris should be destroyed, but the city's commander, Von Cholitz, delayed just long enough. **Liberation** arrived on August 25 in the shape of General Leclerc's tanks, motoring up the Champs-Elysées to the roar of a vast crowd.

## Postwar Paris: 1945 to 2000

**Postwar Paris** remained no stranger to political street battles. Violent demonstrations accompanied the Communist withdrawal from the coalition government in 1947; in the Fifties the Left protested against the colonial wars in Indochina and Algeria; and, in 1961, in one of the most shameful episodes in modern French history, some two hundred Algerians were killed by the police during a civil rights demonstration.

In the extraordinary month of **May 1968**, a radical leftist movement gathered momentum in Paris's universities. Students began by occupying university buildings, and the extreme reaction of the police and government helped the movement to spread until it represented a mass revolt against institutional stagnation that ended with a general strike by nine million workers. The vicious battles between students, workers and police on the streets of Paris shook large sectors of the population – France's silent majority – to the core.

Elections called in June 1968 returned the Right to power, but French institutions and French society had changed – then-president Charles de Gaulle didn't survive a referendum in 1969. His successor, **Georges Pompidou**, only survived long enough to begin the construction of the giant Les Halles development, and the expressways along the *quais* of the Seine.

When **François Mitterrand** became president in 1981, there was a mood of euphoria on the Left. His chief legacy to the city of Paris, however, was not social reform, but the **Grands Projets**, or great architectural projects. Many were extremely controversial. Most shocking of all to conservative Paris was I.M. Pei's **glass pyramid**, erected in the very heart of the historic Louvre palace. It is a testament to a new spirit in the city that most Parisians have now taken this symbol of thrusting modernity to their hearts, along with the **Institut du Monde Arabe** in the Quartier Latin, the **Grande Arche de la Défense** and the **Bibliothèque Nationale**, in the 13<sup>e</sup>. Only one *grand projet* has proved less successful: the ugly **Opéra Bastille**.

In the summer following the presidential election of 1995, which brought **Jacques Chirac** to power, a series of shocks hit Paris and the new regime. **Bombs** planted by an extremist Algerian Islamic group exploded in the RER stations of St-Michel and Port Royal. By November, public confidence in the government of Prime Minister **Alain Juppé** had collapsed, and over a period of three weeks some five million people took to the streets of Paris in protest against arrogant, elitist politicians and economic austerity measures.

The government's standing in the popularity stakes tumbled further as it was hit by a succession of **corruption scandals**. Accusations of cover-ups and perversion of the course of justice followed, punctuated by revelations of illegal funding of election campaigns, politicians taking bribes and dirty money changing hands during privatizations. The home affairs minister, Charles Pasqua, stepped up **anti-immigration measures** which resulted in some 250,000 people living and working in France having their legal status removed.

In a bid to gain influence for his party, Chirac called a snap parliamentary election in May 1997. His gamble failed spectacularly as he was forced into "cohabitation" with triumphant Socialist Prime Minister **Lionel Jospin**, whose government introduced the famous 35-hour working week. It was soon hit by another series of **scandals**, however, as was the Right. In 1998, Jean Tiberi – conservative Paris mayor since Chirac's move to the presidency in 1995 – was implicated in a scandal involving subsidized real-estate and salaries for fake jobs. As if this wasn't bad enough, Chirac himself was also accused of using millions of francs in cash from illegal sources to pay for luxury holidays for himself and his family and friends between 1992 and 1995. When investigating magistrates tried to question him, he claimed presidential immunity. At the time of writing, it seemed as if the great escaper might finally come to trial by early 2011.

Lightening the national mood, in July 1998, Paris – or rather the Paris suburb of St-Denis – was the scene of France's victory in the football **World Cup** at the new Stade de France. The team was proudly multi-ethnic and, for once, support for *les bleus* overrode all other colour distinctions; that night, the Champs-Elysées became a river of a million cheering fans.

## The New Paris: 2000 to 2010

In the first years of the new millennium, two seismic events shook Parisian politics. The first was the election of the quiet, unassuming Socialist candidate, **Bertrand Delanoë**, as Mayor of Paris in March 2001. The fact that this was the first time the Left had won control of the capital since the Paris Commune in 1871 was far more of a shock to most Parisians than the fact that he was gay. Delanoë's brief was to end town-hall corruption, tackle crime and traffic congestion and instil new pride and energy into the city.

The second major upset of the new millennium – not counting the **introduction of the euro** on January 1, 2002 – was the far-Right candidate **Le Pen's shock success** in the presidential election of spring 2002 in the first round. Against all predictions he beat the Socialist candidate Lionel Jospin into third place and went head to head with Chirac for President. On May 1, some 800,000 people packed the boulevards of Paris in the biggest **demonstration** the capital had seen since the student protests of 1968. Two weeks later, in the run-off, Chirac duly swept the board, winning 82 percent – 90 percent in Paris – of the vote: by far the biggest majority ever won by a French president.

France faced serious problems, most stemming from high unemployment and a swollen budget deficit. Chirac and the right wing proposed sweeping **reforms** including relaxations of labour laws and cuts to the generous provision of pensions and free health care. For the next ten years, the government's attempts to impose economic reforms broadly on the "Anglo-Saxon" liberal model, and the French people's fierce attempt to resist them, dominated the domestic agenda. Almost every year, fresh waves of passionate strikers would flood the streets of Paris and other cities across the country. There were half a million strikers out in Paris in October 2005. In March 2006, students protesting against "liberalized" employment laws occupied the Sorbonne, in conscious imitation of May 1968. Once again, they were brutally driven out by riot police – but the proposed reforms were withdrawn. Four years later, with precious little accomplished, a million French workers were out on strike.

There was trouble on the foreign front, too. Responding to the US's refusal to give weapons inspectors in **Iraq** more time, Chirac vowed in March 2003 to use France's Security Council veto against any second resolution committing the UN to war. Throughout France, Chirac was feted for "standing up to the Americans", but Paris's tourist industry suffered. In November 2005, violent civil unrest swept France's urban areas after two teenagers died in a run-down area of the Paris *banlieue* while fleeing police they mistakenly thought were chasing them. Local anger and **rioting** quickly spread to other Parisian suburbs. Over three weeks some nine thousand vehicles went up in smoke, and 2900 people were arrested. Young people living in the suburbs saw the main causes as anger at racism and exclusion from society, especially from employment. In many of the worst-affected areas – home to communities of largely African or North African origin – youth unemployment was (and still is) as high as fifty percent – double the already high average among young people.

As Chirac's presidency limped to its end, the French were attracted to the idea of an economic hard-man who could break down the strikers. In the presidential elections of 2007, they rejected the consensus-seeking charms of the centrist Socialist candidate, Ségolène Royal, and plumped for a confrontational and egotistical right-winger **Nicolas Sarkozy**, known as "Sarko".

Some major surprises quickly ensued. First, he appointed a notably conciliatory cabinet. Next, his wife left him, and he took up with the model, singer and Euro-jetsetter **Carla Bruni**, marrying her in February 2008. Then came the **global financial crisis** of 2008/9. Suddenly, the "Anglo-Saxon" form of market-led, laissez-faire capitalism seemed exactly what French socialists had always said it was: a debt-fuelled castle built on sand. In response, Sarkozy performed an astonishing political about-turn, pledging to wield the power of the state to ensure stability. Strong-state *dirigisme* was back. National reform, again, would have to wait.

## The Paris of the future?

While national reforms stumbled along, Paris raced ahead under its new mayor, Bertrand Delanoë and his energetic Green Party sidekick (and later, Deputy Mayor), Denis Baupin. During the summer of 2002, Delanoë caused apoplexy among Paris's fiercely independent car users by closing a three-kilometre length of the riverbank roads and turning them into a public beach, dubbed **Paris Plage**, from mid-July to mid-August. In October Delanoë launched the first **Nuit Blanche** ("sleepless night"), in which hundreds of galleries, museums, bars, restaurants and public buildings remained open for a city-wide all-night party of poetry readings, live music and performance art. This and Paris Plage are now established events in the city's calendar.

Still more significant have been Delanoë's improvements in **city transport and sustainability**: huge numbers of bus and cycle lanes have been installed throughout Paris; a tramway ringing the entire city is almost complete; the river-bus service has expanded; and the Vélib' bike scheme (see p.23) is a success. And there's more: the existing Batobus ferries will one day be a fully integrated **métro fluvial** service and rentable cars on the Vélib' model – called, inevitably, **Autolib'** – are imminent. There's even a scheme to dramatically extend the number of pedestrian areas in the city, perhaps covering the first four arrondissements of the historic centre, and to install water turbines under four of the capital's bridges.

In the long term, however, Paris faces significant structural issues. High rents and higher property prices have provoked a

**flight of residents** from Paris "intra-muros" to the suburbs, or *banlieue*. There are now 2.1 million residents in central Paris, roughly half the number in 1900, and the city has lost roughly a quarter of its **small food stores** and butcher's shops in the last decade. Even as the centre has become a virtual ghetto of the rich, with government money lavished upon it, the ever-swelling **suburbs** beyond the perimeter fence of the *périphérique* ring road remain riven with poverty, unemployment and discontent. The three administrative *départements* of the "Petite Couronne", the suburban districts encircling Paris, contain some four million people, yet the city government has no remit to be concerned with them or their affairs. **The poor**, including large numbers of immigrants and their families, are effectively excluded from the city centre. The high-paying, white-collar jobs of the shopping, banking and governmental districts just don't seem to be available to non-white youths from the "9–3" – as the depressed *département* of Seine Saint-Denis, officially numbered 93, is known.

Intent on preventing the "museumification" of Paris, the Mairie now buys up private apartment buildings in the historic centre, to be rented out as **social housing**. Furthermore, in 2009 the government invited ten leading architectural firms to submit proposals for **Le Grand Pari**, the Greater, Greener Paris of the future. The architects envisioned new *Grands Axes*, avenues as radical as any bulldozed by Haussmann – but in this case linking city and *banlieue*. President Sarkozy favoured high-speed rail links down the Seine towards the port of Le Havre; Richard Rogers called for a green network covering the train lines leading out of the northern stations; Christian de Portzamparc wanted a high-speed elevated train running circles around the ring road. The radical left-wing architect Roland Castro mildly proposed that perhaps the suburbs might have their share of government offices and cultural institutions. That may never happen. But with climate change, social unrest and economic disturbances all lapping at the city's walls, Paris cannot remain an island much longer.

# Books

In the selected listing of books below, publishers are detailed in the form of British publisher/American publisher. Where books are published in one country only, UK or US follows the publisher's name. The ★ symbol marks titles that are particularly recommended.



## History and politics

**Anthony Beevor & Artemis Cooper** *Paris After the Liberation: 1944–1949* (Penguin). Gripping account of a crucial era in Parisian history, featuring de Gaulle, the Communists, the St-Germain scene and Dior's New Look.

**Robert Cole** *A Traveller's History of Paris* (Windrush Press/Interlink). This brief history of the city from the first Celtic settlement to the present day is an ideal starting point for anyone wishing to delve into the historical archives.

★ **Eric Hazan** *The Invention of Paris* (Verso). Utterly compelling psychogeographical account of the city, picking over its history *quartier* by *quartier* in a thousand aperçus and anecdotes. It's a weighty book, but a zesty, lefty bias nicely brings out the passions behind the rebellions and revolutions.

**Christopher Hibbert** *The French Revolution* (Penguin). Good, concise popular history of the period. The description of events is vivid, but it's not so good on the intellectual background and the meaning of the Revolution.

**Alistair Horne** *The Fall of Paris* (Pan) and *Seven Ages of Paris* (Pan/Vintage). The former is a very readable and humane account of the extraordinary period of the Prussian siege of Paris in 1870 and the ensuing struggles of the Commune, while the latter is a compelling (if rather old-fashionedly fruity) account of significant episodes in the city's history.

**Andrew Hussey** *Paris, the Secret History* (Penguin). Delves into fascinating and little-known aspects of Paris's history, including occultism, freemasonry and the seedy underside of the city.

**Colin Jones** *Paris: Biography of a City* (Allen Lane/Viking). Jones focuses on the actual life and growth of the city, from the Neolithic past to the future. Five hundred pages flow by easily, punctuated by thoughtful but accessible "boxes" on streets, buildings and characters whose lives were especially bound up with Paris's. The best single book on the city's history.

**Philip Mansel** *Paris Between Empires* (Orion/ Phoenix). Serious but gripping tale of an often-ignored patch of Paris's history: the turbulent years of revolutions and restorations that followed in the wake of Napoleon. Brilliantly conjures up the events of the streets and the salons.

**Lucy Moore** *Liberty: The Lives and Times of Six Women in Revolutionary France* (HarperCollins). Follows the fervid lives of six influential women through the Revolution, taking in everything from sexual scandal to revolutionary radicalism.

## Culture and society

**John Ardagh** *France in the New Century: Portrait of a Changing Society* (Penguin). Published in 2000, but still the most useful general book if you want to get to grips with French culture, society and (fairly) recent political history.

**Marc Augé** *In the Metro* (University of Minnesota Press, US). A philosophically minded anthropologist descends deep into métro culture and his own memories of life in Paris. A brief, brilliant and utterly Barthian essay.

**Muriel Barbery** *The Elegance of the Hedgehog* (Gallic Books, UK). This whimsical, philosophically minded novel, published in 2008, is set among the eccentric characters of a Parisian apartment block, and sold over a million copies in France.

**James Campbell** *Paris Interzone* (Vintage/Secker and Warburg). The feuds, passions and destructive lifestyles of Left Bank writers in 1946–60 are evoked here. The cast includes Beckett, Ionesco, Sartre, de Beauvoir, Nabokov and Ginsberg.

**Richard Cobb** *Paris and Elsewhere* (John Murray/New York Review of Books). Selected writings on postwar Paris by the acclaimed historian of the Revolution, with a personal and meditative tone.

**Adam Gopnik** *Paris to the Moon* (Vintage/Random House). Intimate and acutely observed essays from the Paris correspondent of the *New Yorker* on society, politics, family life and shopping. Probably the most thoughtful and enjoyable book by an expat in Paris.

**Ross King** *The Judgement of Paris: The Revolutionary Decade That Gave the World Impressionism* (Pimlico/Walker). High-octane account of the fierce battles in the 1860s and 1870s between Meissonier, the ultimate academic, highly-polished Society painter, and the upstart Manet, who tried to supplant the established style with his outrageous contemporary scenes and impressionistic brushwork. Focuses on the culture and political atmosphere of the times as much as the art.

**Graham Robb** *Parisians* (Picador). This playful, joyfully readable but magnificently researched book tells the story of Paris from 1750 to today, looking through the eyes of the people who have played key roles in its turbulent life. Among other scenes, Robb shows us Marie-Antoinette fleeing the Tuileries, Napoleon losing his virginity in the Palais Royal, Hitler's day-trip conquerer's tour, and the nasty build-up to the suburban riots of 2005.

**Edmund White** *The Flâneur* (Bloomsbury). An American expat novelist muses over Parisian themes and places as diverse as the Moreau museum, gay cruising and the history of immigration, as well as the art of being a good *flâneur* – a loiterer or stroller.

**Theodore Zeldin** *The French* (Harvill Press/ Kodansha). A wise and original book that attempts to describe a country through the thoughts and feelings of its people. Draws on the author's conversations with a fascinating range of French people, about money, sex, phobias, parents and everything else.

## Art, architecture and photography

**Henri Cartier-Bresson** *A propos de Paris* (Bullfinch Press). Some of the greatest photos ever taken: a brilliant blend of the ordinary and the surreal, of photo-journalism and art photography.

**André Chastel** *French Art* (Flammarion). The great French art historian tries to define what is distinctively French about French art in this insightful and superbly illustrated three-volume work.

**Anthony Sutcliffe** *Paris – An Architectural History* (Yale UP). Excellent overview of Paris's changing cityscape, as dictated by fashion, social structure and political power.

## Fiction and travel writing

### In English

**Charles Dickens** *A Tale of Two Cities* (Penguin/Vintage). Melodramatic tale of Paris and London during the 1789 Revolution and before, yet backed up by Dickens's unerring eye for reportage.

**Julien Green** *Paris* (Marion Boyars). Born in Paris in 1900, Green became one of the city's defining writers. This bilingual edition presents twenty-odd short, meditative and highly personal essays on different aspects and *quartiers* of Paris, from Notre-Dame and the 16$^{e}$ to "stairways and steps" and the lost cries of the city's hawkers. Proust meets travel writing.

**Ernest Hemingway** *A Moveable Feast* (Arrow/Scribner). Hemingway's memoirs of his life as a young man in Paris in the 1920s. Includes fascinating accounts of meetings with literary celebrities Ezra Pound, F. Scott Fitzgerald, Gertrude Stein and others.

**Henry Miller** *Tropic of Cancer* (Flamingo/Grove Press); *Quiet Days in Clichy* (New Eng Lib/Grove Press). Erratic, wild, self-obsessed writing, with definite flights of genius.

**George Orwell** *Down and Out in Paris and London* (Penguin/Harvest). Documentary account of breadline living in the 1930s – Orwell at his best.

**Jean Rhys** *Quartet* (Penguin/Norton). A beautiful and evocative story of a lonely young woman's existence on the fringes of 1920s Montparnasse society. In the same vein are the subsequent *After Leaving Mr Mackenzie* and *Good Morning, Midnight*, both exploring sexual politics and isolation in the atmospheric streets, shabby hotel rooms and smoky bars of interwar Paris, all in Rhys's spare, dream-like style.

**Sarah Turnbull** *Almost French: A New Life in Paris* (Nicholas Brealey/Gotham Books). Funny but mostly painful account of a young Australienne falling in love, moving to Paris and failing to fit in. Acute observation lifts it above chick-lit travel status. A must for would-be expats.

## French (in translation)

**Honoré de Balzac** *The Père Goriot* (Oxford Paperbacks). Biting exposé of cruelty and selfishness in the contrasting worlds of the fashionable Faubourg St-Germain and a down-at-heel but genteel boarding house in the Quartier Latin. Like Dickens, but with a tougher heart. Balzac's equally brilliant *Wild Ass's Skin* (Penguin) is a strange moralistic tale of an ambitious young man's fall from grace in early nineteenth-century Paris.

**Louis-Ferdinand Céline** *Death on Credit* (Calder/Riverrun Press). A disturbing and powerful semi-autobiographical novel, in which Céline recounts the delirium of the world as seen through the eyes of an adolescent in working-class Paris at the beginning of the twentieth century.

**Colette** *Chéri* (Vintage/Secker and Warburg). Brilliantly evokes the world of a demi-monde Parisian courtesan who embarks upon a doomed love affair with a younger man.

**Helen Constantine** (translator) *Paris Tales* (OUP). Twenty-two (very) short stories and essays, each chosen for their evocation of a particular place in Paris. From Balzac in the Palais Royal to Perec on the Champs-Elysées.

**Gustave Flaubert** *Sentimental Education* (Penguin). A lively, detailed 1869 reconstruction of the life, manners, characters and politics of Parisians in the 1840s, including the 1848 Revolution.

**Faïza Guene** *Just Like Tomorrow/Kiffe Kiffe Tomorrow* (Chatto and Windus/Harvest). A simple, touching tale of a shy, fifteen-year-old Muslim girl in the Paris housing projects trying to make good.

**Victor Hugo** *Les Misérables* (Penguin). Set among the Parisian poor and low-life in the first half of the nineteenth century, it's probably the greatest treatment of Paris in fiction – unless that title goes to Hugo's haunting (and shorter) *Notre-Dame de Paris* (Penguin/Modern Library), a novel better known in English as "The Hunchback of Notre Dame".

**J.K. Huysmans** *Parisian Sketches* (Dedalus European Classics). Published in 1880, Huysmans' fantastical, intense prose pieces on contemporary Paris drip with decadence and cruelly acute observation. If Manet was a novelist, he might have produced this.

**Guy de Maupassant** *Bel-Ami* (Penguin/Hatier). Maupassant's chef-d'oeuvre is a brilliant and utterly sensual account of corrupt Parisian high society during the *belle époque*. Traces the progress of the fascinating journalist and seducer, Georges Duroy.

**Daniel Pennac** *Monsieur Malaussène* (Harvill Press/ Kiepenheuer & Witsch). The last in the "Belleville Quintet" of quasi-detective novels set in the working-class east of Paris is possibly the most disturbing, centred on a series of macabre killings. Witty, experimental and chaotic, somewhat in the mode of Thomas Pynchon.

**Marcel Proust** *Remembrance of Things Past* (Penguin/ Modern Library). Proust's 3000-page novel, much of it set in Paris, is one of the twentieth century's greatest works of fiction.

**Georges Simenon** *Maigret at the Crossroads* (Penguin/ New York Review Books), or any other of the Maigret novels. Literary crime thrillers; the Montmartre and seedy criminal locations are unbeatable. If you don't like crime fiction you should go for *The Little Saint*, the story of a little boy growing up in the rue Mouffetard when it was a down-at-heel market street.

**Emile Zola** *Nana* (Penguin). The rise and fall of a courtesan in the decadent times of the Second Empire. Not bad on sex, but confused on sexual politics. A great story nevertheless, which brings mid-nineteenth-century Paris alive, direct, to present-day senses. Paris is also the setting for Zola's *L'Assommoir*, *The Masterpiece*, *Money*, *Thérèse Raquin* and *The Debacle*.

# Language

# Language

# French



Paris isn't the easiest place to learn French: many Parisians speak a hurried slang and will often reply to your carefully enunciated question in English. Despite this, it's worth making the effort as knowing a few essentials can make all the difference. Even just saying "Bonjour Monsieur/Madame" and then gesticulating will usually secure you a smile and helpful service.

What follows is a run-down of essential words and phrases. For more detail, get *French: A Rough Guide Dictionary Phrase Book*, which has an extensive vocabulary, a detailed menu reader and useful dialogues.

## Pronunciation

**Vowels** are the hardest sounds to get right. Roughly:

| | | | |
|---|---|---|---|
| a | as in h**a**t | **o** | as in h**o**t |
| e | as in g**e**t | **o/au** | as in **o**ver |
| é | between get and gate | **ou** | as in f**oo**d |
| è | between get and gut | **u** | as in a pursed-lip, clipped version of toot |
| **eu** | like the u in h**ur**t | | |
| **i** | as in mach**i**ne | | |

More awkward are the combinations in/im, en/em, on/om, un/um at the end of words, or followed by consonants other than n or m. Again, roughly:

| | |
|---|---|
| **in/im** | like the "an" in **an**xious |
| **an/am, en/em** | like "on" said with a nasal accent |
| **on/om** | like "on" said by someone with a heavy cold |
| **un/um** | like the "u" in **u**nderstand |

**Consonants** are much as in English, except that ch is always sh, h is silent, th is the same as t, ll is sometimes pronounced like the y in "yes" (there are exceptions, eg ville) when preceded by the letter i; w is v, and r is growled (or rolled).

# Words and phrases

## Basics

| | |
|---|---|
| **Yes** | Oui |
| **No** | Non |
| **Please** | S'il vous plaît |
| **Thank you** | Merci |
| **Excuse me** | Pardon/excusez-moi |
| **Sorry** | Pardon/Je m'excuse |
| **Hello** | Bonjour |
| **Hello (phone)** | Allô |
| **Goodbye** | Au revoir |
| **Good morning/ afternoon** | Bonjour |
| **Good evening** | Bonsoir |
| **Good night** | Bonne nuit |
| **How are you?** | Comment allez-vous?/Ça va? |
| **Fine, thanks** | Très bien, merci |
| **I don't know** | Je ne sais pas |
| **Do you speak English?** | Vous parlez anglais? |
| **How do you say...in French?** | Comment ça se dit...en français? |
| **What's your name?** | Comment vous appelez-vous? |
| **My name is …** | Je m'appelle … |
| **I'm English/ Irish/ Scottish/ Welsh/ American/** | Je suis anglais(e)/ irlandais(e)/ écossais(e)/ gallois(e)/ américain(e)/ |
| **OK/agreed** | D'accord |
| **I understand** | Je comprends |
| **I don't understand** | Je ne comprends pas |
| **Please can you speak more slowly?** | S'il vous plaît, parlez moins vite |
| **Today** | Aujourd'hui |
| **Yesterday** | Hier |
| **Tomorrow** | Demain |
| **In the morning** | Le matin |
| **In the afternoon** | L'après-midi |
| **In the evening** | Le soir |
| **Now** | Maintenant |

| | |
|---|---|
| **Later** | Plus tard |
| **Here** | Ici |
| **There** | Là |
| **This one** | Ceci |
| **That one** | Cela |
| **Open** | Ouvert |
| **Closed** | Fermé |
| **Big** | Grand |
| **Small** | Petit |
| **More** | Plus |
| **Less** | Moins |
| **A little** | Un peu |
| **A lot** | Beaucoup |
| **Half** | La moitié |
| **Expensive** | Cher |
| **Inexpensive** | Bon marché/ pas cher |
| **Good** | Bon |
| **Bad** | Mauvais |
| **Hot** | Chaud |
| **Cold** | Froid |
| **With** | Avec |
| **Without** | Sans |

## Questions

| | |
|---|---|
| **Where?** | Où? |
| **How?** | Comment? |
| **How many** | Combien? |
| **How much is it?** | C'est combien? |
| **When?** | Quand? |
| **Why?** | Pourquoi? |
| **At what time?** | À quelle heure? |
| **What is/ Which is?** | Quel est? |

## Getting around

| | |
|---|---|
| **Which way is it to the Eiffel Tower?** | S'il vous plaît, pour aller à la Tour Eiffel? |
| **Where is the nearest métro?** | Où est le métro le plus proche? |
| **Bus** | Bus |
| **Bus stop** | Arrêt |
| **Train** | Train |
| **Boat** | Bâteau |
| **Plane** | Avion |
| **Railway station** | Gare |
| **Platform** | Quai |
| **What time does it leave?** | Il part à quelle heure? |
| **What time does it arrive?** | Il arrive à quelle heure? |
| **A ticket to …** | Un billet pour … |
| **Single ticket** | Aller simple |
| **Return ticket** | Aller retour |

| | |
|---|---|
| **Where are you going?** | Vous allez où? |
| **I'm going to…** | Je vais à… |
| **I want to get off at …** | Je voudrais descendre à … |
| **Near** | Près/pas loin |
| **Far** | Loin |
| **Left** | À gauche |
| **Right** | À droite |

## Accommodation

| | |
|---|---|
| **A room for one/two people** | Une chambre pour une/deux personne/s |
| **With a double bed** | Avec un grand lit |
| **A room with a shower** | Une chambre avec douche |
| **A room with a bath** | Une chambre avec salle de bain |
| **For one/two/ three nights** | Pour une/deux/ trois nuit(s) |
| **With a view** | Avec vue |
| **Key** | Clé |
| **To iron** | Repasser |
| **Do laundry** | Faire la lessive |
| **Sheets** | Draps |
| **Blankets** | Couvertures |
| **Quiet** | Calme |
| **Noisy** | Bruyant |
| **Hot water** | Eau chaude |
| **Cold water** | Eau froide |
| **Is breakfast included?** | Est-ce que le petit déjeuner est compris? |
| **I would like breakfast** | Je voudrais prendre le petit déjeuner |
| **I don't want breakfast** | Je ne veux pas le petit déjeuner |
| **Youth hostel** | Auberge de jeunesse |

## Eating out

| | |
|---|---|
| **I'd like to reserve a table…** | Je voudrais réserver une table … |
| **…for two people, at eight thirty** | …pour deux personnes, à vingt heures et demie |
| **I'm having the €15 menu** | Je prendrai le menu à quinze euros |
| **Waiter!** | Monsieur/Madame! (never "garçon") |
| **The bill, please** | L'addition, s'il vous plaît |

## Days

| | | | |
|---|---|---|---|
| **Monday** | Lundi | **Friday** | Vendredi |
| **Tuesday** | Mardi | **Saturday** | Samedi |
| **Wednesday** | Mercredi | **Sunday** | Dimanche |
| **Thursday** | Jeudi | | |

## Numbers

| | | | |
|---|---|---|---|
| **1** | un | **20** | vingt |
| **2** | deux | **21** | vingt-et-un |
| **3** | trois | **22** | vingt-deux |
| **4** | quatre | **30** | trente |
| **5** | cinq | **40** | quarante |
| **6** | six | **50** | cinquante |
| **7** | sept | **60** | soixante |
| **8** | huit | **70** | soixante-dix |
| **9** | neuf | **75** | soixante-quinze |
| **10** | dix | **80** | quatre-vingts |
| **11** | onze | **90** | quatre-vingt-dix |
| **12** | douze | **95** | quatre-vingt-quinze |
| **13** | treize | **100** | cent |
| **14** | quatorze | **101** | cent un |
| **15** | quinze | **200** | deux cents |
| **16** | seize | **1000** | mille |
| **17** | dix-sept | **2000** | deux mille |
| **18** | dix-huit | **1,000,000** | un million |
| **19** | dix-neuf | | |

# Menu glossary



## Essentials

| | |
|---|---|
| **déjeuner** | lunch |
| **dîner** | dinner |
| **menu** | set menu |
| **à la carte** | individually priced dishes |
| **entrées** | starters |
| **les plats** | main courses |
| **pain** | bread |
| **beurre** | butter |
| **oeufs** | eggs |
| **lait** | milk |
| **poivre** | pepper |
| **sel** | salt |
| **sucre** | sugar |
| **fourchette** | fork |
| **couteau** | knife |
| **cuillère** | spoon |
| **bio** | organic |
| **à la vapeur** | steamed |
| **au four** | baked |
| **cru** | raw |
| **frit** | fried |
| **fumé** | smoked |
| **grillé** | grilled |
| **rôti** | roast |
| **salé** | salted/savoury |
| **sucré** | sweet |
| **à emporter** | takeaway |

## Drinks

| | |
|---|---|
| **eau minérale** | mineral water |
| **eau gazeuse** | fizzy water |
| **eau plate** | still water |
| **carte des vins** | wine list |
| **une pression** | a glass of beer |
| **un café** | coffee (espresso) |
| **un café américain** | black coffee |
| **un crème** | white coffee |
| **bouteille** | bottle |
| **verre** | glass |
| **un quart/ demi de rouge/ blanc** | a quarter/half-litre of red/ white house wine |
| **un verre de rouge/ blanc** | a glass of red/white wine |

## Snacks

| | |
|---|---|
| **crêpe** | pancake (sweet) |
| **un sandwich/ une baguette** | sandwich |
| **croque-monsieur** | grilled cheese & ham sandwich |
| **panini** | flat toasted Italian sandwich |
| **omelette nature** | omelette plain |
| **aux fines herbes** | with herbs |
| **au fromage** | with cheese |
| **assiette de charcuterie** | plate of cold meats |
| **crudités** | raw vegetables with dressings |

## Fish (poisson) and seafood (fruits de mer)

| | |
|---|---|
| **anchois** | anchovies |
| **brème** | bream |
| **brochet** | pike |
| **cabillaud** | cod |
| **carrelet** | plaice |
| **colin** | hake |
| **coquilles st-jacques** | scallops |
| **crabe** | crab |
| **crevettes** | shrimps/prawns |
| **daurade** | sea bream |
| **flétan** | halibut |
| **friture** | whitebait |
| **hareng** | herring |
| **homard** | lobster |
| **huîtres** | oysters |
| **langoustines** | saltwater crayfish (scampi) |
| **limande** | lemon sole |
| **lotte de mer** | monkfish |
| **loup de mer** | sea bass |
| **maquereau** | mackerel |
| **merlan** | whiting |
| **morue** | dried, salted cod |
| **moules (marinière)** | mussels (with shallots in white wine sauce) |
| **raie** | skate |
| **rouget** | red mullet |
| **saumon** | salmon |
| **sole** | sole |
| **thon** | tuna |
| **truite** | trout |
| **turbot** | turbot |

## Meat (viande) and poultry (volaille)

| | | | |
|---|---|---|---|
| **agneau** | lamb | **jambon** | ham |
| **andouillette** | tripe sausage | **lapin, lapereau** | rabbit, young rabbit |
| **bavette** | beef flank steak | **lard, lardons** | bacon, diced bacon |
| **boeuf** | beef | **merguez** | spicy red sausage |
| **boudin noir** | black pudding | **oie** | goose |
| **caille** | quail | **onglet** | cut of beef |
| **canard** | duck | **pièce de boeuf** | steak |
| **contrefilet** | sirloin roast | **porc** | pork |
| **dinde** | turkey | **poulet** | chicken |
| **entrecôte** | ribsteak | **poussin** | baby chicken |
| **faux filet** | sirloin steak | **rognons** | kidneys |
| **foie** | liver | **tête de veau** | calf's head (in jelly) |
| **foie gras** | fattened (duck/goose) liver | **tournedos** | thick slices of fillet |
| **gigot (d'agneau)** | leg (of lamb) | **veau** | veal |
| **grillade** | grilled meat | **venaison** | venison |
| **hachis** | chopped meat or mince hamburger | | |

## Steaks

| | | | |
|---|---|---|---|
| **bleu** | almost raw | **à point** | medium |
| **saignant** | rare | **bien cuit** | well done |

## Garnishes and sauces

| | | | |
|---|---|---|---|
| **beurre blanc** | sauce of white wine & shallots, with butter | **fricassée** | rich, creamy sauce |
| **chasseur** | white wine, mushrooms & shallots | **mornay** | cheese sauce |
| **forestière** | with bacon & mushroom | **pays d'auge** | cream & cider |
| | | **piquante** | gherkins or capers, vinegar & shallots |
| | | **provençale** | tomatoes, garlic, olive oil & herbs |

## Vegetables (légumes), herbs (herbes) and spices (épices)

| | |
|---|---|
| **ail** | garlic |
| **artichaut** | artichoke |
| **asperges** | asparagus |
| **avocat** | avocado |
| **basilic** | basil |
| **betterave** | beetroot |
| **carotte** | carrot |
| **céleri** | celery |
| **champignons** | mushrooms |
| **chou (rouge)** | (red) cabbage |
| **chou-fleur** | cauliflower |
| **ciboulette** | chives |
| **concombre** | cucumber |
| **cornichon** | gherkin |
| **échalotes** | shallots |
| **endive** | chicory |
| **épinards** | spinach |
| **estragon** | tarragon |
| **fenouil** | fennel |
| **flageolets** | white beans |
| **gingembre** | ginger |
| **haricots** | beans |
| **verts** | string (french) |
| **rouges** | kidney |
| **beurres** | butter |
| **lentilles** | lentils |
| **maïs** | corn (maize) |
| **moutarde** | mustard |
| **oignon** | onion |
| **pâtes** | pasta |
| **persil** | parsley |
| **petits pois** | peas |
| **pois chiche** | chickpeas |
| **pois mange-tout** | snow peas |
| **pignons** | pine nuts |
| **poireau** | leek |
| **poivron (vert, rouge)** | sweet pepper (green, red) |
| **pommes (de terre)** | potatoes |
| **primeurs** | spring vegetables |
| **radis** | radishes |
| **riz** | rice |
| **safran** | saffron |
| **salade verte** | green salad |
| **tomate** | tomato |
| **truffes** | truffles |

## Fruits (fruits) and nuts (noix)

| | |
|---|---|
| **abricot** | apricot |
| **amandes** | almonds |
| **ananas** | pineapple |
| **banane** | banana |
| **brugnon, nectarine** | nectarine |

| | |
|---|---|
| **cacahouète** | peanut |
| **cassis** | blackcurrants |
| **cerises** | cherries |
| **citron** | lemon |
| **citron vert** | lime |
| **figues** | figs |
| **fraises** | strawberries |
| **framboises** | raspberries |
| **groseilles** | redcurrants & gooseberries |
| **mangue** | mango |
| **marrons** | chestnuts |
| **melon** | melon |
| **myrtilles** | bilberries |
| **noisette** | hazelnut |
| **noix** | nuts |
| **orange** | orange |
| **pamplemousse** | grapefruit |
| **pêche** | peach |
| **pistache** | pistachio |
| **poire** | pear |
| **pomme** | apple |
| **prune** | plum |
| **pruneau** | prune |
| **raisins** | grapes |

## Desserts (desserts) and pastries (pâtisserie)

| | |
|---|---|
| **bavarois** | refers to the mould, could be mousse or custard |
| **brioche** | sweet, high-yeast breakfast roll |
| **coupe** | a serving of ice cream |
| **crème chantilly** | vanilla-flavoured & sweetened whipped cream |
| **crème fraîche** | sour cream |
| **crème pâtissière** | thick eggy pastry filling |
| **fromage blanc** | cream cheese |
| **glace** | ice cream |
| **parfait** | frozen mousse, sometimes ice cream |
| **petits fours** | bite-sized cakes/ pastries |
| **tarte** | tart |
| **yaourt, yogourt** | yoghurt |

## Cheese (fromage)

There are over four hundred types of French cheese, most of them named after their place of origin. *Chèvre* is goat's cheese and *brebis* is cheese made from sheep's milk. *Le plateau de fromages* is the cheeseboard, and bread – but not butter – is served with it.

# Small print & Index

## A Rough Guide to Rough Guides

Published in 1982, the first Rough Guide – to Greece – was a student scheme that became a publishing phenomenon. Mark Ellingham, a recent graduate in English from Bristol University, had been travelling in Greece the previous summer and couldn't find the right guidebook. With a small group of friends he wrote his own guide, combining a highly contemporary, journalistic style with a thoroughly practical approach to travellers' needs.

The immediate success of the book spawned a series that rapidly covered dozens of destinations. And, in addition to impecunious backpackers, Rough Guides soon acquired a much broader and older readership that relished the guides' wit and inquisitiveness as much as their enthusiastic, critical approach and value-for-money ethos.

These days, Rough Guides include recommendations from shoestring to luxury and cover more than 200 destinations around the globe, including almost every country in the Americas and Europe, more than half of Africa and most of Asia and Australasia. Our ever-growing team of authors and photographers is spread all over the world, particularly in Europe, the US and Australia.

In the early 1990s, Rough Guides branched out of travel, with the publication of Rough Guides to World Music, Classical Music and the Internet. All three have become benchmark titles in their fields, spearheading the publication of a wide range of books under the Rough Guide name.

Including the travel series, Rough Guides now number more than 350 titles, covering: phrasebooks, waterproof maps, music guides from Opera to Heavy Metal, reference works as diverse as Conspiracy Theories and Shakespeare, and popular culture books from iPods to Poker. Rough Guides also produce a series of more than 120 World Music CDs in partnership with World Music Network.

Visit www.roughguides.com to see our latest publications.

## Publishing information

This fourth edition published March 2011 by
**Rough Guides Ltd,**
80 Strand, London WC2R 0RL
11, Community Centre,
Panchsheel Park,
New Delhi 110017, India
**Distributed by the Penguin Group**
Penguin Books Ltd,
80 Strand, London WC2R 0RL
Penguin Group (USA)
375 Hudson Street, NY 10014, USA
Penguin Group (Australia)
250 Camberwell Road, Camberwell, Victoria 3124, Australia
Penguin Group (NZ)
67 Apollo Drive, Mairangi Bay, Auckland 1310, New Zealand
Rough Guides is represented in Canada by Tourmaline Editions Inc.
662 King Street West, Suite 304, Toronto, Ontario M5V 1M7
Cover concept by Peter Dyer.
Typeset in Bembo and Helvetica to an original design by Henry Iles.
Printed in Singapore

364pp includes index
A catalogue record for this book is available from the British Library
ISBN: 978-1-84836-932-0

1 3 5 7 9 8 6 4 2

## Help us update

We've gone to a lot of effort to ensure that the fourth edition of **The Mini Rough Guide to Paris** is accurate and up-to-date. However, things change – places get "discovered", opening hours are notoriously fickle, restaurants and rooms raise prices or lower standards. If you feel we've got it wrong or left something out, we'd like to know, and if you can remember the address, the price, the hours, the phone number, so much the better.

Please send your comments with the subject line "**Mini Rough Guide Paris Update**" to Ⓔmail @uk.roughguides.com. We'll credit all contributions and send a copy of the next edition (or any other Rough Guide if you prefer) for the very best emails.

Find more travel information, connect with fellow travellers and book your trip on Ⓦwww .roughguides.com.

## Rough Guides credits

**Text editor**: Lara Kavanagh
**Layout**: Ankur Guha, Pradeep Thapliyal
**Cartography**: Deshpal Dabas
**Picture editor**: Nicole Newman
**Production**: Rebecca Short
**Proofreader**: Sam Cook
**Cover design**: Daniel May, Nicole Newman
**Photographers**: Lydia Evans, James McConnachie

## Photo credits

All photos © Rough Guides except the following:

**Introduction**
p.5 Place du Tertre, Montmartre © Sylvain Sonnet/Corbis

**Things not to miss**
Eiffel Tower © Arnaud Chicurel/ Getty
The Pyramid at the Louvre © Bruno De Hogues/Getty
Notre-Dame © fanelie rosier/ iStock

# Index

Map entries are in colour.

# D



# E



# F

# I



# J



# K



# L



# M

# Q



# R

## S

## T



## U



## V



## W



## Z

# 1. PARIS

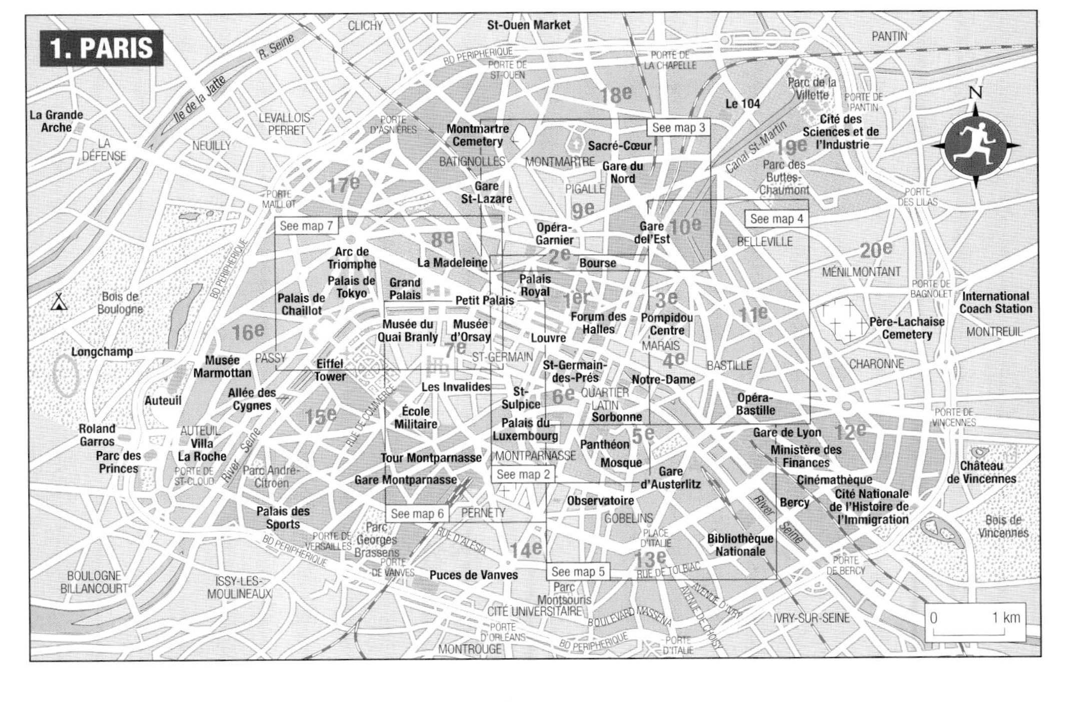

1. PARIS
CLICHY
St-Ouen Market
PANTIN
R. Seine
BD PERIPHERIQUE
PORTE DE ST-OUEN
PORTE DE LA CHAPELLE
18e
Parc de la Villette
PORTE DE PANTIN
Le 104
Ile de la Jatte
La Grande Arche
LEVALLOIS-PERRET
PORTE D'ASNIERES
Montmartre Cemetery
See map 3
Cité des Sciences et de l'Industrie
N
LA DÉFENSE
NEUILLY
Sacré-Cœur
Canal St-Martin
19e
BATIGNOLLES
MONTMARTRE
Gare du Nord
Parc des Buttes-Chaumont
17e
Gare St-Lazare
PIGALLE
PORTE MAILLOT
PORTE DES LILAS
9e
See map 4
See map 7
8e
Opéra-Garnier
Gare del'Est
10e
BELLEVILLE
Arc de Triomphe
La Madeleine
2e
Bourse
20e
MÉNILMONTANT
Palais de Tokyo
Grand Palais
Palais Royal
Bois de Boulogne
Palais de Chaillot
Petit Palais
1er
3e
PORTE DE BAGNOLET
International Coach Station
Forum des Halles
Pompidou Centre
11e
Père-Lachaise Cemetery
16e
Musée du Quai Branly
Musée d'Orsay
Louvre
MARAIS
MONTREUIL
Longchamp
7e
ST-GERMAIN
4e
PASSY
Musée Marmottan
Eiffel Tower
St-Germain-des-Prés
BASTILLE
CHARONNE
Notre-Dame
Les Invalides
Allée des Cygnes
St-Sulpice
6e
QUARTIER LATIN
Auteuil
Opéra-Bastille
École Militaire
Sorbonne
PORTE DE VINCENNES
15e
RUE DE COMMERCE
Palais du Luxembourg
Roland Garros
AUTEUIL
5e
Gare de Lyon
12e
Villa La Roche
Panthéon
Parc des Princes
River Seine
Tour Montparnasse
MONTPARNASSE
Ministère des Finances
Mosque
Château de Vincennes
PORTE DE ST-CLOUD
Parc André-Citroën
See map 2
Gare d'Austerlitz
Gare Montparnasse
Cinémathèque
Cité Nationale de l'Histoire de l'Immigration
Observatoire
Bercy
Palais des Sports
See map 6
PERNETY
GOBELINS
River Seine
Bois de Vincennes
PORTE DE VERSAILLES
Parc Georges Brassens
RUE D'ALESIA
PLACE D'ITALIE
Bibliothèque Nationale
14e
13e
PORTE DE VANVES
BD PERIPHERIQUE
PORTE DE BERCY
BOULOGNE BILLANCOURT
Puces de Vanves
See map 5
RUE DE TOLBIAC
ISSY-LES-MOULINEAUX
Parc Montsouris
AVENUE D'IVRY
AVENUE DE CHOISY
CITÉ UNIVERSITAIRE
BOULEVARD MASSENA
IVRY-SUR-SEINE
0
1 km
PORTE D'ORLÉANS
BD PERIPHERIQUE
PORTE D'ITALIE
MONTROUGE

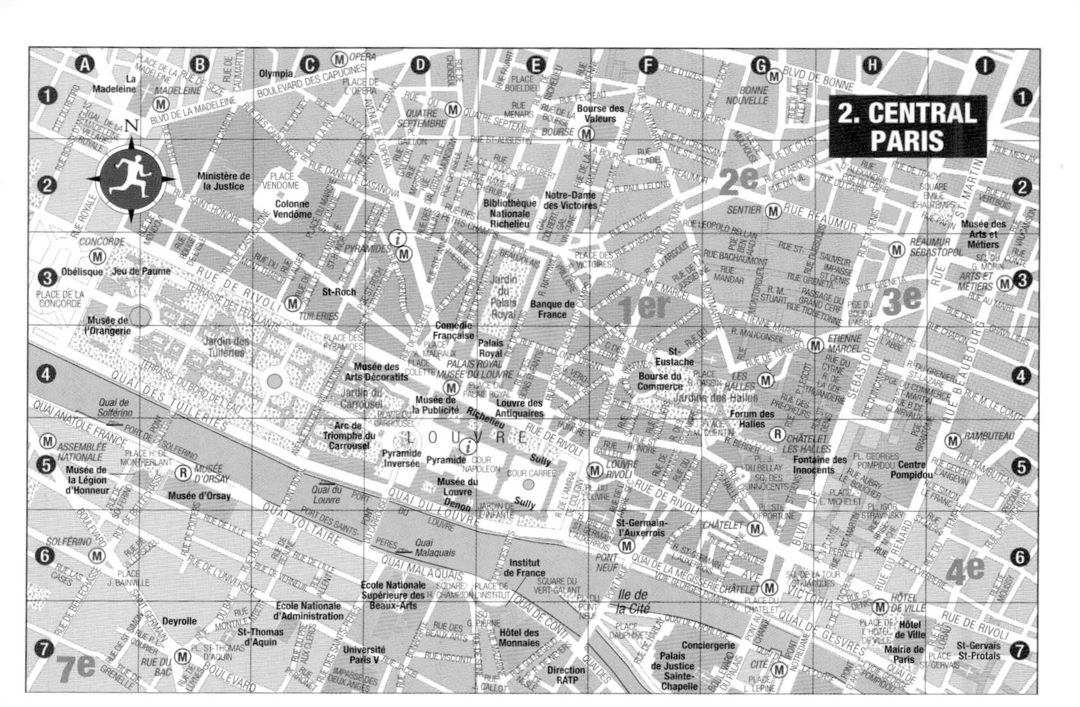
2. CENTRAL PARIS
La Madeleine
Madeleine
Olympia
Opéra
Quatre Septembre
Bourse des Valeurs
Bourse
Bonne Nouvelle
Ministère de la Justice
Place Vendôme
Colonne Vendôme
Bibliothèque Nationale Richelieu
Notre-Dame des Victoires
Sentier
Réaumur Sébastopol
Musée des Arts et Métiers
Arts et Métiers
Concorde
Obélisque
Jeu de Paume
Place de la Concorde
St-Roch
Pyramides
Tuileries
Jardin du Palais Royal
Banque de France
Musée de l'Orangerie
Jardin des Tuileries
Comédie Française
Palais Royal
Palais Royal Musée du Louvre
St-Eustache
Bourse du Commerce
Jardin des Halles
Les Halles
Etienne Marcel
Musée des Arts Décoratifs
Jardin du Carrousel
Musée de la Publicité
Louvre des Antiquaires
Richelieu
Forum des Halles
Châtelet Les Halles
Arc de Triomphe du Carrousel
LOUVRE
Pyramide Inversée
Pyramide
Cour Napoléon
Cour Carrée
Sully
Fontaine des Innocents
Centre Pompidou
Rambuteau
Assemblée Nationale
Musée de la Légion d'Honneur
Musée d'Orsay
Louvre Rivoli
Musée du Louvre
Denon
St-Germain-l'Auxerrois
Châtelet
Solférino
Institut de France
Pont Neuf
Ile de la Cité
Hôtel de Ville
Ecole Nationale Supérieure des Beaux-Arts
Ecole Nationale d'Administration
Deyrolle
St-Thomas d'Aquin
Université Paris V
Hôtel des Monnaies
Direction RATP
Palais de Justice Sainte-Chapelle
Conciergerie
Cité
Mairie de Paris
St-Gervais St-Protais
Rue de Rivoli
Quai des Tuileries
Quai Anatole France
Quai Voltaire
Quai Malaquais
Quai du Louvre
Quai de Conti
Quai de Gesvres
Boulevard des Capucines
Blvd de la Madeleine
Blvd de Bonne
Avenue de l'Opéra
Rue Réaumur
Rue Montmartre
Rue St-Honoré
Rue Etienne Marcel
Blvd de Sébastopol
Rue Beaubourg
Rue St-Martin
Rue du Renard
Avenue Victoria
Boulevard St-Germain
Rue du Bac
Rue de l'Université
Rue de Lille
1er
2e
3e
4e
7e

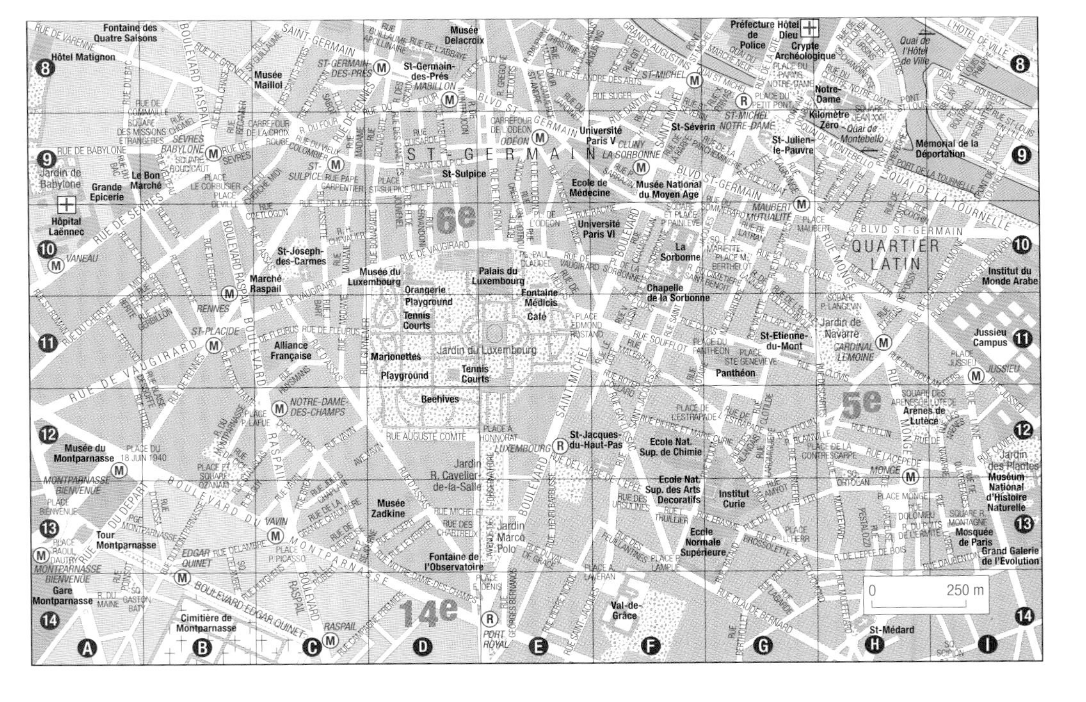
Fontaine des Quatre Saisons
Hôtel Matignon
Musée Maillol
Musée Delacroix
St-Germain-des-Prés
Préfecture de Police
Hôtel Dieu
Crypte Archéologique
Notre-Dame
Kilomètre Zéro
Quai de l'Hôtel de Ville
Quai de Montebello
Mémorial de la Déportation
Université Paris V
St-Séverin
St-Julien-le-Pauvre
ST-GERMAIN
St-Sulpice
Jardin de Babylone
Le Bon Marché
Grande Epicerie
Hôpital Laënnec
Ecole de Médecine
Musée National du Moyen Age
Université Paris VI
6e
QUARTIER LATIN
Institut du Monde Arabe
St-Joseph-des-Carmes
Musée du Luxembourg
Palais du Luxembourg
La Sorbonne
Marché Raspail
Orangerie
Playground
Tennis Courts
Fontaine Médicis
Café
Chapelle de la Sorbonne
Jardin de Navarre
Jussieu Campus
Alliance Française
Marionettes
Jardin du Luxembourg
St-Etienne-du-Mont
Panthéon
Beehives
5e
Arènes de Lutèce
Musée du Montparnasse
Jardin R. Cavelier-de-la-Salle
St-Jacques-du-Haut-Pas
Ecole Nat. Sup. de Chimie
Jardin des Plantes
Muséum National d'Histoire Naturelle
Musée Zadkine
Ecole Nat. Sup. des Arts Decoratifs
Institut Curie
Tour Montparnasse
Jardin Marco Polo
Ecole Normale Supérieure
Mosquée de Paris
Grand Galerie de l'Evolution
Fontaine de l'Observatoire
Gare Montparnasse
Cimitière de Montparnasse
14e
Val-de-Grâce
St-Médard
0
250 m
BOULEVARD ST-GERMAIN
BOULEVARD RASPAIL
BOULEVARD SAINT-MICHEL
BOULEVARD DU MONTPARNASSE
RUE DE VAUGIRARD
RUE DE RENNES
RUE DE SEVRES
RUE MONGE
QUAI DE LA TOURNELLE
A
B
C
D
E
F
G
H
I
8
9
10
11
12
13
14

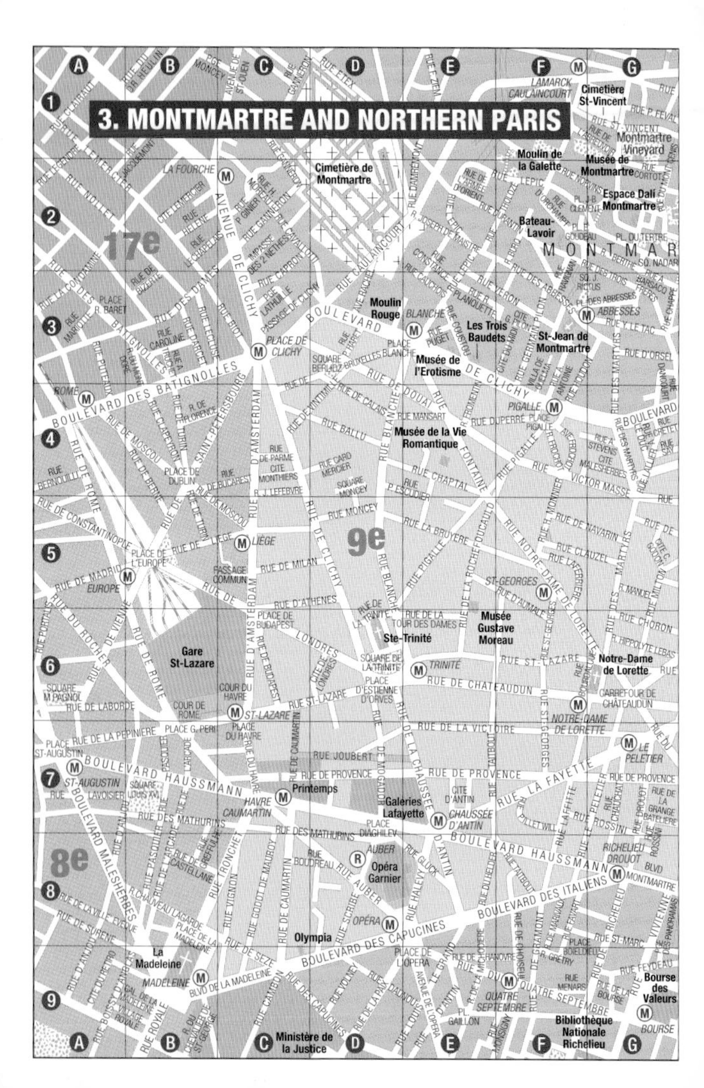
3. MONTMARTRE AND NORTHERN PARIS
A
B
C
D
E
F
G
1
2
3
4
5
6
7
8
9
17e
9e
8e
Cimetière St-Vincent
Montmartre Vineyard
Moulin de la Galette
Musée de Montmartre
Espace Dalí Montmartre
Cimetière de Montmartre
Bateau-Lavoir
MONTMAR
LAMARCK CAULAINCOURT
LA FOURCHE
ABBESSES
Moulin Rouge
BLANCHE
Les Trois Baudets
St-Jean de Montmartre
PLACE DE CLICHY
Musée de l'Erotisme
ROME
PIGALLE
PLACE PIGALLE
Musée de la Vie Romantique
BOULEVARD DES BATIGNOLLES
BOULEVARD DE CLICHY
AVENUE DE CLICHY
RUE DE CLICHY
RUE D'AMSTERDAM
RUE DE ROME
RUE BLANCHE
RUE PIGALLE
RUE FONTAINE
RUE DES MARTYRS
RUE VICTOR MASSE
RUE DE DOUAI
RUE CHAPTAL
RUE LA BRUYERE
RUE NOTRE-DAME DE LORETTE
RUE DE LA ROCHEFOUCAULD
PLACE DE DUBLIN
PLACE DE L'EUROPE
LIEGE
EUROPE
RUE DE MADRID
RUE DE CONSTANTINOPLE
RUE DE LONDRES
RUE DE MILAN
RUE D'ATHENES
ST-GEORGES
Musée Gustave Moreau
Gare St-Lazare
Ste-Trinité
TRINITÉ
Notre-Dame de Lorette
NOTRE-DAME DE LORETTE
RUE ST-LAZARE
RUE DE CHATEAUDUN
RUE DE LA VICTOIRE
COUR DU HAVRE
COUR DE ROME
ST-LAZARE
PLACE DU HAVRE
PLACE ST-AUGUSTIN
ST-AUGUSTIN
RUE DE LA PEPINIERE
BOULEVARD HAUSSMANN
RUE DE PROVENCE
RUE LA FAYETTE
Printemps
HAVRE CAUMARTIN
Galeries Lafayette
CHAUSSÉE D'ANTIN
LE PELETIER
RICHELIEU DROUOT
RUE DES MATHURINS
BOULEVARD MALESHERBES
AUBER
Opéra Garnier
OPÉRA
Olympia
BOULEVARD DES ITALIENS
BOULEVARD DES CAPUCINES
BLVD MONTMARTRE
La Madeleine
MADELEINE
BLVD DE LA MADELEINE
RUE ROYALE
RUE DE LA PAIX
AVENUE DE L'OPERA
PLACE DE L'OPERA
QUATRE SEPTEMBRE
RUE DU QUATRE SEPTEMBRE
Bourse des Valeurs
BOURSE
Bibliothèque Nationale Richelieu
Ministère de la Justice

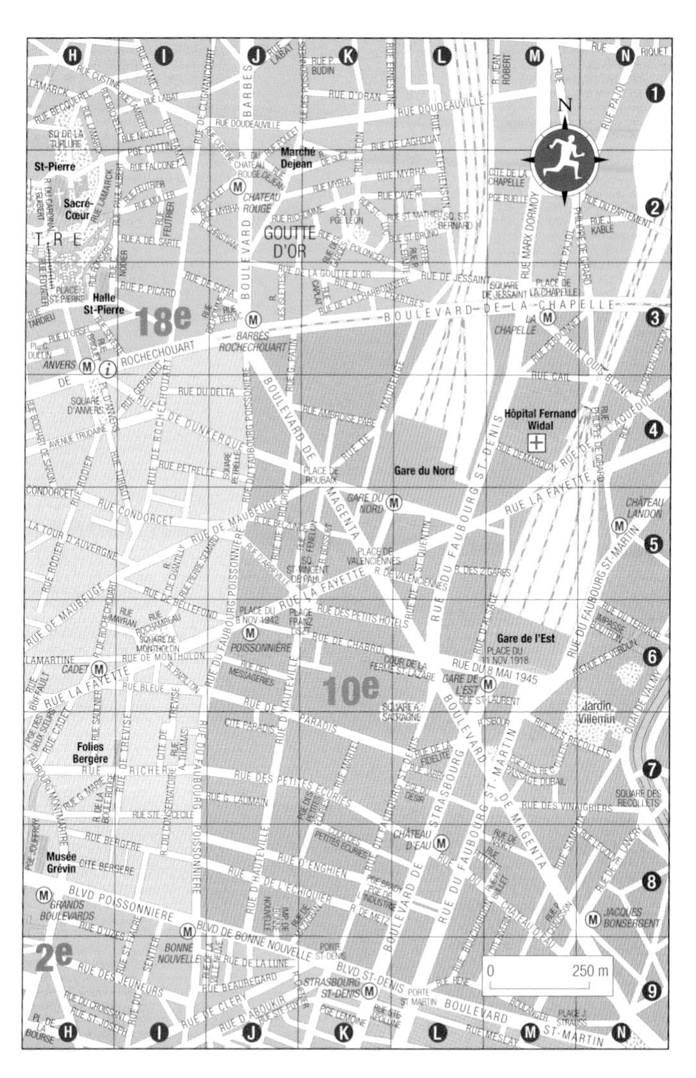

H
I
J
K
L
M
N
1
2
3
4
5
6
7
8
9
N
RUE CUSTINE
LAMARCK
RUE BECQUEREL
RUE LAMARCK
RUE BACHELET
RUE LABAT
RUE NICOLET
RUE RAMEY
RUE DE CLIGNANCOURT
RUE DOUDEAUVILLE
BARBÈS
RUE P. BUDIN
RUE D'ORAN
RUE ERNESTINE
R. JEAN ROBERT
RUE PAJOL
RIQUET
RUE DOUDEAUVILLE
SQ DE LA TURLURE
PGE COTTIN
RUE CUSTINE
PL. DU CHATEAU ROUGE
RUE POULET
Marché Dejean
RUE LÉON
RUE DE LAGHOUAT
St-Pierre
RUE FALCONET
CHATEAU ROUGE
RUE MYRHA
RUE STEPHENSON
CITÉ DE LA CHAPELLE
PGE RUELLE
RUE CAVE
Sacré-Cœur
RUE MULLER
RUE FEUTRIER
RUE RICHOMME
SQ. DU PGE LÉON
RUE ST-MATHIEU
SQ. ST-BERNARD
RUE DU DEPARTEMENT
RUE J. KABLE
RUE MARX DORMOY
PHILIPPE DE GIRARD
RUE A. DEL SARTE
GOUTTE D'OR
RUE POLONCEAU
RUE ST-BRUNO
RUE NODIER
RUE DE LA GOUTTE D'OR
RUE DE JESSAINT
SQUARE DE JESSAINT
PLACE DE LA CHAPELLE
PLACE ST-PIERRE
Halle St-Pierre
RUE P. PICARD
RUE DE SOFIA
RUE DE CHARTRES
RUE DE LA CHARBONNIÈRE
RUE CAPLAT
R. DES ISLETTES
BOULEVARD DE LA CHAPELLE
TARDIEU
18e
RUE BERVIC
BARBÈS ROCHECHOUART
LA CHAPELLE
RUE D'ORSEL
PL. C. DULLIN
ANVERS
ROCHECHOUART
RUE PERDONNET
RUE LOUIS BLANC
RUE CAIL
SQUARE D'ANVERS
RUE DU DELTA
RUE DE DUNKERQUE
RUE AMBROISE PARÉ
BOULEVARD DE MAGENTA
RUE DE MAUBEUGE
Hôpital Fernand Widal
RUE DE L'AQUEDUC
AVENUE TRUDAINE
RUE DE ROCHECHOUART
RUE RODIER
RUE TURGOT
RUE PETRELLE
SQUARE PETRELLE
RUE DU FAUBOURG POISSONNIÈRE
PLACE DE ROUBAIX
Gare du Nord
RUE DEMARQUAY
RUE DU FAUBOURG ST-DENIS
CONDORCET
RUE CONDORCET
GARE DU NORD
RUE LA FAYETTE
CHÂTEAU LANDON
LA TOUR D'AUVERGNE
R. DE BELZUNCE
PLACE DE VALENCIENNES
R. DE VALENCIENNES
RUE DE ST-QUENTIN
R. DES 2 GARES
RUE D'ABBEVILLE
SQ. ST-VINCENT DE PAUL
RUE DU FAUBOURG ST-MARTIN
RUE DE BELLEFOND
RUE DE MAUBEUGE
PLACE DU 8 NOV 1942
PLACE FRANZ LISZT
RUE DES PETITS HÔTELS
RUE D'ALSACE
RUE DU TERRAGE
IMPASSE BOUTRON
RUE MAYRAN
RUE ROCHAMBEAU
SQUARE DE MONTHOLON
POISSONNIÈRE
RUE DE CHABROL
Gare de l'Est
PLACE DU 11 NOV 1918
AVENUE DE VERDUN
LAMARTINE
CADET
RUE DE MONTHOLON
COUR DE LA FERME ST-LAZARE
RUE DU 8 MAI 1945
GARE DE L'EST
RUE LA FAYETTE
RUE BLEUE
R. PAPILLON
RUE DES MESSAGERIES
10e
RUE ST-LAURENT
Jardin Villemin
QUAI DE VALMY
RUE CADET
RUE SAULNIER
RUE DE PARADIS
SQUARE A. SATRAGNE
CITÉ PARADIS
RUE DES RÉCOLLETS
Folies Bergère
RUE RICHER
RUE DE TREVISE
CITÉ DE TREVISE
RUE A. THOMAS
RUE D'HAUTEVILLE
RUE MARTEL
RUE DE LA FIDÉLITÉ
RUE JARRY
BOULEVARD DE STRASBOURG
RUE DES PETITES ÉCURIES
PGE DU DÉSIR
PASSAGE DUBAIL
SQUARE DES RÉCOLLETS
RUE G. LAUMAIN
RUE DES VINAIGRIERS
RUE STE-CÉCILE
RUE DU CONSERVATOIRE
RUE BERGÈRE
CHÂTEAU D'EAU
COUR DES PETITES ÉCURIES
RUE DE NANCY
RUE DE LANCRY
RUE SAMSON
Musée Grévin
CITÉ BERGÈRE
PGE JOUFFROY
RUE D'ENGHIEN
RUE DE L'ÉCHIQUIER
RUE DU CHÂTEAU D'EAU
RUE BOUCHARDON
GRANDS BOULEVARDS
BLVD POISSONNIÈRE
R. DE METZ
JACQUES BONSERGENT
RUE D'UZÈS
BLVD DE BONNE NOUVELLE
BONNE NOUVELLE
PORTE ST-DENIS
2e
RUE DE LA LUNE
BLVD ST-DENIS
0
250 m
RUE DES JEUNEURS
RUE BEAUREGARD
STRASBOURG ST-DENIS
PORTE ST MARTIN
BOULEVARD
RUE DU CROISSANT
RUE ST-JOSEPH
RUE DE CLÉRY
RUE D'ABOUKIR
PGE LEMOINE
RUE STE APOLLINE
PLACE J. STRAUSS
PL. DE LA BOURSE
RUE MESLAY
ST-MARTIN

4. THE MARAIS AND EASTERN PARIS
0 250 m
Gare de l'Est
Jardin Villemin
Hôpital St-Louis
Parc des Buttes-Chaumont
Parc de Belleville
Musée des Arts et Métiers
Musée Edith Piaf
10e
19e
20e
BELLEVILLE
MENILMONTANT
Canal St-Martin
BOULEVARD DE LA VILLETTE
BOULEVARD DE BELLEVILLE
BOULEVARD DE STRASBOURG
BOULEVARD DE MAGENTA
BOULEVARD ST-MARTIN
BOULEVARD DU TEMPLE
BOULEVARD VOLTAIRE
BOULEVARD DE MENILMONTANT
BLVD ST-DENIS
BLVD JULES FERRY
BLVD RICHARD
AVENUE DE LA REPUBLIQUE
AVENUE PARMENTIER
AVENUE SIMON BOLIVAR
AVENUE CLAUDE VELLEFAUX
AVENUE JEAN AICARD
RUE DU FAUBOURG DU TEMPLE
RUE DU FAUBOURG ST-MARTIN
RUE DU FAUBOURG ST-DENIS
RUE DE BELLEVILLE
RUE SAINT-MAUR
RUE DE LA FONTAINE AU ROI
RUE OBERKAMPF
RUE DE TURBIGO
RUE REAUMUR
RUE ST-MARTIN
RUE DU CHATEAU D'EAU
RUE BICHAT
RUE ALIBERT
RUE DE LA GRANGE AUX BELLES
RUE DE PARADIS
RUE DES VINAIGRIERS
RUE DES RECOLLETS
RUE DU 8 MAI 1945
RUE VICQ D'AZIR
RUE DE SAMBRE ET MEUSE
RUE RENÉ BOULANGER
RUE MESLAY
RUE NOTRE-DAME DE NAZARETH
RUE BERANGER
RUE DE MALTE
RUE AMELOT
RUE DE CRUSSOL
RUE DES TROIS BORNES
RUE JEAN-PIERRE TIMBAUD
RUE DES COURONNES
RUE DE MENILMONTANT
RUE DES MARONITES
RUE DES PYRÉNÉES
QUAI DE VALMY
QUAI DE JEMMAPES
PLACE DE LA REPUBLIQUE
PLACE DU COLONEL FABIEN
PLACE J. STRAUSS
PL. ROBERT DESNOS
SQUARE E. VARLIN
SQUARE DES RECOLLETS
SQUARE H. CHRISTINE
SQUARE DU TEMPLE
SQUARE DE REBEVAL
SQUARE EMILE CHAUTEMPS
PORTE ST-DENIS
PORTE ST MARTIN
COLONEL FABIEN
BUTTES CHAUMONT
PYRÉNÉES
GARE DE L'EST
CHÂTEAU D'EAU
JACQUES BONSERGENT
GONCOURT
BELLEVILLE
COURONNE
MÉNILMONTANT
STRASBOURG ST-DENIS
RÉPUBLIQUE
TEMPLE
RÉAUMUR SÉBASTOPOL
ARTS ET METIERS
PARMENTIER
OBERKAMPF

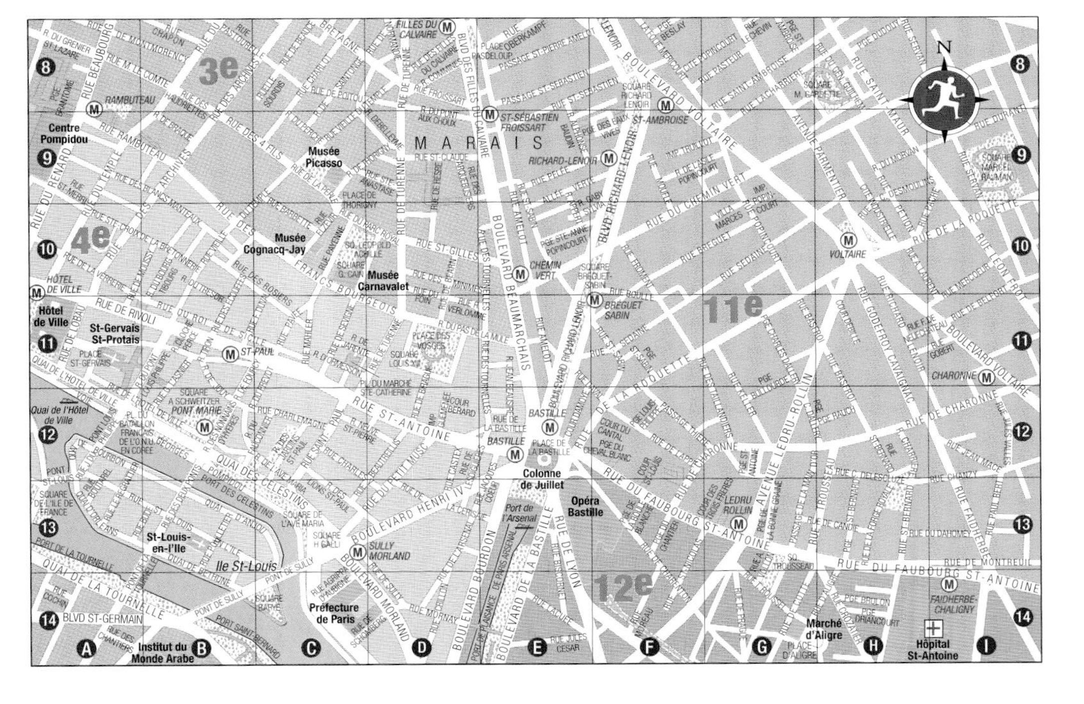

N
3e
4e
11e
12e
MARAIS
Centre Pompidou
Musée Picasso
Musée Cognacq-Jay
Musée Carnavalet
Hôtel de Ville
St-Gervais St-Protais
St-Louis-en-l'Ile
Ile St-Louis
Institut du Monde Arabe
Préfecture de Paris
Colonne de Juillet
Opéra Bastille
Port de l'Arsenal
Marché d'Aligre
Hôpital St-Antoine
Quai de l'Hôtel de Ville
RAMBUTEAU
HÔTEL DE VILLE
ST-PAUL
PONT MARIE
SULLY MORLAND
FILLES DU CALVAIRE
ST-SÉBASTIEN FROISSART
RICHARD-LENOIR
ST-AMBROISE
CHEMIN VERT
BREGUET SABIN
BASTILLE
LEDRU ROLLIN
VOLTAIRE
CHARONNE
FAIDHERBE-CHALIGNY
RUE BEAUBOURG
RUE RAMBUTEAU
RUE DU TEMPLE
RUE DU RENARD
RUE DE RIVOLI
RUE FRANCS BOURGEOIS
RUE ST-ANTOINE
RUE DE TURENNE
BOULEVARD BEAUMARCHAIS
BLVD DES FILLES DU CALVAIRE
BOULEVARD VOLTAIRE
BLVD RICHARD-LENOIR
RUE DU CHEMIN VERT
RUE DE LA ROQUETTE
RUE DE CHARONNE
AVENUE LEDRU-ROLLIN
RUE DU FAUBOURG ST-ANTOINE
RUE DE LYON
BOULEVARD DE LA BASTILLE
BOULEVARD BOURDON
BOULEVARD HENRI IV
BOULEVARD MORLAND
QUAI DES CÉLESTINS
QUAI DE LA TOURNELLE
BLVD ST-GERMAIN
PONT DE SULLY
AVENUE PARMENTIER
RUE SAINT-MAUR
RUE GODEFROY CAVAIGNAC
RUE FAIDHERBE
RUE DE MONTREUIL
RUE LÉON FROT
RUE AMELOT
RUE ST-GILLES
RUE DES TOURNELLES
PLACE DES VOSGES
PLACE DE LA BASTILLE
PLACE D'ALIGRE
A
B
C
D
E
F
G
H
I
8
9
10
11
12
13
14

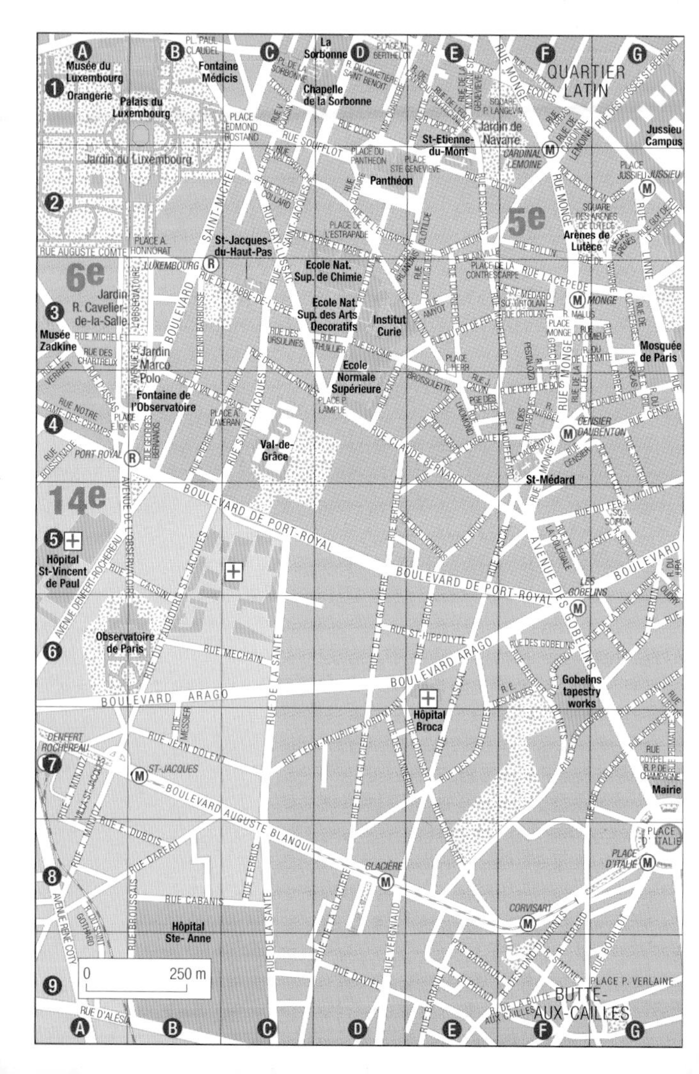

A
B
C
D
E
F
G
1
2
3
4
5
6
7
8
9
Musée du Luxembourg
Orangerie
Palais du Luxembourg
Jardin du Luxembourg
Fontaine Médicis
La Sorbonne
Chapelle de la Sorbonne
QUARTIER LATIN
Jussieu Campus
St-Etienne-du-Mont
Jardin de Navarre
Panthéon
St-Jacques-du-Haut-Pas
Ecole Nat. Sup. de Chimie
Ecole Nat. Sup. des Arts Decoratifs
Institut Curie
Ecole Normale Supérieure
Arènes de Lutèce
Mosquée de Paris
5e
6e
14e
Jardin R. Cavelier-de-la-Salle
Musée Zadkine
Jardin Marco Polo
Fontaine de l'Observatoire
Val-de-Grâce
St-Médard
Hôpital St-Vincent de Paul
Observatoire de Paris
Hôpital Broca
Gobelins tapestry works
Mairie
Hôpital Ste- Anne
BUTTE-AUX-CAILLES
0
250 m
BOULEVARD SAINT-MICHEL
BOULEVARD DE PORT-ROYAL
BOULEVARD ARAGO
BOULEVARD AUGUSTE BLANQUI
AVENUE DES GOBELINS
AVENUE DE L'OBSERVATOIRE
AVENUE DENFERT-ROCHEREAU
RUE DU FAUBOURG ST-JACQUES
RUE SAINT-JACQUES
RUE GAY-LUSSAC
RUE SOUFFLOT
RUE MONGE
RUE MOUFFETARD
RUE CLAUDE BERNARD
RUE DE LA SANTE
RUE DE LA GLACIERE
RUE BROCA
RUE PASCAL
RUE AUGUSTE COMTE
RUE D'ASSAS
RUE CASSINI
RUE MECHAIN
RUE JEAN DOLENT
RUE CABANIS
RUE DAVIEL
RUE D'ALESIA
PLACE D'ITALIE
PLACE P. VERLAINE
LUXEMBOURG
PORT ROYAL
DENFERT ROCHEREAU
ST-JACQUES
GLACIÈRE
CORVISART
LES GOBELINS
CENSIER DAUBENTON
MONGE
CARDINAL LEMOINE
JUSSIEU

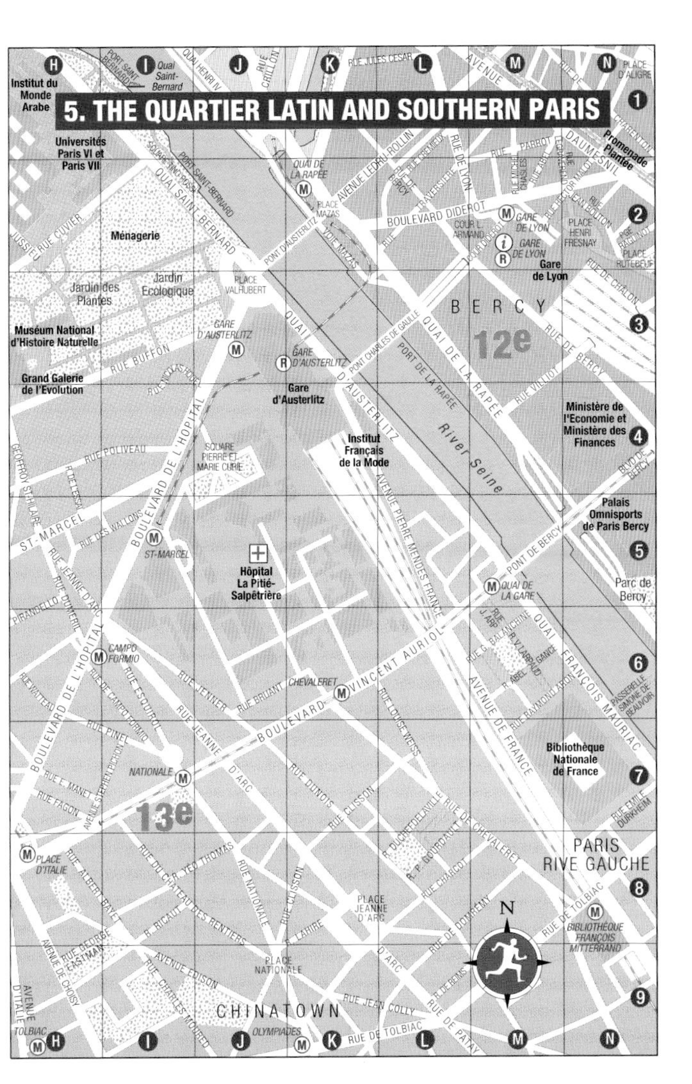

5. THE QUARTIER LATIN AND SOUTHERN PARIS
Institut du Monde Arabe
Universités Paris VI et Paris VII
Ménagerie
Jardin des Plantes
Jardin Ecologique
Muséum National d'Histoire Naturelle
Grand Galerie de l'Evolution
Gare d'Austerlitz
Gare de Lyon
BERCY
12e
Ministère de l'Economie et Ministère des Finances
Institut Français de la Mode
River Seine
Palais Omnisports de Paris Bercy
Parc de Bercy
Hôpital La Pitié-Salpêtrière
Bibliothèque Nationale de France
13e
PARIS RIVE GAUCHE
CHINATOWN
Promenade Plantée
QUAI SAINT-BERNARD
QUAI D'AUSTERLITZ
QUAI DE LA RAPÉE
QUAI FRANÇOIS MAURIAC
BOULEVARD DE L'HOPITAL
BOULEVARD VINCENT AURIOL
BOULEVARD DIDEROT
AVENUE PIERRE MENDES FRANCE
AVENUE DE FRANCE
RUE DE TOLBIAC
RUE DE CHEVALERET
PONT DE BERCY
PONT CHARLES DE GAULLE
PONT D'AUSTERLITZ
RUE BUFFON
RUE POLIVEAU
PLACE VALHUBERT
PLACE D'ITALIE
PLACE NATIONALE
PLACE JEANNE D'ARC
N

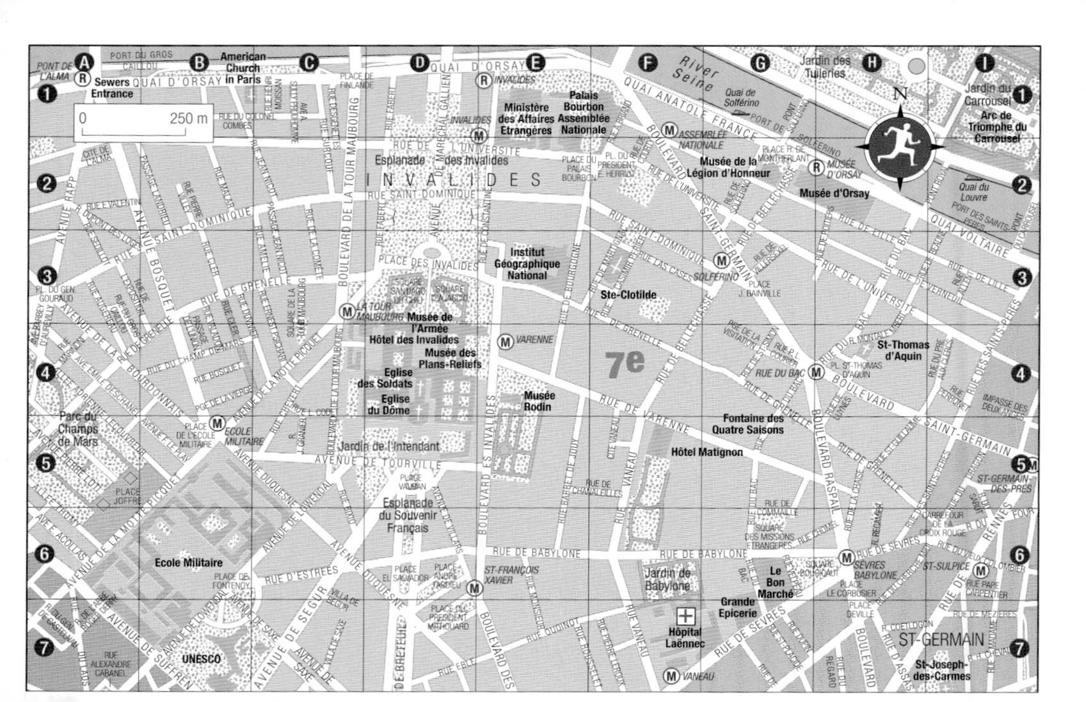

River Seine
Quai d'Orsay
Quai Anatole France
Quai Voltaire
Quai de Solférino
Quai du Louvre
Port du Gros Caillou
Port des Saints-Pères
Pont de l'Alma
Pont Royal
Pont du Carrousel
Pont de Solférino
0 250 m
N
Sewers Entrance
American Church in Paris
Jardin des Tuileries
Jardin du Carrousel
Arc de Triomphe du Carrousel
Musée d'Orsay
Musée de la Légion d'Honneur
Ministère des Affaires Etrangères
Palais Bourbon Assemblée Nationale
Esplanade des Invalides
INVALIDES
Institut Géographique National
Ste-Clotilde
St-Thomas d'Aquin
Musée de l'Armée
Hôtel des Invalides
Musée des Plans-Reliefs
Eglise des Soldats
Eglise du Dôme
Musée Rodin
7e
Fontaine des Quatre Saisons
Hôtel Matignon
Jardin de l'Intendant
Esplanade du Souvenir Français
Parc du Champs de Mars
Ecole Militaire
UNESCO
Jardin de Babylone
Hôpital Laënnec
Le Bon Marché
Grande Epicerie
ST-GERMAIN
St-Joseph-des-Carmes
ST-GERMAIN-DES-PRES
Invalides
Assemblée Nationale
Solférino
Rue du Bac
La Tour Maubourg
Varenne
Ecole Militaire
St-François Xavier
Sèvres Babylone
St-Sulpice
Vaneau
Boulevard Saint-Germain
Boulevard Raspail
Boulevard de la Tour Maubourg
Boulevard des Invalides
Avenue Bosquet
Avenue Rapp
Avenue de la Bourdonnais
Avenue de la Motte Picquet
Avenue de Tourville
Avenue Duquesne
Avenue de Lowendal
Avenue de Ségur
Avenue de Saxe
Avenue de Suffren
Avenue de Breteuil
Avenue de Villars
Rue Saint-Dominique
Rue de Grenelle
Rue de l'Université
Rue de Varenne
Rue de Babylone
Rue de Sèvres
Rue de Lille
Rue du Bac
Rue de Bellechasse
Rue de Bourgogne
Rue Vaneau
Rue Cler
Rue des Saints-Pères
Rue de Rennes
Rue d'Estrées
Place des Invalides
Place Joffre
Place Vauban
Place de Fontenoy

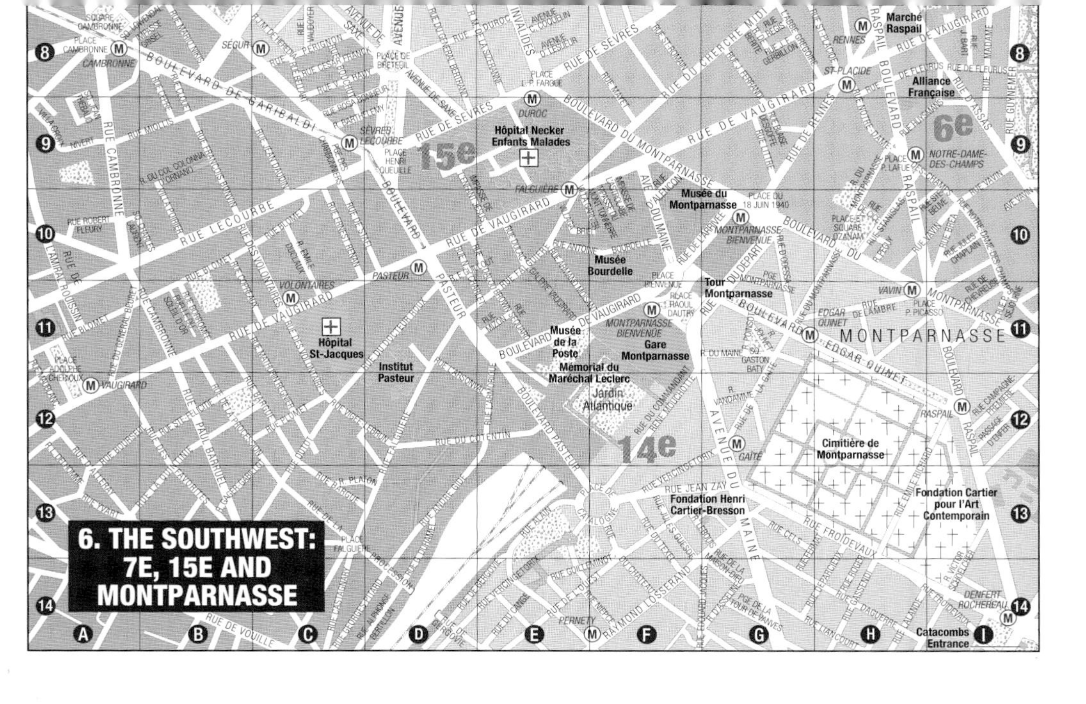
6. THE SOUTHWEST: 7E, 15E AND MONTPARNASSE
15e
14e
6e
MONTPARNASSE
Hôpital Necker Enfants Malades
Hôpital St-Jacques
Institut Pasteur
Musée du Montparnasse
Musée Bourdelle
Musée de la Poste
Tour Montparnasse
Gare Montparnasse
Mémorial du Maréchal Leclerc
Jardin Atlantique
Cimitière de Montparnasse
Fondation Henri Cartier-Bresson
Fondation Cartier pour l'Art Contemporain
Catacombs Entrance
Marché Raspail
Alliance Française
BOULEVARD DE GARIBALDI
BOULEVARD DU MONTPARNASSE
BOULEVARD PASTEUR
BOULEVARD RASPAIL
BOULEVARD EDGAR QUINET
RUE DE VAUGIRARD
RUE LECOURBE
RUE CAMBRONNE
RUE DE SEVRES
RUE DE RENNES
AVENUE DU MAINE
RUE FROIDEVAUX
RUE RAYMOND LOSSERAND
RUE DU CHERCHE MIDI
PLACE CAMBRONNE
CAMBRONNE
SÉGUR
SÈVRES LECOURBE
DUROC
FALGUIÈRE
PASTEUR
VOLONTAIRES
VAUGIRARD
MONTPARNASSE BIENVENÜE
EDGAR QUINET
VAVIN
RASPAIL
GAITÉ
PERNETY
DENFERT ROCHEREAU
RENNES
ST-PLACIDE
NOTRE-DAME-DES-CHAMPS
PLACE DU 18 JUIN 1940
PLACE DE CATALOGNE
A
B
C
D
E
F
G
H
I
8
9
10
11
12
13
14

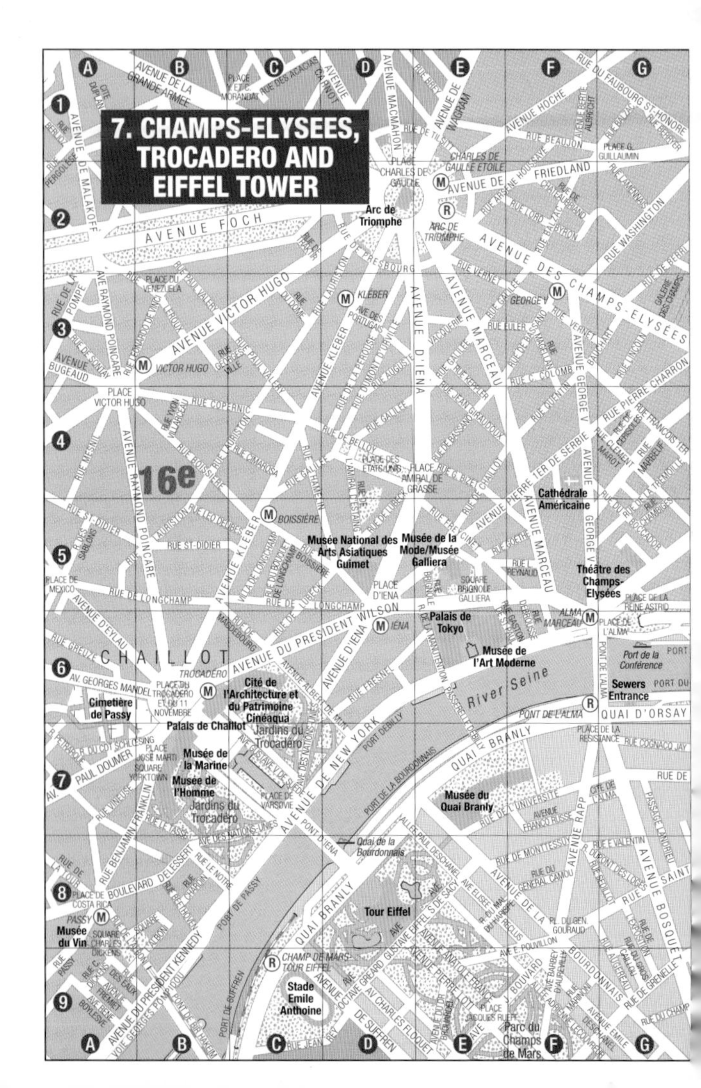

7. CHAMPS-ELYSEES, TROCADERO AND EIFFEL TOWER
A
B
C
D
E
F
G
1
2
3
4
5
6
7
8
9
AVENUE DE LA GRANDE ARMEE
PLACE Y. ET C. MORANDAT
RUE DES ACACIAS
AVENUE CARNOT
AVENUE MACMAHON
RUE BREY
AVENUE DE WAGRAM
AVENUE HOCHE
RUE DU FAUBOURG ST-HONORE
RUE BEAUJON
PLACE G. GUILLAUMIN
RUE DE TILSITT
CHARLES DE GAULLE ETOILE
PLACE CHARLES DE GAULLE
AVENUE DE FRIEDLAND
Arc de Triomphe
ARC DE TRIOMPHE
AVENUE FOCH
AVENUE DE MALAKOFF
RUE PERGOLESE
RUE DE PRESBOURG
RUE LORD BYRON
RUE BALZAC
RUE WASHINGTON
AVENUE DES CHAMPS-ELYSÉES
RUE VERNET
GEORGE V
RUE DE LA POMPE
PLACE DU VENEZUELA
AVENUE VICTOR HUGO
RUE PAUL VALERY
RUE LAURISTON
KLEBER
AVE DES PORTUGAIS
AVENUE D'IENA
AVENUE MARCEAU
RUE EULER
RUE BASSANO
RUE VERNET
RUE LINCOLN
AVENUE RAYMOND POINCARE
AVENUE BUGEAUD
VICTOR HUGO
AVENUE KLEBER
RUE DE LA PEROUSE
RUE GALILEE
RUE C. COLOMB
AVENUE GEORGE V
RUE PIERRE CHARRON
RUE FRANCOIS 1ER
PLACE VICTOR HUGO
RUE COPERNIC
RUE DE BELLOY
RUE BOISSIERE
RUE CIMAROSA
16e
PLACE DES ETATS-UNIS
PLACE AMIRAL DE GRASSE
AVENUE PIERRE 1ER DE SERBIE
Cathédrale Américaine
RUE ST-DIDIER
RUE LEO DELIBES
BOISSIERE
Musée National des Arts Asiatiques Guimet
Musée de la Mode/Musée Galliera
Théâtre des Champs-Elysées
PLACE DE MEXICO
RUE DE LONGCHAMP
PLACE D'IENA
SQUARE BRIGNOLE GALLIERA
Palais de Tokyo
ALMA MARCEAU
PLACE DE LA REINE ASTRID
PLACE DE L'ALMA
AVENUE D'EYLAU
RUE GREUZE
CHAILLOT
AVENUE DU PRESIDENT WILSON
IENA
Musée de l'Art Moderne
Port de la Conférence
TROCADERO
AV. GEORGES MANDEL
PLACE DU TROCADERO ET DU 11 NOVEMBRE
Cité de l'Architecture et du Patrimoine Cinéaqua
River Seine
Sewers Entrance
Cimetière de Passy
Palais de Chaillot
Jardins du Trocadéro
PONT DE L'ALMA
QUAI D'ORSAY
PLACE DE LA RESISTANCE
RUE COGNACQ JAY
QUAI BRANLY
AVENUE DE NEW YORK
PORT DEBILLY
PASSERELLE DEBILLY
PORT DE LA BOURDONNAIS
Musée de la Marine
Musée de l'Homme
PAUL DOUMER
PLACE DE VARSOVIE
Musée du Quai Branly
RUE DE L'UNIVERSITE
AVENUE FRANCO RUSSE
AVENUE RAPP
CITE DE L'ALMA
PONT D'IENA
AVE DES NATIONS-UNIES
Quai de la Bourdonnais
RUE BENJAMIN FRANKLIN
ALLEE PAUL DESCHANEL
RUE DE MONTTESSUY
RUE DU GENERAL CAMOU
AVENUE BOSQUET
RUE SAINT
BOULEVARD DELESSERT
PLACE DE COSTA RICA
PORT DE PASSY
AVENUE DE LA BOURDONNAIS
PASSY
Tour Eiffel
PL. DU GEN. GOURAUD
Musée du Vin
QUAI BRANLY
AVE E. POUVILLON
RUE DE GRENELLE
AVENUE DU PRESIDENT KENNEDY
CHAMP DE MARS-TOUR EIFFEL
AVENUE ANATOLE FRANCE
AVENUE PIERRE LOTI
Stade Emile Anthoine
PORT DE SUFFREN
AV CHARLES FLOQUET
PLACE JACQUES RUEFF
Parc du Champs de Mars
DE SUFFREN

Musée Jacquemart-André
Gare St-Lazare
Boulevard Haussmann
Rue de la Pépinière
St-Augustin
Miromesnil
Rue La Boétie
Rue du Faubourg St-Honoré
St-Philippe-du-Roule
Ministère de l'Intérieur
8e
Franklin D. Roosevelt
Palais de l'Elysée
Boulevard Malesherbes
Madeleine
Rond Point des Champs-Elysées
Avenue des Champs-Elysées
Champs Elysées Clemenceau
Avenue Montaigne
Rue Royale
Ministère de la Justice
Grand Palais
Palais de la Découverte
Université Paris IV
Petit Palais
Concorde
Obélisque
Jeu de Paume
Rue de Rivoli
Place de la Concorde
Cours Albert 1er
Cours la Reine
Musée de l'Orangerie
Tuileries Gardens
Port des Champs-Elysées
Quai des Tuileries
American Church in Paris
Quai d'Orsay
Invalides
Ministère des Affaires Etrangères
Palais Bourbon Assemblée Nationale
Quai Anatole France
Assemblée Nationale
Musée de la Légion d'Honneur
Musée d'Orsay
Esplanade des Invalides
INVALIDES
Rue de l'Université
Boulevard Saint-Germain
Rue Saint-Dominique
7e
Institut Géographique National
Solférino
Ste-Clotilde
Boulevard de la Tour Maubourg
La Tour Maubourg
Musée de l'Armée
Hôtel des Invalides
Musée des Plans-Reliefs
Eglise des Soldats
Varenne
Rue de Varenne
Musée Rodin
Rue du Bac
0
250 m
N

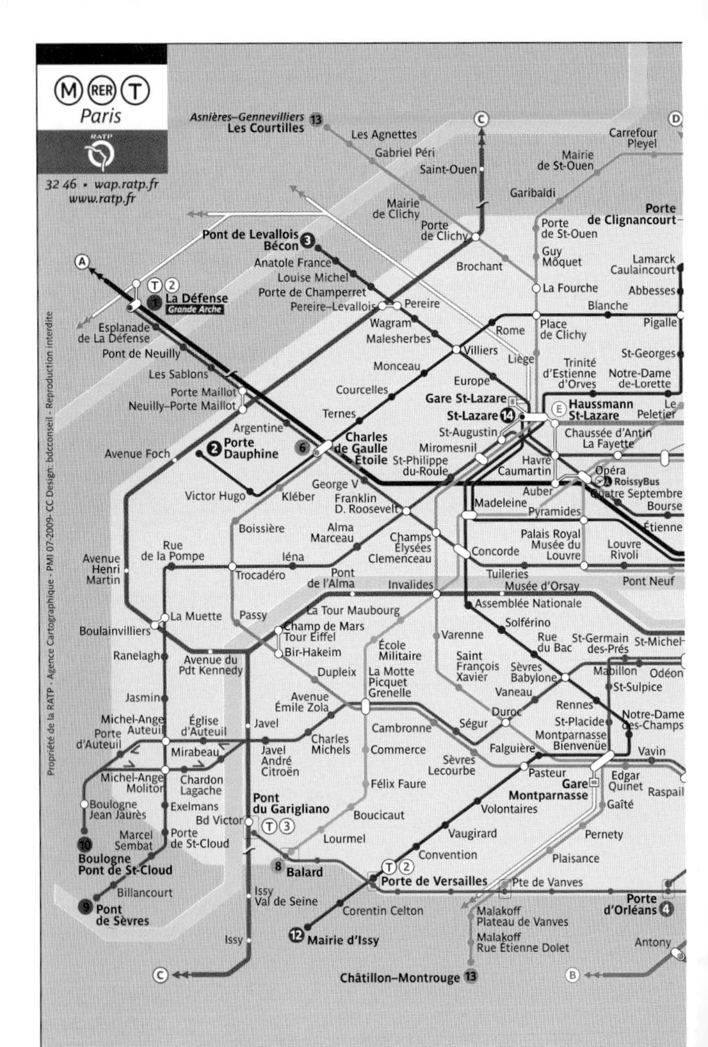

M RER T
Paris
RATP
32 46 • wap.ratp.fr
www.ratp.fr
Propriété de la RATP - Agence Cartographique - PMI 07-2009- CC Design: bdcconseil - Reproduction interdite
Asnières–Gennevilliers
Les Courtilles
Les Agnettes
Gabriel Péri
Saint-Ouen
Mairie de St-Ouen
Carrefour Pleyel
Garibaldi
Mairie de Clichy
Porte de Clichy
Porte de St-Ouen
Porte de Clignancourt
Guy Môquet
Brochant
Lamarck Caulaincourt
Pont de Levallois Bécon
Anatole France
Louise Michel
Porte de Champerret
Pereire–Levallois
Pereire
La Fourche
Abbesses
Blanche
La Défense
Grande Arche
Esplanade de La Défense
Pont de Neuilly
Les Sablons
Porte Maillot
Neuilly–Porte Maillot
Wagram
Malesherbes
Villiers
Rome
Place de Clichy
Pigalle
Liège
Trinité d'Estienne d'Orves
St-Georges
Notre-Dame de-Lorette
Monceau
Europe
Courcelles
Gare St-Lazare
Haussmann St-Lazare
Le Peletier
St-Lazare
Ternes
Argentine
Charles de Gaulle Étoile
St-Augustin
Chaussée d'Antin La Fayette
Porte Dauphine
Avenue Foch
Miromesnil
St-Philippe du-Roule
Havre Caumartin
Opéra
RoissyBus
Quatre Septembre
George V
Auber
Bourse
Victor Hugo
Kléber
Franklin D. Roosevelt
Madeleine
Pyramides
Boissière
Alma Marceau
Champs Élysées Clemenceau
Palais Royal Musée du Louvre
Étienne
Louvre Rivoli
Rue de la Pompe
Iéna
Concorde
Avenue Henri Martin
Trocadéro
Pont de l'Alma
Invalides
Tuileries
Musée d'Orsay
Pont Neuf
Assemblée Nationale
La Muette
Passy
La Tour Maubourg
Solférino
Boulainvilliers
Champ de Mars Tour Eiffel
Varenne
Rue du Bac
St-Germain des-Prés
St-Michel
Ranelagh
Bir-Hakeim
École Militaire
Avenue du Pdt Kennedy
Saint François Xavier
Sèvres Babylone
Mabillon
Odéon
Dupleix
La Motte Picquet Grenelle
St-Sulpice
Jasmin
Vaneau
Rennes
Avenue Émile Zola
Duroc
St-Placide
Notre-Dame des-Champs
Michel-Ange Auteuil
Église d'Auteuil
Javel
Cambronne
Ségur
Montparnasse Bienvenüe
Porte d'Auteuil
Charles Michels
Mirabeau
Javel André Citroën
Commerce
Falguière
Vavin
Sèvres Lecourbe
Michel-Ange Molitor
Chardon Lagache
Pasteur
Edgar Quinet
Gare Montparnasse
Raspail
Félix Faure
Boulogne Jean Jaurès
Exelmans
Pont du Garigliano
Volontaires
Gaîté
Bd Victor
Boucicaut
Marcel Sembat
Porte de St-Cloud
Vaugirard
Pernety
Lourmel
Boulogne Pont de St-Cloud
Convention
Plaisance
Balard
Porte de Versailles
Pte de Vanves
Billancourt
Issy Val de Seine
Porte d'Orléans
Pont de Sèvres
Corentin Celton
Malakoff Plateau de Vanves
Mairie d'Issy
Malakoff Rue Étienne Dolet
Antony
Issy
Châtillon–Montrouge

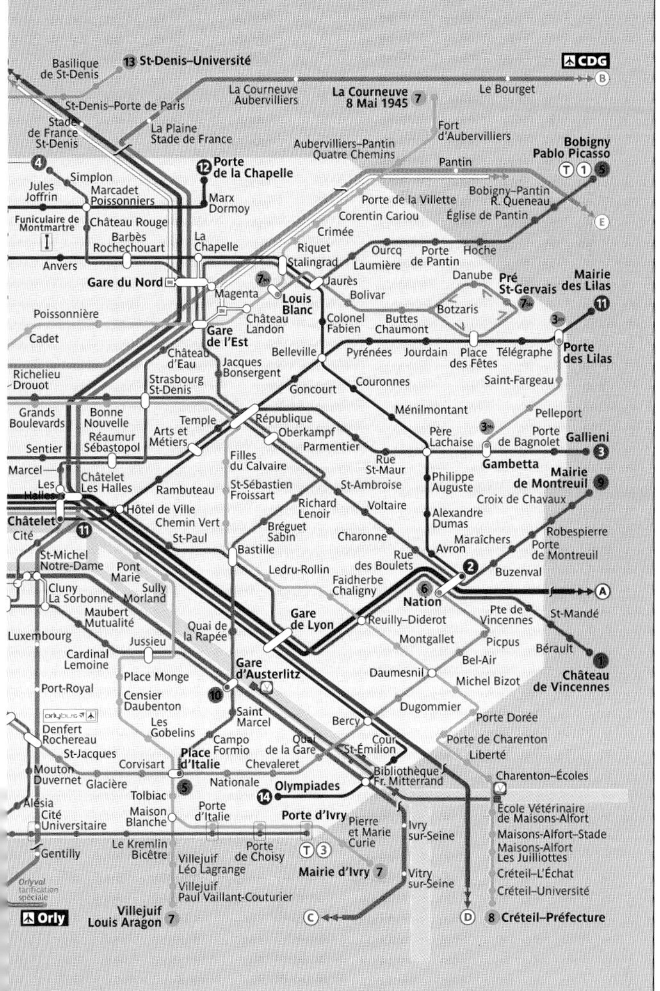

Basilique de St-Denis
13 St-Denis–Université
CDG
St-Denis–Porte de Paris
La Courneuve Aubervilliers
La Courneuve 8 Mai 1945 7
Le Bourget
B
Stade de France St-Denis
La Plaine Stade de France
Fort d'Aubervilliers
Aubervilliers–Pantin Quatre Chemins
Bobigny Pablo Picasso
4
Simplon
12 Porte de la Chapelle
Pantin
T 1 5
Jules Joffrin
Marcadet Poissonniers
Marx Dormoy
Porte de la Villette
Bobigny–Pantin R. Queneau
Funiculaire de Montmartre
Château Rouge
Corentin Cariou
Église de Pantin
E
Barbès Rochechouart
La Chapelle
Crimée
Anvers
Riquet
Stalingrad
Ourcq
Laumière
Porte de Pantin
Hoche
Gare du Nord
Jaurès
Danube
Pré St-Gervais
Mairie des Lilas
Magenta
Louis Blanc
Bolivar
11
Poissonnière
Château Landon
Colonel Fabien
Botzaris
Buttes Chaumont
Cadet
Gare de l'Est
Belleville
Pyrénées
Jourdain
Place des Fêtes
Télégraphe
Porte des Lilas
Château d'Eau
Jacques Bonsergent
Richelieu Drouot
Strasbourg St-Denis
Goncourt
Couronnes
Saint-Fargeau
Ménilmontant
Grands Boulevards
Bonne Nouvelle
Temple
République
Pelleport
Réaumur Sébastopol
Arts et Métiers
Oberkampf
Parmentier
Père Lachaise
Porte de Bagnolet
Gallieni
Sentier
Filles du Calvaire
Rue St-Maur
Gambetta
3
Marcel
Châtelet Les Halles
Mairie de Montreuil
9
Les Halles
Rambuteau
St-Sébastien Froissart
St-Ambroise
Philippe Auguste
Croix de Chavaux
Châtelet
Hôtel de Ville
Richard Lenoir
Voltaire
Alexandre Dumas
Cité
11
Chemin Vert
Bréguet Sabin
Robespierre
St-Paul
Charonne
Maraîchers
St-Michel Notre-Dame
Bastille
Avron
Porte de Montreuil
Pont Marie
Ledru-Rollin
Rue des Boulets
2
Buzenval
Sully Morland
Faidherbe Chaligny
6
A
Cluny La Sorbonne
Nation
Maubert Mutualité
Quai de la Rapée
Gare de Lyon
Pte de Vincennes
St-Mandé
Luxembourg
Reuilly–Diderot
Jussieu
Montgallet
Picpus
Bérault
Cardinal Lemoine
1
Gare d'Austerlitz
Bel-Air
Place Monge
Daumesnil
Château de Vincennes
Port-Royal
Michel Bizot
10
Censier Daubenton
Dugommier
orlybus
Denfert Rochereau
Saint Marcel
Bercy
Porte Dorée
Les Gobelins
Campo Formio
Quai de la Gare
Cour St-Émilion
Porte de Charenton
St-Jacques
Liberté
Mouton Duvernet
Corvisart
Place d'Italie
Chevaleret
Bibliothèque Fr. Mitterrand
Charenton–Écoles
Glacière
Nationale
Olympiades
5
14
Tolbiac
Alésia
École Vétérinaire de Maisons-Alfort
Cité Universitaire
Maison Blanche
Porte d'Italie
Porte d'Ivry
Pierre et Marie Curie
Ivry sur-Seine
Maisons-Alfort–Stade
Gentilly
Le Kremlin Bicêtre
Porte de Choisy
T 3
Maisons-Alfort Les Juilliottes
Villejuif Léo Lagrange
Mairie d'Ivry 7
Vitry sur-Seine
Créteil–L'Échat
Orlyval tarification spéciale
Villejuif Paul Vaillant-Couturier
Créteil–Université
Orly
Villejuif Louis Aragon 7
C
D
8 Créteil–Préfecture

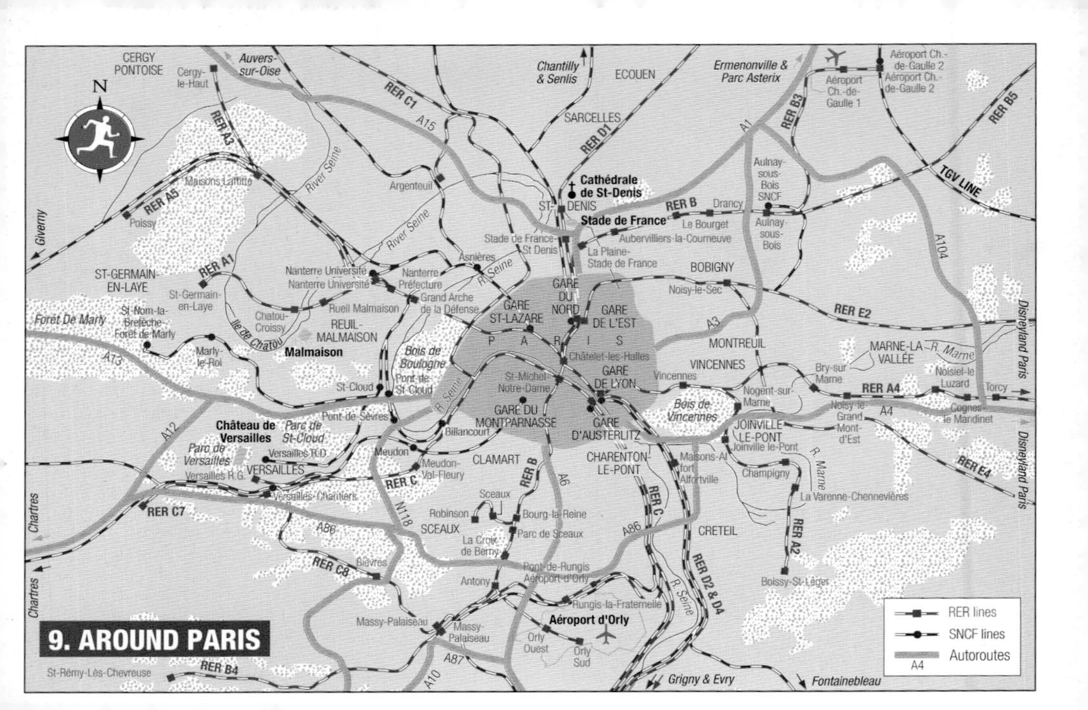
9. AROUND PARIS
N
RER lines
SNCF lines
Autoroutes
A4
CERGY PONTOISE
Cergy-le-Haut
Auvers-sur-Oise
Chantilly & Senlis
ECOUEN
Ermenonville & Parc Asterix
Aéroport Ch.-de-Gaulle 1
Aéroport Ch.-de-Gaulle 2
SARCELLES
Cathédrale de St-Denis
ST-DENIS
Stade de France
Stade de France-St Denis
La Plaine-Stade de France
Aubervilliers-la-Courneuve
Le Bourget
Drancy
Aulnay-sous-Bois SNCF
Aulnay-sous-Bois
BOBIGNY
Noisy-le-Sec
MONTREUIL
VINCENNES
Vincennes
Bois de Vincennes
MARNE-LA-VALLÉE
R. Marne
Bry-sur-Marne
Noisiel-le Luzard
Torcy
Cognes-le Mardinet
Noisy-le-Grand
Mont-d'Est
Nogent-sur-Marne
JOINVILLE LE-PONT
Joinville le-Pont
Champigny
La Varenne-Chennevières
Boissy-St-Léger
Disneyland Paris
TGV LINE
Maisons Laffitte
Poissy
Giverny
River Seine
Argenteuil
Asnières
R. Seine
ST-GERMAIN-EN-LAYE
St-Germain-en-Laye
St-Nom-la-Bretèche-Forêt de Marly
Forêt De Marly
Marly-le-Roi
Chatou-Croissy
Ile de Chatou
Malmaison
REUIL-MALMAISON
Rueil Malmaison
Nanterre Université
Nanterre Préfecture
Grand Arche de la Défense
Bois de Boulogne
St-Cloud
Pont-de-St-Cloud
Pont-de-Sèvres
Billancourt
GARE ST-LAZARE
GARE DU NORD
GARE DE L'EST
P A R I S
Châtelet-les-Halles
St-Michel-Notre-Dame
GARE DE LYON
GARE DU MONTPARNASSE
GARE D'AUSTERLITZ
CHARENTON-LE-PONT
Maisons-Alfort Alfortville
CRETEIL
Château de Versailles
Parc de St-Cloud
Parc de Versailles
Versailles R.D.
Versailles R.G.
VERSAILLES
Versailles-Chantiers
Meudon
Meudon-Val-Fleury
CLAMART
Sceaux
Robinson
SCEAUX
Bourg-la-Reine
Parc de Sceaux
La Croix de Berny
Antony
Pont-de-Rungis Aéroport d'Orly
Rungis-la-Fraternelle
Aéroport d'Orly
Orly Ouest
Orly Sud
Massy-Palaiseau
Bièvres
St-Rémy-Lès-Chevreuse
Chartres
Grigny & Evry
Fontainebleau
RER A1
RER A2
RER A3
RER A4
RER A5
RER B
RER B3
RER B4
RER B5
RER C
RER C1
RER C7
RER C8
RER D1
RER D2 & D4
RER E2
RER E4
A1
A3
A4
A6
A10
A12
A13
A15
A86
A87
A104
N118